The Foreign Relations
of the People's Republic of China

The Foreign Relations of the People's Republic of China

EDITED WITH INTRODUCTION AND COMMENTARY

BY *Winberg Chai*

G. P. PUTNAM'S SONS, *New York*

To Carolyn,
With love and gratitude

Preface

General readers and nonspecialists on Chinese affairs when confronted with foreign policy questions on the People's Republic of China are often handicapped by their inability to locate original documents and policy papers and, further, to place the documents and policy papers in their proper context. This book offers sixty-six basic documents, treaties, correspondence, and policy statements, as well as editorials by Chinese officials, that constitute the strategics and operational guides to today's Chinese foreign affairs.

In order to place these documents in their meaningful context, I have written an introduction and commentaries on seven important subjects: the meaning of Maoism; Sino-American relations; Sino-Soviet disputes; Chinese strategies in developing nations; Chinese policies on economic aid, trade, and cultural relations; overseas Chinese, boundaries and disputed territories; and war, peace, world order, and ecology. I have also written brief explanatory notes preceding each of the sixty-six documents. Because of the multitude and complexity of foreign policy questions, there are many variables that must be considered beyond the scope of this book, but it will be found to be an indispensable first tool for those readers wishing to gain a deeper knowledge of China's foreign relations.

In preparation of this work, I am indebted to many friends and many sources. I am grateful to my parents, Dr. and Mrs. Ch'u Chai, formerly of Nanking, now of New York City, for their devotion and love. I also wish to acknowledge valuable assistance freely rendered to me by my colleagues in the Los Angeles Modern China Seminar, Berkeley Regional Seminar, and Diplomat-Scholar Seminar in Washington, D.C., and many China-scholars, China "Watchers," and "on-the-spot" reporters. Thanks are due also to the staff of Armacost Library of the University of Redlands for their friendly assistance, to Mr. Walter C. Betkowski for his appreciation of the need for this work, to my wife, Carolyn, for editorial advice, to Mrs. Virginia

Templeton, who typed part of the manuscript, and to my children, May-Lee and Jeffrey, for their patience and understanding.

For all my appreciation to those who assisted me, however, I alone bear the responsibility for any errors of judgment and omission of facts.

WINBERG CHAI

Redlands, California
December 1, 1971

Contents

INTRODUCTION
Understanding Chinese Foreign Policies

"The next 50 to 100 years, beginning from now, will be a great era of radical change in the social system throughout the world, an earth-shaking era without equal in any previous historical period. Living in such an era, we must be prepared to engage in great struggles which will have many features different in form from those of the past"[1]—so stated Chairman Mao Tse-tung, supreme teacher of the largest country in the world, with a population of one-fourth of the human race.

"The twenty-two-year-old hostility between ourselves and the People's Republic of China is another unresolved problem. . . . It is a truism that an international order cannot be secure if one of the major powers remains largely outside it and hostile toward it,"[2] reported the President of the United States in February, 1971.

Abolishing hostility and the establishment of closer relations between the two giants of the world is indeed not an easy task. It calls for sympathetic and sound understanding, as well as objective knowledge of the people, their culture, current problems, needs, and aspirations. This is a minimum requirement, because Chinese foreign policy, like that of other major world powers, rests on multiple determinants, including China's historical experience and political culture, as well as international environment.

---

1 Quoted in Lin Piao's "Report of the Ninth National Congress of the Communist Party of China," *Peking Review* (April 28, 1969), p.30. See Document 59.

2 *U.S. Foreign Policy for the 1970's* (Washington, D.C., U.S. Printing House, February 25, 1971), p. 105.

I.

Historical Experience: Opium War

The 130 years in China's history from the 1840's to the 1970's might be viewed as the vital link between the waning of the old order—feudal political system, social institutions, and cultural values—and the beginning of a new era, the era of the People's Republic of China and Mao Tse-tung. To understand this dramatic transformation in China, one must examine the historical background, especially the foreign influences and internal developments of the past century which were responsible for eventually toppling the traditional order.

The years between 1839, when China was opened to the West, and 1949, when it became a closed Communistic society, may be divided into two stages of revolutionary development: (1) from the Opium War (1839-41) to the Sino-Japanese War of 1894, with the Treaty of Tientsin (1858) a decisive turning point, and (2) from 1895, when the old dynasty began to crumble, to 1949, when the Communists took possession of the mainland. The first phase was a period of external humiliation and internal turmoil, the second a time of economic difficulties, political chaos and ideological conflicts, all leading to the total destruction of the old order.

For centuries prior to the Opium War, China had lived in self-imposed isolation, with a belief in her cultural superiority rooted in the past when there was a sharp distinction between the *Hua Hsia* (the Chinese) and the *Yi Ti* (the barbarians). The regions surrounding China—Korea, Japan, Burma, Annam (Indochina), and Nepal—were all under her military control or treated as satellite areas. It was the rule that those "barbarian peoples" who wished to "come and be transformed," and so share in the benefits of Chinese civilization, must recognize the imperial supremacy of the Middle Kingdom. This supremacy was ritually acknowledged either in the performance of the *kowtow*—the

2

three kneelings and nine prostrations—or by the bringing of tributes. (See Appendix D.)

When China began to have contacts with Western nations in the beginning of the sixteenth century she regarded them as barbarians and their special envoys as tribute bearers. With the exception of Russia, foreign traders were not allowed to enter Peking and were restricted to the port of Canton, where business was conducted without treaty arrangements.

In 1793, the British government sent Lord Macartney on a mission to the Chinese Imperial Court in an attempt to improve trade relations. On his arrival at Peking, Macartney presented a letter from King George III requesting that a diplomat be accredited to the Manchu court and that trade conditions be improved. To these requests, Chinese Emperor Ch'ien Lung replied:

> As to your entreaty to send one of your nationals to be accredited to my Celestial Court and to be in control of your country's trade with China, this request is contrary to all usage of my dynasty and cannot possibly be entertained. . . . Our dynasty's majestic virtue has penetrated into every country under Heaven and Kings of all nations have offered their costly tribute by land and sea. As your Ambassador can see for himself, we possess all things. I set no value on objects strange or ingenious, and have no use for your country's manufactures. . . .[1]

In 1816 the British sent another mission under Lord Amherst. He was not treated as hospitably as Macartney had been, and when he complained, he was ordered to leave the country. Unrealistically, Peking refused to open its door to the West.

The Opium War

In the search for commodities which the Chinese would buy, the Western traders finally discovered a very profitable product—opium. In fact, the immediate profits of the opium trade were so high that practically all Western traders took part in it, including the Americans.

1 Sir Frederick Whyte, *China and Foreign Powers* (London, Oxford University Press, 1927), p. 39.

In 1839, the Chinese emperor appointed a special commissioner, Lin Tse-hsu, to enforce the prohibition of the opium trade at Canton. Commissioner Lin forced the foreign traders to surrender all their opium and then had it burned in Canton. The Americans submitted to the Chinese demands, while the British decided to use force to obtain satisfaction and reparation from the Chinese.

This resulted in the Opium War, which lasted from November, 1839, to August, 1842, and ended in complete victory for the British. A treaty was signed in Nanking in 1842 providing for the opening of five Chinese ports—Canton, Amoy, Foochow, Ningpo, and Shanghai—to British traders. It also imposed on China an indemnity of 21,000,000 taels and provided for the cession to England of the island of Hong Kong, which controls the sea entrance to Canton. Most incriminating of all, the British introduced into the supplementary Treaty of Bogus, concluded with China in 1843, the infamous "most-favored-nation" clause, guaranteeing the British any further concessions which China might subsequently grant to other nations. From that time all treaties with China by foreign powers contained this clause.

The Treaty of Wanghia, signed in July, 1844, allowed American citizens a special legal protection to compensate for the lack of a naval base such as the British had secured in Hong Kong. This is known as the principle of extraterritoriality, which granted resident aliens and corporations exemptions from Chinese law and authority in both civil and criminal cases. Another treaty with the French was signed in October, 1844. These treaties set a pattern for China's relations with the West that lasted for 100 years.

Foreign "Spheres of Influence"

During the two decades following these treaties, China had to surrender more and more of its sovereignty to foreign powers. For example, foreigners administered China's maritime customs and postal service until 1929. They also had the right to establish factories, open mines, navigate in coastal and inland waters, and build railways for the expansion of their commerce. The closing decades of the nineteenth century also found foreign powers engaged in a battle of concessions, through which they leased territory from the Chinese government. In addition, foreign troops were permitted to be stationed in the concessions and foreign warships patrolled Chinese coasts and rivers.

As China's weakness grew, so did foreign aggression. This was revealed in the loss of some of China's outlying possessions. By 1860 Russia had penetrated into Manchuria, Mongolia, and Chinese Turkestan. France, victorious in a small-scale war (1884-85), acquired a protectorate over Annam; Great Britain coerced China again to yield sovereignty over Upper Burma in 1886; the Portuguese, who had occupied Macao for 300 years, obtained its formal cession in 1887; Japan, only recently emerged from its centuries-long isolation, enforced a claim to suzerainty over the Ryukyu Islands (1881) by defeating the Chinese in Korea (1894-95). In addition, Japan also acquired the island of Formosa.

Japan's defeat of China in 1895 stripped her of any remaining prestige and precipitated a scramble for new concessions. By the year 1898, the leading powers had acquired leaseholds on the coast of China, ranging from twenty-five to ninety-nine years.

In the continuing scramble for China, foreign powers negotiated the partition of China into spheres of influence, with Russia in Manchuria, Germany in Shantung, and Great Britain in the Yangtze Valley. They even wrested assurance that China would not grant concessions to any other power in their respective spheres of influence. The powers understood the leased territories and spheres of influence as the first steps toward annexation. The complete disintegration of China, which seemed to be imminent, was checked by the bitter rivalries among the powers themselves. Thus, in the course of a few decades after the Opium War, these concessions not only discredited the Celestial Dynasty once and for all but also made China an economic dependency of the great powers—a fatal blow both against the welfare of the state and the livelihood of the people.

The Impact of the Opium War

The course of Chinese history has been marked by the changes in the relationship of the peasants to agriculture. Three-fourths of the people are peasants, and four-fifths of national revenue is derived from agricultural production. The age-long superiority of the root (agriculture) over the branch (commerce), the principle of fair distribution of wealth, the ideal of the well-field system, and the various measures for limiting the ownership of land adopted by the various dynasties all were intended to rehabilitate the traditional agrarian economy and maintain agricultural land in due proportion all over the country, with the exception of the outlying areas.

The development of agrarian economy in China had its roots in the Yellow River basin, then gradually was focused in the Yangtze Valley, and finally moved to the coast in the southeast. What is significant is the fact that although economic development changed from the river basin to the seacoast, there had been no great tendency toward overlocalization. Then the main problem of the farmers was that of water. When water failed, crops failed and famine quickly spread. Famine, flood, irrigation, and water control shaped the policies of the empires.

This type of agrarian economy was by no means unprofitable or destructive. In fact, Chinese economy had been a balanced one up to 1800 and the efficient use of water was a most notable achievement. The water transport network throughout central and south China was remarkably serviceable and well developed. And the methods of application of abundant manpower to the process of the economy had been utilized well. But for the new factors from abroad, China would have been self-contained and economically sound.

The economic situation was greatly worsened by the failure of the Manchu government to suppress the trade in opium. During the late eighteenth century, about 1,000 chests (a chest equals some 133 pounds) of opium were being imported from India to China per year. From 1800 to 1810, the average was about 4,500 chests a year. By 1838, the annual growth was increased to 40,000 chests. The following table gives some indication of the increase in the opium trade:

Years	Annual Average in Chests	Est. Value in Mexican Dollars*
1800-10	4,500	4,500,000
1811-20	10,000	10,000,000
1821-30	16,000	16,000,000
1831-35	18,712	18,712,000
1835	26,000	26,000,000
1838	40,000	40,000,000

*A chest of opium sold at somewhere between 1,000 and 2,000 Mexican dollars.

The tragedy of the opium trade was a dual one. On one hand, it became a social problem for China, as somewhere between 2,000,000 to 10,000,000 Chinese had become opium addicts. It also caused a great flow of silver out of China, thereby depleting the treasury.

After the opening of China, foreigners seized local points along the seacoast and made them trade ports for the penetration of the interior. By 1899 there were 32 "treaty ports" in China, and the number increased to 48 in 1913. Under the Inland Navigation Regulation of 1898 foreigners could travel and do business freely along the seacoast of 5,000 nautical miles and through the inland rivers as long as 10,000 nautical miles. After 1895 some 7,671 miles of railroads were built, mostly with foreign capital, cutting the major portion of the mainland from north to south as well as east to west. Foreign commerce not only greatly increased but also quickly penetrated to the rural areas of China.

Foreign trade grew as foreign governments extended political control. Consequently, the traditional political social structure disintegrated and new groups emerged. Urban development spread from the city to the village and changed ways of life and patterns of values. Rural communities were affected to a degree that was deep and far-reaching.

But urbanization brought no significant increase in industrialization. Industry was centered in the trade cities, and China derived no benefit that could in any way help the development of its industry or agricultural production. Moreover, foreign goods, under the protection of unequal treaties, were dumped on the Chinese market, and native products could not successfully compete with them. Machine-made cotton goods were proving cheaper and better than those hand made by peasants. The existing handicraft industries, once an important source of supplementary income to the farmers, began to disappear; and yet, at the same time, the few newly founded Chinese industries failed to prosper due to foreign competition.

Consequently, the ever-increasing excess of imports over exports, together with the imbalance between the high market value of manufactured goods and low market value of agricultural products, plus the population increase, caused the bankruptcy of China's agrarian economy.

II.
Reform, Rebellion, and Revolution

As China entered the nineteenth century, the symptoms of dynastic decay were evident in the failure of the Manchu government to handle its external and internal problems. The reasons for this are not hard to find. Under the emperor K'ang Hsi (1654-1722) and his grandson Ch'ien Lung (1736-95), the Middle Kingdom, which enjoyed almost 150 years of internal peace and prosperity, might be compared to Great Britain. However, by the middle of the Tao Kuang period (1821-50), Britain had undergone the Industrial Revolution, pacified the Chartist Movement, passed the Great Reform Bill of 1832, and witnessed tremendous economic, political, and intellectual progress; the Manchu Empire still followed the traditional system of government and clung slavishly to the family tradition, such as K'ang Hsi's Sacred Edict:

> Be filial to parents and affectionate to brothers; Be loyal to clans and friendly to neighbors; Pay attention to agriculture and sericulture; Practice thrift and be frugal; Devote one's own pursuit.[1]

This unshaken faith in the past as a guide to the present prevented China from perceiving the desirability of any change or apprehending the danger of having unwelcome change forced on it.

In the nineteenth century, China had found herself in an entirely new kind of decline, but the Manchu rulers remained stubbornly unaware of the danger. When coercion and war broke upon the empire from the onslaught of the West, they turned to the past for time-tested solutions and held wistfully

[1] *Cf.* John K. Fairbank, Edwin O. Reischauer, and Albert M. Craig, *East Asia: The Modern Transformation* (Boston, Houghton Mifflin, 1965), p. 276.

to the illusion that the Europeans would ultimately submit to China's civilizing influence, as had her previous invaders. However, these illusions were dispelled by the events of the late 1800's, for this time the new invaders brought weapons, machines, and ideas that could not be fitted into the imperial system without destroying the roots of its basic traditions.

Decadence in Bureaucracy

The nineteenth century was also the period of decadence in the imperial system of government in which political life was monopolized less by the bureaucracy and centered more in the personality of the emperor.

The early Manchu (Ch'ing) emperors exercised not only the usual prerogatives of the Chinese sovereign but also the power of appointment and removal for all official posts. The Manchu emperors made sure that social position reinforced political subjection by degrading their officials from the proud status of functionaries of state to the status of slaves. Nu-tsai (slave) was the term Manchu officials used in referring to themselves when addressing the emperor.

As a result, the emperors were less apt to listen to the suggestions of their officials about good government or against the abuses of personal power, despite the extensive setup of a bureaucratic government.

Contributing to the inertia of the Manchu leaders were their vested interests in maintaining the power structure that ensured their wealth and position. During the T'ung chih reign (1862-75), for example, the emperor was a young boy under a regency dominated by his mother, the Empress Dowager Tzu Hsi (1835-1908), who became entrenched in power, governing with the aid of palace eunuchs and trusted personal friends. The Empress Dowager had no grasp whatsoever of China's problem of modernization. Her government suffered from the evils of nepotism and cliquish favoritism and the lack of risk-taking initiative.

This incapacity of the empress' court was, of course, inherited from a long past. For instance, the imperial government's fiscal system was based on the antiquated system of tax-farming, which means that local officials were expected to make certain tax quotas available to the imperial court while maintaining themselves and their administrations on the remainder of what they collected. There was no budgeting, accounting, or central planning.

Even the time-honored system of civil service and literary examinations had completely disintegrated. The content and direction of education was under the rigid control of the Department of Civil Service of the Metropolitan Administration, which made memorizing the Confucian classics the cornerstone of all education.

Disinterest and apathy in the Metropolitan Administration was reflected also in the activities and attitudes of local authorities. During the Manchu Dynasty, there were some 1,500 *Chou* or *Hsien* governments distributed among some 18 to 22 provinces under the personal supervision of the viceroys and governors. Provincial administrative functions were divided among several commissioners who were independently appointed by the Metropolitan Administration and responsible to the emperor. At the very bottom were the district magistrates, called *chih-hsien* or, more popularly, the father and mother official of a district.

Each of the magistrates was in charge of an area of some 300 square miles with a population of 250,000 people. They were aided by a varied retinue of personal and semiofficial assistants, at times their personal servants.

The local governments had always occupied a semiautonomous status in relation to the Metropolitan authorities. Although legally they were all responsible to the emperor, they were free from interference as long as they furnished their quota in taxes, supported the vague general policies of the Metropolitan Administration, and avoided outrage to the general scheme of Confucian morality.

After the Tao Kuang period, there was a general decline of imperial power in the provincial and local regions. Often independent groups emerged and some organized into secret societies which became the vehicle for all sorts of illegal activities as well as open rebellion.

The Taiping Rebellion

The decadent Manchu government both was undermined by and in turn escalated the rise and progress of internal revolts and rebellion. In the two decades before the Opium War, revolts had already occurred in Honan (1822), Taiwan (1826), Hunan (1833), Shansi (1835), and many other parts of the country.

After the Opium War, there were six serious rebellions: one in the south by the Taipings (1850-64), one in the north by the Niens (1853-68), and four by the Moslems—in the northwest (1855-72), the southwest (1862-73), and Central Asia (1862-76, 1866-78).

More often than not these rebellions gained momentum through affiliation with one or another of the secret societies such as the White Lotus Sect in the north and the Hung Society in the south which were motivated by nationalism and religious ideology. These internal uprisings succeeded one another with shocking military violence and political disturbance, resulting in a tremendous loss of life and serious property damage throughout the empire.

The most formidable of all uprisings in China was the movement known as the Taiping Rebellion, which was an almost fatal challenge to the Manchu Dynasty. It began in 1850 as a series of local conflicts in south China but rapidly grew into a popular movement which affected 17 out of the then 18 provinces of China and resulted in the death of between 20,000,000 and 40,000,000 people.

The Taiping Rebellion was in many ways a standard Chinese antidynastic movement, born of agrarian distress and justified by the "Mandate of Heaven." Such movements generally combined political and economic purposes: A new dynasty was to replace the old and the have-nots were to become the haves. However, it was its religious tenets and political ideology that gave the Taiping movement a distinctive character.

The leader of the revolt, Hung Hsiu-ch'uan (1814-64), frustrated in office-seeking and influenced by the tracts of Protestant missionaries, was convinced that he had a divine mission to perform. In 1848 he inaugurated the Shang Ti Hui, or the Worshipers of Shang Ti (a Protestant term for God), which later became a political as well as a religious movement to overthrow the Manchu Dynasty and to establish a new Heavenly Kingdom (Taiping T'ien Kuo).

From the outset the movement acquired tremendous momentum by preaching utopian and Socialist ideology (independent of European Socialism), such as land redistribution, communal property, the brotherhood of man, and the equality of sexes. The rebel movement made rapid progress and by 1853 occupied Nanking and much of central and south China. For a time, the Taipings appeared to have succeeded in overthrowing the Manchu Dynasty and establishing their Heavenly Kingdom.

In a certain sense the Taiping Rebellion was a social and economic revolt, an uprising of impoverished peasants against oppressive landlords and corrupt officials. Their reform program was an admixture of Christian ideas and ideas of ancient China. Serious efforts were made at public ownership of money and property, the reduction of taxes on the peasantry, prohibition of bribery and opium, and the demand for a new calendar and colloquial literature, among other reforms.

The Taipings, in fact, had all the ingredients for a successful revolution, such as inspiring ideology, an audacious leader, an oppressed people, and a real program of reform. However, they were unable to make the best of their opportunities. They lacked qualified personnel and were unable to devise an effective administrative system over all the regions they conquered. In addition, the failure of the Taipings had been accelerated by their inability to establish relations with the Western powers. After the new treaties of 1858 and 1860 between the Manchu Court and the Western powers, the imperial government received Western support and was able to crush the revolution.

The Reform Movement

During the Taiping Rebellion, men like Tseng Kuo-fan (1811-72) and Li Hung-chang (1823-1901) launched a movement of "enriching the nation and strengthening the army." Tseng and Li commanded the famous Hunan and Anhwei armies that suppressed the Taipings and various other rebellions. They had restored order for the Manchu government and encouraged the manufacture of arms, the building of ships, the construction of railways, and improvements in telegraphic communication as part of their goal to establish an industrial base in China. They also instituted foreign language schools, as well as sending Chinese students abroad. Li Hung-chang established a modern foreign office, the Tsungli Yamen, and he later played an indispensable role in foreign diplomacy for the Manchu Dynasty.

Li Hung-chang also introduced a new operational principle for the government based upon "government supervision and merchant operation." Under this principle, profit-oriented enterprises were managed by merchants while the government maintained its control of policy much like a board of directors. Among Li's projects were included the China Merchant's Steamship Line, a modern coal mine in the Kaiping area, and a Chinese textile mill to compete with foreign imports. The slow progress of reform initiated by Li in the 1870's and 1880's could have proved to be successful to modernize the Manchu Dynasty if it had not been obstructed by additional foreign encroachment and aggression.

Russia began an invasion of the Manchu Empire's territories in Central Asia; France attacked China's tributary states in the south, such as Annam (Vietnam) and other parts of Indochina. The outbreak of domestic rebellion in Korea provided the occasion in 1894 for Japanese intervention, which led to the disastrous Sino-Japanese War (1894-95).

China signed a treaty in Shimonoseki with Japan in which the independence of Korea was recognized, the islands of Taiwan and Pescadores and the Liaotung peninsula were ceded to Japan, an indemnity of 200,000,000 taels of silver was to be paid to Japan, and four more ports were to be opened to foreign trade. With this treaty began the mad scramble for concessions on the part of the great European powers.

The Hundred Days' Reform

The defeat of China by Japan in the war of 1894-95 was destined to have profound effects on the Chinese mind. A progressive reformer, K'ang Yu-wei (1858-1927), led 1,200 young scholars who were candidates for the Metropolitan examination to submit an important memorial to the emperor in which they called for a repudiation of the treaty, a move of the capital to the safer interior of the country, and the total reform of the government. This demand had no effect, but in 1898 K'ang submitted to the emperor another critical memorial in which he set forth a whole new program for the government.

In the summer of 1898, the emperor began to issue a series of reform edicts based on the program spelled out by K'ang and instituted what was later known as the Hundred Days' Reform, which lasted from June 11 to September 16. K'ang wanted a constitutional monarchy similar to that of the Meiji era in Japan. He also proposed the abolition of the traditional examination and a complete renovation of the educational system in which Western sciences and practical arts would be studied together with the Chinese classics. K'ang also proposed to use Buddhist temples for modern schools and the establishment of a bureau of translation of Western works.

K'ang's general economic plans were to encourage commerce and industry through the construction of railways and factories in various parts of China. Steps were also to be taken to develop mining and to promote agricultural improvements. A modern budget system was to be introduced. And there were many other measures aimed at social and institutional reforms. To pave the way for his reform program, K'ang tried to reorganize government machinery and eliminate the old officialdom.

K'ang's reform aroused a storm of opposition from those who by conviction or interest were wedded to the old order. The situation was complicated by the rivalries of two factions at the imperial court, one of them advocating reforms and the other taking a conservative position. The conservatives looked to the Empress Dowager for support and leadership. When the empress saw that the young emperor was actually launching reforms, she resumed her regency and made the emperor a prisoner, arresting and executing many reformers in the process. Finally all the reform edicts were annulled.

After the failure of the reform movement, K'ang Yu-wei went abroad and continued to write and raise funds on behalf of the movement. However, he no longer played any important part in Chinese politics and his place was soon taken over by Sun Yat-sen (1866-1925), who turned the reform movement into a national revolution.

Kuomintang Revolution

In contrast to K'ang Yu-wei, Sun Yat-sen was not only a republican revolutionary but also a man of magnetic political personality. He came of a poor peasant family and received his education in Western schools. Hence he was not bound to conventional Chinese scholarship and became an ardent believer in Western culture and science.

In 1879, at the age of twelve, Sun joined his brother in Honolulu, where he learned about Western democracy, whose influence was later to play an important part in the formation of his own political philosophy. From 1884 to 1886 he continued his education in Hong Kong, where he studied Western medicine, and after graduation he practiced medicine in Macao. But his professional career did not last long, for he soon took active part in the revolutionary movement.

After the calamities of the Sino-Japanese War, Sun founded the China Regeneration Society (Hsing Chung-hui) in Honolulu in 1894 for the purpose of overthrowing the Manchu Dynasty. His early efforts were not very successful. He then reorganized his society in a new organization, the League of Common Alliance (T'ung Meng Hui), in Japan in order to express his political philosophy through an organized political movement. He offered the following reforms:

1. The expulsion of the Manchus and the restoration of China—later formulated as the Principle of People's Rule (*Min-tsu*, translated as "nationalism").
2. The establishment of a republic—later formulated as the Principle of People's Authority (*Min-ch'uan*, translated as "democracy").
3. Equal distribution and nationalization of land—later formulated as the Principle of People's Livelihood (*Min-sheng*, translated as "Socialism").

This program included the main points which served as the basic text of the nationalist movement and was later known as the Three People's Principles. Although there were many reverses, persecutions, and rebuffs, the revolutionary work led by Sun Yat-sen succeeded in the overthrow of the Manchu Dynasty in October, 1911.

The success of Sun's revolution did not, however, free China from the economic difficulties, ideological conflicts, political chaos, and foreign intervention of the Manchu Dynasty. Governmental power was in fact soon passed into the hands of political opportunists and militarists and for thirteen years China was torn by civil wars.

During these years of crisis, Sun Yat-sen continued his revolutionary work in China. He reorganized his League of Common Alliance into the Kuomintang (the Nationalist Party), a democratic political party with open membership, for the purpose of implanting his own program, the Three People's Principles, in the minds and lives of the people.

Since he was ignored by Western powers, Sun accepted offers of assistance and guidance from the newly formed Soviet government and in 1923 invited a host of Soviet advisers to come to China to reorganize the Kuomintang and to train Chinese cadres. By 1924 a new Kuomintang was patterned after the Soviet model and a military school was established at Whampoa to train future Chinese military officers. Chiang Kai-shek was named its first president and Chou En-lai its chief political officer.

At the end of 1924 Sun Yat-sen with some of his advisers went to Peking to negotiate a reconciliation between various factions in China. Before any definite results could be realized, he died in Peking on March 12, 1925, leaving a last testament which urged his followers to continue to work for the solution of China's complex problems.

The death of Sun split the party into two opposing factions: Members of the left, who advocated the continuation of the revolution patterned on the Soviet model, which demanded the expulsion of China's capitalists, warlords, and landholders; and those of the right, who wanted an alliance with the gentry in order to preserve China's traditional cultural heritage.

After it became apparent that a negotiated settlement with China's warlords was impossible, the Kuomintang armies, officered by cadres of the Whampoa Military Academy under the supreme command of Chiang Kai-shek, set out in the summer of 1926 on the long-planned Northern Expedition. With the continued success of the expedition, Chiang Kai-shek had to make a decision: Should he lend his support to the right or the left? At the siege of Shanghai, Chiang Kai-shek decided on the first alternative, and Shanghai came into his hands without a struggle and the enormous capital of the Shanghai financiers and industrialists was placed at his disposal. At the same time, Russian advisers were dismissed and members of the Chinese Communist Party were purged from the party. The latter established themselves as a guerrilla force in rural areas, where they remained the archenemy of the Kuomintang and its government.

The decision arrived at by Chiang Kai-shek and his advisers secured him the party leadership and at the same time deepened the nation's schisms. In addition to the warlord forces and the Communists, Chiang Kai-shek now faced a struggle for power within the Kuomintang itself. In order to strengthen his position he tried to consolidate his control over the party machine, thereby revealing not only his strength but also his weakness.

Chiang Kai-shek was undoubtedly a good strategist and skillful in politics as it was practiced in the Kuomintang power struggle; but he was not a man who abided by law or believed in the rule of law. He always made the first criterion for his support of a subordinate the quality of personal loyalty rather than any ability or devotion to particular political programs. Chiang Kai-shek allowed the Kuomintang to be segmented into rival cliques that he played off against each other. Personal rivalry and clique antagonisms paralyzed the Kuomintang in their struggle with the Communists.

Even the Reform Movement of 1950-52 in Taiwan after the fall of the mainland, while bringing some new and younger members into the party, failed to rejuvenate its organization by reducing the animosities of the rival cliques. Some changes in the pattern of cliques might nevertheless have resulted from the Reform Movement, but this is simply the same old package with a new wrapping. Indeed, the Kuomintang lost the vitality and resourcefulness that characterized it in the early revolutionary days.

Another important factor that contributed to the collapse of the Nationalists was Chiang's persistent conviction that political, social, and economic reforms must be delayed until threats from the Communists and from Japan could be removed. The Japanese attack that led to the Sino-Japanese War of 1937 destroyed the last hope for the reform programs of the Nationalist government and paved the way for the final victory of Communism in China.

Finally, Chiang Kai-shek and his party made little effort to present to the Chinese people an attractive postwar political, social, and economic program. In particular, during the last stage of civil war, 1946-49, the Kuomintang was not prepared to take any dramatic steps to alleviate the plight of the millions of China's peasants, the backbone of the Chinese nation.

Meanwhile, the Chinese Communist Party, under the leadership of Mao Tse-tung, had increased its membership from 57 members in 1921 to more than 4,000,000 during the final phase of civil war in 1948. When Mao Tse-tung established his People's Republic of China in Peking on October 1, 1949, the party's membership had reached over 5,000,000 members.

III.
Communist Ideological Revolutions

Historically speaking, the use of ideology as an instrument of social and political control in China has been carried over from the imperial system to the present republic form. Both the Kuomintang and the Communist regimes have bolstered their rule by championing an ideology and indoctrinating the people with its principles.

The Chinese Communist Party founders had envisioned the necessity of ideological remolding along Soviet lines for the construction of a new China because of the inability of the traditional Chinese ideology, Confucianism in particular, to cope with the aggressive twentieth-century world. However, the Chinese never quite felt at home with Marxist-Leninist principles borrowed directly from the Soviet Union, and the Communist leadership in China began to concoct a new formula to continue the revolution.

The Rise of Mao Tse-tung

The most successful leader in China, the man who finally developed a new ideology and transformed all of China into a modern state, is Mao Tse-tung. The long and tortuous road which led Mao to power in China explains his unceasing passion to uplift China's living standards and to improve China's international position. Mao was born to a peasant family in Hunan in 1893, a time when China had suffered great humiliation from foreign encroachments. During his student days in Hunan, he was under the influence of Confucian scholars and reformers K'ang Yu-wei (1858-1927) and Liang Ch'i-ch'ao (1873-1929) and was delighted with the reform movement (1898). At the end of World War I, Mao went to work as a clerk in the library of the Peking University, where the May 4th Movement (1919) originated.

The May 4th Movement was fostered by two groups of intellectuals. One represented the Western-educated scholars, under the leadership of Hu Shih (1891-1962). He launched a new cultural movement which led to attacks on the ideas and customs of the traditional society and advocated democracy, science, and modern education. The second group, inspired by the Russian Bolshevik Revolution, was under the leadership of Ch'en Tu-hsiu (1897-1942) and Li Ta-ch'ao (1888-1927) and advocated Marxism as the effective method for achieving social revolution. Under the influence of this second group, Mao Tse-tung became a student of Marxism.[1]

In the formative years of the Chinese Communist Party, Mao's role is not clearly known.[2] We do know that many factions existed within the Chinese Communist Party, which included a diversity of philosophy and views regarding the party strategy. From his "Report on the Peasant Movement in Hunan" (1927), Mao Tse-tung seemed opposed to the strategy based on the urban proletariat which was then pursued by the leaders of the party Central Committee. Mao insisted on a strategy based on the culture of the peasantry with encirclement and subsequently seizure of the "cities occupied by the counterrevolutionaries, by means of armed, revolutionary rural areas."[3]

In the early years of the Civil War, Mao talked and practiced the tactics of guerrilla war rather than the formation of a new peasants' culture. However, Mao did link the mobilization of the masses to the tactics of the guerrilla war. In his important essay "On Protracted War" (1938), Mao wrote: "The mobilization of the common people throughout the country will create a vast sea in which to drown the enemy, create the

1 For a study of the origin of Communism in China and Li Ta-ch'ao's influence upon Mao Tse-tung see Maurice Meisner, *Li Ta-ch'ao and the Origins of Chinese Marxism* (Cambridge, Harvard University Press, 1967).

2 For a detailed study of Mao's role in the Chinese Communist Party see Benjamin I. Schwartz, *Chinese Communism and the Rise of Mao* (Cambridge, Mass., Harvard University Press, 1951); Jerome Ch'en, *Mao and the Chinese Revolution* (New York, Oxford University Press, 1965); also cf. Hsiao Tso-liang, *Power Relations within the Chinese Communist Movement, 1930-1934* (Seattle, University of Washington Press, 1961); and articles and debate on Chinese Communist history published by *The Chinese Quarterly* (London), No. 1 (January-March, 1960) and No. 2 (April-June, 1960).

3 *Selected Works of Mao Tse-tung*, Vol. 1 (Peking, Foreign Language Press, 1965), pp. 41-42.

conditions that will make up for our inferiority in arms and other things, and create the prerequisites for overcoming every difficulty in the war. To win victory, we must persevere in the War of Resistance, in the united front and in the protracted war. But all these are inseparable from the mobilization of the common people."[1]

Sinification of Communism

During the Sino-Japanese War period (1937-45), the Chinese Communists under Mao's leadership not only gained territory and organizational strength but also built up a very powerful army and a highly disciplined party. It is also during this period that Mao again raised the issue of cultural revolution (*wen-hua ke-ming*), which he expounded in his "On New Democracy"[2] (1940), often quoted as the classic document of "Sinification of Communism."[3]

> On the cultural or ideological front, the two periods preceding and following the May 4th Movement form two distinct historical periods. Before the May 4th Movement, the struggle on China's cultural front was one between the new culture of the bourgeoisie and the old culture of the feudal class . . . . But since the May 4th Movement things have been different. A brand-new cultural force came into being in China, that is, the Communist culture and ideology guided by the Chinese Communists, or the Communist world outlook and theory of social revolution. . . .The new democratic culture is the anti-imperialist and anti-feudal culture of the broad masses. . . .The culture can be led only by the culture and ideology of the proletariat, by the ideology of Communism . . . to form a national, scientific and mass culture . . . . [4]

In addition, the "new democracy" was aimed at the development of a new democratic state ruled by an alliance of several revolutionary classes under "proletarian hegemony." The Chinese revolution, as Mao envisioned, would be continued in two stages: the democratic and the Socialist. Though of

1 *Ibid.*, Vol. II, p. 1954.
2 *Ibid.*, pp. 339-84.
3 John King Fairbank, *et al.*, *East Asia: The Modern Transformation* (Boston, Houghton Mifflin, 1965), p. 855.
4 *Selected Works of Mao Tse-tung*, Vol. II, pp. 380-82.

different natures, the two stages could be homogenized in a continuous process if conducted by a coalition of all revolutionary classes.

As soon as the Sino-Japanese War ended, open and intensified struggles between the Kuomintang and the Communists began. Mao consolidated and controlled the Chinese Communist Party with the emergence of a new constitution in 1945 in which "Mao Tse-tung's theory of Chinese revolution" was added to Marxism-Leninism as the party's guiding principle.[1] Finally, with the whole of China unified under the Chinese Communist Party, he began to implement his basic strategies and thought.

In 1949 the first plan was adopted by the Peking regime and was called the Common Program. It demanded economic reforms and a revitalized government. An ideological remolding campaign was also begun with the introduction of the new tactic of group study *(hsueh-hsi)*, a program of political indoctrination. To the peasantry reforms such as rent reduction, land redistribution, public health, and the need for literacy were explained. For the elites, group study was one way to encourage them to study Marxist-Leninist theory and the thought of Mao Tse-tung.

The official study group was under the leadership of a propagandist. The propagandist not only put up posters, prepared wall newspapers, gave street-corner shows, and shouted slogans at mass meetings, but he also constantly created agitation among the people in his study group.

The propagandists were chosen from among members of the party and the new Democratic Youth Corps. They represented and reported to party branch officials. It is estimated that by December, 1950, there were more than 1,920,000 propagandists in the country. The estimated figures for the number of propagandists in each of the six regional administrative areas were as follows:

North China	606,000
Northeast	300,000
East	650,000
Central South	236,000
Southwest	85,000
Northwest	30,000

1 The Constitution of Communist Party of China (1945) in Liu Shao-chi, *On the Party* (Peking, Foreign Language Press, 1954), p. 155.

The method the study group used was criticism. The ideas of each member of the study group were criticized by the others against the correct standard. Every member was required to express an opinion; there was no freedom of silence and every member knew how the others valued his thinking and his future.

The outbreak of the Korean War in 1951 turned the milder forms of study to a more coercive method in the form of "reformative study" (*kai-tsao hsueh-hsi*). New programs eradicating deviant ideologies were introduced, such as the "Three Anti" (against corruption, waste, and bureaucratism) and the "Five Anti" (against crimes of bribery, tax evasion, fraud, theft of state assets, and leakage of state economic secrets) campaigns. These drives set out not only to eliminate the evils of the bourgeoisie but also the bourgeois ideology.

Successfully completing the initial stage of political consolidation as well as economic rehabilitation, the Chinese government then announced in October, 1953, the beginning of another new program, defined as the "general line of the state during the period of transition to Socialism." Politically, the new line was signaled by the announcement of nationwide elections and led to the convocation of the National People's Congress and the new constitution's adoption in 1954.[1]

The 1954 Constitution was designed to bring the policy and operation of the new government into close collaboration with the social and economic developments of China. Its provisions for highly centralized direction and control of many facets of state and local affairs gave the new government a free hand to bring about "Socialist industrialization and social transformation."

In addition, a Five-Year Plan was outlined, to be carried out during the years 1953-57. By the end of 1957 it appeared that many of the goals had been reached, and Peking claimed that it actually had surpassed its investment target. Foreign visitors at that time were impressed by the new buildings and wide streets in the major cities of China as well as the immense energy of the population engaged in construction of dams, buildings, and new industries.

This primary success led the Communist leaders to seek an

1 See A. Doak Barnett, *Communist China—The Early Years, 1949-1955* (New York, Praeger, 1964).

unusually ambitious expansion of production and power under the Second Five-Year Plan, including the creation of People's Communes and the Great Leap Forward movement of 1958. However, these radical changes met with tremendous resistance from the peasants, and the situation became aggravated by the Sino-Soviet disputes which led to the total withdrawal of Soviet experts and Soviet aid to China. Nature even added to the difficulties with three successive years of drought, flood, and bad crops.

Ideological Disputes

The economic crisis, which became acute after 1959, led various prominent party leaders to question seriously and openly the efficiency of Mao Tse-tung's leadership and the reliability of his thought.[1] It would be wrong to assume that the dispute over Mao's leadership and his thought had not occurred until this time within the Chinese Communist Party. While the Chinese Communists often hid most of their internal factional strifes, the changes of high-ranking personnel and the purges of party leadership often split the party leadership right to the peak of the hierarchy.

Often, it was the ideological aspect of the dispute which posed serious problems for the regime. Many ideological remolding campaigns were launched to rectify the deviation from the party line, such as the anti-rightist campaigns that followed the "Hundred schools and hundred flowers contending" campaigns of 1957 and subsequent Socialist Education campaigns which included several mass movements.

One such mass movement was called the Four Withs, under which policy cadres were sent to the countryside to investigate abuses of Socialist morality by (1) eating, (2) living, (3) working, and (4) communicating with the poor and lower-middle peasants. Another was called the Four Clearance movement, which was to correct cadre corruption in respect to (1) financial affairs, (2) work points, (3) accounts, and (4) storage of produce.

In addition to its economic implications, the Socialist Education campaigns also involved the intensive study of Mao

---

1 Mu Fu-sheng, *The Wilting of the Hundred Flowers* (New York, Praeger, 1962).

Tse-tung's thought as well as uplifting the educational standards of the peasantry. There were, for example, some 19,000 sales stations established for Mao's works during the campaign, and more than 12,000,000 copies of his works were published for the peasants during the initial stage of the campaign. Moreover, many mass educational schools were expanded into the rural areas. The Communists also utilized other media, such as newspapers, operas, dramas, novels, motion pictures, and radio broadcasts, in carrying out their campaign. Although the Socialist education campaigns had met some success in rural areas, this movement encountered stiff and stubborn resistance in the intellectual community. For example, Mao Tse-tung himself complained in December, 1963, that in the various fields of literature and art "very little had been achieved so far in Socialist transformation" and termed "absurd" the fact that "many Communists showed enthusiasm in advancing feudal and capitalist art, but not zeal in promoting socialist art."[1]

There was some truth to this charge by Mao. During the period 1961-62 there was definitely renewed interest in traditional Chinese literature, China's old popular novels, and particularly China's traditional history. In line with this awakened interest in ancient literature, there were large reprints of old, popular works. It was alleged that 7,500 tons of paper were used to reprint ancient Chinese classics in 1962, while only 70 tons were devoted to Mao's works. In fact, in 1961-62 there was a sort of cultural renaissance for Communist China, and many leading intellectuals, both inside and outside of the party, used this opportunity to criticize Mao Tse-tung and his policies.

As a result, the party launched a thoroughgoing rectification in 1964 "on the front of literature and art" against intellectual cadres. This rectification campaign, initiated in September, 1964, and extending to mid-1965, had pushed the Socialist education movement into a new stage. Many eminent philosophers, party historians, novelists, and playwrights were purged.

It seems, however, that the rectification campaigns had divided the Chinese Communist Party. Not all of the party members were committed to the Maoist interpretation of

1 *The Great Socialist Cultural Revolution in China*, No. 5 (Peking, Foreign Language Press, 1966). See Richard Baum and Frederick C. Teiwes, *Ssu-Ch'ing—The Socialist Education Movement of 1962-1966* (Berkeley, Calif., Center for Chinese Studies, 1968).

Marxism-Leninism, nor were they readily accepting Maoism as the guiding ideology for China as a developing nation. Consequently, a new phase of rectification campaign, the "Great Proletarian Cultural Revolution," became inevitable.

The Great Proletarian Cultural Revolution

In the summer of 1966 volcanic mass movement swept over the mainland of China. Article after article appeared in the Chinese newspapers attacking "anti-party, anti-Socialist" elements. Many of China's leaders had been removed from power. P'eng Chen, the powerful mayor of Peking, disappeared from the public scene, and the Peking Municipal Party Committee was reorganized on June 4. Mao demoted Liu Shao-chi, Chairman of the Republic, from the second to the eighth position in the party, while Lin Piao, backed by the Army, became the second in command. In the universities and secondary schools, "left-wing" students began to form bands which publicly attacked leading university officials. From cities to countryside, the tremors were felt.

Despite the involvement of plots and counterplots in the initial stage of the Cultural Revolution, one must not assume that a power struggle was underway. In fact, a power struggle was merely the by-product of the Cultural Revolution, a continuation of the earlier ideological campaigns. Furthermore, the Cultural Revolution was a form of mass mobilization, with Mao himself as the catalyst to revitalize as well as to destroy. Phase by phase the revolt progressed toward a goal established by Mao. His aim was to create, as previously noted, a "new national, scientific, and mass culture" and to shape China by total mass mobilization to "catch up and surpass the advanced world levels in the not too distant future."[1]

However, the Cultural Revolution suffered a serious setback from the very beginning because of the opposition it created within the party organization. It has been estimated that Mao Tse-tung could not summon more than thirty percent support from the present membership in the ruling Central Committee

---

1 *Peking Review* (November 3, 1967), p. 15. Also see Thomas Robinson *et al.*, *The Cultural Revolution in China* (Berkeley, Calif., University of California Press, 1971).

(52 out of 172 full and alternate members in 1967).[1] The extent and seriousness of the opposition can also be seen from the publication of a list of 127 prominent party officials and intellectuals as "Monsters and Demons" or "Black Gangsters" in November, 1966.[2]

At times the opposition was composed of government officials who had held office for seventeen or eighteen years; they fought back by whatever means at their disposal, including inciting work stoppages, strikes, and sabotage of production. Another tactic often used was to trick the followers of the Cultural Revolution to return to cities from the countrysides, thereby swamping transportation and distribution systems. In some cases the opponents engaged in street fighting with the Maoists.

Mao's reaction toward his opposition was repeatedly one of arrest, dismissal, retention, and transfer. For example, all cadres who were accused of being "anti-party, anti-Socialist rightists" were to be arrested or dismissed. Other cadres who made "serious mistakes but have not become anti-party, anti-Socialist rightists" were retained by "giving them a chance to make up for their mistakes."[3]

To ensure the successful implementation of his policy and at the same time prevent an outright civil war, Mao relied heavily upon the youthful Red Guards—or as Mao Tse-tung colored it, "large numbers of revolutionary young people, previously unknown, who have become courageous and daring path-breakers. They are vigorous in action and intelligent. Through the media of big-character posters and great debates, they argue things out, expose and criticize thoroughly, and launch resolute attacks on the open and hidden representatives of the bourgeoisie."[4]

Thus, within three months of the official debut of the Red Guards at a Peking rally on August 18, 1966, some 15,000,000

1 See Winberg Chai, "The Reorganization of the Chinese Communist Party, 1966-1968," *Asian Survey*, Vol. VIII, No. 11 (November, 1968).

2 For the complete list see Asia Research Center (Hong Kong), *The Great Cultural Revolution in China* (1967).

3 See Chalmers Johnson, "China, The Cultural Revolution in Structure Perspective," *Asian Survey* (January, 1968).

4 See *Decision of the Central Committee on Cultural Revolution* (Peking, Foreign Language Press, 1966), p. 2.

to 20,000,000 young people had formed themselves into the movement, organized on the basis of their educational institutions. The initial goals were (1) to revolt against *(tsao-fan)* the "four olds" (old thought, old culture, old custom, and old habits), (2) to exchange "revolutionary experiences," and (3) to become "revolutionary successors" *(ke-ming chieh-pan jen)*.

In order to achieve these goals, the Red Guards were told to become *chuang-chiang*—to exhibit a strong touch of bravado, to be somewhat like outlaws. And these desperadoes certainly ignited a great mass revolt against those who opposed Mao and the party machines as well.

However, as the Red Guards accomplished Mao's initial goals, they began to get out of hand, and Mao ordered a more constructive approach of indoctrination using concepts such as "a mountainous task can be surmounted," "selflessness," the "discipline of criticism," "constant improvement," and "close links with the masses to build a modern society" (see Documents 2 and 4). To ensure that his new directives were carried out without further delay and complication, Mao ordered the People's Liberation Army to reestablish "law and order."[1] Thus today in Communist China the military not only wields most of the power but also has the responsibility of training new party cadres to propagate Mao's program and ideology for years to come.[2]

1 See Winberg Chai, "The Reorganization of the Chinese Communist Party," *op. cit.*
2 For a complete evaluation of Chinese policy, see Winberg Chai, *New Politics of Communist China* (Pacific Palisades, Calif., Goodyear Publishing Co., 1972).

IV.

Chinese Foreign Policy Themes

Prior to the 1966 Cultural Revolution, Chinese foreign policy was made under the joint control of the Chinese Communist Party Central Committee and the State Council of the People's Republic. The Foreign Minister's role was then strictly limited to that of foreign affairs spokesman and administrator of his ministry, which was merely an "executive instrumentality for carrying out policies decided by the Party."[1]

After the launching of the Cultural Revolution, Mao Tse tung changed the control apparatus of the Chinese Communist Party into a "troika" system consisting of the Military Affairs Committee of the Party Central Committee, the newly established Central Cultural Revolution Group, and the State Council. Policy-making power was taken away from the Central Committee of the Chinese Communist Party and placed in the hands of the Military Affairs Committee after the reorganization of that committee in 1966.[2]

In international relations, the Cultural Revolution resulted in an unprecedented degree of hostility and violence directed toward foreign nations' diplomatic missions and personnel in China. There was increasing tension and conflict within the ministry, including clashes between senior and junior officials, which together with the hostility toward foreigners by Red Guards paralyzed the routine operation of the ministry. As a result, many lower- and middle-echelon personnel in Chinese

1 *Staffing Procedures and Problems in Communist China* (Subcommittee on National Security Staffing and Operations, U.S. Senate, 1963), p. 21.

2 Winberg Chai, "The Reorganization of the Chinese Communist Party, 1966-1968," *Asian Survey*, Vol. VIII, No. 11 (November, 1968), pp. 901-10.

embassies abroad came to play important roles in performing the conduct of China's foreign relations. [1]

However, the extremely unfavorable reactions abroad with respect to Chinese attitudes during the Cultural Revolution made it imperative for the leadership in Peking to reverse the trend. After the Ninth National Congress of the Chinese Communist Party ended on April 24, 1969, Premier Chou En-lai was given a free hand to reorganize the Chinese government and to correct past mistakes in order to increase its responsiveness to the international environment (see Appendix B).

And 1970-71 rendered convincing evidence that the temporary militance of the Cultural Revolution did not represent a permanent change in China's foreign policy. Five major themes are now dominant in China's relations with foreign countries:

1. Maoism as a theory and practice in international relations
2. People's war as a strategy for the seizure of political power
3. Self-reliance as a model for Socialist construction in developing nations
4. Paper-tiger concept as a psychological deterrent to big-power hegemony
5. Antiimperialism as a condition for peaceful coexistence and world peace.

Maoism as Theory and Practice in International Relations

It has now become evident that China will emerge as one of the dominant forces in world politics; and Maoism, from the Chinese standpoint, must be a guiding principle in international relations.

The term "Maoism," according to Jerome Ch'en, a noted China specialist, is a "handy coinage of Western, or more precisely, of Harvard scholars" [2] which has now gained wide circulation. The Chinese describe it as "Mao Tse-tung Thought" *(Mao Tse-tung ssu-hsiang)* which has been incorporated into the revised Constitution of China (see Appendix A). In Article 2 of

1 Melvin Gurtov, "The Foreign Ministry and Foreign Affairs During the Cultural Revolution," *The China Quarterly*, No. 40 (October-December, 1969), pp. 65-102.

2 Jerome Ch'en, *Mao and the Chinese Revolution* (New York, Oxford University Press, 1965), p. 3.

the Constitution, it states that "Mao Tse-tung's Thought is the guiding compass of all the work of the people of the whole nation."

The practice of Maoism, in fact, operates on two different levels. On the philosophical level, Maoism as the variant of Marxism-Leninism becomes a theoretical system. The Chinese claim that Mao Tse-tung has made a major contribution to the theory of dialectical materialism, as illustrated in Mao's published works "On Practice" (1937) and "On Contradiction" (allegedly written in 1937 but not published until 1952). [1]

In "On Practice," Mao perpetuates dialectical materialism and the neo-Confucian school of idealism. He states that the process of knowledge has three stages: perception, conception, and verification. Mao also emphasizes the relevancy of ideology to action—that is, the unity of theory and practice. On the basis of this analysis, Mao is said to have discovered "the criterion of scientific truth" which can be applied to the criticism of opposing policies as well as to the maintenance of leadership infallibility.

An illustration of this theory can be found in a 1971 study by the Writing Group of the Communist Party: "Chairman Mao not only affirmed in clear terms the Marxist viewpoint of practice but scientifically summarized the practical contents as something applied in the practice of production, in the practice of revolutionary class struggle and revolutionary national struggle and in the practice of scientific experiment" (see Document 8).

The other essay, "On Contradiction," was a companion piece to "On Practice." Again taking the Marxist-Leninist doctrine as a base, Mao insists that contradictions are inherent in human relations and, therefore, govern politics. In this work he on the one hand stresses the "universality of contradiction," such as in war, offense and defense, advance and retreat, etc., and on the other their "particularity" as determined by the needs of time and place.

Since the essay's publication, the theory of contradictions has played a prominent part in the official ideology of the Chinese Communists. This essay became supremely important

---

1 Winberg Chai, ed., *Essential Works of Chinese Communism* (New York, Bantam Books, 1969), pp. 83-117.

in Chinese Communist ideology after Mao's speech "On the Correct Handling of Contradictions Among the People," published in 1957. In it he differentiates two types of contradictions. "The first, called antagonistic contradictions, . . . exist[s] between hostile classes and hostile social systems." These are contradictions, he explains, "between the enemy and ourselves," and being essentially violent, these contradictions can be resolved only by force (though not necessarily war). "The second is called non-antagonistic contradictions," which exist within the Socialist society; being essentially nonviolent, these contradictions can be resolved through the process of "uniting, criticizing and education." [1]

There is another level of Maoism which serves as the day-to-day operational guide for carrying out governmental policies. In international relations, we find that the Chinese use this guide for conducting conventional diplomatic and commercial relations within the accepted nation-state system, often practicing the principles of negotiation and compromise (see Chapter One).

People's Wars as a Strategy for the Seizure of Political Power

This second major theme of China's foreign policy was first developed by Mao Tse-tung and later expanded by Lin Piao, China's Defense Minister. Lin's essay "Long Live the Victory of People's War" has been widely publicized as a comprehensive, systematic, and profound analysis of Mao's theory and strategic concept of "people's war" (see Document 58).

Mao originally developed this strategy in his report to the Central Committee of the Chinese Communist Party in November, 1928, commonly known as Mao's report on "Struggle in the Chingkang Mountains."[2] In this report, Mao stated that in order for an "armed independent base" to survive and grow, it requires the following conditions: "(1) a round mass base, (2) a sound Party organization, (3) a fairly strong Red Army, (4) terrain favorable to military operations, and (5) economic resources sufficient for sustenance."[3]

1 Winberg Chai, ed., *Essential Works of Chinese Communism, op. cit.* pp. 327-40.

2 *Ibid.*, pp. 65-71.

3 *Ibid.*

It is in this report that Mao stressed his policy of transferring "the revolutionary bases, and muster[ing] and develop[ing] their strength in order to surround, and eventually capture, cities,"[1] or, in the words of Chinese Communist Party theoretician Chen Po-ta, that this policy "as the starting point of the road along which Comrade Mao Tse-tung led the revolution to nation-wide victory."[2] Because of its eventual success, this policy, while it was not originally part of Marxism-Leninism, became a further development of the thought of Mao Tse-tung as a guiding ideology of the revolutionary movement of all underdeveloped nations.

Moreover, the strategy and tactics of guerrilla warfare is associated with the theory of people's wars. Again according to Chen Po-ta, "the main strategy of the revolutionary war as expounded by Comrade Mao Tse-tung was to develop guerrilla warfare to the fullest possible extent and on a large scale and then, under certain conditions, after the growth of our strength, to transform it into regular warfare."[3] And Mao is famous for his sixteen-word formulation of guerrilla warfare:

> Enemy advances, we withdraw;
> Enemy withdraws, we progress;
> Enemy weakens, we fight;
> Enemy retreats, we pursue.[4]

Many Soviet writers paid Mao special tribute in discussing his treatise on guerrilla warfare, but the Chinese insisted that Mao's strategy of "people's war must not be mistaken as mere military tactics." Mao, in fact, insists that the Army is to have three types of political relationships in a people's war: with the party, with the people, and with the enemy. Although Mao Tse-tung did say that "political power grows out the barrel of a gun," he qualified the statement by restating that "Our principle is that the party commands the gun, but the gun must never be allowed to command the Party."[5]

1 Chen Po-ta, "Mao Tse-tung's Theory of the Chinese Revolution is the Integration of Marxism-Leninism with the Chinese Revolution," Hsueh-hsi (July 1, 1951), quoted in Arthur A. Cohen, *The Communism of Mao Tse-tung* (Chicago, University of Chicago Press, 1964), pp. 54-55.
2 *Ibid.*
3 *Ibid.*
4 *Jen-min Jih-pao* (February 23, 1953) (author's translations).
5 See I. Plyshevskiy and A. Sobolev in *Pravda*, June 13, 1953, as quoted in Arthur A. Cohen, *The Communism of Mao Tse-tung, op. cit.*, p.56.

Self-Reliance as a Model for Socialist Construction in Developing Nations

The third major theme in China's foreign relations deals with the principle of self-reliance, which China uses as its policy on economic aid and trade. There are four fundamental principles: (1) "self-reliance means to rely on the strength and diligent labor of our people to carry on economic construction," (2) "to build socialism self-reliantly means to make full use of all available resources in our country," (3) "to build socialism self-reliantly means to get the necessary funds for construction through internal accumulation," and (4) "self-reliance in building socialism also means that we must gain and accumulate our own experience in building socialism and gain knowledge of the laws of socialist construction through our own efforts instead of copying the experience of other nations" (see Document 41).

As early as January, 1945, Mao Tse-tung wrote that "We stand for self-reliance. We hope for foreign aid but cannot be dependent on it; we depend on our own efforts, on the creative power of the whole army and the entire people."[1] In fact, Lin Piao speaks of self-reliance even in a people's war: "In order to make a revolution and to fight a people's war and be victorious, it is imperative to adhere to the policy of self-reliance, rely on the strength of the masses in one's own country and prepare to carry on the fight independently even when all material aid from outside is cut off" (see Document 58).

Since Maoism itself evolved out of successful practice in handling political work and military affairs during the Sino-Japanese War period, China's policy of self-reliance is a direct result of that experience. This can be illustrated by Sino-Soviet relations. The Soviet Union, despite its massive aids in terms of industrial projects, credits, and loans to China, had not given the Maoist government a single free grant for economic development. In fact, the Chinese government has been repaying Soviet loans since 1954, and at times the payment included a minimal interest charge of one percent.

In addition, contrary to the trade with Western countries, prices of import commodities from the Soviet Union, when

1 See Mao's "Problems of War and Strategy," *Selected Works, op. cit.*, Vol. II, p. 219.

converted into Chinese currencies at the official rate, were generally much higher than prices of similar goods produced in Communist China (at least prior to the open Sino-Soviet rifts in 1960).[1] For example, a Chinese economist wrote in 1957 that "According to our statistical results from a survey on 33 types of lathes, the prices of imported lathes (from the Soviet Union) are on the average 61% higher than the prices of lathes domestically produced with exactly the same specifications."[2]

The Chinese are also very much against aid from the Western countries, including the United States. Another Chinese economist, Kuo Wen, wrote an article for the benefit of developing nations: "The imperialists, especially the U.S. imperialists, are doing all they can to use 'aid' as a means to buy over influential politicians, support reactionary regimes, foster financial dependence, maintain and supply satellite troops, 'rent' military bases and try to suppress the people's revolution, etc., in the 'aid' recipient countries. One of the main aims in doing this is to maintain colonialist political control and influence in these countries, thus providing general political guarantees for investments" (see Document 42).

However, the stress of self-reliance does not necessarily mean the absence of international cooperation. In the same article, the Chinese economist continues: "self-reliance, however, by no means excludes international economic cooperation on the basis of equality and mutual benefit. In combatting imperialism and colonialism, and developing independent national economics, it is necessary for the Asian, African and Latin American peoples to strengthen their militant unity and relations of mutual help" (see Document 42).

Here he again refers to their own experiences as a model: "In order to successfully carry on the struggle against imperialism and colonialism and implement the policy of self-reliance effectively, democratic reforms, especially land reforms, are necessary. These reforms will . . . enhance the initiative and creativeness of the people in national revolution and economic development. . . . It is the only one which will enable the 'underdeveloped' countries to become strong and prosperous" (see Document 42).

1 See Kang Chao, "Sino-Soviet Exchange Rates," *China Quarterly* (July/September, 1971), pp. 546-52.

2 Han Yuan-tso, "Problems of Economy in Basic Construction," *Chi Hsieh Kung Yeh*, No. 8 (1957), p. 7.

Paper-Tiger Concept as a Psychological Deterrent to Big-Power Hegemony

The Communist Chinese have many fears: first, the fear of annihilation by the Kuomintang forces; then, the fear of nuclear attack by the United States and the USSR; and, finally, the fear of eventual take-over by the industrialized and aggressive Japanese. However, for Mao Tse-tung the revolutionary process had always been one of turning weakness into strength. And in the psychological field, according to Arthur A. Cohen, Mao has succeeded remarkably well "to instill into the Party and Army firm revolutionary confidence and determination by advancing slogans, or concepts of optimism."[1] One of the most important concepts of optimism is Mao's "paper tiger."

Mao derived the concept from an old Chinese fairy tale of the T'ang Dynasty. There was a "Kweichow donkey" which brayed and kicked ferociously before a tiger. As the tiger had never seen such a creature before, he was at first terrified. Then the tiger discovered that the donkey could only bray and kick, so he devoured it. The moral in this story is simply that things are not always as fearsome as they appear.[2]

Mao developed this thought later into a philosophy of "strategic optimism," as he explained to the American correspondent Anna Louise Strong in an interview in August, 1946: "All reactionaries are paper tigers. In appearance, they are frightening, but in reality they don't amount to much. From the long-term point of view, it is the people who really have great strength, and not the reactionaries" (see Document 6). This was at the time when his revolutionary prospects were dimmed because of the overwhelming military strengths of Chiang Kai-shek. Mao was using the late American correspondent to gain international sympathy and to save his own forces from drowning in "a sea of pessimism."

However, Mao is not "an impetuous man blind to the reality of his enemy's superiority."[3] His action at that time showed him to have been a very cautious man. When Chiang Kai-shek's forces under General Hu Tsung-nan's command advanced and captured his capital, Yenan, Mao was retreating, conserving his

1 Arthur A. Cohen, *The Communism of Mao Tse-tung, op. cit.*, p. 59.
2 J. S. Simmonds, *China's World* (New York, Columbia University Press, 1970), p. 165.
3 Arthur A. Cohen, *The Communism of Mao Tse-tung, op. cit.*, p. 60.

own troops rather than fighting, and using guerrilla tactics for survival. But his paper-tiger concept had lifted the morale of his men, and eventually he was able to turn the tide of defeat into victory.

The second time the paper-tiger concept was introduced was during the 1958 U.S.-China confrontation in the Taiwan Strait. Mao used this strategy to provide his own forces with confidence, and he was determined not to be blackmailed by nuclear threats from the then Secretary of State John Foster Dulles. As in the previous time, the Chinese action was cautious and reflected the consideration that the "enemy's power must not be underestimated."[1]

This time a special collection of Mao's remarks was published by the editorial department of the Chinese *Jen-min Jih-pao (People's Daily)*: "We are certainly able and have the confidence to defeat all the enemies of the Chinese people at home and abroad. But in regard to each individual part and in each concrete struggle (whether military, political, economic or ideological) we must never underestimate the enemy. On the contrary, we should take full account of the enemy, concentrate all our efforts on the fight. Only in this way can victory be achieved."[2]

By 1957, Mao Tse-tung himself had revised his original concept of the paper tiger by the inclusion of "real tigers" as well. This is illustrated in the secret speech Mao delivered before the party's Politburo held at Wuchang on December 1, 1958. "Just as there is not a single thing in the world without a dual nature (this is the law of Unity of Opposites), so imperialism and all reactionaries have a dual nature—they are real tigers and paper tigers at the same time. . . . Imperialism and all reactionaries, looked at in essence, from a long-term point of view, from a strategic point of view, must be seen for what they are—paper tigers. On the other hand, they are also living tigers, iron tigers, real tigers, which can eat people. On this we should build our tactical thinking."[3]

1 Allen Whiting, "What Nixon Must Do to Make It in Peking," *The New York Review of Books* (October 7, 1971), pp. 10-13.

2 Mao Tse-tung, *Imperialism and All Reactionaries Are Paper-Tigers* (Peking, Foreign Language Press, 1958), pp. 23-24.

3 Quoted in Arthur A. Cohen, *The Communism of Mao Tse-tung, op. cit.*, p. 65.

The risk of invasion or nuclear attack is theoretically diminished by the fact the Chinese now possess nuclear weapons. However, the paper-tiger concept helped Mao Tse-tung bluff his way through a time in which China did not have and both the United States and the USSR did have nuclear weapons. However, Chinese foreign policy continues to use this important theme in order to convince other developing nations that they too are not militarily weak or psychologically unfit to combat "big-power hegemony and imperialist aggression." And "the Chinese people," a Peking editorial declares, "will fight together with the people of the whole world to resolutely smash the doctrine of big-nation hegemony" (see Document 63).

Anti-Imperialism as a Condition for Peaceful Coexistence and World Peace

From 1960 until 1970, the leaders of China, in a torrential output of publication due to the Sino-Soviet disputes as well as the Cultural Revolution, developed their Maoist vision of today's world: anti-imperialism as a condition for peaceful coexistence and world peace. Here imperialism denotes the policies and practices of the world's two superpowers, the United States and the USSR.

The Chinese experience with both the United States and the USSR has indeed been a sad one (see Chapters Two and Three). From the very beginning, Sino-American relations have been caught in a hopeless deadlock over a variety of major issues including the Korean War and the status of Taiwan, as well as China's role in the international community.

China was in close alliance with the Soviet Union in the 1950's, but that alliance soon turned to bitterness, hatred, and finally open hostility. And the only friends China seemed to be able to count on were the small countries of the third world—Asia, Africa, and Latin America.

To be assured, the People's Republic of China is the largest country on earth, with a population of more than 750,000,000—one-fourth of the human race. But in terms of gross national product, China has been ranked in the eighth position, after the United States, the USSR, Japan, West Germany, the United Kingdom, France, and Italy. Also, if we measure China's per capita GNP, it stands far lower on the ladder.[1] China's needs include massive economic and technical assistance, which no superpower at the present time is willing or capable of providing.

From the Chinese point of view, the policies and practice of "imperialist powers" have been the great obstacle to the economic development of the underdeveloped countries. For example, the Chinese complained that during the period of industrial capitalism the "advanced" capitalist countries in Europe and North America, backed by gunboat diplomacy, had already begun the large-scale export of commodities to Asia, Africa, and Latin America. This led to the destruction of the handicrafts of the colonial and semicolonial countries and the throttling of their national industries, thereby turning them into suppliers of raw materials. In the period of imperialism, by means of capital exports, the monopolies took a direct part in developing the production of primary products in the underdeveloped countries which they themselves needed, particularly raw mineral materials. At the same time, they established more factories there. As a result, the national industries suffered both from competition from imported goods and directly from local factories operated by foreign capital. The economics of the underdeveloped countries thus became more lopsided (see Document 42).

And the Soviet record, in the eye of the Chinese, is equally corrupt and gives equal cause for apprehension. " 'The specialization of production' and 'international division of Labor,' brayed about and put into operation by the Soviet revisionists have brought about a lopsided development of the economics of those East European countries and turned them into workshops of the Soviet revisionists for processing raw materials and a dumping grounds for their goods. Moreover, by 'granting credits,' Soviet revisionism has savagely plundered these countries and grabbed fabulous profits from them" (see Document 60).

This is why Mao Tse-tung wrote, "revolutions and revolutionary wars are inevitable in class society and without them, it is impossible to accomplish any leap in social development and to

1 China ranks 101 in terms of per capita GNP. See Alexander Eckstein, *Communist China's Economic Growth and Foreign Trade* (New York, McGraw-Hill, 1966), p. 249.

overthrow the reactionary ruling classes and therefore impossible for the people to win political power."[1] And Mao continued, "history shows that wars are divided into two kinds, just and unjust. All wars that are progressive are just, and all wars that impede progress are unjust. We Communists oppose all unjust wars that impede progress, but we do not oppose progressive, just wars." [2]

Does this mean that China will unleash a "just" nuclear war to liberate the third world from the "imperialists' " oppression? In the fifth comment on the "Open Letter of the Central Committee of the CPSU," the Chinese stated on November 19, 1963: "We have always maintained that socialist countries must not use nuclear weapons to support the people's wars of national liberation and revolutionary civil wars and have no need to do so. We have always maintained that the socialist countries must achieve and maintain nuclear superiority. Only this can prevent the imperialists from launching a nuclear war and help bring about the complete prohibition of nuclear weapons." [3]

Although China has not produced Vasquez, or Ayala, or Grotius to define the rights of war between states, it imparts the maxim that "it never pays, and it is never right to wage a war of aggression against any state."[4] Peking has certainly profited by its mistakes in foreign relations during the 1950's and the 1960's and is now seeking to avoid a repetition by a more cautious move.

However, in the years ahead, the Chinese Communists may be expected to fight imperialism and imperialist policies of superpowers, whether the brand is U.S., Soviet, or the emerging Japanese, short of war. And China will continue to utilize other methods, as every powerful nation does, such as propaganda, subversion, trade, foreign aid, and cultural activities, to support its foreign policies objectives.

1 Mao Tse-tung, "On Contradiction," *Selected Works, op.cit.,* Vol. I, p. 344.

2 Mao Tse-tung, "On Protracted War," *Selected Works, op.cit.,* Vol. II, p. 150.

3 *The Polemic on the General Line of the International Communist Movement* (Peking, Foreign Language Press, 1965), pp. 245-46.

4 See Winberg Chai, "International Law and Diplomacy in Ancient China (771-221 B.C.): An Introduction," *Chinese Culture Quarterly,* Vol. V, No. 2 (October, 1963), pp. 47-58.

CHAPTER ONE:
Maoism: Basic Operational Guides

The practice of Maoism, as already stated in the Introduction, operates on two different levels. In fact, Maoism remains to some extent within the Chinese tradition with its repeated moral exhortation. Therefore, on a day-to-day operational level, it serves as the basic guide for the Communist cadres to carry out governmental policies which may be summarized as follows:

1. The importance of assuming the leadership role, based upon "correct political orientation," "faith and self-sacrifices," and "courage." (See Documents 2, 3, 4, 6.)
2. The importance of practicing "investigation and research" before making a decision or implementing a decision. (See Documents 1, 8.)
3. The importance of practicing "negotiation" and "compromise" and avoiding "one-sidedness." (See Documents 5, 7.)

According to Mao, the transformation and construction of a modern China depends on the correct leadership role assumed by the Communist cadres. The Communist Party has outlined many rules and guides for the training of the cadres based on Mao's teachings, such as five of the eight documents in this chapter known as "five constantly read articles," or simply practicing Mao's basic rules, such as learning "the four firsts," the "three-eight" working style, and the "three main rules of discipline," as well as the "eight points for attention," to name but a few.[1]

1 *Peking Review* (March 15, 1968), p. 10. *Cf.* Franz Schurmann, *Ideology and Organization in Communist China*, rev. ed. (Berkeley, Calif., University of California Press, 1968).

The so-called "four firsts" are "first place to man, first place to political work, first place to ideological work and first place to living (creative) ideas." The "three-eight" working style is derived from Mao's three famous Chinese phrases (firm, correct political orientation; a plain, hard-working style; flexibility in strategy and tactic) and eight additional Chinese characters, which in English mean unity, alertness, earnestness, and liveliness. The other rules, such as the three main rules of discipline and the eight points for attention are basically used by the Chinese People's Liberation Army as a guide for their day-to-day relationship with the common people.[1]

When applying these rules to the conduct of foreign relations, Mao insists that diplomatic personnel must be associated with correct political orientation, as well as all the other requirements identified with the party's training in leadership. Mao often reminds his cadres that China is an underdeveloped country, that she cannot afford the "luxury" and "casualness" of the "imperialist" advanced nations of the West. In fact, all Chinese working abroad must follow Mao's teachings at all times.

As an illustration, the Chinese *People's Daily* reported the experiences of Chinese technicians in Tanzania by stating that "during their stay of more than two years in Tanzania they had kept in mind the teachings of Chairman Mao, taking the internationalist fighter Norman Bethune as their example, lived and worked with the Tanzanian people and established close friendly relations with them."[2]

Secondly, the training of Chinese cadres at all levels is impressively thorough, with great emphasis on the principle of practicing "research and investigation." As explained by Arthur Lall, an experienced Indian negotiator with the Chinese, this process involves five stages: (1) research on the assigned subjects, (2) research on the relevant party policies, regulations, directives, and resolutions which may have bearings upon such subjects, (3) research on concrete experiences arising in the work of the relevant department, (4) research on the historical

---

1 See Winberg Chai, "The Reorganization of the Chinese Communist Party, 1966-1968," *Asian Survey*, Vol. VIII, No. 11 (November, 1968), p. 908.

2 *Jen-min Jih-pao* (June 19, 1968).

background of each department's work relating to the subjects, and (5) research and investigation on the "scientific principles" pertinent to a full knowledge of the subjects.[1]

Such "research and investigation" is never limited to book or library research; rather, it must involve the investigation of the actual situation—*i.e.*, be based on practical experience of the researcher himself (see Document 1). As the 1971 Writing Group of the Chinese Communist Party wrote, "If one wants to know anything, one must directly participate in the practical struggle to change reality for only thus can one come into contact with it as a phenomenon; only through personal participation in the practical struggle to change reality can one uncover the essence of what one wants to know and know the law of things. This is the path to knowledge" (see Document 8).

A third major operational guide based upon Maoism involves the importance of practicing negotiation, compromising, and avoiding one-sidedness. Mao Tse-tung, in an inner-party circular, set forth the principal conditions under which the Chinese Communist may find it desirable to negotiate with his opponent (see Document 5).

Franklin W. Houn, in an analysis of Mao's circular, maintained that there are five conditions under which the Chinese Communists will hold negotiation:

1. Chinese Communists will negotiate when they have fallen into the "quagmire of an indecisive struggle, armed or otherwise."

2. Chinese Communists will negotiate when confronted with "so strong an enemy that a combative posture would surely invite catastrophe, yet a strategic retreat or truce might enable them to conserve strength and wait for a more favorable change in the balance of power."

3. Chinese Communists will negotiate when "negotiation appears to be a promising way of resolving a specific conflict, whereas struggle (war) would entail a cost incommensurate with the anticipated gain."

4. Chinese Communists will negotiate when they "wish to devote their attention and resources to a more important or urgent project (or problem) at home or abroad."

---

1 Arthur Lall, *How Communist China Negotiates* (New York, Columbia University Press, 1968), p. 10.

5. Chinese Communists will negotiate when they can "win the sympathy of the concerned public (public opinion) and to expose the plots, hypocrisy, and other evil acts of the opponent (in other words, a propaganda victory)."[1]

In fact, in the views of this author, in certain respects Mao's conditions for negotiation resemble those of Hans Morgenthau's classic "fundamental rules of diplomacy," such as "nationals must be willing to compromise on all issues that are not vital to them" and "the objectives of foreign policy must be defined in terms of the national interest and must be supported with adequate power."[2]

Although Mao had probably never heard of Morgenthau, he nevertheless wrote, "We on our side are prepared to make such concessions as are necessary and as do not damage the fundamental interest of the people," and "You must definitely not rely on the negotiations, must definitely not hope that the Kuomintang (opposition) will be kind-hearted, because it will never be kind-hearted. You must rely on your own strength"[3] (see Document 5).

Of course, Mao Tse-tung is now an old man (born in 1893) and there must be anticipation of the time when he will die. What will be the status of Maoism after his death? After all, as A. Doak Barnett wrote, "In an age of nuclear weapons, computers, and space capsules, an age which China, however slowly, is starting to enter, these prescriptions of Mao's for the future sound oddly antiquarian. It seems evident, in fact, that as the Maoist period in China approaches its end, Mao himself is in many respects looking backward rather than forward."[4]

Of course, as time moves on the contents of cultural heritage change. Some of the old elements drop out while new elements develop and are integrated into the cultural system. In any event, no culture of any nation stands still, and Maoism of the future is likely to be different in content from that of the

1 Franklin W. Houn, "The Principles and Operational Code of Communist China's International Conduct," *Journal of Asian Studies*, Vol. XXVII, No. 1 (November, 1967), pp. 36-37.

2 Hans J. Morgenthau, *Politics Among Nations*, 4th ed. (New York, Alfred A. Knopf, 1967), pp. 542-43.

3 *Selected Works of Mao Tse-tung, op. cit.*, IV, pp. 49-50.

4 A. Doak Barnett, *China After Mao* (Princeton, Princeton University Press, 1967), p. 57.

present. However, the stream of Maoism has been broad enough to encompass not only the current of change, both gradual and rapid, but also the current of continuity, always latent and often active.

1. MAO TSE-TUNG: OPPOSE BOOK WORSHIP (May, 1930)*

This work was first written as an article and was included in a training manual for the Red Fourth Army during the guerrilla war days of the 1930's. Because of its proven practical values on the "techniques of investigation," it was reprinted in 1965 and became required reading for all of China's cadres and Red Guards.

I. No Investigation, No Right to Speak

Unless you have investigated a problem, you will be deprived of the right to speak on it. Isn't that too harsh? Not in the least. When you have not probed into a problem, into the present facts and its past history, and know nothing of its essentials, whatever you say about it will undoubtedly be nonsense. Talking nonsense solves no problems, as everyone knows, so why is it unjust to deprive you of the right to speak? Quite a few comrades always keep their eyes shut and talk nonsense, and for a Communist that is disgraceful. How can a Communist keep his eyes shut and talk nonsense?

It won't do!
It won't do!
You must investigate!
You must not talk nonsense!

II. To Investigate a Problem Is to Solve It

You can't solve a problem? Well, get down and investigate the present facts and its past history! When you have investigated the problem thoroughly, you will know how to solve it. Conclusions invariably come after investigation, and not before. Only a blockhead cudgels his brains on his own, or together with a group, to "find a solution" or "evolve an idea"

*Oppose Book Worship (Peking, Foreign Language Press, 1966), pp. 1-5, 13-16 (extract; footnotes omitted).

without making any investigation. It must be stressed that this cannot possibly lead to any effective solution or any good idea. In other words, he is bound to arrive at a wrong solution and a wrong idea.

There are not a few comrades doing inspection work, as well as guerrilla leaders and cadres newly in office, who like to make political pronouncements the moment they arrive at a place and who strut about, criticizing this and condemning that when they have only seen the surface of things or minor details. Such purely subjective nonsensical talk is indeed detestable. These people are bound to make a mess of things, lose the confidence of the masses and prove incapable of solving any problem at all.

When they come across difficult problems, quite a number of people in leading positions simply heave a sigh without being able to solve them. They lose patience and ask to be transferred on the ground that they "have not the ability and cannot do the job". These are cowards' words. Just get moving on your two legs, go the rounds of every section placed under your charge and "inquire into everything" as Confucius did, and then you will be able to solve the problems, however little your ability; for although your head may be empty before you go out of doors, it will be empty no longer when you return but will contain all sorts of material necessary for the solution of the problems, and that is how problems are solved. Must you go out of doors? Not necessarily. You can call a fact-finding meeting of people familiar with the situation in order to get at the source of what you call a difficult problem and come to know how it stands now, and then it will be easy to solve your difficult problem.

Investigation may be likened to the long months of pregnancy, and solving a problem to the day of birth. To investigate a problem is, indeed, to solve it.

III. Oppose Book Worship

Whatever is written in a book is right—such is still the mentality of culturally backward Chinese peasants. Strangely enough, within the Communist Party there are also people who always say in a discussion, "Show me where it's written in the book." When we say that a directive of a higher organ of leadership is correct, that is not just because it comes from "a higher organ of leadership" but because its contents conform with both the objective and subjective circumstances of the struggle and meet its requirements. It is quite wrong to take a formalistic attitude and blindly carry out directives without discussing and examining them in the light of actual conditions simply because they come from a higher organ. It is the mischief done by this formalism which explains why the line and tactics of the Party do not take deeper root among the masses. To carry out a directive of a higher organ blindly, and seemingly without any disagreement, is not really to carry it out but is the most artful way of opposing or sabotaging it.

The method of studying the social sciences exclusively from the book is likewise extremely dangerous and may even lead one onto the road of counter-revolution. Clear proof of this is provided by the fact that whole batches of Chinese Communists who confined themselves to books in their study of the social sciences have turned into counter-revolutionaries. When we say Marxism is correct, it is certainly not because Marx was a "prophet" but because his theory has been proved correct in our practice and in our struggle. We need Marxism in our struggle. In our acceptance of his theory no such formalistic or mystical notion as that of "prophecy" ever enters our minds. Many who have read Marxist books have become renegades from the revolution, whereas illiterate workers often grasp Marxism very well. Of course we should study Marxist books, but this study must be integrated with our country's actual conditions. We need books, but we must overcome book worship, which is divorced from the actual situation.

How can we overcome book worship? The only way is to investigate the actual situation.

* * *

VII. The Technique of Investigation

1. Hold fact-finding meetings and undertake investigation through discussions.

This is the only way to get near the truth, the only way to draw conclusions. It is easy to commit mistakes if you do not hold fact-finding meetings for investigation through discussions but simply rely on one individual relating his own experience.

You cannot possibly draw more or less correct conclusions at such meetings if you put questions casually instead of raising key questions for discussion.

2. What kind of people should attend the fact-finding meetings?

They should be people well acquainted with social and economic conditions. As far as age is concerned, older people are best, because they are rich in experience and not only know what is going on but understand the causes and effects. Young people with experience of struggle should also be included, because they have progressive ideas and sharp eyes. As far as occupation is concerned, there should be workers, peasants, merchants, intellectuals, and occasionally soldiers, and sometimes even vagrants. Naturally, when a particular subject is being looked into, those who have nothing to do with it need not be present. For example, workers, peasants and students need not attend when commerce is the subject of investigation.

3. Which is better, a large fact-finding meeting or a small one?

That depends on the investigator's ability to conduct a meeting. If he is good at it, a meeting of as many as a dozen or even twenty or more people can be called. A large meeting has its advantages; from the answers you get fairly accurate statistics (*e.g.*, in finding out the percentage of poor peasants in the total peasant population) and fairly correct conclusions (*e.g.*, in finding out whether equal or differentiated land redistribution is better). Of course, it has its disadvantages too; unless you are skillful in conducting meetings, you will find it difficult to keep order. So the number of people attending a meeting depends on the competence of the investigator. However, the minimum is three, or otherwise the information obtained will be too limited to correspond to the real situation.

4. Prepare a detailed outline for the investigation.

A detailed outline should be prepared beforehand, and the investigator should ask questions according to the outline, with those present at the meeting giving their answers. Any points which are unclear or doubtful should be put up for discussion. The detailed outline should include main subjects and sub-headings and also detailed items. For instance, taking commerce as a main subject, it can have such sub-headings as cloth, grain, other necessities and medicinal herbs; again, under cloth, there can be such detailed items as calico, homespun and silk and satin.

5. Personal participation.

Everyone with responsibility for giving leadership—from the chairman of the township government to the chairman of the central government, from the detachment leader to the commander-in-chief, from the secretary of a Party branch to the general secretary—must personally undertake investigation into the specific social and economic conditions and not merely rely on reading reports. For investigation and reading reports are two entirely different things.

6. Probe deeply.

Anyone new to investigation work should make one or two thorough investigations in order to gain full knowledge of a particular place (say, a village or a town) or a particular problem (say, the problem of grain or currency). Deep probing into a particular place or problem will make future investigation of other places or problems easier.

7. Make your own notes.

The investigator should not only preside at fact-finding meetings and give proper guidance to those present but should also make his own notes and record the results himself. To have others do it for him is no good.

2. MAO TSE-TUNG: IN MEMORY OF NORMAN BETHUNE (December, 1939) and SERVE THE PEOPLE (September, 1944)*

These two articles were Mao's eulogies for China's war heroes during the earlier periods of revolution. Norman Bethune came to China as the head of a Canadian medical team to serve the Chinese Red Army and died during his service in China. Chang Sze-teh (in the second article) was a soldier who participated in the Long March with the Red Army and was killed in military action. These articles were both required readings during the Cultural Revolution.

In Memory of Norman Bethune

Comrade Norman Bethune, a member of the Communist Party of Canada, was around fifty when he was sent by the Communist Parties of Canada and the United States to China;

Serve the People (Peking, Foreign Language Press, 1966), pp. 1-8 (footnotes omitted).

he made light of travelling thousands of miles to help us in our War of Resistance Against Japan. He arrived in Yenan in the spring of last year, went to work in the Wutai Mountains, and to our great sorrow died a martyr at his post. What kind of spirit is this that makes a foreigner selflessly adopt the cause of the Chinese people's liberation as his own? It is the spirit of internationalism, the spirit of communism, from which every Chinese Communist must learn. Leninism teaches that the world revolution can only succeed if the proletariat of the capitalist countries supports the struggle for liberation of the colonial and semi-colonial peoples and if the proletariat of the colonies and semi-colonies supports that of the proletariat of the capitalist countries. Comrade Bethune put this Leninist line into practice. We Chinese Communists must also follow this line in our practice. We must unite with the proletariat of all the capitalist countries, with the proletariat of Japan, Britain, the United States, Germany, Italy and all other capitalist countries, for this is the only way to overthrow imperialism, to liberate our nation and people and to liberate the other nations and peoples of the world. This is our internationalism, the internationalism with which we oppose both narrow nationalism and narrow patriotism.

Comrade Bethune's spirit, his utter devotion to others without any thought of self, was shown in his great sense of responsibility in his work and his great warm-heartedness towards all comrades and the people. Every Communist must learn from him. There are not a few people who are irresponsible in their work, preferring the light and shirking the heavy, passing the burdensome tasks on to others and choosing the easy ones for themselves. At every turn they think of themselves before others. When they make some small contribution, they swell with pride and brag about it for fear that others will not know. They feel no warmth towards comrades and the people but are cold, indifferent and apathetic. In truth such people are not Communists, or at least cannot be counted as devoted Communists. No one who returned from the front failed to express admiration for Bethune whenever his name was mentioned, and none remained unmoved by his spirit. In the Shansi-Chahar-Hopei border area, no soldier or civilian was unmoved who had been treated by Dr. Bethune or had seen how he worked. Every Communist must learn this true communist spirit from Comrade Bethune.

Comrade Bethune was a doctor, the art of healing was his profession and he was constantly perfecting his skill, which stood very high in the Eighth Route Army's medical service. His example is an excellent lesson for those people who wish to change their work the moment they see something different and for those who despise technical work as of no consequence or as promising no future.

Comrade Bethune and I met only once. Afterwards he wrote me many letters. But I was busy, and I wrote him only one letter and do not even know if he ever received it. I am deeply grieved over his death. Now we are all commemorating him, which shows how profoundly his spirit inspires everyone. We must all learn the spirit of absolute selflessness from him. With this spirit everyone can be very useful to the people. A man's ability may be great or small, but if he has this spirit, he is already noble-minded and pure, a man of moral integrity and above vulgar interests, a man who is of value to the people.

Serve the People

Our Communist Party and the Eighth Route and New Fourth Armies led by our Party are battalions of the revolution. These battalions of ours are wholly dedicated to the liberation of the people and work entirely in the people's interests. Comrade Chang Sze-teh was in the ranks of these battalions.

All men must die, but death can vary in its significance. The ancient Chinese writer Ssuma Ch'ien said, "Though death befalls all men alike, it may be heavier than Mount Tai or lighter than a feather." To die for the people is heavier than Mount Tai, but to work for the fascists and die for the exploiters and oppressors is lighter than a feather. Comrade Chang Sze-teh died for the people, and his death is indeed heavier than Mount Tai.

If we have shortcomings, we are not afraid to have them pointed out and criticized, because we serve the people. Anyone, no matter who, may point out our shortcomings. If he is right, we will correct them. If what he proposes will benefit the people, we will act upon it. The idea of "better troops and simpler administration" was put forward by Mr. Li Ting-ming, who is not a Communist. He made a good suggestion which is of benefit to the people, and we have adopted it. If, in the interests of the people, we persist in doing what is right and correct what is wrong, our ranks will surely thrive.

We hail from all corners of the country and have joined together for a common revolutionary objective. And we need the vast majority of the people with us on the road to this objective. Today, we already lead base areas with a population of 91 million, but this is not enough; to liberate the whole nation more are needed. In times of difficulty we must not lose sight of our achievements, must see the bright future and must pluck up our courage. The Chinese people are suffering; it is our duty to save them and we must exert ourselves in struggle. Wherever there is struggle there is sacrifice, and death is a common occurrence. But we have the interests of the people and the sufferings of the great majority at heart, and when we die for the people it is a worthy death. Nevertheless, we should do our best to avoid unnecessary sacrifices. Our cadres must show concern for every soldier, and all people in the revolutionary ranks must care for each other, must love and help each other.

From now on, when anyone in our ranks who has done some useful work dies, be he soldier or cook, we should have a funeral ceremony and a memorial meeting in his honour. This should become the rule. And it should be introduced among the people as well. When someone dies in a village, let a memorial meeting be held. In this way we express our mourning for the dead and unite all the people.

3. MAO TSE-TUNG: TO BE ATTACKED BY THE ENEMY IS NOT A BAD THING BUT A GOOD THING (May, 1939)*

Mao developed his educational policy for the training of Communist cadres in this speech which he made before the Chinese People's Anti-Japanese Military and Political College on May 26, 1939. This article is also one of the "five constantly read" articles in today's China.

Why is it that the Anti-Japanese Military and Political College has become famous all over the country and even enjoys some reputation abroad? Because, of all the anti-Japanese military institutes, it is the most revolutionary, the most progressive, and the best fighter for national liberation and social emancipation.

*To Be Attacked by the Enemy Is not a Bad Thing but a Good Thing (Peking, Foreign Language Press, 1966), pp. 1-5 (footnotes omitted).

This, I think, is also the reason why visitors to Yenan are so keen on seeing it.

The college is revolutionary and progressive because both its staff members and teachers and its courses are revolutionary and progressive. Without this revolutionary and progressive character, it could never have won the praise of revolutionary people at home and abroad.

Some people attack the college; they are the country's capitulationists and die-hards. This only goes to show that the college is a most revolutionary and progressive one, or otherwise they would not attack it. The vigorous attacks by the capitulationists and die-hards testify to its revolutionary and progressive nature and add to its lustre. It is a glorious military institute not only because the majority of the people support and praise it, but also because the capitulationists and die-hards strenuously attack and slander it.

I hold that it is bad as far as we are concerned if a person, a political party, an army or a school is not attacked by the enemy, for in that case it would mean that we have sunk to the level of the enemy. It is good if we are attacked by the enemy, since it proves that we have drawn a clear line of demarcation between the enemy and ourselves. It is still better if the enemy attacks us wildly and paints us as utterly black and without a single virtue, since it demonstrates that we have not only drawn a clear line of demarcation between the enemy and ourselves but achieved a great deal in our work.

In the past three years, the Anti-Japanese Military and Political College has made a great contribution to the country, to the nation and to society by training tens of thousands of promising, progressive and revolutionary young students. It will certainly go on making its contribution to the country, the nation and society, because it will continue to train such young students in large numbers. In speaking of the college, people often compare it to the Whampoa Military Academy before the Northern Expedition. In fact, there are points of both similarity and difference between the two institutes. The similarity is the presence of Communists among the teachers and students in both. The difference is that, while the chief leaders and the majority of the students at the Whampoa Military Academy were members of the Kuomintang, the entire leadership of the Anti-Japanese Military and Political College is in the hands of the Communist Party and the vast majority of the students are communist or communist-inclined. For this reason, the Anti-Japanese Military and Political College of today cannot but be more revolutionary and more progressive than was the Whampoa Military Academy of the past, and it will certainly make a greater contribution to national liberation and social emancipation.

The educational policy of the college is to cultivate a firm and correct political orientation, an industrious and simple style of work, and flexible strategy and tactics. These are the three essentials in the making of an anti-Japanese revolutionary soldier. It is in accordance with these essentials that the staff teach and the students study.

The progress and development of the college over the past few years have been accompanied by certain shortcomings. It has grown, but difficulties have arisen too. The main difficulty is the shortage of funds, teachers and teaching materials. But led by the Communist Party, the college does not fear any difficulties and will certainly overcome them. There are no such things as difficulties for Communists, for they can surmount them.

It is my hope and the hope of the people of the whole country that the college will eliminate its shortcomings and become still more progressive after its third anniversary.

Teachers, staff members and students of the college, let us redouble our efforts!

4. MAO TSE-TUNG: THE FOOLISH OLD MAN WHO RE-MOVED THE MOUNTAINS (June, 1945)*

> *This was Mao's concluding speech made at the Seventh National Congress of the Chinese Communist Party on June 11, 1945, at the beginning of the Civil War in China. Mao's goal was to introduce a sense of confidence to members of his party for the forthcoming struggle against the Kuomintang. This speech was also made a required reading in 1966.*

We have had a very successful congress.

We have done three things. First, we have decided on the line of our Party, which is boldly to mobilize the masses and expand

The Foolish Old Man Who Removed the Mountains (Peking, Foreign Language Press, 1966), pp. 1-6 (footnotes omitted).

the people's forces so that, under the leadership of our Party, they will defeat the Japanese aggressors, liberate the whole people and build a new-democratic China. Second, we have adopted the new Party Constitution. Third, we have elected the leading body of the Party—the Central Committee. Henceforth our task is to lead the whole membership in carrying out the Party line. Ours has been a congress of victory, a congress of unity. The delegates have made excellent comments on the three reports. Many comrades have undertaken self-criticism and, setting out with unity as the objective, have arrived at unity through self-criticism. This congress is a model of unity, of self-criticism and of inner-Party democracy.

When the congress closes, many comrades will be leaving for their posts and the various war fronts. Comrades, wherever you go, you should propagate the line of the congress and, through the members of the Party, explain it to the broad masses.

Our aim in propagating the line of the congress is to build up the confidence of the whole Party and the entire people in the certain triumph of the revolution. We must first raise the political consciousness of the vanguard so that, resolute and unafraid of sacrifice, they will surmount every difficulty to win victory. But this is not enough; we must also arouse the political consciousness of the entire people so that they may willingly and gladly fight together with us for victory. We should ignite the whole people with the conviction that China belongs not to the reactionaries but to the Chinese people. There is an ancient Chinese fable called "The Foolish Old Man Who Removed the Mountains". It tells of an old man who lived in northern China long, long ago and was known as the Foolish Old Man of North Mountain. His house faced south and beyond his doorway stood the two great peaks, Taihang and Wangwu, obstructing the way. With great determination, he led his sons in digging up these mountains hoe in hand. Another greybeard, known as the Wise Old Man, saw them and said derisively, "How silly of you to do this! It is quite impossible for you few to dig up these two huge mountains." The Foolish Old Man replied, "When I die, my sons will carry on; when they die, there will be my grandsons, and then their sons and grandsons, and so on to infinity. High as they are, the mountains cannot grow any higher and with every bit we dig, they will be that much lower. Why can't we clear them away?" Having refuted the Wise Old Man's wrong view, he went on digging every day, unshaken in his conviction. God was moved by this, and he sent down two angels, who carried the mountains away on their backs. Today, two big mountains lie like a dead weight on the Chinese people. One is imperialism, the other is feudalism. The Chinese Communist Party has long made up its mind to dig them up. We must persevere and work unceasingly, and we, too, will touch God's heart. Our God is none other than the masses of the Chinese people. If they stand up and dig together with us, why can't these two mountains be cleared away?

Yesterday, in a talk with two Americans who were leaving for the United States, I said that the U.S. government was trying to undermine us and this would not be permitted. We oppose the U.S. government's policy of supporting Chiang Kai-shek against the Communists. But we must draw a distinction, firstly, between the people of the United States and their government and, secondly, within the U.S. government between the policy-makers and their subordinates. I said to these two Americans, "Tell the policy-makers in your government that we forbid you Americans to enter the Liberated Areas because your policy is to support Chiang Kai-shek against the Communists, and we have to be on our guard. You can come to the Liberated Areas if your purpose is to fight Japan, but there must first be an agreement. We will not permit you to nose around everywhere. Since Patrick J. Hurley has publicly declared against cooperation with the Chinese Communist Party, why do you still want to come and prowl around in our Liberated Areas?"

The U.S. government's policy of supporting Chiang Kai-shek against the Communists shows the brazenness of the U.S. reactionaries. But all the scheming of the reactionaries, whether Chinese or foreign, to prevent the Chinese people from achieving victory is doomed to failure. The democratic forces are the main current in the world today, while reaction is only a counter-current. The reactionary counter-current is trying to swamp the main current of national independence and people's democracy, but it can never become the main current. Today, there are still three major contradictions in the old world, as Stalin pointed out long ago: first, the contradiction between the proletariat and the bourgeoisie in the imperialist countries; second, the contradiction between the various imperialist powers; and third, the contradiction between the colonial and semi-colonial countries and the imperialist metropolitan countries. Not only do these three contradictions continue to exist but they are becoming more acute and widespread. Because of their existence and growth, the time will come when the reactionary anti-Soviet, anti-Communist and anti-democratic counter-current still in existence today will be swept away.

At this moment two congresses are being held in China, the Sixth National Congress of the Kuomintang and the Seventh National Congress of the Communist Party. They have completely different aims: the aim of one is to liquidate the Communist Party and all the other democratic forces in China and thus to plunge China into darkness; the aim of the other is to overthrow Japanese imperialism and its lackeys, the Chinese feudal forces, and build a new-democratic China and thus to lead China to light. These two lines are in conflict with each other. We firmly believe that, led by the Chinese Communist Party and guided by the line of its Seventh Congress, the Chinese people will achieve complete victory, while the Kuomintang's counter-revolutionary line will inevitably fail.

5. MAO TSE-TUNG: ON PEACE NEGOTIATIONS WITH THE KUOMINTANG (August, 1945)*

This is the classic document on the rules of negotiation which Mao wrote on August 26, 1945, as a secret inner party circular two days before his trip to Chungking to negotiate with Chiang Kai-shek and the Nationalists. It was reprinted in Chinese newspapers in 1971 as a justification of the Nixon-Chou En-lai summit meeting.

The speedy surrender of the Japanese invaders has changed the whole situation. Chiang Kai-shek has monopolized the right to accept the surrender, and for the time being (for a stage) the big cities and important lines of communication will not be in our hands. Nevertheless, in northern China we should still fight hard, fight with all our might to take all we can. In the past two weeks our army has recovered fifty-nine cities of various sizes and vast rural areas, and including those already in our hands we

*From *Selected Works of Mao Tse-tung*, Vol. IV (Peking, Foreign Language Press, 1965), pp. 47-51 (footnotes omitted).

now control 175 cities, thus winning a great victory. In northern China, we have recovered Weihaiwei, Yentai, Lungkou, Itu, Tsechuan, Yangliuching, Pikechi, Po-ai, Changchiakou, Chining and Fengchen. The might of our army has shaken northern China and, together with the sweeping advance of the Soviet and Mongolian forces to the Great Wall, has created a favourable position for our Party. In the coming period we should continue the offensive and do our best to capture the Peiping-Suiyuan Railway, the northern section of the Tatung-Puchow Railway and the Chengting-Taiyuan, Tehchow-Shihchiachuang, Paikuei-Chincheng and Taokou-Chinghua Railways; and also to cut up the Peiping-Liaoning, Peiping-Hankow, Tientsin-Pukow, Tsingtao-Tsinan, Lunghai and Shanghai-Nanking Railways. We should gain control of whatever we can, even though temporarily. At the same time, the necessary forces should be employed to take as many villages, county and higher administrative centres and small towns as possible. For example, a highly favourable situation has been created because the New Fourth Army has occupied many county towns lying between Nanking, Taihu Lake and the Tienmu Mountains and between the Yangtse and the Huai Rivers, because our forces in Shantung have occupied the whole of the Eastern Shantung Peninsula and because our forces in the Shansi-Suiyuan Border Region have occupied many cities and towns north and south of the Peiping-Suiyuan Railway. After another period of offensive operations, it will be possible for our Party to control most of the areas north of the lower Yangtse River and the Huai River, most of Shantung, Hopei, Shansi and Suiyuan Provinces, all of Jehol and Chahar Provinces and a part of Liaoning Province.

At present the Soviet Union, the United States and Britain all disapprove of civil war in China; at the same time our Party has put forward the three great slogans of peace, democracy and unity and is sending Comrades Mao Tse-tung, Chou En-lai and Wang Jo-fei to Chungking to discuss with Chiang Kai-shek the great issues of unity and national reconstruction; thus it is possible that the civil war plot of the Chinese reactionaries may be frustrated. The Kuomintang has now strengthened its position by recovering Shanghai, Nanking and other places, reopening sea communications, taking over the arms of the enemy and incorporating the puppet troops into its own forces. Nevertheless, it is riddled with a thousand gaping wounds, torn by innumerable inner contradictions and beset with great difficulties. It is possible that after the negotiations the Kuomintang, under domestic and foreign pressure, may conditionally recognize our Party's status. Our Party too may conditionally recognize the status of the Kuomintang. This would bring about a new stage of cooperation between the two parties (plus the Democratic League, etc.) and of peaceful development. In that event, our Party should strive to master all methods of legal struggle and intensify its work in the Kuomintang areas in the three main spheres, the cities, the villages and the army (all weak points in our work there). During the negotiations, the Kuomintang is sure to demand that we drastically reduce the size of the Liberated Areas, cut down the strength of the Liberation Army and stop issuing currency. We on our side are prepared to make such concessions as are necessary and as do not damage the fundamental interests of the people. Without such concessions, we cannot explode the Kuomintang's civil war plot, cannot gain the political initiative, cannot win the sympathy of world public opinion and the middle-of-the-roaders within the country and cannot obtain in exchange legal status for our Party and a state of peace. But there are limits to such concessions; the principle is that they must not damage the fundamental interests of the people.

If the Kuomintang still wants to launch civil war after our Party has taken the above steps, it will put itself in the wrong in the eyes of the whole nation and the whole world, and our Party will be justified in waging a war of self-defence to crush its attacks. Moreover, our Party is powerful, and if anyone attacks us and if the conditions are favourable for battle, we will certainly act in self-defence to wipe him out resolutely, thoroughly, wholly and completely (we do not strike rashly, but when we do strike, we must win). We must never be cowed by the bluster of reactionaries. But we must at all times firmly adhere to, and never forget, these principles: unity, struggle, unity through struggle; to wage struggles with good reason, with advantage and with restraint; and to make use of contradictions, win over the many, oppose the few and crush our enemies one by one.

In Kwangtung, Hunan, Hupeh, Honan and some other provinces our Party forces are in a more difficult position than in northern China and the area between the Yangtse and the Huai Rivers. The comrades in those places are much in the thoughts of the Central Committee. But the Kuomintang has many weak spots and its areas are vast; our comrades will be fully able to deal with the situation, provided they make no big mistakes in military policy (movements and operations) and in the policy of uniting with the people, and provided they are modest and prudent, not conceited or rash. Besides receiving the necessary directives from the Central Committee, the comrades in these areas must use their own judgement to analyse the situation, solve their problems, surmount difficulties, maintain themselves and expand their forces. When the Kuomintang becomes unable to do anything with you [the Communists], it may be compelled in the negotiations between the two parties to give your forces recognition and agree to arrangements advantageous to both sides. But you must definitely not rely on the negotiations, must definitely not hope that the Kuomintang will be kind-hearted, because it will never be kind-hearted. You must rely on your own strength, on correct guidance of activities, on brotherly unity within the Party and good relations with the people. Firmly rely on the people, that is your way out.

To sum up, our Party is confronted with many difficulties which must not be ignored, and all Party comrades must be well prepared mentally. But the general trend of the international and internal situation is favourable to our Party and to the people. So long as the whole Party is united as one, we shall be able to overcome all difficulties step by step.

6. MAO TSE-TUNG: TALKS WITH AMERICAN CORRESPONDENT: ANNA LOUISE STRONG (August, 1949)*

This is the original interview on the international and domestic situation with the American correspondent in 1949 when Mao introduced the new "paper tiger" concept, which he later developed into a philosophy of "strategic optimism." For a full discussion of the importance of this concept in Chinese foreign relations, read this editor's analysis in the Introduction.

Strong: Do you think there is hope for a political, a peaceful settlement of China's problems in the near future?

Mao: That depends on the attitude of the U.S. government.

*From *Selected Works of Mao Tse-tung*, Vol. IV (Peking, Foreign Language Press, 1965), pp. 97-101 (footnotes omitted).

If the American people stay the hands of the American reactionaries who are helping Chiang Kai-shek fight the civil war, there is hope for peace.

Strong: Suppose the United States gives Chiang Kai-shek no help, besides that already given, how long can Chiang Kai-shek keep on fighting?

Mao: More than a year.

Strong: Can Chiang Kai-shek keep on that long, economically?

Mao: He can.

Strong: What if the United States makes it clear that it will give Chiang Kai-shek no more help from now on?

Mao: There is no sign yet that the U.S. government and Chiang Kai-shek have any desire to stop the war within a short time.

Strong: How long can the Communist Party keep on?

Mao: As far as our own desire is concerned, we don't want to fight even for a single day. But if circumstances force us to fight, we can fight to the finish.

Strong: If the American people ask why the Communist Party is fighting, what should I reply?

Mao: Because Chiang Kai-shek is out to slaughter the Chinese people, and if the people want to survive they have to defend themselves. This the American people can understand.

Strong: What do you think of the possibility of the United States starting a war against the Soviet Union?

Mao: There are two aspects to the propaganda about an anti-Soviet war. On the one hand, U.S. imperialism is indeed preparing a war against the Soviet Union; the current propaganda about an anti-Soviet war, as well as other anti-Soviet propaganda, is political preparation for such a war. On the other hand, this propaganda is a smoke-screen put up by the U.S. reactionaries to cover many actual contradictions immediately confronting U.S. imperialism. These are the contradictions between the U.S. reactionaries and the American people and the contradictions of U.S. imperialism with other capitalist countries and with the colonial and semi-colonial countries. At present, the actual significance of the U.S. slogan of waging an anti-Soviet war is the oppression of the American people and the expansion of the U.S. forces of aggression in the rest of the capitalist world. As you know, both Hitler and his partners, the Japanese warlords, used anti-Soviet slogans for a long time as a pretext for enslavement of the people at home and aggression against other countries. Now the U.S. reactionaries are acting in exactly the same way.

To start a war, the U.S. reactionaries must first attack the American people. They are already attacking the American people—oppressing the workers and democratic circles in the United States politically and economically and preparing to impose fascism there. The people of the United States should stand up and resist the attacks of the U.S. reactionaries. I believe they will.

The United States and the Soviet Union are separated by a vast zone which includes many capitalist, colonial and semi-colonial countries in Europe, Asia and Africa. Before the U.S. reactionaries have subjugated these countries, an attack on the Soviet Union is out of the question. In the Pacific the United States now controls areas larger than all the former British spheres of influence there put together; it controls Japan, that part of China under Kuomintang rule, half of Korea, and the South Pacific. It has long controlled Central and South America. It seeks also to control the whole of the British Empire and Western Europe. Using various pretexts, the United States is making large-scale military arrangements and setting up military bases in many countries. The U.S. reactionaries say that the military bases they have set up and are preparing to set up all over the world are aimed against the Soviet Union. True, these military bases are directed against the Soviet Union. At present, however, it is not the Soviet Union but the countries in which these military bases are located that are the first to suffer U.S. aggression. I believe it won't be long before these countries come to realize who is really oppressing them, the Soviet Union or the United States. The day will come when the U.S. reactionaries find themselves opposed by the people of the whole world.

Of course, I do not mean to say that the U.S. reactionaries have no intention of attacking the Soviet Union. The Soviet Union is a defender of world peace and a powerful factor preventing the domination of the world by the U.S. reactionaries. Because of the existence of the Soviet Union, it is absolutely impossible for the reactionaries in the United States and the world to realize their ambitions. That is why the U.S. reactionaries rabidly hate the Soviet Union and actually dream of destroying this socialist state. But the fact that the U.S.

reactionaries are now trumpeting so loudly about a U.S.-Soviet war and creating a foul atmosphere, so soon after the end of World War II, compels us to take a look at their real aims. It turns out that under the cover of anti-Soviet slogans they are frantically attacking the workers and democratic circles in the United States and turning all the countries which are the targets of U.S. external expansion into U.S. dependencies. I think the American people and the peoples of all countries menaced by U.S. aggression should unite and struggle against the attacks of the U.S. reactionaries and their running dogs in these countries. Only by victory in this struggle can a third world war be avoided; otherwise it is unavoidable.

Strong: That is very clear. But suppose the United States uses the atom bomb? Suppose the United States bombs the Soviet Union from its bases in Iceland, Okinawa and China?

Mao: The atom bomb is a paper tiger which the U.S. reactionaries use to scare people. It looks terrible, but in fact it isn't. Of course, the atom bomb is a weapon of mass slaughter, but the outcome of a war is decided by the people, not by one or two new types of weapon.

All reactionaries are paper tigers. In appearance, the reactionaries are terrifying, but in reality they are not so powerful. From a long-term point of view, it is not the reactionaries but the people who are really powerful. In Russia, before the February Revolution in 1917, which side was really strong? On the surface the tsar was strong but he was swept away by a single gust of wind in the February Revolution. In the final analysis, the strength in Russia was on the side of the Soviets of Workers, Peasants and Soldiers. The tsar was just a paper tiger. Wasn't Hitler once considered very strong? But history proved that he was a paper tiger. So was Mussolini, so was Japanese imperialism. On the contrary, the strength of the Soviet Union and of the people in all countries who loved democracy and freedom proved much greater than had been foreseen.

Chiang Kai-shek and his supporters, the U.S. reactionaries, are all paper tigers too. Speaking of U.S. imperialism, people seem to feel that it is terrifically strong. Chinese reactionaries are using the "strength" of the United States to frighten the Chinese people. But it will be proved that the U.S. reactionaries, like all the reactionaries in history, do not have much strength. In the United States there are others who are really strong—the American people.

Take the case of China. We have only millet plus rifles to rely on, but history will finally prove that our millet plus rifles is more powerful than Chiang Kai-shek's aeroplanes plus tanks. Although the Chinese people still face many difficulties and will long suffer hardships from the joint attacks of U.S. imperialism and the Chinese reactionaries, the day will come when these reactionaries are defeated and we are victorious. The reason is simply this: the reactionaries represent reaction, we represent progress.

7. *MAO TSE-TUNG: ON PROPAGANDA, CULTURAL, AND EDUCATIONAL WORK (March, 1957)**

This is an important policy speech made by Mao at the party's national conference on propaganda work on March 12, 1957. More than 380 leading cadres of the party's propaganda, cultural, and educational departments at both the national and local levels attended the conference. In addition, many important nonparty personalities of China's arts and sciences were invited. This is the last of the "five constantly read" articles in China.

Comrades! Our conference has gone very well. Many questions have been raised during the conference and we have learned about many things. I shall now make a few remarks on questions the comrades have been discussing.

We are living in a period of great social change. Chinese society has been going through great changes for a long time. The War of Resistance Against Japan was one period of great change and the War of Liberation another. But the present change is much more profound in character than the earlier ones. We are now building socialism. Hundreds of millions of people are taking part in the movement for socialist transformation. Class relations are changing throughout the country. The petty bourgeoisie in agriculture and handicrafts and the bourgeoisie in industry and commerce have both undergone a

*From Mao Tse-tung, *Speech at the Chinese Communist Party's National Conference on Propaganda Work* (Peking, Foreign Language Press, 1966), pp. 1-3, 6-10, 12-19, 21-23, 28-29 (extract; footnotes omitted). Propaganda has a positive connotation within the Communist framework.

change. The social and economic system has been changed; individual economy has been transformed into collective economy, and capitalist private ownership is being transformed into socialist public ownership. Changes of such magnitude are of course reflected in people's minds. Man's social being determines his consciousness. People of different classes, strata and social groups react differently to the great changes in our social system. The masses eagerly support them, for life itself has confirmed that socialism is the only way out for China. Overthrowing the old social system and establishing a new one, the system of socialism, is a great struggle, a great change in the social system and in men's relations with each other. It should be said that the situation is basically sound. But the new social system has only just been established and requires time for its consolidation. It must not be assumed that the new system can be completely consolidated the moment it is established, for that is impossible. It has to be consolidated step by step. To achieve its ultimate consolidation, it is necessary not only to bring about the socialist industrialization of the country and persevere in the socialist revolution on the economic front, but to carry on constant and arduous socialist revolutionary struggles and socialist education on the political and ideological fronts. Moreover, various contributory international factors are required. In China the struggle to consolidate the socialist system, the struggle to decide whether socialism or capitalism will prevail, will still take a long historical period. But we should all realize that the new system of socialism will unquestionably be consolidated. We can assuredly build a socialist state with modern industry, modern agriculture, and modern science and culture.

* * *

Thirdly, there is the question of the remoulding of the intellectuals. Ours is a culturally undeveloped country. For a vast country like ours, five million intellectuals are too few. Without intellectuals our work cannot be done well, and we should therefore do a good job of uniting with them. Socialist society mainly comprises three sections of people, the workers, the peasants and the intellectuals. Intellectuals are mental workers. Their work is in the service of the people, that is, in the service of the workers and the peasants. As far as the majority of intellectuals are concerned, they can serve the new China as they did the old, and serve the proletariat as they did the bourgeoisie. When the intellectuals served the old China, the left wing resisted, the intermediate section wavered, and only the right wing was resolute. Now, when it comes to serving the new society, the situation is reversed. The left wing is resolute, the intermediate section wavers (this wavering in the new society is different from that in the old society), and the right wing resists. Moreover, intellectuals are educators. Our newspapers are educating the people every day. Our writers and artists, scientists and technicians, professors and teachers are all educating students, educating the people. Being educators and teachers, they themselves must first be educated. And all the more so in the present period of great change in the social system. They have had some Marxist education in the last few years, and some have studied very hard and made great progress. But the majority still have a long way to go before they can completely replace the bourgeois world outlook with the proletarian world outlook. Some people have read a few Marxist books and think themselves quite learned, but what they have read has not penetrated, has not struck root in their minds, so that they do not know how to use it and their class feelings remain as of old. Others are very conceited and having learned some book-phrases, think themselves terrific and are very cocky; but whenever a storm blows up, they take a stand very different from that of the workers and the majority of the peasants. They waver while the latter stand firm, they equivocate while the latter are forthright. Hence it is wrong to assume that people who educate others no longer need to be educated and no longer need to study, or that socialist remoulding means remoulding others—the landlords, the capitalists and the individual producers—but not the intellectuals. The intellectuals, too, need remoulding, and not only those who have not changed their basic stand; everybody should study and remould himself. I say "everybody," and this includes us who are present here. Conditions are changing all the time, and to adapt one's thinking to the new conditions, one must study. Even those who have a better grasp of Marxism and are comparatively firm in their proletarian stand have to go on studying, have to absorb what is new and tackle new problems. Unless they rid their minds of what is unsound, intellectuals cannot undertake the task of educating others. Naturally, we have to learn while teaching and be pupils while serving as teachers. To be a good teacher, one must first be a good pupil. There are many things which cannot be learned from books alone; one must learn from those engaged in production, from the workers, from the poor and lower middle peasants and, in schools, from the students, from those one teaches. In my opinion, the majority of our intellectuals are willing to learn. It is our task to help them warm-heartedly and in a proper way on the basis of their willingness to study; we must not resort to compulsion and force them to study.

Fourthly, there is the question of the integration of the intellectuals with the masses of workers and peasants. Since their task is to serve the masses of workers and peasants, the intellectuals must, first and foremost, know them and be familiar with their life, work and ideas. We encourage the intellectuals to go among the masses, to go to factories and villages. It is very bad if you never in all your life meet a worker or a peasant. Our government workers, writers, artists, teachers and scientific research workers should seize every opportunity to get close to the workers and peasants. Some can go to factories or villages just to look around; this may be called "looking at the flowers while on horseback" and is better than nothing at all. Others can stay there for a few months, conducting investigations and making friends; this may be called "dismounting to look at the flowers". Still others can stay and live there for a considerable time, say, two or three years or even longer; this may be called "settling down". Some intellectuals do live among the workers and peasants, for instance, the industrial technicians in factories and the agricultural technicians and rural school teachers in the countryside. They should do their work well and integrate themselves with the workers and peasants.

* * *

Fifthly, there is rectification. Rectification means correcting one's way of thinking and style of work. Rectification movements were conducted within the Communist Party during the anti-Japanese war, during the War of Liberation, and in the early days after the founding of the People's Republic of China. Now the Central Committee of the Communist Party has decided on another rectification within the Party to be started this year. Non-Party people may take part in it, or they need not if they do not wish to. The main thing in this rectification movement is to criticize the following three errors in one's way of thinking and style of work—subjectivism, bureaucracy and sectarianism. As in the rectification movement in the anti-Japanese war, the method this time will be first to study a number of documents, and then, on the basis of such study, to examine one's own thinking and work and unfold criticism and self-criticism to expose shortcomings and mistakes and promote what is right and good. On the one hand, we must be strict and conduct criticism and self-criticism of mistakes and short-comings seriously, and not perfunctorily, and correct them; on the other hand, we must not be rough but must follow the principle of "learning from past mistakes to avoid future ones and curing the sickess to save the patient", and we must oppose the method of "finishing people off with a single blow".

* * *

The transformation and construction of China depend on us for leadership. When we have rectified our way of thinking and style of work, we shall enjoy greater initiative in our work, become more capable and work better. Our country has need of many people who wholeheartedly serve the masses and the cause of socialism and who are determined to bring about changes. We Communists should all be people of this kind. In old China it was a crime to talk about reforms, and offenders would be beheaded or imprisoned. Nevertheless there were determined reformers who, fearing nothing, published books and newspapers, educated and organized the people and waged indomitable struggles under every kind of difficulty. The people's democratic dictatorship has paved the way for the rapid economic and cultural development of our country. It is only a few years since the establishment of our state, and yet people can already see the unprecedented flowering of the economy, culture, education and science. In building up the new China we Communists are not daunted by any difficulties whatsoever. But we cannot accomplish this on our own. We need a good number of non-Party people with great ideals who will fight dauntlessly together with us for the transformation and construction of our society in the direction of socialism and communism. It is an arduous task to ensure a better life for the several hundred million people of China and to build our economically and culturally backward country into a prosperous and powerful one with a high level of culture. Therefore, in order to be able to shoulder this task more competently and work better together with all non-Party people who are actuated by high ideals and determined to institute reforms, we must conduct rectification movements both now and in the future, and constantly rid ourselves of whatever is wrong. Thoroughgoing materialists are fearless; we hope that all our fellow fighters will courageously shoulder their responsibilities and overcome all difficulties, fearing no setbacks or gibes, nor hesitating to criticize us Communists and give us their suggestions. "He who is not afraid of death by a thousand cuts dares to unhorse the emperor"—this is the indomitable spirit needed in our struggle to build socialism and communism. On our part, we Communists should create conditions helpful to those who co-operate with us, establish good comradely relations with them in our common work and unite with them in our joint struggle.

Sixthly, there is the question of one-sidedness. One-sidedness means thinking in terms of absolutes, that is, a metaphysical approach to problems. In the appraisal of our work, it is one-sided to regard everything either as all positive or as all negative. There are quite a few people inside the Communist Party and very many outside it who do just that. To regard everything as positive is to see only the good and not the bad, and to tolerate only praise and no criticism. To talk as though our work is good in every respect is at variance with the facts. It is not true that everything is good; there are still shortcomings and mistakes. But neither is it true that everything is bad, and that, too, is at variance with the facts. We must analyse things concretely. To negate everything is to think, without having made any analysis, that nothing has been done well and that the great work of socialist construction, the great struggle in which hundreds of millions of people are participating, is a complete mess with nothing in it worth commending. Although there is a difference between the many people who hold such views and those who are hostile to the socialist system, these views are very mistaken and harmful and can only dishearten people. It is wrong to appraise our work either from the viewpoint that everything is positive, or from the viewpoint that everything is negative. We should criticize those people who take such a one-sided approach to problems, though of course in criticizing them we should help them, keeping to the principle of "learning from past mistakes to avoid future ones and curing the sickness to save the patient".

Some people say: Since there is to be a rectification movement and since everyone is to be asked to express his opinions, one-sidedness is unavoidable, and therefore in calling for the elimination of one-sidedness, it seems that you really don't want people to speak up. Is this assertion right? It is naturally difficult for everyone to avoid any trace of one-sidedness. People always examine and handle problems and express their views in the light of their own experience, and unavoidably they sometimes show a little one-sidedness. However, should we not ask them gradually to overcome their one-sidedness and to look at problems in a relatively all-sided way? In my opinion, we should. Otherwise, we would be stagnating; we would be approving one-sidedness and contradicting the whole purpose of rectification if we did not make the demand that, from day to day and from year to year, more and more people should view problems in a relatively all-sided way. One-sidedness is a violation of dialectics. We want gradually to disseminate dialectics, and to ask everyone gradually to learn the use of the scientific dialectical method. Some of the articles now being published are extremely pompous but devoid of any content, any analysis of problems and any reasoned argument, and they carry no conviction. There should be fewer and fewer of such articles. When writing an article, one should not be thinking all the time, "How brilliant I am!" but should regard one's readers as on a completely equal footing with oneself. You may have been in the revolution for a long time, but all the same if you say something wrong, people will refute you. The more airs you put on, the less people will stand for it and the less they will care to read your articles. We should do our work honestly, analyse things concretely, write articles that carry conviction and never overawe people by striking a pose.

Seventhly, to "open wide" or to "restrict"? This is a question of policy. "Let a hundred flowers blossom and a hundred schools of thought contend" is a long-term as well as a fundamental policy; it is not just a temporary policy. In the discussion, comrades expressed disapproval of "restriction", and I think this view is the correct one. The Central Committee of the Party is of the opinion that we must "open wide", not "restrict".

In leading our country, two alternative methods, or in other words two alternative policies, can be adopted—to "open wide" or to "restrict". To "open wide" means to let all people express their opinions freely, so that they dare to speak, dare to criticize and dare to debate; it means not being afraid of wrong views and anything poisonous; it means to encourage argument and criticism among people holding different views, allowing freedom both for criticism and for counter-criticism; it means not suppressing wrong views but convincing people by reasoning with them. To "restrict" means to forbid people to air differing opinions and express wrong ideas, and to "finish them off with a single blow" if they do so. That is the way to aggravate rather than to resolve contradictions. To "open wide", or to "restrict."—we must choose one or the other of these two policies. We choose the former, because it is the policy which will help to consolidate our country and develop our culture.

We are prepared to use the policy of "opening wide" to unite with the several million intellectuals and change their present outlook. As I have said above, the overwhelming majority of the intellectuals in our country want to make progress and remould themselves, and they are quite capable of remoulding themselves. In this connection, the policy we adopt will play a tremendous role. The question of the intellectuals is above all one of ideology, and it is not helpful but harmful to resort to crude and high-handed measures for solving ideological questions. The remoulding of the intellectuals, and especially the changing of their world outlook, is a process that requires a long period of time. Our comrades must understand that ideological remoulding involves long-term, patient and painstaking work, and they must not attempt to change people's ideology, which has been shaped over decades of life, by giving a few lectures or by holding a few meetings. Persuasion, not compulsion, is the only way to convince them. Compulsion will never result in convincing them. To try to convince them by force simply won't work. This kind of method is permissible in dealing with the enemy, but absolutely impermissible in dealing with comrades or friends. What if we don't know how to convince others? Then we have to learn. We must learn to conquer erroneous ideas through debate and reasoning.

* * *

Eighthly and lastly, the Party committees of the provinces, municipalities and autonomous regions must tackle the question of ideology. This is the point some of the comrades present here wanted me to touch upon. In many places, the Party committees have not yet tackled the question of ideology, or have done very little in this respect. The main reason is that they are busy. But they must tackle it. By "tackling it" I mean that it must be put on the agenda and studied. The large-scale, turbulent class struggles of the masses characteristic of the previous revolutionary periods have in the main come to an end, but there is still class struggle—mainly on the political and ideological fronts—and it is very acute too. The question of ideology has now become very important. The first secretaries of the Party committees in all localities should personally tackle this question, which can be solved correctly only when they have given it serious attention and gone into it. All localities should call meetings on propaganda work, similar to our present one, to discuss local ideological work and all related problems. Such meetings should be attended not only by Party comrades but also by people outside the Party, and moreover by people with different opinions. This is all to the good and no harm can come of it, as the experience of the present meeting has proved.

8. PARTY WRITING GROUP: GUIDING PRINCIPLE FOR KNOWING AND CHANGING THE WORLD (May, 1971)*

This is the current interpretation of Mao's important philosophic work "On Practice" (1937). The Chinese claim that Mao has made a major contribution to the theory of dialectical materialism as illustrated in "On

*Hongqi, No. 5 (1971). This abridged translation was published in *Peking Review* (June 18, 1971), pp. 6-10.

> *Practice" and "On Contradiction" (see editor's analysis in Introduction). This new interpretation was allegedly written by the Writing Group of Liaoning Provincial Committee of the Chinese Communist Party.*

For a long period in the history of our Party there were Wang Ming and renegades of his sort who rejected applying the universal truth of Marxism-Leninism to the study of practice in the Chinese revolution. Tearing words and phrases from Marxist works, they overawed people with them. There were also people who for a long time limited themselves to their own fragmentary experience and did not understand the importance of theory in guiding revolutionary practice and thus became captives of the sham Marxists. Using bourgeois idealism and metaphysics as the ideological basis, Wang Ming and company wildly opposed Chairman Mao's revolutionary line and thereby caused enormous losses to the Chinese revolution.

Thirty-three years ago our great leader Chairman Mao issued this brilliant work *On Practice* to expose the anti-Marxist world outlook and methodology of these renegades. In accordance with the principle of the Marxist theory of knowledge, Chairman Mao systematically summed up the historical experiences of the struggle between the two lines in the Party, penetratingly criticized the idealist apriorism of renegade Wang Ming and other sham Marxists, and thus greatly raised the whole Party's Marxist-Leninist theoretical level and guided the Chinese revolution from victory to victory.

Using Marxism-Leninism-Mao Tsetung Thought as their weapon, the whole Party and the people of the whole country are now sharply criticizing "apriorism," the "theory of productive forces," the "theory of human nature," the "theory of the dying out of class struggle" and other reactionary fallacies spread by Wang Ming, Liu Shao-chi and other political swindlers. This is a most important task on the political and ideological front. Conscientious study of Chairman Mao's *On Practice* in connection with this struggle is of great practical and far-reaching historical significance in further determining what is materialism and what is idealism, distinguishing between genuine and sham Marxism, heightening our consciousness of implementing Chairman Mao's proletarian revolutionary line, successfully fulfilling the various fighting tasks set forth by the

Ninth Party Congress and the Second Plenary Session of the Party's Ninth Central Committee and greeting the 50th anniversary of the birth of the Communist Party of China.

I

Social practice is the foundation of knowledge and this is the fundamental viewpoint of Marxist philosophy. Recognizing or not recognizing the dependence of knowledge on social practice is an important hallmark distinguishing between the materialist theory of reflection and idealist apriorism and the touchstone distinguishing genuine Marxism from sham Marxism.

As far back as more than 100 years ago, the great revolutionary teacher Marx explicitly pointed out: "The question whether objective (*gegenstandliche*) truth can be attributed to human thinking is not a question of theory but is a *practical* question. In practice man must prove the truth, that is, the reality and power, the this-sidedness (*Diesseitigkeit*) of his thinking. The dispute over the reality or non-reality of thinking which is isolated from practice is a purely *scholastic* question." (*Theses on Feuerbach.*) By introducing the viewpoint of practice to the theory of knowledge, Marx correctly settled the question of the relations between thinking and being and brought about a great revolution unprecedented in the history of human knowledge.

In his *On Practice*, Chairman Mao upheld and developed the Marxist theory of knowledge and incisively expounded the primary place and decisive role of social practice in the course of cognition. He emphatically pointed out: "The standpoint of practice is the primary and basic standpoint in the dialectical-materialist theory of knowledge." "There can be no knowledge apart from practice."

If one wants to know anything, one must directly participate in the practical struggle to change reality, for only thus can one come into contact with it as a phenomenon; only through personal participation in the practical struggle to change reality can one uncover the essence of what one wants to know and know the laws of things. This is the path to knowledge which everyone actually travels. The fallacy of "intuitive knowledge" runs counter to the materialist theory of reflection. This is nothing but drivel which all exploiting classes as well as Wang Ming, Liu Shao-chi and their kind used to deceive the masses of people. Chairman Mao ridiculed the "know-all" who completely divorced himself from reality. Such a person "picks up a smattering of hearsay knowledge and proclaims himself 'the world's Number One authority'; this merely shows that he has not taken a proper measure of himself."

Chairman Mao not only affirmed in clear terms the Marxist viewpoint of practice but scientifically summarized the practical contents as something applied "in the practice of production, in the practice of revolutionary class struggle and revolutionary national struggle and in the practice of scientific experiment." In his famous essay *Where Do Correct Ideas Come From?* Chairman Mao further pointed out: "They (correct ideas) come from social practice, and from it alone; they come from three kinds of social practice, the struggle for production, the class struggle and scientific experiment." This is a great development of Marxist philosophy. Activity in production is the primary source from which human knowledge develops. In class society, it is done by members of different social classes who enter into definite relations of production. Therefore, "class struggle . . ., in all its various forms, exerts a profound influence on the development of man's knowledge." The prejudice of the exploiting classes invariably blocks the road to knowing the truth. Only by constantly removing the brand of the bourgeoisie and all other exploiting classes stamped into our thinking, can we know the truth about objective things.

Chairman Mao pointed out: "The Marxist philosophy of dialectical materialism has two outstanding characteristics. One is its class nature: it openly avows that dialectical materialism is in the service of the proletariat. The other is its practicality. it emphasizes the dependence of theory on practice, emphasizes that theory is based on practice and in turn serves practice." Grasping the essence of dialectical materialism, this scientific thesis of Chairman Mao's was an effective criticism of Wang Ming, Liu Shao-chi and their like who denied the Marxist viewpoints of classes and practice.

For a long period Wang Ming, Liu Shao-chi and the rest had all along used reactionary idealist apriorism to counter the materialist theory of reflection, preaching that man's knowledge preceded his experience and his ability preceded his practice. Liu Shao-chi advertised that man's "intelligence" or "stupidity" was "endowed by nature." His aim was to portray the working people as being "born" to be "stupid," and create the theoretical basis for his reactionary theory that "the masses are backward." Counterposing the Marxist viewpoint against this, Chairman Mao pointed out: "The lowly are most intelligent; the elite are most ignorant." "The lowly" here refers to the broad masses of the working people who stand opposed to the exploiting classes and "the elite" refers to the reactionaries and intellectual aristocrats of the exploiting classes, including Liu Shao-chi and his bunch who fancied themselves clever and vainly tried to turn back the wheel of history.

In refuting the Right opportunists during the agricultural collectivization movement, Chairman Mao pointed out: "Both cadres and peasants will remould themselves in the course of the struggles they themselves experience. Let them go into action and learn while doing, and they will become more capable. In this way, fine people will come forward in large numbers." (*On the Question of Agricultural Co-operation.*) From the viewpoint of dialectical materialism, this instruction of Chairman Mao's points out the fundamental way for us to discover and train outstanding people of the proletariat and the fundamental way for our outstanding revolutionary cadres to mature. At the same time, it shows that man's knowledge (ability and capability belong to the category of knowledge) is not inborn but is acquired after birth by summing up the experience in social practice. In different historical periods, large numbers of outstanding revolutionary persons, without exception, came forward in the storm of revolutionary practice. Describing capability and ability as transcending practice and as something endowed by nature is nothing but self-glorification and fabrication by the arrogant idealists and such capability and ability are non-existent in social life.

Chairman Mao regards Marx as "a most completely developed intellectual, representing the acme of human wisdom" (*Rectify the Party's Style of Work*) and, with the viewpoint of dialectical materialism and historical materialism, gives a scientific explanation of the historical conditions of the birth of Marxism-Leninism. Chairman Mao pointed out: "Marxism could be the product only of capitalist society. Marx, in the era of laissez-faire capitalism, could not concretely know certain laws peculiar to the era of imperialism beforehand, because imperialism, the last stage of capitalism, had not yet emerged and the relevant practice was lacking; only Lenin and Stalin could undertake this task. Leaving aside their genius, the reason why

Marx, Engels, Lenin and Stalin could work out their theories was mainly that they personally took part in the practice of the class struggle and the scientific experimentation of their time; lacking this condition, no genius could have succeeded." Here Chairman Mao pointed out with special emphasis that lacking the condition of participation in the practice of class struggle and scientific experimentation "no genius could have succeeded." This Marxist-Leninist scientific thesis of Chairman Mao's must be comprehensively and profoundly understood and no attempt by Wang Ming, Liu Shao-chi and company to distort or quote it out of context is tolerated.

In advertising the reactionary fallacy that ability preceded practice, Wang Ming, Liu Shao-chi and other renegades did not mean to acknowledge that others were capable but vainly hoped that the people recognized counter-revolutionary revisionists like themselves as born "supermen," and that the masses of the people were "backward" and "reactionary." In the eyes of these careerists and conspirators, once their myths became reality, they could change history and turn the dictatorship of the proletariat into the dictatorship of the bourgeoisie and socialism into capitalism. However, the wheel of history cannot be turned back and the truth of Marxism-Leninism cannot be resisted. Those who slander the masses of the people are most stupid and can come to no good end.

Chairman Mao pointed out: "Idealism and mechanical materialism, opportunism and adventurism, are all characterized by the breach between the subjective and the objective, by the separation of knowledge from practice. The Marxist-Leninist theory of knowledge, characterized as it is by scientific social practice, cannot but resolutely oppose these wrong ideologies." The "Left" and Right opportunist lines pushed by Wang Ming, Liu Shao-chi and their cronies took idealist apriorism as their ideological basis. Proceeding from such a reactionary world outlook, they tried to make everything dependent on their own subjective will and denied the law of the development of objective things. Now from the Right and now from the "Left," they interfered with and sabotaged Chairman Mao's revolutionary line and caused great harm to the revolutionary cause.

Chairman Mao's proletarian revolutionary line is based on the dialectical materialist theory of knowledge. It comes from practice and stands higher than practice. It scientifically sums up the historical experience of the proletarian revolution and the dictatorship of the proletariat, and correctly reflects the objective law of social development. It is the lifeline of our Party. Only by adhering to the materialist theory of reflection and going deep into reality to investigate and study can we master the present state and history of the struggle between the two classes, the two roads and the two lines, grasp the principal contradictions and work out our plans, measures and methods conforming to Chairman Mao's revolutionary line and translate them into the masses' conscious revolutionary actions. The plans, measures and methods must be put into the test of practice so that the correct things can be popularized and the erroneous ones can be corrected. Through such repeated practice, our knowledge will become deeper and more comprehensive and will all the more conform with objective law.

II

How does man's cognition arise and develop in social practice? Lenin pointed out: "From living perception to abstract thought, *and from this to practice*,—such is the dialectical path of the cognition of *truth*, of the cognition of objective reality." ("Conspectus of Hegel's Book *The Science of Logic*.")

In his *On Practice*, Chairman Mao, through analysis of the two leaps in the process of cognition, profoundly elucidates the materialism and dialectics of the theory of knowledge and further develops Lenin's great thinking on the dialectical movement of cognition. Chairman Mao pointed out: "Knowledge begins with experience—this is the materialism of the theory of knowledge." "That knowledge needs to be deepened, that the perceptual stage of knowledge needs to be developed to the rational stage—this is the dialectics of the theory of knowledge."

When the phenomena of the objective world are reflected through his sense organs to man's brain in practice and perceptual knowledge is thus formed, this is the first step in man's cognition. Negating taking part in practice and negating perceptual knowledge means negating materialism. But it should be noted that perceptual knowledge reflects only the phenomena, the separate aspects and the external relations of things and sometimes even presents a false picture completely contrary to the essence of things. Chairman Mao has said: "Perception only solves the problem of phenomena; theory alone can solve the problem of essence." Conclusions drawn from data based on perceptual experience alone will inevitably give rise to subjectivity, one-sidedness and superficiality and cannot correctly and completely reflect objective things. Chairman Mao seriously criticized the vulgar "practical men," saying they "respect experience but despise theory, and therefore cannot have a comprehensive view of an entire objective process, lack clear direction and long-range perspective, and are complacent over occasional successes and glimpses of the truth. If such persons direct a revolution, they will lead it up a blind alley." Therefore, all comrades who have gained experience in their work should pay attention to preventing and overcoming empiricist tendencies, use Marxism-Leninism-Mao Tsetung Thought to conscientiously sum up experience and raise it to the level of rational knowledge.

Chairman Mao pointed out: "The real task of knowing is, through perception, to arrive at thought, to arrive step by step at the comprehension of the internal contradictions of objective things, of their laws and of the internal relations between one process and another, that is, to arrive at logical knowledge." Rational knowledge is characterized by its scientific abstraction, comprehensiveness and systematism, its reflection of the objective world in a deeper, truer and fuller way and its reflection of the essence and mainstream of things. Therefore, rational knowledge is a higher stage in the process of cognition and a more important stage compared with perceptual knowledge.

To carry out the leap from perceptual knowledge to rational knowledge, "it is necessary through the exercise of thought to reconstruct the rich data of sense perception, discarding the dross and selecting the essential, eliminating the false and retaining the true, proceeding from the one to the other and from the outside to the inside." The important work methods consistently advocated by Chairman Mao, including investigation and study, summing up experience and from the masses and to the masses, are scientific methods to raise perceptual knowledge to rational knowledge. The process of making investigation and study and summing up experience is one of concentrating the masses' scattered and unsystematic ideas and turning them into concentrated and systematic ideas. To raise rich experience to the level of theory, it is necessary to seriously study Marxism-Leninism-Mao Tsetung Thought and under its guidance to give full play to the brain, the organ of thought. Only in this way can we bring about the qualitative change of the rich data of perception in our minds and achieve the leap to rational knowledge.

The active function of knowledge manifests itself not only in the leap from perceptual knowledge to rational knowledge, but—and this is more important—it also manifests itself in the leap from rational knowledge to revolutionary practice. The second leap is of greater significance than the first. Chairman Mao said: "Marxist philosophy holds that the most important problem does not lie in understanding the laws of the objective world and thus being able to explain it, but in applying the knowledge of these laws actively to change the world." Whether or not rational knowledge correctly reflects the laws of objective world cannot be solved in the first leap. To solve this question, it is necessary to return rational knowledge to practice, using it to actively guide practice and ascertaining whether it can achieve the expected goal. Generally speaking, what succeeds is correct and what fails is incorrect. "In social struggle, the forces representing the advanced class sometimes suffer defeat not because their ideas are incorrect but because, in the balance of forces engaged in struggle, they are not as powerful for the time being as the forces of reaction; they are therefore temporarily defeated, but they are bound to triumph sooner or later." *(Where Do Correct Ideas Come From?)*

The revolutionary practice of the masses keeps developing. Even correct knowledge must also be returned to practice and develop continuously with the development of practice. If correct knowledge is not used to guide practice, it becomes meaningless.

Wang Ming, Liu Shao-chi, Yang Hsien-chen and those like them denied that theory comes from practice and its role in guiding revolutionary practice. They even openly made the slander that the great truth that matter is transformed into consciousness and vice versa is "idealist." Actually, it was specifically this gang who, proceeding from idealist apriorism, separated the interrelations and mutual transformation between consciousness and matter and between thinking and being on the basis of practice. Their vicious efforts were to oppose using Marxism-Leninism-Mao Tsetung Thought to actively change the world, and thereby realize their plot to subvert the dictatorship of the proletariat and restore capitalism.

In this great work Chairman Mao specially stressed the guiding role of revolutionary theory in correctly knowing and changing the world. He pointed out: "From the Marxist viewpoint, theory is important, and its importance is fully expressed in Lenin's statement, 'Without revolutionary theory there can be no revolutionary movement.' But Marxism emphasizes the importance of theory precisely and only because it can guide action." We must follow Chairman Mao's teaching "Read and study seriously and have a good grasp of Marxism." This is of great significance to us, because if we fail to grasp Marxism we will be unable to use revolutionary theory to guide our action and perceive political swindlers who proclaim themselves supporters of Marxism but actually oppose Marxism. Wang Ming, Liu Shao-chi and their bunch dressed themselves up as Marxists to cheat and bluff persons with a relatively low theoretical level. If we do not conscientiously study Marxist-Leninist theory, then we might take the false for the true and regard poisonous weeds as fragrant flowers when such political swindlers present the false as the true.

III

In his *On Practice* Chairman Mao pointed out: "The struggle of the proletariat and the revolutionary people to change the world comprises the fulfilment of the following tasks: to change the objective world and, at the same time, their own subjective world—to change their cognitive ability and change the relations between the subjective and the objective world." This teaching of Chairman Mao's profoundly explains the dialectics of changing the subjective world and changing the objective world and points out to us the orientation in remoulding our world outlook.

Vice-Chairman Lin further expounded this great thinking of Chairman Mao's, pointing out: "We should regard ourselves as a part of the strength in the revolution and at the same time constantly make ourselves a target of revolution. We should revolutionize ourselves in the revolution. Without doing this, it is impossible to make the revolution a success."

Man's struggle to change the objective world is realized through conscious actions under the guidance of a certain world outlook. "This change in world outlook is something funda- mental." (*On the Correct Handling of Contradictions Among the People.*) Remoulding world outlook means remoulding one into a thoroughgoing dialectical and historical materialist and a staunch fighter of continuing the revolution under the dictatorship of the proletariat, making thinking conform to the objective world's law of development and to the needs of the development of the revolutionary situation, and achieving the concrete and historical unity of the subjective and the objective and of knowledge and practice. Chairman Mao pointed out: "In the building of a socialist society, everybody needs remoulding." (*On the Correct Handling of Contradictions Among the People.*) Both veteran cadres tested in the prolonged revolutionary struggle and new cadres who emerged in the tempering of the Great Proletarian Cultural Revolution have the urgent task of conscientiously remoulding their world outlook. High-ranking cadres should set still higher demands on themselves in remoulding their world outlook. Denying the necessity of this remoulding is actually negating continued revolution under the dictatorship of the proletariat and negating dialectical materialism and historical materialism.

Remoulding the subjective world cannot be separated from the struggle to change the objective world. Marx and Engels pointed out: "In revolutionary activity the changing of oneself coincides with the changing of circumstances." (*The German Ideology.*) The road to remoulding the subjective world lies in integrating the conscientious study of Marxist-Leninist works and Chairman Mao's works with taking part in the three great revolutionary movements. Only by mastering the weapon of Marxism-Leninism-Mao Tsetung Thought, unconditionally going deep among the worker and peasant masses for a long time, going deep into practical struggles and experiencing strenuous tempering can we achieve a relatively thorough transformation in our thinking and feelings and gradually move our stand to the side of the proletariat. When one is divorced from practical struggle and the worker and peasant masses, talking about remoulding one's subjective world is out of the question.

Proceeding from idealist apriorism, Wang Ming, Liu Shao-chi and their like consistently opposed remoulding world outlook in the course of revolutionary practice. They babbled that "seeing more and talking more" will "naturally" "foster one's proletarian world outlook." According to this fallacy, there is no need at all for people to take part in the three great revolutionary movements—the struggle for production, class struggle and scientific experiment—or go among the masses; as long as they devote themselves to studying the "teachings of Confucius and Mencius" and "examine themselves three times a day" behind the closed doors of "studies and academies," they could "cultivate" themselves into "excellent and politically matured revolutionaries." This is pure nonsense. How can "revolutionaries" be "cultivated" in this way? It can only produce intellectual aristocrats trained by Liu Shao-chi and his gang for restoring capitalism.

As long as one makes revolution all his life, one needs to remould his world outlook throughout his life for it is a long-term task. As class struggle in the socialist period is prolonged, complex and tortuous, remoulding world outlook must be a prolonged and arduous task. Once we slacken our efforts to do this, we will be unable to resist corruption by bourgeois and revisionist ideas and will lose our bearings and commit serious mistakes. Only by raising the consciousness of remoulding one's world outlook, studying revolutionary theory and persisting in revolutionary practice, and making ourselves a target of revolution and regarding ourselves as a part of the strength in the revolution can we keep our thinking in conformity with the ever-changing revolutionary situation and march ahead to guide the chariot of society.

In his great work *On Practice* Chairman Mao pointed out to us: "In the present epoch of the development of society, the responsibility of correctly knowing and changing the world has been placed by history upon the shoulders of the proletariat and its party." Studying this teaching of Chairman Mao's makes us profoundly realize that the task entrusted to us by history is extremely important, arduous and glorious. Guided by Marxism-Leninism-Mao Tsetung Thought and with the revolutionary spirit of seizing the day and seizing the hour, we will make a big effort to remould our world outlook so as to more effectively change the objective world, make still more and greater contributions to the Chinese revolution and the world revolution and advance triumphantly to the great goal of communism.

CHAPTER TWO:
Sino-American Relations

When the People's Republic was established in Peking on October 1, 1949, it was not at all certain whether or not the United States would recognize the new regime. A series of complicating events already made the "normalization" a difficult and complex task.

First of all, the failure of the Marshall Mission (1945-47) to mediate the cessation of hostilities between the Kuomintang and the Chinese Communist forces and the newly formed coalition government in China made it difficult for the United States to negotiate again in good faith with the Chinese; then the precipitated release of the State Department's White Paper on China by Dean Acheson angered both the Nationalists and the Communists and made negotiation almost impossible (see Document 9).

Acheson himself also believed that there was no immediate advantage for the United States to recognize the Peking government. He declared, "The Communist leaders have foresworn their Chinese heritage and have publicly announced their subservience to a foreign power, Russia, which during the last fifty years, under Czars and Communist alike, has been most assiduous in its efforts to extend its control in the Far East."[1]

The Chinese, on the other hand, at this point also made no effort to encourage and reassure or win the approval of the United States. Mao Tse-tung made an important policy statement in July, 1949, in which he declared himself to be "leaning to one side" with the Soviet Union. He wrote: "The forty years' experience of Sun Yat-sen and the twenty-eight years' experience of the Communist Party have taught us to

[1] Department of State, *United States Relations with China* (Washington, D.C., Government Printing Office, 1949, reprinted, Stanford; Stanford University Press, 1967), p. x.

lean to one side, and we are firmly convinced that in order to win victory and consolidate it we must lean to one side. In the light of the experiences accumulated in these forty years, and those twenty-eight years, all Chinese without exception, must lean either to the side of imperialism or to the side of socialism. Sitting on the fence will not do, nor is there a third road."[1]

In response to Mao's article, the editors of *Life* magazine wrote in a preface to a proposal by General Claire Chennault advocating a program of aid to save part of China "that Mao's article had shattered the illusion cherished by many an American—the illusion that China's Communists are 'different.' "[2]

The Chinese Communists also failed to negotiate with U. S. Ambassador John Leighton Stuart, who was instructed by his government to remain in Nanking after the capture of the city by the Communist forces on April 24, 1949. After all efforts to contact the Chinese Communist leadership was unsuccessful and his official residence was illegally "entered" by the local troops, Stuart left China for Washington on August 2, and three days later the State Department released its critical White Paper (see Document 10).

These incidents, together with a series of other fateful events—the threatening of lives or confiscation of property of Americans in China; the fears and doubts of American public attitudes as a result of Senator Joseph McCarthy's investigation and accusations; the effective publicity and promotional programs on behalf of Chiang Kai-shek by the China Lobby; and the outbreak of the Korean War on June 25, 1950—destroyed hopes for any sort of political settlement with the Chinese.

The invasion by the North Koreans of South Korea precipitated a decision by President Harry Truman on June 27 to interpose the U.S. Seventh Fleet to protect Taiwan from possible future attacks by the Chinese Communists. This protective action by the United States was viewed with extreme hostility by the Chinese, who insisted that the liberation of Taiwan was an internal affair of China. And in subsequent years

1 Mao Tse-tung, *Selected Works*, Vol. IV (Peking, Foreign Language Press, 1967), p. 415.
2 Quoted in Tsang Tsou, *America's Failure in China; 1941-50*, Vol. 2 (Chicago, University of Chicago Press, 1963), p. 506.

three crises involving Taiwan developed, in 1955, 1958, and 1962 (see Document 11).

The Korean War, extending from 1950 to 1953, resulted in a total of 455,000 casualties, of whom 300,000 were South Koreans and 150,000 were Americans. Estimates of Communist casualties range from 1,500,000 to 2,000,000. Finally, an armistice was signed on July 26, 1953, after the longest truce negotiation in history—575 separate meetings in two years and seventeen days.[1]

Scars of the war were shared by both the Chinese and the Americans; but China, under U.S. sponsorship, was declared guilty of aggression in Korea by the United Nations. Meanwhile, the United States was engaged with China in another indirect conflict in Indochina. Communist China had already committed her support to the Viet Minh offense in Indochina against the French effort which was then partially financed by the United States.[2]

In an effort to prevent a repetition of the Korean tragedy in Indochina, especially after the defeat of French forces in Dienbienphu, an Indochina settlement was reached in Geneva on July 21, 1954, under the joint sponsorship of China, Great Britain, the USSR, and the United States.

Unfortunately, under Dulles, the United States refused to sign the final Geneva Declaration, continued to oppose Chinese admission to the United Nations, created SEATO to contain China in Asia (see Document 29), and signed a separate mutual defense pact with the Nationalists on Taiwan (see Document 12).

Perhaps as a direct reaction to the United States' extreme hostile attitude, China began applying pressure on Taiwan, including military attacks upon the Nationalist-held offshore islands. On January 24, 1955, President Eisenhower requested that Congress pass the first Formosa Resolution (the H. J. Res. 159) to defend "the U.S. security interest in the area," which he signed into public law (PL 84-4).[3]

1 For Chinese involvement in Korean War see Allen S. Whiting, *China Crosses the Yalu* (Stanford, Stanford University Press, 1960).

2 See Jean Lacoutoure, *Vietnam: Between Two Truces* (New York, Vintage Books, 1966).

3 George McTurnay Kahin and John W. Lewis, *The U.S. in Vietnam* (New York, Dial Press, 1967).

Meanwhile, a new spirit of Asian nationalism and a different international Communist strategy (developed during the Nineteenth Communist Party Congress at Moscow) stressed a policy of peaceful coexistence. On April 18, 1955, the first major conference of Afro-Asian nations was held in Bandung, Indonesia, in which the Chinese were among the major participants (see Document 27).

Afterward, Communist China released some of the American prisoners held in China and Chou En-lai announced his willingness to negotiate with the United States during the Bandung Conference, resulting in the first U.S.-China ambassadorial talks in August, 1955.

There was considerable opposition again in the United States with respect to negotiation with the Chinese Communists, as represented by the views of the then Senate Minority Leader William F. Knowland (Republican, California).[1] Secretary of State Dulles suspended the ambassadorial talks on December 6, 1955, and continued his hard-line "containment policy" with a new strategy of "brinkmanship" to deal with China, including the "tactical use of atomic arms."[2]

China reacted with great disappointment and anger, which resulted in renewal of bombardment of Quemoy and Matsu islands. But this new Taiwan Strait crisis permitted the China Lobby to intensify its anti-China campaign in the United States and strengthen its power base in the Congress with the enlistment of twenty-three Senators and eighty-three Representatives as supporters.[3]

Meanwhile, Chinese domestic politics forced Mao Tse-tung temporarily out of office and Liu Shao-chi was named Chairman of the Republic on April 27, 1959. There was considerable internal unrest in China, including a revolt in Tibet which China successfully crushed (see Document 49). In foreign relations, China began to develop differences with the Soviet Union (see Document 21), and Chinese-Indian relations worsened because of border disputes (see Document 51).

Chou En-lai then proposed a peace pact on August 1, 1960, between China, the United States, and other Pacific powers, to

1 *China-U.S. Far East Policy, 1945-1966* (Washington, D.C., Washington Congressional Quarterly Service, 1967), p. 74.
2 *Life* (January 11, 1956).
3 *China-U.S. Far East Policy, 1945-1966, op. cit.*, p. 87.

establish a nonnuclear zone in Asia and the western Pacific. Chou added that China had not "given up its policy of seeking peaceful relations with countries with different social systems." [1] However, the United States was not in a mood to accept the Chinese offer and the State Department termed Chou's proposal a "propaganda gesture."

Fresh sources of tension were developing between China and the United States: Chinese involvement in "wars of Liberation" in Indochina, U.S. involvement in Japan and Korea, U.S. embargo on trade and cultural relations with China and continuing opposition to Chinese representation in the United Nations, and Sino-American competition in the "Third World" nations. After John F. Kennedy was elected President of the United States, his counterinsurgency planning, the Bay of Pigs invasion of Cuba, and the U.S.-USSR thaw made the Chinese feel that he was "worse than Eisenhower." And finally, after President Lyndon B. Johnson's massive involvement of U.S. troops in Vietnam, all hopes were shattered for better China-U.S. relations (see Document 15).

China then developed a new policy differentiating American people from the government in Washington, a sort of "Two America" policy. China continued to stress friendship with the American people and her support for their struggle for civil rights (see Document 14) and the American antiwar movement, while opposing the U.S. government, especially its policies of "imperialism" in Asia, Africa, and Latin America. In fact, immediately following the U.S.-South Vietnamese invasion of Cambodia in May, 1970, China withdrew her suggestion of resumption of the ambassadorial talks (see Document 16).

Because of the rise of China as a nuclear power and the long, barbarous war in Vietnam, public opinion in the United States began to exert pressure on the government to relax its tension with the Chinese regime in Peking. The U.S. ban on travel to China was revoked in July, 1969, for scholars, scientists, and journalists. And in March, 1971, all U.S. restrictions for travel to China were lifted.

After July, 1969, Americans abroad were allowed to buy and bring back $100 worth of Chinese-made goods. In December, 1969, the $100 ceiling on purchases was removed, and two significant steps were taken by the Nixon administration to

1 *Ibid*, p. 99.

allow American businessmen to trade with China, resulting in the end of a twenty-one-year embargo on trade with China. On June 10, 1971, President Nixon authorized the export of a wide range of nonstrategic items and lifted all controls on imports from China with the goal of stimulating the "business of diplomacy" between the two countries[1] (see Appendix F).

At that time, Premier Chou En-lai, greeting a U.S. table tennis team and news correspondents in Peking's Great Hall of the People, said, "You have opened a new page in the relations of the Chinese and American people. I am confident that this beginning again of our friendship will certainly meet with the majority support of our two peoples."[2] And in Hong Kong, some Communist Chinese stores already began to run ads for their products in the English-language *South China Morning Post*, apparently in an attempt to attract American tourists.

Finally, with the announcement on July 15, 1971, of President Nixon's impending trip to China, the future relations of China and the United States are indeed brighter (see Document 17). With a more enlightened policy of the two countries, removed from the fears of the past, away from the military and political confrontations of yesteryears and with a generous America offering its help in the development of the Chinese economy,[3] the next generation of Americans and Chinese may be able to grow up in a far more peaceful and better world, without the dangerous ignorance and barbarous wars of today.

9. MAO TSE-TUNG: "FRIENDSHIP" OR AGGRESSION? (August, 1949)*

The U.S. State Department's White Paper, released on August 8, 1949, attempted to clarify U.S. policy toward China for the American public and to silence the criticism made by conservative Republican leaders. The Chinese reactions to it, as illustrated in

1 New York *Times* (June 11, 1971).
2 *Newsweek* (April 26, 1971), p. 16.
3 Harry Schwartz wrote that "it would be surprising if U.S. economic and technical assistance to China were not high on the agenda of the historic meeting." New York *Times* (July 19, 1971), p. 25.
*From *Selected Works of Mao Tse-tung*, Vol. IV (Peking, Foreign Language Press, 1967), pp. 447-50 (footnotes omitted).

this statement of Mao on August 30, proved the White Paper to be a disappointment to the Chinese Communists.

Seeking to justify aggression, Dean Acheson harps on "friendship" and throws in lots of "principles".

Acheson says:

> The interest of the people and the Government of the United States in China goes far back into our history. Despite the distance and broad differences in background which separate China and the United States, our friendship for that country has always been intensified by the religious, philanthropic and cultural ties which have united the two peoples, and has been attested by many acts of good will over a period of many years, including the use of the Boxer indemnity for the education of Chinese students, the abolition of extra-territoriality during the Second World War, and our extensive aid to China during and since the close of the War. The record shows that the United States has consistently maintained and still maintains those fundamental principles of our foreign policy toward China which include the doctrine of the Open Door, respect for the administrative and territorial integrity of China, and opposition to any foreign domination of China.

Acheson is telling a bare-faced lie when he describes aggression as "friendship".

The history of the aggression against China by U.S. imperialism, from 1840 when it helped the British in the Opium War to the time it was thrown out of China by the Chinese people, should be written into a concise textbook for the education of Chinese youth. The United States was one of the first countries to force China to cede extraterritoriality—witness the Treaty of Wanghia of 1844, the first treaty ever signed between China and the United States, a treaty to which the White Paper refers. In this very treaty, the United States compelled China to accept American missionary activity, in addition to imposing such terms as the opening of five ports for trade. For a very long period, U.S. imperialism laid greater stress than other imperialist countries on activities in the sphere of spiritual aggression, extending from religious to "philanthropic" and cultural under-takings. According to certain statistics, the investments of U.S. missionary and "philanthropic" organizations in China totalled

41,900,000 U.S. dollars, and 14.7 per cent of the assets of the missionary organizations were in medical service, 38.2 per cent in education and 47.1 per cent in religious activities. Many well-known educational institutions in China, such as Yenching University, Peking Union Medical College, the Huei Wen Academies, St. John's University, the University of Nanking, Soochow University, Hangchow Christian College, Hsiangya Medical School, West China Union University and Lingnan University, were established by Americans. It was in this field that Leighton Stuart made a name for himself; that was how he became U.S. ambassador to China. Acheson and his like know what they are talking about, and there is a background for his statement that "our friendship for that country has always been intensified by the religious, philanthropic and cultural ties which have united the two peoples." It was all for the sake of "intensifying friendship," we are told, that the United States worked so hard and deliberately at running these undertakings for 105 years after the signing of the Treaty of 1844.

Participation in the Eight-Power Allied Expedition to defeat China in 1900, the extortion of the "Boxer indemnity" and the later use of this fund "for the education of Chinese students" for purposes of spiritual aggression—this too counts as an expression of "friendship."

Despite the "abolition" of extraterritoriality, the culprit in the raping of Shen Chung was declared not guilty and released by the U.S. Navy Department on his return to the United States—this counts as another expression of "friendship". [An incident involved U. S. troops in Peking after World War II.]

"Aid to China during and since the close of the War", totalling over 4,500 million U.S. dollars according to the White Paper, but over 5,914 million U.S. dollars according to our computation, was given to help Chiang Kai-shek slaughter several million Chinese—this counts as yet another expression of "friendship".

All the "friendship" shown to China by U.S. imperialism over the past 109 years (since 1840 when the United States collaborated with Britain in the Opium War), and especially the great act of "friendship" in helping Chiang Kai-shek slaughter several million Chinese in the last few years—all this had one purpose, namely, it "consistently maintained and still maintains those fundamental principles of our foreign policy toward China which include the doctrine of the Open Door, respect for the administrative and territorial integrity of China, and opposition to any foreign domination of China".

Several million Chinese were killed for no other purpose than first, to maintain the Open Door, second, to respect the administrative and territorial integrity of China and, third, to oppose any foreign domination of China.

Today, the only doors still open to Acheson and his like are in small strips of land, such as Canton and Taiwan, and only in these places is the first of these sacred principles "still maintained". In other places, in Shanghai for instance, the door was open after liberation, but now some one is using U.S. warships and their big guns to enforce the far from sacred principle of the Blockaded Door.

Today, it is only in small strips of land, such as Canton and Taiwan, that thanks to Acheson's second sacred principle administrative and territorial "integrity" is "still maintained". All other places are out of luck, and administration and territory have fallen to pieces.

Today, it is only in places such as Canton and Taiwan that thanks to Acheson's third sacred principle all "foreign domination", including U.S. domination, has been successfully done away with through the "opposition" of Acheson and his like; therefore such places are still dominated by the Chinese. The rest of the land of China—the mere mention makes one weep—is all gone, all dominated by foreigners, and the Chinese there have one and all been turned into slaves. Up to this point in his writing, His Excellency Dean Acheson did not have time to indicate what country these foreigners came from, but it becomes clear as one reads on, so there is no need to ask.

Whether non-interference in China's domestic affairs also counts as a principle, Acheson didn't say; probably it does not. Such is the logic of the U.S. mandarins. Anyone who reads Acheson's Letter of Transmittal to the end will attest to its superior logic.

10. MAO TSE-TUNG: FAREWELL, LEIGHTON STUART (August, 1949)*

> *John Leighton Stuart, who was born in China in 1876, served as U.S. missionary in China from 1905*

*From *Selected Works of Mao Tse-tung*, Vol. IV (Peking, Foreign Language Press, 1967), pp. 433-40 (footnotes omitted).

to 1919, when he became the president of Yenching University in Peking. On July 11, 1946, he was named U.S. ambassador to China, a position he held until August 2, 1949, when he left Nanking for Washington after his failure to negotiate a political settlement with the Chinese Communists. Following is another statement by Mao published on August 18, commenting on Stuart's departure and on the State Department's White Paper.

It is understandable that the date chosen for the publication of the U.S. White Paper was August 5, a time when Leighton Stuart had departed from Nanking for Washington but had not yet arrived there, since Leighton Stuart is a symbol of the complete defeat of the U.S. policy of aggression. Leighton Stuart is an American born in China; he has fairly wide social connections and spent many years running missionary schools in China; he once sat in a Japanese gaol during the War of Resistance; he used to pretend to love both the United States and China and was able to deceive quite a number of Chinese. Hence, he was picked out by George C. Marshall, was made U.S. ambassador to China and became a celebrity in the Marshall group. In the eyes of the Marshall group he had only one fault, namely, that the whole period when he was ambassador to China as an exponent of their policy was the very period in which that policy was utterly defeated by the Chinese people; that was no small responsibility. It is only natural that the White Paper, which is designated to evade this responsibility, should have been published at a time when Leighton Stuart was on his way to Washington but had not yet arrived.

The war to turn China into a U.S. colony, a war in which the United States of America supplies the money and guns and Chiang Kai-shek the men to fight for the United States and slaughter the Chinese people, has been an important component of the U.S. imperialist policy of world-wide aggression since World War II. The U.S. policy of aggression has several targets. The three main targets are Europe, Asia and the Americas. China, the centre of gravity in Asia, is a large country with a population of 475 million; by seizing China, the United States would possess all of Asia. With its Asian front consolidated, U.S. imperialism could concentrate its forces on attacking Europe. U.S. imperialism considers its front in the Americas relatively secure. These are the smug over-all calculations of the U.S. aggressors.

But in the first place, the American people and the peoples of the world do not want war. Secondly, the attention of the United States has largely been absorbed by the awakening of the peoples of Europe, by the rise of the People's Democracies in Eastern Europe, and particularly by the towering presence of the Soviet Union, this unprecedentedly powerful bulwark of peace bestriding Europe and Asia, and by its strong resistance to the U.S. policy of aggression. Thirdly, and this is most important, the Chinese people have awakened, and the armed forces and the organized strength of the people under the leadership of the Communist Party of China have become more powerful than ever before. Consequently, the ruling clique of U.S. imperialism has been prevented from adopting a policy of direct, large-scale armed attacks on China and instead has adopted a policy of helping Chiang Kai-shek fight the civil war.

U.S. naval, ground and air forces did participate in the war in China. There were U.S. naval bases in Tsingtao, Shanghai and Taiwan. U.S. troops were stationed in Peiping, Tientsin, Tangshan, Chinwangtao, Tsingtao, Shanghai and Nanking. The U.S. air force controlled all of China's air space and took aerial photographs of all China's strategic areas for military maps. At the town of Anping near Peiping, at Chiutai near Changchun, at Tangshan and in the Eastern Shantung Peninsula, U.S. troops and other military personnel clashed with the People's Liberation Army and on several occasions were captured. Chennault's air fleet took an extensive part in the civil war. Besides transporting troops for Chiang Kai-shek, the U.S. air force bombed and sank the cruiser *Chungking*, which had mutinied against the Kuomintang. All these were acts of direct participation in the war, although they fell short of an open declaration of war and were not large in scale, and although the principal method of U.S. aggression was the large-scale supply of money, munitions and advisers to help Chiang Kai-shek fight the civil war.

The use of this method by the United States was determined by the objective situation in China and the rest of the world, and not by any lack of desire on the part of the Truman-Marshall group, the ruling clique of U.S. imperialism, to launch direct aggression against China. Moreover, at the outset of its help to Chiang Kai-shek in fighting the civil war, a crude farce was staged in which the United States appeared as mediator in the conflict between the Kuomintang and the Communist Party; this was an attempt to soften up the Communist Party of China, deceive the Chinese people and thus gain control of all China without fighting. The peace negotiations failed, the deception fell through and the curtain rose on the war.

Liberals or "democratic individualists" who cherish illusions about the United States and have short memories! Please look at Acheson's own words:

> When peace came the United States was confronted with three possible alternatives in China: (1) it could have pulled out lock, stock and barrel; (2) it could have intervened militarily on a major scale to assist the Nationalists to destroy the Communists; (3) it could, while assisting the Nationalists to assert their authority over as much of China as possible, endeavor to avoid a civil war by working for a compromise between the two sides.

Why didn't the United States adopt the first of these policies? Acheson says:

> The first alternative would, and I believe American public opinion at the time so felt, have represented an abandonment of our international responsibilities and of our traditional policy of friendship for China before we had made a determined effort to be of assistance.

So that's how things stand: the "international responsibilities" of the United States and its "traditional policy of friendship for China" are nothing but intervention against China. Intervention is called assuming international responsibilities and showing friendship for China, as to non-intervention, it simply won't do. Here Acheson defiles U.S. public opinion; his is the "public opinion" of Wall Street, not the public opinion of the American people.

Why didn't the United States adopt the second of these policies? Acheson says:

> The second alternative policy, while it may look attractive theoretically and in retrospect, was wholly impracticable. The Nationalists had been unable to destroy the Communists during the 10 years before the war. Now after the war the

Nationalists were, as indicated above, weakened, demoralized, and unpopular. They had quickly dissipated their popular support and prestige in the areas liberated from the Japanese by the conduct of their civil and military officials. The Communists on the other hand were much stronger than they had ever been and were in control of most of North China. Because of the ineffectiveness of the Nationalist forces which was later to be tragically demonstrated, the Communists probably could have been dislodged only by American arms. It is obvious that the American people would not have sanctioned such a colossal commitment of our armies in 1945 or later. We therefore came to the third alternative policy. . . .

What a splendid idea! The United States supplies the money and guns and Chiang Kai-shek the men to fight for the United States and slaughter the Chinese people, to "destroy the Communists" and turn China into a U.S. colony, so that the United States may fulfil its "international responsibilities" and carry out its "traditional policy of friendship for China".

Although the Kuomintang was corrupt and incompetent, "demoralized and unpopular", the United States nevertheless supplied it with money and guns and made it fight. Direct armed intervention was all right, "theoretically". It also seems all right "in retrospect" to the rulers of the United States. For direct armed intervention would really have been interesting and it might "look attractive". But it would not have worked in practice, for "it is obvious that the American people would not have sanctioned" it. Not that the imperialist group of Truman, Marshall, Acheson and their like did not desire it—they very much desired it—but the situation in China, in the United States and in the world as a whole (a point Acheson does not mention) did not permit it; they had to give up their preference and take the third way.

Let those Chinese who believe that "victory is possible even without international help" listen. Acheson is giving you a lesson. Acheson is a good teacher, giving lessons free of charge, and he is telling the whole truth with tireless zeal and great candour. The United States refrained from dispatching large forces to attack China, not because the U.S. government didn't want to, but because it had worries. First worry: the Chinese people would oppose it, and the U.S. government was afraid of getting hopelessly bogged down in a quagmire. Second worry: the American people would oppose it, and so the U.S.

government dared not order mobilization. Third worry: the people of the Soviet Union, of Europe and of the rest of the world would oppose it, and the U.S. government would face universal condemnation. Acheson's charming candour has its limits and he is unwilling to mention the third worry. The reason is he is afraid of losing face before the Soviet Union, he is afraid that the Marshall Plan in Europe, which is already a failure despite pretences to the contrary, may end dismally in total collapse.

Let those Chinese who are short-sighted, muddle-headed liberals or democratic individualists listen. Acheson is giving you a lesson; he is a good teacher for you. He has made a clean sweep of your fancied U.S. humanity, justice and virtue. Isn't that so? Can you find a trace of humanity, justice or virtue in the White Paper or in Acheson's Letter of Transmittal?

True, the United States has science and technology. But unfortunately they are in the grip of the capitalists, not in the hands of the people, and are used to exploit and oppress the people at home and to perpetrate aggression and to slaughter people abroad. There is also "democracy" in the United States. But unfortunately it is only another name for the dictatorship of the bourgeoisie by itself. The United States has plenty of money. But unfortunately it is willing to give money only to the Chiang Kai-shek reactionaries, who are rotten to the core. The United States, it is said, is and will be quite willing to give money to its fifth column in China, but is unwilling to give it to the ordinary run of liberals or democratic individualists, who are much too bookish and do not know how to appreciate favours, and naturally it is even more unwilling to give money to the Communists. Money may be given, but only conditionally. What is the condition? Follow the United States. The Americans have sprinkled some relief flour in Peiping, Tientsin and Shanghai to see who will stoop to pick it up. Like Chiang Tai Kung fishing, they have cast the line for the fish who want to be caught. But he who swallows food handed out in contempt will get a bellyache.

We Chinese have backbone. Many who were once liberals or democratic individualists have stood up to the U.S. imperialists and their running dogs, the Kuomintang reactionaries. Wen Yi-to rose to his full height and smote the table, angrily faced the Kuomintang pistols and died rather than submit. Chu Tse-ching, though seriously ill, starved to death rather than accept U.S. "relief food". Han Yu of the Tang Dynasty wrote a "Eulogy of Po Yi", praising a man with quite a few "democratic individualist" ideas, who shirked his duty towards the people of his own country, deserted his post and opposed the people's war of liberation of that time, led by King Wu. He lauded the wrong man. We should write eulogies of Wen Yi-to and Chu Tse-ching who demonstrated the heroic spirit of our nation.

What matter if we have to face some difficulties? Let them blockade us! Let them blockade us for eight or ten years! By that time all of China's problems will have been solved. Will the Chinese cower before difficulties when they are not afraid even of death? Lao Tzu said, "The people fear not death, why threaten them with it?" U.S. imperialism and its running dogs, the Chiang Kai-shek reactionaries, have not only "threatened" us with death but actually put many of us to death. Besides people like Wen Yi-to, they have killed millions of Chinese in the last three years with U.S. carbines, machine-guns, mortars, bazookas, howitzers, tanks and bombs dropped from aeroplanes. This situation is now coming to an end. They have been defeated. It is we who are going in to attack them, not they who are coming out to attack us. They will soon be finished. True, the few problems left to us, such as blockade, unemployment, famine, inflation and rising prices, are difficulties, but we have already begun to breathe more easily than in the past three years. We have come triumphantly through the ordeal of the last three years, why can't we overcome these few difficulties of today? Why can't we live without the United States?

When the People's Liberation Army crossed the Yangtse River, the U.S. colonial government at Nanking fled helter-skelter. Yet His Excellency Ambassador Stuart sat tight, watching wide-eyed, hoping to set up shop under a new signboard and to reap some profit. But what did he see? Apart from the People's Liberation Army marching past, column after column, and the workers, peasants and students rising in hosts, he saw something else—the Chinese liberals or democratic individualists turning out in force, shouting slogans and talking revolution together with the workers, peasants, soldiers and students. In short, he was left out in the cold, "standing all alone, body and shadow comforting each other". There was nothing more for him to do, and he had to take to the road, his briefcase under his arm.

There are still some intellectuals and other people in China who have muddled ideas and illusions about the United States. Therefore we should explain things to them, win them over, educate them and unite with them, so they will come over to the side of the people and not fall into the snares set by imperialism. But the prestige of U.S. imperialism among the Chinese people is completely bankrupt, and the White Paper is a record of its bankruptcy. Progressives should make good use of the White Paper to educate the Chinese people.

Leighton Stuart has departed and the White Paper has arrived. Very good. Very good. Both events are worth celebrating.

11. CHOU EN-LAI: REFUTING TRUMAN'S STATEMENT (June, 1950)*

> *On June 27, 1950, two days after the outbreak of the Korean War, President Truman ordered the U.S. Seventh Fleet to protect Taiwan from being attacked by the Chinese Communists. This is the official Chinese reaction, made by Foreign Minister Chou En-lai and published on June 28.*

After instigating the puppet government of Syngman Rhee in South Korea to provoke civil war in Korea, President Truman of the United States of America made a statement on June 27, declaring that the United States Government had decided to prevent by armed force our liberation of Taiwan.

On Truman's order, the U.S. Seventh Fleet has moved to the coast of Taiwan.

On behalf of the Central People's Government of the People's Republic of China, I declare that Truman's statement of June 27 and the action of the U.S. navy constitute armed aggression against the territory of China and are a gross violation of the United Nations Charter. This violent, predatory action by the United States Government comes as no surprise to the Chinese people but only increases their wrath, because the Chinese people have, over a long period, consistently exposed all the conspiratorial schemes of U.S. imperialism to commit aggression against China and seize Asia by force. In his statement, Truman

*From *Oppose U.S. Occupation of Taiwan and "Two-China's" Plot* (Peking, Foreign Language Press, 1958), pp. 5-7.

merely discloses his premeditated plan and puts it into practice. In fact the attack by the puppet Korean troops of Syngman Rhee on the Korean Democratic People's Republic at the instigation of the United States Government was a premeditated move by the United States, designed to create a pretext for the United States to invade Taiwan, Korea, Vietnam and the Philippines. It is nothing but a further act of intervention by U.S. imperialism in the affairs of Asia.

On behalf of the Central People's Government of the People's Republic of China, I declare that, no matter what obstructive action U.S. imperialists may take, the fact that Taiwan is part of China will remain unchanged for ever. This is not only a historical fact; it has also been confirmed by the Cairo and Potsdam Declarations and the situation since the surrender of Japan. All the people of our country will certainly fight as one man and to the end to liberate Taiwan from the grasp of the U.S. aggressors. The Chinese people, who have defeated Japanese imperialism and Chiang Kai-shek, the hireling of U.S. imperialism, will surely succeed in driving out the U.S. aggressors and in recovering Taiwan and all other territories belonging to China.

The Central People's Government of the People's Republic of China calls on all peoples throughout the world who love peace, justice and freedom, and especially on all the oppressed nations and peoples of the East, to rise as one and halt the new aggression of U.S. imperialism in the East. Such aggression can be completely defeated if we do not yield to threats but resolutely mobilize the broad mass of the people to take part in the struggle against the war-makers. The Chinese people express their sympathy and respect for the peoples of Korea, Vietnam, the Philippines and Japan who are similarly victims of U.S. aggression and are similarly fighting against it. The Chinese people firmly believe that all the oppressed nations and peoples of the East will certainly destroy the vicious and hated U.S. imperialist war-makers once and for all in the great flames of struggle for national independence.

12. CHOU EN-LAI: ON U.S.-CHIANG KAI-SHEK "MUTUAL SECURITY TREATY" (December, 1954)*

*From *Oppose U.S. Occupation of Taiwan and "Two-China's" Plot* (Peking, Foreign Language Press, 1958), pp. 18-27.

> *On December 2, 1954, Secretary of State Dulles signed a mutual security pact for the defense of Taiwan. The treaty, ratified by the Senate on February 9, 1955, and signed by President Eisenhower three days later, required the United States and Nationalist China to (1) maintain and develop "jointly by self-help and mutual aid" their individual and collective capacity to resist armed attack and Communist subversion directed against the two countries "from without," (2) cooperate in economic development, (3) consult on implementation of the treaty, and (4) act to meet an armed attack. The following is Foreign Minister Chou En-lai's official response given on December 8, 1954.*

On December 2, 1954 the United States Government, disregarding the repeated protests and warnings of the Chinese people, concluded a so-called Mutual Security Treaty with the Chiang Kai-shek traitor gang fugitive on Taiwan. The United States Government is trying, by means of this treaty, to legalize its armed seizure of Chinese territory of Taiwan, and make Taiwan a base for further aggression against China and the preparation for a new war. This act is a grave warlike provocation against the People's Republic of China and the Chinese people.

On behalf of the Government of the People's Republic of China, I hereby declare: Taiwan is China's territory, and Chiang Kai-shek is the public enemy of the Chinese people. To liberate Taiwan and liquidate the Chiang Kai-shek gang of traitors is entirely within the purview of China's sovereignty and a purely internal affair of China, and no interference by any foreign country will be tolerated. Threats of war cannot shake the determination of the Chinese people to liberate Taiwan but can only heighten their indignation. The Chiang Kai-shek traitor gang has no authority whatsoever to conclude any treaty with any country. The "Mutual Security Treaty" concluded between the United States and Chiang Kai-shek has no legal basis whatsoever and is null and void. This treaty is a betrayal of China's sovereign and territorial rights and the Chinese people oppose it resolutely. If the United States Government does not withdraw all its armed forces from Taiwan, the Penghu Islands and the Taiwan Straits, and persists in interfering in China's internal affairs, it must take upon itself all the grave consequences.

The "Mutual Security Treaty" which the United States Government has entered into with the Chiang Kai-shek traitor gang is, in every sense, a treaty of war and aggression. United States imperialism is hostile to the Chinese people. Refusing to reconcile itself to the defeat of its imperialist policy in China, the United States Government occupied Taiwan by armed force in June 1950 at the same time as it launched its war of aggression in Korea. Since then it has been shielding the Chiang Kai-shek traitor gang and directing it in its uninterrupted war of harassment and destruction against the mainland and coastal islands of China. Now that the Korean war has ended, the United States Government no longer finds it possible to use that war as a pretext for the continued occupation of Taiwan. That is why it has come out openly and fabricated this U.S.-Chiang Kai-shek "Mutual Security Treaty" for the purpose of outright seizure of China's territories of Taiwan and the Penghu Islands.

The "Mutual Security Treaty" between the United States and Chiang Kai-shek cannot be called defensive in any sense; it is a treaty of naked aggression. The aggressive circles of the United States and those who follow them pretend that the treaty is defensive in character; but such a pretence cannot hide its aggressive nature in any way. Taiwan is China's territory. This is a fact which the United States Government has recognized in such international agreements as the Cairo and Potsdam Declarations and the Instrument of Japanese Surrender, all of which bear its own signature. For the Chinese people to liberate Taiwan is an internal affair of China. Here too the United States Government, in January 1950, acknowledged China's exercise of her sovereign rights over Taiwan and declared its intention not to become involved in the civil conflict in China.

Now the United States Government is erecting fortifications and establishing military bases on the Chinese territories of Taiwan and the Penghu Islands, which are 5,000 miles away from the United States. It is shielding the Chiang Kai-shek gang of traitors which has been repudiated by the 600 million people of China. It is endeavouring to prevent the Chinese people from liberating their own territory of Taiwan. In so doing, the United States Government is committing flagrant violations of international good faith, seizing Chinese territory, infringing upon China's sovereignty and interfering in China's internal affairs—

acts which can in no way be described as defensive. It is a genuine act of defence, on the other hand, for the Chinese people to liberate their own territory of Taiwan and to safeguard their national sovereignty and the territorial integrity of their country. The Japanese militarists, in their time, also represented their seizure of North-east China in 1931 as an act of self-defence. But nobody believed them. Everyone knows that to seize another country's territory, to infringe upon another country's sovereignty and to interfere in another country's internal affairs is to commit acts of aggression. The Chinese people, tempered in victorious struggle against the Japanese militarist aggression, will never tolerate United States aggression, undertaken under the name of "defence," against China's Taiwan and Penghu Islands.

The "Mutual Security Treaty" between the United States and Chiang Kai-shek is designed to extend aggression and prepare for a new war. It has nothing to do with the maintenance of peace. The aggressive circles of the United States, and those who follow them, are advancing all kinds of arguments to conceal the warlike purpose of this treaty. But this purpose cannot be concealed. It is well-known that since it undertook its armed aggression on Taiwan, the United States Government has been aiding and abetting the Chiang Kai-shek traitor gang in its war of harassment and destruction against the Chinese mainland, and has never relaxed its efforts in this regard. By this treaty, the United States Government now attempts to legalize the occupation of Taiwan by its naval and air forces, and to secure the right to dispose its ground forces "in and about Taiwan and the Pescadores" with a view to strengthening its military base in Taiwan. By this treaty the United States Government openly attempts to use the threat of war to hinder the Chinese people from liberating Taiwan; and at the same time provides for further aggression against "other territories" of China. There can be no doubt that the signing of the "Mutual Security Treaty" between the United States and Chiang Kai-shek has increased the danger of the extension of the United States aggression against China.

In his statement on December 1, the United States Secretary of State, John Foster Dulles, openly asserted that this treaty forms "another link" in the so-called system of security established by the United States in the Pacific. This shows that the aggressive circles of the United States not only intend to occupy Taiwan and extend their aggression against China, but that they also intend to prepare a new war. The danger of war in South-east Asia has also been increased by the Manila treaty recently concluded under United States manipulation. It is clear that the aggressive circles of the United States are now trying to form a system of aggression in the East by linking the U.S.-Chiang Kai-shek treaty with the Manila treaty and other war treaties in Asia and the Pacific region. These moves of the aggressive circles of the United States dovetail with their action in Europe, where they master-minded the conclusion of the Paris agreements to revive German militarism and expand the system of aggression in the West. Their aim is to deepen the division of the world, to enslave the peoples in these areas and to accelerate their preparations for a new world war.

All that has been said above shows that the aim pursued by the United States Government in this "Mutual Security Treaty" is not peace, but war. The aggressive circles of the United States are in fact copying the old tactics used by Japanese militarism in its aggression against China. Nevertheless, there are some who want the Chinese people to forget the lessons of history and accept as the status quo the U.S. occupation of Taiwan, just as they wish. But the Chinese people will never forget the calamities that ensued from the Mukden Incident of 1931; nor will they forget that the Lukouchiao Incident of 1937 was a sequel to the Mukden Incident [beginning of the Sino-Japanese War]. The peoples of Asia and of the Pacific, whose memory of the attack on Pearl Harbour in 1941 is still fresh, will also never forget how disastrous were the consequences of the policy of appeasing Japanese militarist aggression. Similarly, the peoples of Europe will never forget that the Munich policy of giving rein to German militarist aggression, was precisely the thing that led to the Second World War. The mistakes of history must not be repeated. The Chinese people are firmly opposed to this U.S.-Chiang Kai-shek treaty for war which endangers the security of China and the peace of Asia. They are also firmly opposed to the Paris agreements which endanger the security of Europe and the peace of the world.

The "Mutual Security Treaty" between the United States and Chiang Kai-shek has created new tensions in the Far East. Nevertheless, there are some who maintain that this treaty will lead to an easing of tension in the Far East. This is the complete opposite of the truth. The United States Government undertook its armed occupation of Taiwan at the same time as it unleashed its war of aggression against Korea and intensified its intervention in the war in Indo-China. Hence from the very beginning this act has been part of the whole scheme to create tensions in the Far East.

Thanks to the armistice in Korea and the restoration of peace in Indo-China, the tense situation in the Far East began to relax. After the Geneva Conference, with a view to further reducing the tension in the Far East, we reaffirmed in clear terms that the United States should withdraw all its armed forces from Taiwan, the Penghu Islands and the Taiwan Straits and stop interfering in China's internal affairs. But the United States Government, far from withdrawing all its armed forces from Taiwan, the Penghu Islands and the Taiwan Straits, directed the Chiang Kai-shek gang of traitors to become even more reckless in its war of harassment and destruction against the Chinese mainland. As a matter of fact, the incessant creation of tensions has been the consistent policy of the United States Government. For years the United States armed forces have repeatedly invaded China's territorial air and territorial waters. It is not the Chinese armed forces that have invaded the United States territorial air or territorial waters. The United States has dispatched spies to the Chinese mainland to carry out subversive activities. It is not China that has carried out subversive activities against the United States.

In the Korean armistice, the Korean and Chinese side faithfully implemented the Armistice Agreement and the agreement on the repatriation of prisoners of war. The United States side, on the other hand, violated the agreement on the repatriation of prisoners of war by forcibly retaining more than 20,000 Korean and Chinese prisoners of war and pressing them into the armies of Syngman Rhee and Chiang Kai-shek. Even up to now the United States side has not accounted for these 20,000 Korean and Chinese prisoners of war.

With regard to the restoration of peace in Indo-China, China has guaranteed the execution of the Geneva agreements. The United States, on the other hand, not only refused to join in guaranteeing the agreements, but on the contrary concluded the Manila treaty—and is now preparing to arm and train Bao Dai's troops for the purpose of undermining the Geneva agreements.

And now, in an attempt to increase the threat of war and create new tensions in the Far East, the United States

Government has concluded its treaty of aggression and war with the Chiang Kai-shek gang of traitors. All the above facts show that the responsibility for the failure to lessen the tension in the Far East rests entirely on the United States.

The United Nations Charter categorically forbids any infringement of the territorial integrity and political independence of any nation. This principle constitutes the basis of peace between nations. The treaty the United States Government has concluded with the Chiang Kai-shek traitor gang, like other so-called treaties of defence engineered by the United States, includes a reaffirmation of faith in the purposes and principles of the United Nations Charter. But all these so-called treaties of defence are in their essence diametrically opposed to the purposes and principles which the United Nations Charter proclaims. These treaties can only lead to war. They cannot possibly promote peaceful co-existence between nations. These treaties make a mockery of the United Nations Charter. They cannot possibly contribute to the realization of the purposes and principles of the United Nations Charter or the safeguarding of international peace.

By contrast, the People's Republic of China consistently upholds the principles of safeguarding the national rights of all peoples, and of mutual respect by all states for each other's national sovereignty and territorial integrity. The five principles of peaceful co-existence jointly advocated by China, India and Burma are in full accord with the purposes of the United Nations Charter. We hold the firm conviction that, so long as the nations of the world abide by the five principles, strive to establish and expand areas of peace, and refrain from creating division, states with different social systems can co-exist in peace and a world system of collective peace and security can be built up.

The Moscow Conference of European Countries which has just been concluded has exerted great efforts in this direction, and has won wide support from the peace-loving countries and peoples of the world. But the aggressive circles of the United States and those who follow them are doing all they can to undermine the five principles of peaceful co-existence and obstruct the establishment of a world system of collective peace and security. By these means they are steadily worsening the current international situation both in the East and the West.

We hold that all peace-loving countries and peoples of the world are in duty bound to put an end to the deterioration in the international situation and to redouble their efforts for the safeguarding of international peace.

To this end, the Chinese people make the following declaration solemnly before the world:

Taiwan is China's territory. The Chinese people are determined to liberate Taiwan. Only by liberating Taiwan from the tyranny of the Chiang Kai-shek gang of traitors can the Chinese people achieve the complete unity of their motherland and further safeguard the peace of Asia and the world. All proposals to set up a so-called "independent state" of Taiwan, to "neutralize" Taiwan or to place Taiwan under "trusteeship" mean, in practice, dismemberment of China's territory, infringement upon China's sovereignty and interference in China's internal affairs. All are therefore utterly unacceptable to the Chinese people.

In order to ease the situation in the Far East, eliminate the threat of war against China and safeguard peace in Asia and the world, the U.S. Government must withdraw all its armed forces from Taiwan, the Penghu Islands and the Taiwan Straits. There is no justification whatsoever for the action of the United States in crossing vast oceans to occupy China's territory of Taiwan.

The Chinese people are resolutely opposed to war, but no threats of war will ever frighten them into submission. Should anybody insist on imposing war on the Chinese people, the Chinese people will, without fail, deal determined counterblows to those who commit such acts of intervention and provocation.

The Chinese people fervently desire peace, but they will never beg for peace at the expense of their territory and sovereignty. To sacrifice territory and sovereignty can only lead to further aggression; it cannot possibly bring about genuine peace. The Chinese people understand that only by resisting aggression can peace be defended.

13. GOVERNMENT STATEMENT: ON SINO-AMERICAN AMBASSADORIAL TALKS (June, 1958)*

*From *Oppose U.S. Occupation of Taiwan and "Two-China's" Plot* (Peking, Foreign Language Press, 1958), pp. 59-63.

Sino-American ambassadorial talks were first held in Geneva in 1955. However, Secretary of State Dulles had always had reservations about these negotiations. Shortly before the chief U.S. negotiator, Ambassador U. Alexis Johnson, was transferred to Thailand in December, 1957, Dulles suspended the ambassadorial talks and reduced the negotiations to the second-secretary level. Meanwhile, Sino-American relations were reaching a dangerous point because of the new Taiwan Strait crisis in 1958. The following is the Chinese proposal made on June 30, 1958, for the resumption of U.S.-China ambassadorial talks. Although the State Department rejected the ultimatum mentioned in this proposal, the American and Chinese ambassadors to Poland did reopen new talks on the Taiwan crisis on September 15.

More than half a year has passed since the U.S. Government suspended the Sino-American ambassadorial talks. The Chinese Government considers that this state of affairs should not continue. The U.S. ruling circles have been playing all sorts of tricks in an attempt to create the false impression that the Sino-American talks are still continuing in order to cover up its continued occupation of China's territory of Taiwan and its activities to create world tension. Such sinister designs must not be allowed to bear fruit. The Chinese Government agreed to hold the Sino-American ambassadorial talks with the aim of settling questions. The U.S. Government must answer clearly whether it is sincere about the talks.

Since December 12, 1957, when the U.S. Government broke the agreement between China and the United States on holding talks on an ambassadorial level by refusing to designate a representative of ambassadorial rank, thereby suspending the talks, the Chinese side, on January 14 and March 26, 1958, repeatedly urged the U.S. Government to designate a representative with the rank of ambassador to resume the talks. The U.S. Government, however, not only refused to do this but did not even consider it necessary to reply to the March 26 letter of the Chinese side. Moreover, a spokesman of the State Department of the United States recently even remarked nonchalantly that a First Secretary of its foreign service was ready to hold talks with us at any time, as if there had never been an agreement between China and the United States on the holding of talks on an ambassadorial level. This cannot but rouse the indignation of the Chinese people.

The imperialist attitude consistently maintained by the United States is proven by the record of nearly three years of the Sino-American ambassadorial talks. The U.S. occupation of China's territory of Taiwan has created tension in the Taiwan area. This is a naked act of aggression against China and the Chinese people have every right to take any measures to repulse it. Nevertheless, the Chinese side, in order to relax the tension in the Taiwan area, expressed its willingness to sit down and talk matters over with the United States and, during the Sino-American ambassadorial talks, put forward a series of reasonable proposals for the peaceful settlement of the international dispute between China and the United States in the Taiwan area. But the American side rejected all these proposals. They attempted to confuse China's domestic affair, a matter between the Chinese Government and the Taiwan local authorities, with the international dispute between China and the United States in the Taiwan area, and demanded that China give up its right of exercising sovereignty over its own territory and recognize the right of "self-defence" for the United States on China's territory. This demonstrates clearly that the aim of the United States is not to relax the tension in the Taiwan area at all, but to insist that China recognize the status quo of U.S. occupation of Taiwan and to maintain and heighten tension. It is due to the imperialist policy of the United States that discussion on this crucial question of Sino-American relations has bogged down since the latter part of 1956.

In order to break the deadlock and gradually improve Sino-American relations, the Chinese side further put forward a series of proposals on certain questions that are comparatively easy to settle, such as removing the trade barriers between the two countries, eliminating the obstacles in the way of mutual contacts and cultural exchange between the two peoples, exchanging correspondents for news coverage on an equal and reciprocal basis, and rendering judicial assistance between the two countries. Although questions such as the entry of correspondents for news coverage and judicial assistance were first raised by those concerned on the American side to those concerned on the Chinese side, and all the proposals of the Chinese side were fully in accord with the principles of equality and mutual benefit, the U.S. Government nonetheless rejected them. What is even more intolerable is the fact that the United States, in disregard of the agreement reached in 1955 on the return of civilians of both sides, continues to detain thousands upon thousands of Chinese civilians in the United States and prevent them from returning to their motherland.[1]

Irrefutable facts show that what the United States was after in the Sino-American ambassadorial talks was by no means a peaceful settlement of the international disputes between China and the United States on the basis of equality and mutual respect for territorial integrity and sovereignty, but to impose its imperialist will on the Chinese people and, failing that, to make use of the ambassadorial talks to deceive the people of the world and cover up its sinister designs to continue its aggression against China and to create international tension. During the past three years, the United States has been intensifying its interference and control of all aspects of life in Taiwan, establishing on it bases for guided missiles to threaten the Chinese people and utilizing the reactionary clique in Taiwan to carry out subversive activities and armed intervention against South-east Asian countries. At the same time, the United States is endeavouring to bring about, at many international conferences and organizations, a situation of "two Chinas," to create eventually such a *fait accompli* in the international arena, and thereby to prolong its occupation of Taiwan. This is the crux of the reason for the failure of the Sino-American ambassadorial talks to make progress. U.S. Secretary of State Dulles recently declared that it is in the best interests of the United States to persist in its policy of enmity towards the People's Republic of China but that it will deal with China when its interest so demands. This demonstrates most clearly that, in the minds of the U.S. ruling circles, the Sino-American ambassadorial talks are but a means serving the imperialist policy of the United States. The reason China agreed to hold the ambassadorial talks was to try by peaceful means to eliminate armed aggression and the threat of force in the Taiwan area on the part of the United States. However, the Chinese people are by no means afraid of U.S. aggression, and there is no reason whatsoever why they

1 The most distinguished Chinese detained by U.S. authorities was Chien Hsüeh-shen, a Cal Tech rocket specialist who was repatriated from the United States after the Geneva Talks.

should pine for talks with the United States. Building socialism with lightning speed, the Chinese people are perfectly strong enough to liberate their territory of Taiwan. No force on earth can stop the great cause of the Chinese people in building up and uniting their motherland. The handful of U.S. imperialists can only suffer isolation and defeat from their policy of enmity towards the 600 million Chinese people.

The Chinese Government hereby declares once again that it can neither agree to the unilateral changing of the level of the Sino-American ambassadorial talks, nor can it agree to the continued suspension of the talks on any administrative pretext. The Chinese Government demands that the United States Government designate a representative of ambassadorial rank and resume the talks within fifteen days counting from today, otherwise, the Chinese Government cannot but consider that the United States has decided to break off the Sino-American ambassadorial talks.

14. MAO TSE-TUNG: SUPPORTING THE AMERICAN NEGROES IN THEIR JUST STRUGGLE AGAINST RACIAL DISCRIMINATION BY U.S. IMPERIALISM (August, 1963)*

> *This is both a policy and a propaganda statement which was made during the critical days of China's foreign relations. 1963 was the year when Sino-Soviet negotiations failed to reach any agreement; the United States and the USSR had concluded an "anti-China" test-ban treaty; the United States began heavy involvement in Vietnam; and Sino-Indian relations deteriorated because of border wars. China developed a new policy that she must look for friendship in the Third World and its "colored people." On August 8, 1963, when receiving a group of African visitors in Peking, Mao made the following statement.*

An American Negro leader now taking refuge in Cuba,[1] Mr. Robert Williams, the former President of the Monroe, North

*From *Jen-min Jih-pao* (August 12, 1963).
1 Robert Williams has since returned to the United States—ed.

Carolina, Chapter of the National Association for the Advancement of Coloured People, has twice this year asked me for a statement in support of the American Negroes' struggle against racial discrimination. On behalf of the Chinese people, I wish to take this opportunity to express our resolute support for the American Negroes in their struggle against racial discrimination and for freedom and equal rights.

There are more than 19 million Negroes in the United States, or about 11 per cent of the total population. They are enslaved, oppressed and discriminated against—such is their position in society. The overwhelming majority are deprived of their right to vote. In general, only the most backbreaking and despised jobs are open to them. Their average wages are barely a third or a half those of the white people. The proportion of unemployment among the Negroes is the highest. In many states they are forbidden to go to the same school, eat at the same table, or travel in the same section of a bus or train as the white people. Negroes are often arrested, beaten up or murdered at will by the U.S. authorities at various levels and by members of the Ku Klux Klan and other racists. About half the American Negroes are concentrated in eleven southern states, where the discrimination and persecution they suffer are especially shocking.

The American Negroes are awakening and their resistance is growing stronger and stronger. Recent years have witnessed a continuous expansion of their mass struggle against racial discrimination and for freedom and equal rights.

In 1957 the Negro people in Little Rock, Arkansas, waged a fierce struggle against the barring of their children from public schools. The authorities used armed force against them, creating the Little Rock incident which shocked the world.

In 1960 Negroes in more than twenty states held "sit-in" demonstrations protesting against racial segregation in local restaurants, shops and other public places.

In 1961 the Negroes launched the "freedom riders" campaign to oppose racial segregation in public transportation, a campaign which rapidly spread to many states.

In 1962 the Negroes in Mississippi fought for the equal right to enrol in colleges and met with bloody suppression by the authorities.

This year, the American Negroes started their struggle early in April in Birmingham, Alabama. Unarmed and bare-handed Negro people were arrested en masse and most barbarously suppressed merely for holding meetings and parades against racial discrimination. On June 12 Mr. Medgar Evers, a leader of the Negro people in Mississippi, was murdered in cold blood.

Defying brutality and violence, the indignant Negro masses waged their struggle even more heroically and quickly won the support of Negroes and other people of various strata throughout the United States. A gigantic and vigorous nation-wide struggle is going on in nearly every city and state, and the struggle is mounting. American Negro organizations have decided to start a "freedom march" on Washington on August 28, in which 250,000 people will take part.

The speedy development of the struggle of the American Negroes is a manifestation of sharpening class struggle and sharpening national struggle within the United States; it has been causing increasing anxiety among U.S. ruling circles. The Kennedy Administration is insidiously using dual tactics. On the one hand, it continues to connive at and take part in discrimination against Negroes and their persecution, and it even sends troops to suppress them. On the other hand, in the attempt to numb the fighting will of the Negro people and deceive the masses of the country, the Kennedy Administration is parading as an advocate of "the defence of human rights" and "the protection of the civil rights of Negroes", calling upon the Negro people to exercise "restraint" and proposing the "civil rights legislation" to Congress. But more and more Negroes are seeing through these tactics of the Kennedy Administration. The fascist atrocities of the U.S. imperialists against the Negro people have exposed the true nature of so-called American democracy and freedom and revealed the inner link between the reactionary policies pursued by the U.S. government at home and its policies of aggression abroad.

I call on the workers, peasants, revolutionary intellectuals, enlightened elements of the bourgeoisie and other enlightened persons of all colours in the world, whether white, black, yellow or brown, to unite to oppose the racial discrimination practised by U.S. imperialism and support the American Negroes in their struggle against racial discrimination. In the final analysis, national struggle is a matter of class struggle. Among the whites in the United States it is only the reactionary ruling circles who oppress the Negro people. They can in no way represent the workers, farmers, revolutionary intellectuals and other enlightened persons who comprise the overwhelming majority of the white people. At present, it is the handful of imperialists headed by the United States, and their supporters, the reactionaries in different countries, who are oppressing, committing aggression against and menacing the overwhelming majority of the nations and peoples of the world. We are in the majority and they are in the minority. At most, they make up less than 10 per cent of the 3,000 million population of the world. I am firmly convinced that, with the support of more than 90 per cent of the people of the world, the American Negroes will be victorious in their just struggle. The evil system of colonialism and imperialism arose and throve with the enslavement of Negroes and the trade in Negroes, and it will surely come to its end with the complete emancipation of the black people.

15. CONGRESS RESOLUTION: RESOLUTE AND UNRESERVED SUPPORT FOR VIETNAM (April, 1965)*

On April 14, 1965, in a joint statement issued by Soviet Premier Alexei Kosygin and North Vietnamese Premier Pham Van Dong, a four-point program for negotiation was outlined which involved the removal of foreign bases and troops from Vietnam and reunification of both Vietnams at a later date through free elections. The four-point program was also adopted by the National Assembly of North Vietnam. The following is the official statement of the Standing Committee of the National People's Congress of Communist China in support of this program, adopted at its enlarged sixth session on April 20.

Having discussed the Appeal to All Parliaments of the World adopted by the Second Session of the Third National Assembly of the Democratic Republic of Viet Nam, the Standing Committee of the National People's Congress of the People's Republic of China warmly responds to the solemn appeal of the National Assembly of the D.R.V.

The Chinese people have always resolutely supported the fraternal Vietnamese people in the joint struggle against U.S.

*From *Peking Review* (April 23, 1965), pp. 6-7.

imperialist aggression. Now, in the name of the 650 million Chinese people, the Standing Committee of the National People's Congress solemnly declares that China will continue to do everything in its power to give resolute and unreserved support to the Vietnamese people in their patriotic and just struggle to resist U.S. aggression.

The present grave situation in Viet Nam is entirely the handiwork of U.S. imperialism. The U.S. imperialists have torn the 1954 Geneva agreements on the Viet Nam problem to shreds, launched a frenzied war of aggression against south Viet Nam and engaged in repeated and wanton bombing of the Democratic Republic of Viet Nam, thus flagrantly escalating the war. U.S. imperialism is the most ferocious enemy of the Vietnamese people and all the peace-loving people of the world.

Closely united and imbued with the revolutionary spirit of determination to fight and win, the entire people of Viet Nam are today engaged in a fight of immense historical significance to liberate the south and defend the north, to defeat the U.S. aggressors and achieve complete national reunification.

The Appeal to All the Parliaments of the World adopted by the National Assembly of the Democratic Republic of Viet Nam solemnly reiterated the four point proposition on the implementation of the Geneva agreements and the solution of the Vietnamese problem, namely:

1) Recognition of the basic national rights of the Vietnamese people which are independence, sovereignty, unity and territorial integrity. In strict conformity with the Geneva agreements, the U.S. Government must withdraw its troops, military personnel and weapons, ammunition and war materials of all kinds from south Viet Nam, dismantle the U.S. military bases there, abolish its military alliance with the south Viet Nam administration and at the same time stop its policy of intervention and aggression in south Viet Nam. The U.S. Government must stop all its acts of war against north Viet Nam and put a definite end to all acts of encroachment upon the territory and sovereignty of the Democratic Republic of Viet Nam.

2) Pending the realization of the peaceful reunification of Viet Nam, while Viet Nam is still temporarily divided in two, the military provisions of the 1954 Geneva agreements on Viet Nam must be strictly respected: the two zones must refrain from joining any military alliance with foreign countries, there

must be no foreign military bases, troops or military personnel in their respective territory.

3) The affairs of south Viet Nam must be settled by the south Vietnamese people themselves in accordance with the programme of the South Viet Nam National Front for Liberation without any foreign intervention.

4) The realization of the peaceful reunification of Viet Nam must be settled by the people in the two zones without foreign intervention.

The Standing Committee of the National People's Congress of the People's Republic of China holds that this four-point proposition put forward by the National Assembly of the Democratic Republic of Viet Nam is wholly reasonable and that it is the only correct road to the solution of the Vietnamese problem. The Chinese Government and the Chinese people fully approve and firmly support this four-point proposition. We hold that the necessary conditions for a political settlement of the Vietnamese problem can be created only by resolutely putting an end to U.S. imperialist aggression against Viet Nam and forcing the United States to withdraw all its armed forces from Viet Nam. Together with the Vietnamese people, we firmly oppose the U.S. imperialists' "peaceful negotiations" plot, and firmly oppose all despicable collusion with the U.S. imperialists to betray the fundamental interests of the Vietnamese people.

China is a signatory to the 1954 Geneva agreements. China and Viet Nam are fraternal socialist neighbours, as interdependent as man's lips and teeth. The Chinese and Vietnamese peoples are close comrades-in-arms, sharing the same destiny. The Chinese Government and people have already solemnly declared that aggression by the U.S. imperialists against the Democratic Republic of Viet Nam means aggression against China. The Chinese people will absolutely not stand idly by without lending a helping hand. In accordance with the requests of the Vietnamese people and with the needs of the joint struggle against U.S. imperialist aggression, the Chinese people have done and will continue to do their utmost to assist the Vietnamese people to defeat the U.S. aggressors completely. The Chinese people have always been infinitely loyal in fulfilling their proletarian internationalist obligations, they have never spared any sacrifice whatever in this respect, and they always mean what they say. Both past and present struggles testify to this.

The aggression which U.S. imperialism is committing against Viet Nam is an important step in its counterrevolutionary global strategy. The Vietnamese people's heroic resistance to this aggression is an important part of the common struggle of the people of the whole world against U.S. imperialism and in defence of world peace. As President Ho Chi Minh said, "Our country is an outpost of the socialist camp and of the peoples of the world engaged in the struggle against imperialism, colonialism and neo-colonialism. To us, this is a great honour." Glory to the valorous Vietnamese people! They are entitled to every assistance from the people of all the countries in the socialist camp, from the revolutionary people throughout the world and from all peace-loving countries and people.

The Standing Committee of the National People's Congress calls on the people's organizations and the people throughout the country:

—to publicize widely President Ho Chi Minh's April 10 address to the National Assembly of the Democratic Republic of Viet Nam, Premier Pham Van Dong's report on government work at the Second Session of the Third National Assembly of the Democratic Republic of Viet Nam and the Appeal of the National Assembly of the Democratic Republic of Viet Nam to All Parliaments of the World; to publicize widely the March 22 statement of the Central Committee of the South Viet Nam National Front for Liberation; to support the stand taken by the Democratic Republic of Viet Nam and the South Viet Nam National Front for Liberation; and to expose still further the U.S. imperialists' crime of aggression;

—to study conscientiously the relevant statements issued by our Government and the relevant editorials of *Renmin Ribao*, to carry out education on patriotism and internationalism and, together with the people throughout the world, to launch a mighty mass movement to compel the U.S. aggressors to get out of Viet Nam;

—to heighten vigilance, strengthen national defence, take an active part in labour, increase production, study hard and work hard, and by actual deeds assist the Vietnamese people in their just and patriotic struggle of resistance to U.S. aggression;

—to make full preparations to send our own people to fight together with the Vietnamese people and drive out the U.S. aggressors in the event that U.S. imperialism continues to escalate its war of aggression and the Vietnamese people need them.

The Standing Committee of the National People's Congress sincerely hopes that:

the people of the countries in the socialist camp will give the Vietnamese people all-out support, oppose the U.S. aggressors and defend the southeastern outpost of the socialist camp;

the people of all the countries of Indo-China and Southeast Asia will fully support the Vietnamese people, frustrate the criminal U.S. imperialist plan of escalating its war of aggression and safeguard peace and security in Southeast Asia;

the people of the Asian, African and Latin American countries will give the Vietnamese people full support, deal blows to the U.S. imperialist forces of aggression, and strive for still greater victories in the national-liberation movement and the people's revolutionary movement;

all countries and people throughout the world that oppose U.S. imperialism and love peace will warmly respond to the Appeal of the National Assembly of the Democratic Republic of Viet Nam, take emergency action and launch an unprecedentedly powerful mass movement on a worldwide scale to compel the U.S. aggressors to get out of Viet Nam, Indo-China and all other places they occupy.

The heroic Vietnamese people are sure to win! The diabolical U.S. imperialists are sure to be defeated!

16. GOVERNMENT STATEMENT: ON U.S. INVASION OF CAMBODIA (May, 1970)*

1970 was the most eventful year in the modern history of Cambodia: (1) the ouster of the nation's leader of twenty-nine years, Prince Norodom Sihanouk, who went to China; (2) the demand by General Lon Nol, the new Cambodian leader, for the withdrawal of North Vietnamese and National Liberation Front forces in the border regions of Cambodia; and (3) the unprecedented direct U.S. intervention in Cambodia. The following is the first official Chinese response to the U.S. military intervention in that country, published on May 4, 1970.

*From *Peking Review* (May 8, 1970), p. 14.

On April 30, 1970, U.S. President Nixon, tearing off all masks of "peace," brazenly declared the sending of U.S. troops and south Vietnamese mercenaries to make a massive invasion of Cambodia and launched a barbarous war of aggression against the Cambodian people. At the same time, on May 1 and 2, U.S. imperialism resumed bombing of Quang Binh and Nghe An Provinces of the Democratic Republic of Viet Nam. This is an extremely grave step taken by U.S. imperialism to further expand its war of aggression in Indo-China. This fully proves that the reactionary coup d'etat staged on March 18 by the Lon Nol-Sirik Matak Rightist clique with the aim of illegally overthrowing the Cambodian Head of State Samdech Norodom Sihanouk was entirely plotted and engineered by the Nixon government.

On May 2, Samdech Norodom Sihanouk, Head of State of Cambodia and Chairman of the National United Front of Kampuchea [Cambodian government in exile], issued a solemn and just statement sternly condemning U.S. imperialism for its towering crime of aggression against Cambodia and solemnly calling on the valiant Cambodian people to unite closely with the fraternal Vietnamese and Laotian peoples and strengthen to the maximum their common struggle against the U.S. aggressors in accordance with the resolutions of the Summit Conference of the Indo-Chinese Peoples.

In condemnation of these new atrocious acts of aggression and war perpetrated by U.S. imperialism, the Government of the Democratic Republic of Viet Nam on May 2 and the Provisional Revolutionary Government of the Republic of South Viet Nam and the Central Committee of the Laotian Patriotic Front on May 3 also issued strong statements.

The Chinese Government and people express their most resolute support to the statement of the Cambodian Head of State Samdech Norodom Sihanouk and to the statements of the Government of the Democratic Republic of Viet Nam, the Provisional Revolutionary Government of the Republic of South Viet Nam and the Central Committee of the Laotian Patriotic Front.

The Chinese Government solemnly declares:

U.S. imperialism's aggression against Cambodia and expansion of its war of aggression in Indo-China are not only frantic provocations against the three Indo-Chinese peoples, but also frantic provocations against the Chinese people, the Southeast Asian people and the revolutionary people of the whole world. Following their great leader Chairman Mao Tse-tung's teachings, the 700 million Chinese people pledge to provide a powerful backing for the three Indo-Chinese peoples and give all-out support and assistance to the fraternal peoples of Cambodia, Laos and Viet Nam in carrying to the end until complete victory the war against U.S. aggression and for national salvation.

Chairman Mao has long pointed out: "The U.S. imperialists and reactionaries of all countries are paper tigers." The three Indo-Chinese peoples, uniting together, daring to fight, persevering in protracted war, defying difficulties and advancing wave upon wave, will certainly defeat the U.S. aggressors and all their running dogs.

Victory surely belongs to the three heroic Indo-Chinese peoples!

17. NEWS ANNOUNCEMENT: NIXON'S VISIT TO CHINA (July, 1971)*

A dramatic change was internationally heralded in Sino-American relations shortly after Peking invited an American table tennis team and journalists to visit China in April, 1971 (see Document 45).

China needs to improve her relations with the United States because of her realistic appraisal of the current international situation, recognizing an aggressive Soviet Union as well as the emerging industrial giant, Japan.

The United States, on the other hand, because of her own pressing domestic needs and her utmost desire to get out of the long, barbarous war in Vietnam, needs China to exert her powerful influence in North Vietnam.

*From Hsin Hua News Release, July 16, 1971, in *Peking Review* (July 16, 1971), p. 3.

The following joint communiqué was issued simul-
taneously in Peking and San Clemente, California, on
July 15, after Henry Kissinger's secret visit in Peking
from July 9 to 11. The Peking radio merely read the
official communiqué without comment and Jen-min
Jih-pao published the announcement in only a few
lines. However, according to Edgar Snow, "The whole
subject is undoubtedly being cautiously discussed and
explained."[1]

Premier Chou En-lai and Dr. Henry Kissinger, President
Nixon's Assistant for National Security Affairs, held talks in
Peking from July 9 to 11, 1971. Knowing of President Nixon's
expressed desire to visit the People's Republic of China, Premier
Chou En-lai on behalf of the Government of the People's
Republic of China has extended an invitation to President
Nixon to visit China at an appropriate date before May, 1972.

President Nixon has accepted the invitation with pleasure.

The meeting between the leaders of China and the United
States is to seek the normalization of relations between the two
countries and also to exchange views on questions of concern to
the two sides.

1 *Time* (August 2, 1971), p. 13.

CHAPTER THREE:
Sino-Soviet Disputes

Although the founding of the Chinese Communist Party can be traced to the formation of many Marxist study societies in China around 1918,[1] it was not until several agents of the Third International from Moscow, including Gregory Voitinsky, Yang Ming-chai, and later, G. Maring, brought these groups together that the Chinese Communist Party was formally established in Shanghai on July 1, 1921.[2] The first organizational meeting, which opened a new chapter in Chinese history, began with 12 delegates, representing only 57 members. That young organization grew to be the largest communist party in the world.

The Communist Party's struggle for power went through many phases, including the first "revolutionary civil war" from 1921-27, the second "revolutionary civil war" from 1927-37, the "war of resistance against Japanese aggression" from 1937-45, and finally, the third "revolutionary civil war" from 1945-49, when the People's Republic was formally promulgated by Mao Tse-tung in Peking on October 1, 1949.[3]

The role which Moscow played with respect to the growth of the Chinese Communist Party was a complicated one, permeated with contradictions and controversy. However, Moscow certainly kept a watchful eye if not actually an "iron arm" on the situation in China. At times there was a certain lack of confidence on the part of the Soviet leaders in the ability of the Chinese to play a primary role in the war against Japan. But the USSR did provide the only material help, however limited, to the Chinese Communists. This is perhaps why Mao Tse-tung, in

1 See Maurice Meisner, *Li Tao-chao and the Origins of Chinese Communism* (Cambridge, Mass., Harvard University Press, 1967).

2 Robert C. North, *Moscow and Chinese Communists*, 2d ed. (Stanford, Stanford University Press, 1963).

3 *Cf.* O. Edmund Clubb, *Twentieth Century China* (New York, Columbia University Press, 1964).

spite of the shortcomings and mistakes made by Stalin, called him "friend of the Chinese people" (see Document 18).

After the establishment of the People's Republic in 1949, the Chinese Communists' foreign policy was unequivocally pro-Soviet, at least until the death of Stalin in 1953, as evidenced by the number of treaties and agreements signed between the two countries[1] (see Document 19).

There were a total of forty-two economic, trade, and technical aid agreements from February 7, 1950, to December 31, 1952, between China and the USSR.[2] These agreements were mainly concerning (1) military cooperation, including the use of military bases in China and training of Chinese military personnel, (2) economic cooperation, including Sino-Soviet joint stock companies, and (3) cultural cooperation, including exchange of students, scientists, and advisers.

The "Peking-Moscow Axis" soon revealed its joint foreign policy line. O. Edmund Clubb writes, "The Chinese and Soviet press treatment of the subject of Formosa and of American relations with the Nationalists followed a common pattern from December, 1949 onward. Peking's anti-American propaganda was broadened to include General MacArthur's administration of Japan, American relations with the Philippines, American military aid to the French in Indo-china, and the alleged organization of an American espionage apparatus for subversive activities in China."[3] China was also following the Soviet Union in instigating the uprising and "revolution" in Korea resulting in three years of conflict.

The Sino-Soviet alliance also called for China to make economic concessions, in spite of massive Soviet technical assistance to China, which included Soviet participation in the administration of China's principal railways in Manchuria, Soviet exploitation of the petroleum and nonferrous metals in Sinkiang, Soviet use of naval bases in Chinese Port Arthur and Dairen, and China's acceptance of the independence of pro-Soviet Outer Mongolia.

1 A. Doak Barnett, *Communist China, the Early Years, 1949-55* (New York, Praeger, 1964).

2 Douglas M. Johnston and Hungdah Chiu, *Agreements of the People's Republic of China, 1949-1967; A Calendar* (Cambridge, Mass., Harvard University Press, 1968).

3 O. Edmund Clubb, *Twentieth Century China, op. cit.,* p. 337.

During the period following the death of Stalin, Mao Tse-tung's prestige rose internationally and Stalin's successors began almost immediately to show increasing deference to Chinese leadership. China and the Soviet Union then signed an additional sixty-five agreements from 1953 to 1957, involving the construction of ninety-one industrial projects in China in 1953, fifteen in 1954, and fifty-five in 1956. In 1957 the Soviet Union further agreed to assist Peking in the development of nuclear weapons, which they continued to do until 1959.

Thus, Soong Ching-ling, Vice Chairman of the People's Republic, wrote in 1960, "the great Communist parties of the Soviet Union and China are today leading our peoples in works that inspire all of mankind . . . and these great victories on the economic front have far reaching historical meaning" (see Document 20).

What, then, brought about the sudden striking change in relations between these two Communist states which were almost at war with each other in the 1970's?

According to Robert C. North, "Between June and December, 1957 the Soviet Union and the People's Republic of China appeared to reverse roles, that is, the Chinese seemed to argue for greater centralization within the bloc, at the same time urging a more aggressive response to the West, whereas the Russians, at least relatively, seemed to be in favor of a certain pluralism, a loose confederation of Soviet states, and a somewhat more flexible policy toward the West."[1]

While one may disagree with North's analysis with respect to the Chinese position, it is unquestionable that Khrushchev's decision to "de-Stalinize" the Soviet party set in motion a process that soon led to a loosening of controls throughout the Communist bloc, and it marked the beginning of a critical period of instability in Communist bloc affairs.

To be sure, the Chinese Communist Party was no longer subservient to the Soviet vested position as the senior party within the international Communist movement. As A. Doak Barnett writes, "At almost every stage in these turbulent events the Chinese Communist leaders gave evidence that, instead of being content merely to parrot Moscow lines, they were

---

1 Robert C. North, *The Foreign Relations of China* (Belmont, Calif., Dickenson Publishing Co., 1969), p. 105.

determined to make their own independent evaluation and to define their own position."[1]

In fact, immediately after the Hungarian uprising in 1956, China began a new and significant political move as a mediator between the USSR and its East European satellites, much to the dismay of the Russians, especially when China bolstered Rumania's opposition to new Soviet pressures.

The Chinese diplomatic move in East European countries, traditionally Russia's stronghold, was not always successful, however. For example, Rumania was the only East European country, other than Albania, to send a warm message of greeting to the post-Cultural Revolution Ninth Congress of the Chinese Communist Party in April, 1969—a gathering described by the Soviet Union as a "Maoist farce."

Meanwhile, the USSR began to extend its influence in the Pacific and challenge the traditionally Chinese stronghold in Asia. After the Soviet's open expression of sympathy and aid to the Indians in the 1959 and 1962 Sino-Indian border wars, the tempo of the Chinese attack on the Russians increased with: "modern revisionism," "phony Communism," and finally, "Soviet Socialist imperialism" (see Document 22).

Beyond the ideological polemics, there are indeed many serious areas of disagreement which precluded improvement of political and economic relations of the two countries for many years to come[2] (see Documents 21-25). Specifically, for example, there are the problems of Chinese indebtedness as a result of Soviet loans totaling $700,000,000 to finance China's participation in the Korean War; Soviet political interference in Albania, China's major East European ally; the USSR's unilateral suspension of nuclear tests in 1958 and subsequent agreement with the United States on the nuclear test-ban treaty, considered by China as an attempt to preclude Chinese nuclear development; Khrushchev's alleged tearing up of old agreements and economic contracts, including the withdrawal of all Soviet technicians in 1959; and finally, the USSR's involvement to move more than 60,000 Chinese minorities (Kazakh nomads) in Sinkiang to the Soviet Union in 1962.

1 A. Doak Barnett, *Communist China and Asia* (New York, Council on Foreign Relations, 1960), p. 349.

2 Donald S. Zagoria, *The Sino-Soviet Conflict, 1956-61* (New York, Atheneum, 1962).

There is, in addition, Chinese anger at Soviet aid to India in construction of a plant to produce military aircraft and in supplying India with MIG-21's during the Sino-Indian border clashes and at *Pravda's* calling on Mao's dissidents in China in 1966 to halt his "erroneous policies,"[1] a move considered by the Chinese to be interference in China's internal affairs. Then arose the dangerous military confrontations over border areas, including those at Chenpao Island, Ussuri River, March 2 and 15, 1969; Yumin County, Sinkiang, May 2, June 10, and August 13, 1969; and Pachao Island, Amur River, July 8, 1969. The Chinese, in fact, protested on August 19, 1969, against 429 Soviet-provoked incidents during June and July of that year; and the Soviet Union responded on September 10 that the Chinese had deliberately violated the border 488 times between June and mid-August.[2]

In addition to these serious political and economic differences, there are also environmental differences, not to mention the differences in historical experiences. China and the Soviet Union share a common border in three distinct sectors: 1,850 miles in the "inner Asia" zone, 2,700 miles in the "Mongolian sector," and 2,300 miles in the "Far Eastern sector."[3] Many of the boundaries negotiated in the early days of the Manchu Empire were never formally accepted by the modern Chinese (see Chapter Six and Appendix E).

The Soviet Union is, after all, an aggressive industrial and military giant, second only to the United States, with a larger territory (22,403,000 square kilometers) than China's (9,761,012 square kilometers) and more resources. China, while she has the greatest asset in population (800,000,000),[4] is, in fact, an underdeveloped country with rather limited resources to fulfill her needs. How these countries resolve their tremendous differences and conflicts will certainly affect world peace and the prosperity of mankind.[5]

1 *Pravda* (November 27, 1966).

2 New York *Times* (September 11, 1969).

3 W. A. Douglas Jackson, *The Russo-Chinese Borderlands*, 2d ed. (Princeton, D. Van Nostrand Co., 1968).

4 U. S. Department of State estimates; see Department of State Publication 8499, East Asian and Pacific Series 173 (December, 1969).

5 Sino-Soviet relations improved in 1970, following the American invasion of Cambodia. The two nations apparently decided to "dissociate four groups of issues: ideology, the border, diplomatic relations, and economics." In July, 1970, the two nations did exchange ambassadors. See Harry Harding, "China: Toward Revolutionary Pragmatism," *Asian Survey*, Vol. XI, No. 1 (January, 1971), pp. 62-63.

18. MAO TSE-TUNG: STALIN, FRIEND OF THE CHINESE PEOPLE (December, 1939)*

The relations between China and the USSR during the 1930's and 1940's are still obscure in many respects. In spite of the Soviets' dual role in giving rather limited material aid to Mao's revolution in China and at times simultaneously providing assistance to Chiang Kai-shek's Nationalist government, the only outside help Mao received was from the Soviet Union, including the training of large groups of Chinese Communists. There was never any serious doubt about the fidelity of Mao's party to Stalin,[1] as illustrated in the following congratulatory article on Stalin's sixtieth birthday.

On the Twenty-first of December, Comrade Stalin will be sixty years old. We can be sure that his birthday will evoke warm and affectionate congratulations from the hearts of all revolutionary people throughout the world who know of the occasion.

Congratulating Stalin is not a formality. Congratulating Stalin means supporting him and his cause, supporting the victory of socialism, and the way forward for mankind which he points out, it means supporting a dear friend. For the great majority of mankind today are suffering, and mankind can free itself from suffering only by the road pointed out by Stalin and with his help.

Living in a period of the bitterest suffering in our history, we Chinese people most urgently need help from others. The *Book of Odes* says, "A bird sings out to draw a friend's response." This aptly describes our present situation.

But who are our friends?

There are so-called friends, self-styled friends of the Chinese people, whom even some Chinese unthinkingly accept as friends. But such friends can only be classed with Li Lin-fu, the prime minister in the Tang Dynasty who was notorious as a man with "honey on his lips and murder in his heart". They are

*From *Selected Works of Mao Tse-tung*, Vol. II (Peking, Foreign Language Press, 1967), pp. 335-36 (footnotes omitted).

1 Scholars differ; however, this editor agrees with the views of Tso-liang Hsiao in his *Power Relations Within the Chinese Communist Movement, 1930-1934* (Seattle, University of Washington Press, 1961).

indeed "friends" with "honey on their lips and murder in their hearts". Who are these people? They are the imperialists who profess sympathy with China.

However, there are friends of another kind, friends who have real sympathy with us and regard us as brothers. Who are they? They are the Soviet people and Stalin.

No other country has renounced its privileges in China; the Soviet Union alone has done so.

All the imperialists opposed us during our First Great Revolution; the Soviet Union alone helped us.

No government of any imperialist country has given us real help since the outbreak of the War of Resistance Against Japan; the Soviet Union alone has helped China with its aviation and supplies.

Is not the point clear enough?

Only the land of socialism, its leaders and people, and socialist thinkers, statesmen and workers can give real help to the cause of liberation of the Chinese nation and the Chinese people, and without their help our cause cannot win final victory.

Stalin is the true friend of the cause of liberation of the Chinese people. No attempt to sow dissension, no lies and calumnies, can affect the Chinese people's whole-hearted love and respect for Stalin and our genuine friendship for the Soviet Union.

19. TREATY OF FRIENDSHIP, ALLIANCE, AND MUTUAL ASSISTANCE BETWEEN THE USSR AND THE PEOPLE'S REPUBLIC OF CHINA (February, 1950)*

The Soviet Union was the first nation to recognize Communist China after it established the People's Republic on October 1, 1949, in Peking. Two months later, in December, Mao personally paid his first official visit to the USSR and during his nine-week stay there signed this important thirty-year treaty, among a number of other agreements, on February 14. Although this treaty has not been formally declared null and void, the enforcement of it is most unlikely in view of the Sino-Soviet disputes since the 1960's.

*From *Soviet Monitor* (London), No. 11 (February 15, 1950), p. 311.

The Presidium of the Supreme Soviet of the Union of Soviet Socialist Republics and the Central People's Government of the People's Republic of China;

Filled with determination jointly to prevent, by the consolidation of friendship and co-operation between the Union of Soviet Socialist Republics and the People's Republic of China, the rebirth of Japanese imperialism and a repetition of aggression on the part of Japan or any other state, which should unite in any form with Japan in acts of aggression;

Imbued with the desire to consolidate lasting peace and universal security in the Far East and throughout the world in conformity with the aims and principles of the United Nations Organization;

Profoundly convinced that the consolidation of good neighborly relations and friendship between the Union of Soviet Socialist Republics and the People's Republic of China meets the fundamental interests of the peoples of the Soviet Union and China;

Resolved for this purpose to conclude the present Treaty and appointed as their plenipotentiary representatives;

The Presidium of the Supreme Soviet of the Union of Soviet Socialist Republics—Andrei Yanuaryevich Vyshinsky, Minister of Foreign Affairs of the Union of Soviet Socialist Republics;

The Central People's Government of the People's Republic of China—Chou En-lai, Prime Minister of the State Administrative Council and Minister of Foreign Affairs of China;

Who, after exchange of their credentials, found in due form and good order, agreed upon the following:

Article I. Both High Contracting Parties undertake jointly to take all the necessary measures at their disposal for the purpose of preventing a repetition of aggression and violation of peace on the part of Japan or any other state which should unite with Japan, directly or indirectly, in acts of aggression. In the event of one of the High Contracting Parties being attacked by Japan or states allied with it, and thus being involved in a state of war, the other High Contracting Party will immediately render military and other assistance with all the means at its disposal.

The High Contracting Parties also declare their readiness in the spirit of sincere co-operation to participate in all international actions aimed at ensuring peace and security throughout the world, and will do all in their power to achieve the speediest implementation of these tasks.

Article II. Both the High Contracting Parties undertake by means of mutual agreement to strive for the earliest conclusion of a peace treaty with Japan, jointly with the other Powers which were allies during the Second World War.

Article III. Both High Contracting Parties undertake not to conclude any alliance directed against the other High Contracting Party, and not to take part in any coalition or in actions or measures directed against the other High Contracting Party.

Article IV. Both High Contracting Parties will consult each other in regard to all important international problems affecting the common interests of the Soviet Union and China, being guided by the interests of the consolidation of peace and universal security.

Article V. Both the High Contracting Parties undertake, in the spirit of friendship and co-operation and in conformity with the principles of equality, mutual interests, and also mutual respect for the state sovereignty and territorial integrity and non-interference in internal affairs of the other High Contracting Party—to develop and consolidate economic and cultural ties between the Soviet Union and China, to render each other every possible economic assistance, and to carry out the necessary economic co-operation.

Article VI. The present Treaty comes into force immediately upon its ratification; the exchange of instruments of ratification will take place in Peking.

The present Treaty will be valid for 30 years. If neither of the High Contracting Parties gives notice one year before the expiration of this term of its desire to renounce the Treaty, it shall remain in force for another five years and will be extended in compliance with this rule.

Done in Moscow on February 14, 1950, in two copies, each in the Russian and Chinese languages, both texts having equal force.

[Signatures]

20. SOONG CHING-LING: THE BASIS OF ETERNAL FRIENDSHIP (February, 1960)*

> *This is an important last minute plea and propaganda statement made by the widow of Dr. Sun Yat-sen,*

*From *Sino-Soviet Alliance* (Peking, Foreign Language Press, 1960), pp. 8-18.

*father of the Chinese Republic and a friend of the
Soviet Union. Although the Sino-Soviet dispute had
already begun in 1957, Soong (and some other
Chinese leaders) was obviously hoping that perhaps
there could still be ways to reunite the two former
allies.*

The Sino-Soviet Treaty of Friendship, Alliance and Mutual
Assistance has been in existence for ten years. From its first
appearance on the world scene on February 14, 1950, this
Treaty has been a vivid expression of the close fraternal ties
between the Soviet and Chinese peoples, ties formed in the
momentous victories of the Great October Socialist Revolution
and the Chinese people's revolution, and rooted in the
invincible truths of Marxism-Leninism. The Chinese people,
fully comprehending the historical significance of this great
alliance, commemorate each anniversary with wholehearted
rejoicing.

The Sino-Soviet Treaty is based on common ideas, interests
and objectives. Ours are socialist societies, without vested
interests exerting their will solely for the sake of private profit.
In the Soviet Union and China, the people are in power, the
means of production are in their hands. Exploitation within our
countries has been eliminated. The possibility of our exploiting
others does not exist, being incompatible with our whole
revolutionary concept of life. We ourselves are rich in labour
power, resources and territory, and we do not need nor do we
covet the wealth of others. Above all, we are one with the
working people of the world, united with them in the prime
cause of the 20th Century—the transition of human society
from capitalism to communism.

Starting from this bed rock, everything that takes place
within our countries and in our relations with others is
simultaneously aimed at enhancing the welfare and prosperity
of our own peoples, and in promoting peace and progress for all
peoples.

These are the new and higher type of international relations.
They can only spring from the world outlook of
Marxism-Leninism. Ten years of practice has proved that the
economic, political and cultural co-operation between the
Soviet Union and China has been in absolute conformity with
the principles of equality and mutual benefit; and that it has
enabled both our countries, which being the largest components

have special responsibilities, to carry out with consummate success our obligations towards guaranteeing the solidarity of the socialist camp, the bastion of world tranquillity and human advancement.

Just three days after the signing of the Sino-Soviet Treaty, Chairman Mao Tse-tung said: "Everybody sees that the unity of the peoples of the two great countries, China and the Soviet Union, sealed by the Treaty, will be lasting and indestructible and no one can split it. This unity will inevitably influence not only the prosperity of the two great countries—China and the Soviet Union—but also the future of mankind and the victory of peace and justice throughout the world."

Utilizing Marxism-Leninism, this was the evaluation Chairman Mao placed on Sino-Soviet friendship, and from this he predicted a brilliant future for it in regard to international affairs. One must remember that this was said ten years ago, when the development of neither the Soviet Union nor of China had reached such a height as we know today. In fact, China, just newly liberated, was most weak and backward economically speaking. This led some commentators at that time to express doubt about the validity of Chairman Mao's conclusion. These people struck a simple balance between the material assets of imperialism and socialism. This crude method enabled them to see only the surface features of the situation, completely neglecting the main features, that of the justness of socialism and the great unconquerable spirit that grew in the people once they had taken power into their own hands.

In this decade, it has been these half-blind doubters who have been proven totally wrong, while Chairman Mao's foresight has been borne out to the full. Today, the Soviet Union and China, representing the new, the bright, the growing, enjoy high prestige throughout the world, and the stand we take for peace and justice has the sympathy and support of tens of millions of people. What is more, the great benefits which accrue from this stand to our own peoples and the people of the world in general, are in sharp contrast to the detriment which the imperialist policy of "cold war" and struggle over markets bring to the security and livelihood of vast populations. The peoples see this; they learn from it; and they soon begin to act from a new point of view, one derived from the universal desire to lead peaceful and useful lives.

It is thus that the great friendship of the Soviet and Chinese peoples has become a key element in the present world situation. This unprecedented harmony between two great nations plays an especially important role at this particular moment in history. In conjunction with the close fraternal relations of the whole socialist camp, and in co-ordination with the irrepressible movement for national independence and world peace, in the decade of the fifties it changed the balance of world forces; and it has already cast its mark on the coming decade of the sixties. For if, as Chairman Mao pointed out in 1957, the East wind has begun to prevail over the West wind, then it is all the more obvious now that in this next ten years the East wind will continue to prevail, and the imperialist sphere will further shrink while the forces for peace, democracy, national independence and socialism will experience further successive victories.

Naturally, these victories for peace and progress will not come without struggle. The imperialist forces, led by the United States monopoly capitalists, will spare no effort in their attempt to gain a world dominating position. Here of late, we have seen some adjustment in their tactics. Their methods are less raucous, but their objective is the same: to split the unity of the socialist camp, and first the unity between China and the Soviet Union, and the unity of the socialist countries and the countries of Asia and Africa supporting peace and neutrality.

One central spearhead is the drive to isolate China. The imperialists have been trying every way to divide us from our neighbours, with whom we have flesh and blood bonds growing out of our common struggle against colonialism. But anyone respecting the truth can see through this attempt to make of China's progress against poverty and backwardness a threat to others. No matter what degree of success we might achieve, this does not change China's fundamental position as a socialist nation with the working people in power; and as such it can be a threat to no one, but it definitely will remain loyal to the stand of internationalism, the anti-imperialist cause and the Five Principles of Peaceful Coexistence. Part of the struggle is to assure that this truth is protected from the slander and violence of the imperialist propaganda, thereby preserving the basis for co-operation and mutual assistance between China and the other Asian and African countries. This is vital to our efforts in national construction, whereby we achieve economic independence from imperialism, and in the struggle for peace and against aggression.

Realizing the immense vitality for the cause of peace and justice emanating from Sino-Soviet friendship, the imperialists have from the beginning made this a point of concentrated attack. In keeping with their overall assault against China, this attempt to cause stress and strain in our relationship has been intensified. But it will never succeed. Fraternal unity between the Soviet Union and China, and between all the socialist countries, is too important to our own peoples and to the peoples of the whole world. The imperialists may use every device at their command, but the results will always be the same: they will break their heads against our proletarian solidarity.

This will not make them give up their plan, however, and we can see they use a variety of methods. On the one hand, hard reality—the Soviet superiority in modern weaponry, the demonstrated superiority of socialism in the matter of the rate of economic development, the overwhelming peace sentiment—has caused the imperialists to make some adjustment in their approach to the "cold war" and the "roll back" of the socialist camp. This, on the other hand, does not alter their main objectives. There may be less public philosophizing of the order that Dulles gave us, but the essence of his policy is still the guiding force in Western foreign relations. Eisenhower may junket over half the world acting as a ceremonial "messenger of peace," but his own actions, as well as those of Nixon, certain leading members of the Democratic Party and the sabre-rattling American generals and admirals show us that in the last analysis they are bent on salvaging as much as possible of the "positions of strength" strategy.

It is true, words of peace have been forced out of the mouths of the imperialists by mass pressure and the new balance of power in the world. This indicates that for all their bellicosity the Western policy-makers can be made to respond to reality. There has been a certain relaxation of international tensions, and the general situation continues to develop in a direction favourable to peace. The Chinese and Soviet peoples join the rest of the world in welcoming this. However, at the same time we listen to these professions of peace, we cannot but give our attention to two new danger signals which are sure to heighten tensions once again.

The first of these is the outcropping of fascist activity throughout the world, especially the outburst of vicious anti-semitism. Some people have termed this "neo-fascism," but in my opinion it is no such thing. It is the same old Hitlerite racism which the Western imperialist powers, purposely ignoring the lessons of history, never stamped out in Western Germany and other places throughout the world. The truth is that they have been carefully protecting, nurturing and fostering the surviving leading Hitler fascists in their maniacal hope of using them in a concerted thrust against Communist Parties and everything progressive, and in a war against the socialist countries. Bonn, United States and London politicians are trying to point in all directions but their own as the source of this scourge, but this fools no one. It is the result of their doings, and nothing exposes the real imperialist policy more than this.

What demands the attention of people everywhere is that it is in these hands, bloodied with the murders of millions of innocent people in the death camps of Europe, that the United States imperialists are insisting on placing rockets and atomic weapons. Can one imagine a more dangerous and irresponsible move against world peace than this? Can the people sit back and take this and the revival of fascist racism without protest? It is obvious we cannot, and we must serve warning on those who make such policy: you will never be able to evade the responsibility for this terrible deed!

The second of these two recent events is the signing of the so-called "security treaty" between the United States and Japan. In character this differs not in the least from the first event, but is just the second phase of one single development, that is, the preparation for a general offensive against the progressive cause and the socialist camp. For here, as in the first case, the imperialists are reviving a bitter enemy of the peoples of Asia and the world—the Japanese militarists.

This treaty is a new and firmer linking of American imperialism and Japanese militarism in an aggressive military alliance. It aims at restoring the latter's position in Japanese society without restrictions, stepping up the nuclear rearmament of Japan, all to be placed at the disposal of the

American imperialists. Through this act, one of the East's most industrialized nations has once again been put onto the path of aggression and war, openly threatening to drive to the heart of the Soviet Union and China, and endangering the peace of the Far East and the world.

Kishi, a representative of the most reactionary forces in Japan, signed this treaty in face of protests from all sides, including broad sections of the Japanese people, who have put up a heroic struggle. The Japanese people are burning with national indignation at the thought of placing the fate of their country in the hands of the American imperialists, and at the idea of American troops occupying their land for another ten years, making a total of twenty-five years since the end of World War II. The Chinese people, having suffered untold misery and loss during the occupation of our own land by the Japanese militarists, can well understand these feelings of anger. We join the Japanese people with full heart, giving them every support in their just fight for peace, democracy, national independence, neutrality and the re-establishment of normal relations with China.

We cannot but once again warn the imperialists: you are playing with fire! This is not the 1930s; and this is not the Soviet Union and China of twenty-five years ago you are facing. The peoples are today more mature politically, for they still suffer the scars of fascism and militarism. And the firm stand maintained by the Soviet Union and China on the question of suppressing the criminal activities of the fascists and militarists of Germany and Japan is backed not only by the great might of the world socialist camp, but has the support of all decent-minded people in every country.

On the occasion of the 10th anniversary of the Sino-Soviet Treaty of Friendship, Alliance and Mutual Assistance, we would also like to remind certain political figures that an important provision of this document calls for common action against "the rebirth of Japanese imperialism and the resumption of aggression on the part of Japan or any other state that may collaborate in any way with Japan in acts of aggression." In other words, if there is a miscalculation and there are those foolish enough to want to test the determination and dispatch with which this obligation will be fulfilled, such people should here and now understand that this is an invitation to their own funeral.

The Soviet Union and China, for ten years carrying out the intent and purpose of the Friendship Treaty, have been engaged in great feats of peaceful construction, and using our multiplying resources for the betterment of the life of our peoples and for the protection of peace in the Far East and the world. That we will continue in these next ten years to work for the same goals, is beyond question.

The great Communist Parties of the Soviet Union and China are today leading our peoples in works that inspire all of mankind. In the Soviet Union, the Seven-Year Plan, which is the extended construction of communism in its initial stage, is proceeding ahead of schedule. In China, our people, using the great leap forward in both 1958 and 1959, are now in the process of making this phenomenon a permanent part of our economic and cultural development. Our achievements are a direct result of the Sino-Soviet Friendship Treaty, are inseparable from the aid rendered us by the Soviet Union and the other socialist countries. During the First Five-Year Plan (1953-57), the Soviet Union helped China build 166 large-scale modern enterprises. Between 1958 and 1967, it will assist with another 125 such projects. On this anniversary occasion, we wish once again to express our warmest thanks to the great Soviet people and their Communist Party for their tremendous and selfless assistance.

These great victories on the economic front have far-reaching historical meaning. They are the fore runners of the inevitable final victory which socialism will win over capitalism. This is a fact which is daily penetrating deeper into the political consciousness of the peoples, leading them by the millions so to appreciate the validity of the Marxist-Leninist doctrines that they make this treasure-trove of human thought their own. They see that this holds the only solution to the old antagonisms between individuals, between individuals and society, and between nations. They see that only by basing society on Marxism-Leninism can the inequalities in the distribution of man's necessities of life be abolished, opening up before him a boundless and peaceful existence. They see that herein lies the method by which class, national and racial inequalities can once and for all be sent to the museum cases, their only use then being to educate the future generations on man's cruelty to man before he became enlightened.

These are the very objectives to which Sino-Soviet friendship is dedicated. It is a union of two great nations and peoples, not of a temporary, transient nature, but permanent and eternal, continuous in its development. Here is the hope of mankind.

Long live the unbreakable friendship between the Soviet and Chinese peoples!

Long live world peace!

21.   CHINESE EDITORIAL: THE ORIGIN AND DEVELOPMENT OF THE DIFFERENCES BETWEEN THE LEADERSHIP OF THE CPSU AND OURSELVES (September, 1963)*

This statement, although written as a joint editorial by Jen-min Jih-pao (People's Daily) *and* Hongqi *(the party theoretical journal) published on September 6, 1963, was in fact China's "white paper" on Sino-Soviet relations, a most significant policy document.*

There is a saying, "It takes more than one cold day for the river to freeze three feet deep." The present differences in the international communist movement did not, of course, begin just today.

The Open Letter of the Central Committee of the CPSU spreads the notion that the differences in the international communist movement were started by "Long Live Leninism!" and two other articles which we published in April 1960. This is a big lie.

"What is the truth?"

The truth is that the whole series of differences of principle in the international communist movement began more than seven years ago.

To be specific, it began with the 20th Congress of the CPSU in 1956.

The 20th Congress of the CPSU was the first step along the road of revisionism taken by the leadership of the CPSU. From the 20th Congress to the present, the revisionist line of the leadership of the CPSU has gone through the process of emergence, formation, growth and systematization. And by a

*From *The Polemic on the General Line of the International Communist Movement* (Peking, Foreign Language Press, 1965), pp. 59-62, 92-99 (extract; footnotes omitted).

gradual process, too, people have come to understand more and more deeply the revisionist line of the CPSU leadership.

From the very outset we held that a number of views advanced at the 20th Congress concerning the contemporary international struggle and the international communist movement were wrong, were violations of Marxism-Leninism. In particular, the complete negation of Stalin on the pretext of "combating the personality cult" and the thesis of peaceful transition to socialism by "the parliamentary road" are gross errors of principle.

The criticism of Stalin at the 20th Congress of the CPSU was wrong both in principle and in method.

Stalin's life was that of a great Marxist-Leninist, a great proletarian revolutionary. For thirty years after Lenin's death, Stalin was the foremost leader of the CPSU and the Soviet Government, as well as the recognized leader of the international communist movement and the standard-bearer of the world revolution. During his lifetime, Stalin made some serious mistakes, but compared to his great and meritorious deeds his mistakes are only secondary.

Stalin rendered great services to the development of the Soviet Union and the international communist movement. In the article "On the Historical Experience of the Dictatorship of the Proletariat" published in April 1956, we said:

> After Lenin's death Stalin creatively applied and developed Marxism-Leninism as the chief leader of the Party and the state. Stalin expressed the will and aspirations of the people, and proved himself an outstanding Marxist-Leninist fighter, in the struggle in defence of the legacy of Leninism against its enemies—the Trotskyites, Zinovievites and other bourgeois agents. Stalin won the support of the Soviet people and played an important role in history primarily because, together with the other leaders of the Communist Party of the Soviet Union, he defended Lenin's line on the industrialization of the Soviet Union and the collectivization of agriculture. By pursuing this line, the Communist Party of the Soviet Union brought about the triumph of socialism in the Soviet Union and created the conditions for the victory of the Soviet Union in the war against Hitler; these victories of the Soviet people accorded with the interests of the working class of the world and all progressive mankind. It was therefore natural that the name of Stalin was greatly honoured throughout the world.

It was necessary to criticize Stalin's mistakes. But in his secret report to the 20th Congress, Comrade Khrushchov completely negated Stalin, and in doing so defamed the dictatorship of the proletariat, defamed the socialist system, the great CPSU, the great Soviet Union and the international communist movement. Far from using a revolutionary proletarian party's method of criticism and self-criticism for the purpose of making an earnest and serious analysis and summation of the historical experience of the dictatorship of the proletariat, he treated Stalin as an enemy and shifted the blame for all mistakes on to Stalin alone.

Khrushchov viciously and demagogically told a host of lies in his secret report, and threw around charges that Stalin had a "persecution mania", indulged in "brutal arbitrariness", took the path of "mass repressions and terror", "knew the country and agriculture only from films" and "planned operations on a globe", that Stalin's leadership "became a serious obstacle in the path of Soviet social development", and so on and so forth. He completely obliterated the meritorious deeds of Stalin who led the Soviet people in waging resolute struggle against all internal and external foes and achieving great results in socialist transformation and socialist construction, who led the Soviet people in defending and consolidating the first socialist country in the world and winning the glorious victory in the anti-fascist war, and who defended and developed Marxism-Leninism.

In completely negating Stalin at the 20th Congress of the CPSU, Khrushchov in effect negated the dictatorship of the proletariat and the fundamental theories of Marxism-Leninism which Stalin defended and developed. It was at that Congress that Khrushchov, in his report, began the repudiation of Marxism-Leninism on a number of questions of principle.

* * *

An Adverse Current That Is Opposed to Marxism-Leninism and Is Splitting the International Communist Movement

In the Open Letter the leaders of the CPSU try hard to make people believe that after the 22nd Congress they "made fresh efforts" to improve relations between the Chinese and Soviet Parties and to strengthen unity among the fraternal Parties and countries.

This is another lie.

What are the facts?

They show that since the 22nd Congress the leadership of the CPSU has become more unbridled in violating the principles guiding relations among fraternal Parties and countries and in pursuing policies of great-power chauvinism, sectarianism and splittism in order to promote its own line of systematic revisionism, which is in complete violation of Marxism-Leninism. This has brought about a continuous deterioration in Sino-Soviet relations and grave damage to the unity of the fraternal Parties and countries.

The following are the main facts about how the leaders of the CPSU have sabotaged Sino-Soviet unity and the unity of fraternal Parties and countries since the 22nd Congress:

1. The leaders of the CPSU have tried hard to impose their erroneous line upon the international communist movement and to replace the Declaration and the Statement with their own revisionist programme. They describe their erroneous line as the "whole set of Leninist policies of the international communist movement of recent years", and they call their revisionist programme the "real Communist Manifesto of our time" and the "common programme" of the "Communist and Workers' Parties and of the people of countries of the socialist community".

Any fraternal Party which rejects the erroneous line and programme of the CPSU and perseveres in the fundamental theories of Marxism-Leninism and the revolutionary principles of the Declaration and the Statement is looked upon as an enemy by the leaders of the CPSU, who oppose, attack and injure it and try to subvert its leadership by every possible means.

2. Disregarding all consequences, the leadership of the CPSU broke off diplomatic relations with socialist Albania, an unprecedented step in the history of relations between fraternal Parties and countries.

3. The leadership of the CPSU has continued to exert pressure on China and to make outrageous attacks on the Chinese Communist Party. In its letter of February 22, 1962 to

the Central Committee of the CPC, the Central Committee of the CPSU accused the CPC of taking a "special stand of their own" and pursuing a line at variance with the common course of the fraternal Parties, and even made a crime out of our support for the Marxist-Leninist Albanian Party of Labour. As pre-conditions for improving Sino-Soviet relations, the leaders of the CPSU attempted to compel the CPC to abandon its Marxist-Leninist and proletarian internationalist stand, abandon its consistent line, which is in full conformity with the revolutionary principles of the Declaration and the Statement, accept their erroneous line, and also accept as a *fait accompli* their violation of the principles guiding relations among fraternal Parties and countries. In its Open Letter, the Central Committee of the CPSU boasted of its letters to the Central Committee of the CPC during this period of Khrushchov's remarks about his desire for unity in October 1962 to our Ambassador to the Soviet Union and so on, but in fact these were all acts for realizing their base attempt.

4. The Central Committee of the CPSU rejected the proposals made by the fraternal Parties of Indonesia, Viet Nam, New Zealand, etc., that a meeting of representatives of the fraternal Parties should be convened, as well as the five positive proposals made by the Central Committee of the CPC in its letter of April 7, 1962 to the Central Committee of the CPSU for the preparation for the meeting of fraternal Parties. In its reply of May 31, 1962 to the Central Committee of the CPC, the Central Committee of the CPSU went so far as to make the demand that the Albanian comrades abandon their own stand as a pre-condition for improving Soviet-Albanian relations and also for convening a meeting of the fraternal Parties.

5. In April and May 1962 the leaders of the CPSU used their organs and personnel in Sinkiang, China, to carry out large-scale subversive activities in the Ili region and enticed and coerced several tens of thousands of Chinese citizens into going to the Soviet Union. The Chinese Government lodged repeated protests and made repeated representations, but the Soviet Government refused to repatriate these Chinese citizens on the pretext of "the sense of Soviet legality" and "humanitarianism". To this day this incident remains unsettled. This is indeed an astounding event, unheard of in the relations between socialist countries.

6. In August 1962 the Soviet Government formally notified China that the Soviet Union would conclude an agreement with the United States on the prevention of nuclear proliferation. This was a joint Soviet-U.S. plot to monopolize nuclear weapons and an attempt to deprive China of the right to possess nuclear weapons to resist the U.S. nuclear threat. The Chinese Government lodged repeated protests against this.

7. The leadership of the CPSU has become increasingly anxious to strike political bargains with U.S. imperialism and has been bent on forming a reactionary alliance with Kennedy, even at the expense of the interests of the socialist camp and the international communist movement. An outstanding example was the fact that, during the Caribbean crisis, the leadership of the CPSU committed the error of capitulationism by submitting to the nuclear blackmail of the U.S. imperialists and accepting the U.S. Government's demand for "international inspection" in violation of Cuban sovereignty.

8. The leadership of the CPSU has become increasingly anxious to collude with the Indian reactionaries and is bent on forming a reactionary alliance with Nehru against socialist China. The leadership of the CPSU and its press openly sided with Indian reaction, condemned China for its just stand on the Sino-Indian border conflict and defended the Nehru government. Two thirds of Soviet economic aid to India have been given since the Indian reactionaries provoked the Sino-Indian border conflict. Even after large-scale armed conflict on the Sino-Indian border began in the autumn of 1962, the leadership of the CPSU has continued to extend military aid to the Indian reactionaries.

9. The leadership of the CPSU has become increasingly anxious to collude with the Tito clique of Yugoslavia and is bent on forming a reactionary alliance with the renegade Tito to oppose all Marxist-Leninist Parties. After the 22nd Congress, it took a series of steps to reverse the verdict on the Tito clique and thus openly tore up the 1960 Statement.

10. Since November 1962 the leadership of the CPSU has launched still fiercer attacks, on an international scale, against the Chinese Communist Party and other Marxist-Leninist Parties and whipped up a new adverse current in order to split the socialist camp and the international communist movement. Khrushchov made one statement after another and the Soviet

press carried hundreds of articles attacking the Chinese Communist Party on a whole set of issues. Directed by the leaders of the CPSU, the Congresses of the fraternal Parties of Bulgaria, Hungary, Czechoslovakia, Italy and the Democratic Republic of Germany became stages for anti-China performances, and more than forty fraternal Parties published resolutions, statements or articles attacking the Chinese Communist Party and other Marxist-Leninist Parties.

The facts cited above cannot possibly be denied by the leaders of the CPSU. These iron-clad facts prove that the "fresh efforts" they made after the 22nd Congress of the CPSU were aimed, not at improving Sino-Soviet relations and strengthening unity between the fraternal Parties and countries, but on the contrary, at further ganging up with the U.S. imperialists, the Indian reactionaries and the renegade Tito clique in order to create a wider split in the socialist camp and the international communist movement.

In these grave circumstances, the Chinese Communist Party had no alternative but to make open replies to the attacks of some fraternal Parties. Between December 15, 1962 and March 8, 1963 we published seven such replies. In these articles we continued to leave some leeway and did not criticize the leadership of the CPSU by name.

Despite the serious deterioration in Sino-Soviet relations resulting from the errors of the leadership of the CPSU, the Chinese Communist Party agreed to send its delegation to Moscow for the talks between the Chinese and Soviet Parties, and, in order that there might be a systematic exchange of views in the talks, put forward its proposal concerning the general line of the international communist movement in its letter of reply to the Central Committee of the CPSU dated June 14.

As subsequent facts have shown, the leaders of the CPSU were not only insincere about eliminating differences and strengthening unity, but used the talks as a smokescreen for covering up their activities to further worsen Sino-Soviet relations.

On the eve of the talks, the leaders of the CPSU publicly attacked the Chinese Communist Party by name, through statements and resolutions. At the same time, they unjustifiably expelled a number of Chinese Embassy personnel and research students from the Soviet Union.

On July 14, that is, on the eve of the U.S.-British-Soviet talks, while the Sino-Soviet talks were still in progress, the leadership of the CPSU hastily published the Open Letter of the Central Committee of the CPSU to Party organizations and all Communists in the Soviet Union and launched unbridled attacks on the Chinese Communist Party. This was another precious presentation gift made by the leaders of the CPSU to the U.S. imperialists in order to curry favour with them.

Immediately afterwards in Moscow, the leadership of the CPSU signed the treaty on the partial halting of nuclear tests with the United States and Britain in open betrayal of the interests of the Soviet people, the people in the socialist camp including the Chinese people, and the peace-loving people of the world; there was a flurry of contacts between the Soviet Union and India; Khrushchov went to Yugoslavia for a "vacation"; the Soviet press launched a frenzied anti-Chinese campaign; and so on and so forth. This whole train of events strikingly demonstrates that, disregarding everything, the leadership of the CPSU is allying with the imperialists, the reactionaries of all countries and the renegade Tito clique in order to oppose fraternal socialist countries and fraternal Marxist-Leninist Parties. All this completely exposes the revisionist and divisive line which the leadership of the CPSU is following.

At present, the "anti-Chinese chorus" of the imperialists, the reactionaries of all countries and the revisionists is making a lot of noise. And the campaign led by Khrushchov to oppose Marxism-Leninism and split the socialist camp and the international communist ranks is being carried on with growing intensity.

* * *

22. CHINESE EDITORIAL: ON KHRUSHCHOV'S PHONY COMMUNISM (July, 1964)*

This is officially described as the "ninth comment" on the open letter of the Central Committee of the CPSU by the editorial departments of Jen-min Jih-pao

*From *The Polemic On the General Line of the International Movement* (Peking, Foreign Language Press, 1965), pp. 459-63 (extract; footnotes omitted).

and Hongqi, *released on July 14, 1964. It is a classic example of the ideological polemics used by the Chinese in disputes with the Russians, and in the words of A. Doak Barnett, "this document is the closest thing we have to a personal testament of Mao's."*[1]

At the 22nd Congress of the CPSU, Khrushchov announced that the Soviet Union had already entered the period of the extensive building of communist society. He also declared that "we shall, in the main, have built a communist society within twenty years". This is pure fraud.

How can there be talk of building communism when the revisionist Khrushchov clique are leading the Soviet Union onto the path of the restoration of capitalism and when the Soviet people are in grave danger of losing the fruits of socialism?

In putting up the signboard of "building communism" Khrushchov's real aim is to conceal the true face of his revisionism. But it is not hard to expose this trick. Just as the eyeball of a fish cannot be allowed to pass as a pearl, so revisionism cannot be allowed to pass itself off as communism.

Scientific communism has a precise and definite meaning. According to Marxism-Leninism, communist society is a society in which classes and class differences are completely eliminated, the entire people have a high level of communist consciousness and morality as well as boundless enthusiasm for and initiative in labour, there is a great abundance of social products and the principle of "from each according to his ability, to each according to his needs" is applied, and in which the state has withered away.

Marx declared:

> In a higher phase of communist society, after the enslaving subordination of the individual to the division of labour, and therewith also the antithesis between mental and physical labour, has vanished; after labour has become not only a means of life but life's prime want; after the productive forces have also increased with the all-round development of the individual, and all the springs of cooperative wealth flow more

1 A. Doak Barnett, *China After Mao* (Princeton, Princeton University Press, 1967), p. 47.

abundantly—only then can the narrow horizon of bourgeois
right be crossed in its entirety and society inscribe on its
banners: From each according to his ability, to each according
to his needs!

According to Marxist-Leninist theory, the purpose of
upholding the dictatorship of the proletariat in the period of
socialism is precisely to ensure that society develops in the
direction of communism. Lenin said that "forward
development, i.e., towards Communism, proceeds through the
dictatorship of the proletariat, and cannot do otherwise". Since
the revisionist Khrushchov clique have abandoned the
dictatorship of the proletariat in the Soviet Union, it is going
backward and not forward, going backward to capitalism and
not forward to communism.

Going forward to communism means moving towards the
abolition of all classes and class differences. A communist
society which preserves any classes at all, let alone exploiting
classes, is inconceivable. Yet Khrushchov is fostering a new
bourgeoisie, restoring and extending the system of exploitation
and accelerating class polarization in the Soviet Union. A
privileged bourgeois stratum opposed to the Soviet people now
occupies the ruling position in the Party and government and in
the economic, cultural and other departments. Can one find an
iota of communism in all this?

Going forward to communism means moving towards a
unitary system of the ownership of the means of production by
the whole people. A communist society in which several kinds
of ownership of the means of production coexist is
inconceivable. Yet Khrushchov is creating a situation in which
enterprises owned by the whole people are gradually
degenerating into capitalist enterprises and farms under the
system of collective ownership are gradually degenerating into
units of a kulak economy. Again, can one find an iota of
communism in all this?

Going forward to communism means moving towards a great
abundance of social products and the realization of the
principle of "from each according to his ability, to each
according to his needs". A communist society built on the
enrichment of a handful of persons and the impoverishment of
the masses is inconceivable. Under the socialist system the great

Soviet people developed the social productive forces at unprecedented speed. But the evils of Khrushchov's revisionism are creating havoc in the Soviet socialist economy. Constantly beset with innumerable contradictions, Khrushchov makes frequent changes in his economic policies and often goes back on his own words, thus throwing the Soviet national economy into a state of chaos. Khrushchov is truly an incorrigible wastrel. He has squandered the grain reserves built up under Stalin and brought great difficulties into the lives of the Soviet people. He has distorted and violated the socialist principle of distribution of "from each according to his ability, to each according to his work", and enabled a handful of persons to appropriate the fruits of the labour of the broad masses of the Soviet people. These points alone are sufficient to prove that the road taken by Khrushchov leads away from communism.

Going forward to communism means moving towards enhancing the communist consciousness of the masses. A communist society with bourgeois ideas running rampant is inconceivable. Yet Khrushchov is zealously reviving bourgeois ideology in the Soviet Union and serving as a missionary for the decadent American culture. By propagating material incentive, he is turning all human relations into money relations and encouraging individualism and selfishness. Because of him, manual labour is again considered sordid and love of pleasure at the expense of other people's labour is again considered honourable. Certainly, the social ethics and atmosphere promoted by Khrushchov are far removed from communism, as far as far can be.

Going forward to communism means moving towards the withering away of the state. A communist society with a state apparatus for oppressing the people is inconceivable. The state of the dictatorship of the proletariat is actually no longer a state in its original sense, because it is no longer a machine used by the exploiting few to oppress the overwhelming majority of the people but a machine for exercising dictatorship over a very small number of exploiters, while democracy is practised among the overwhelming majority of the people Khrushchov is altering the character of Soviet state power and changing the dictatorship of the proletariat back into an instrument whereby a handful of privileged bourgeois elements exercise dictatorship over the mass of the Soviet workers, peasants and intellectuals.

He is continuously strengthening his dictatorial state apparatus and intensifying his repression of the Soviet people. It is indeed a great mockery to talk about communism in these circumstances.

A comparison of all this with the principles of scientific communism readily reveals that in every respect the revisionist Khrushchov clique are leading the Soviet Union away from the path of socialism and onto the path of capitalism and, as a consequence, further and further away from, instead of closer to, the communist goal of "from each according to his ability, to each according to his needs".

Khrushchov has ulterior motives when he puts up the signboard of communism. He is using it to fool the Soviet people and cover up his effort to restore capitalism. He is using it to deceive the international proletariat and the revolutionary people the world over and betray proletarian internationalism. Under this signboard, the Khrushchov clique has itself abandoned proletarian internationalism and is seeking a partnership with U.S. imperialism for the partition of the world; moreover, it wants the fraternal socialist countries to serve its own private interests and not to oppose imperialism or to support the revolutions of the oppressed peoples and nations, and it wants them to accept its political, economic and military control and be its virtual dependencies and colonies. Furthermore, the Khrushchov clique wants all the oppressed peoples and nations to serve its private interests and abandon their revolutionary struggles, so as not to disturb its sweet dream of partnership with imperialism for the division of the world, and instead submit to enslavement and oppression by imperialism and its lackeys.

In short, Khrushchov's slogan of basically "building a communist society within twenty years" in the Soviet Union is not only false but also reactionary.

The revisionist Khrushchov clique say that the Chinese "go to the length of questioning the very right of our Party and people to build communism". This is a despicable attempt to fool the Soviet people and poison the friendship of the Chinese and Soviet people. We have never had any doubt that the great Soviet people will eventually enter into communist society. But right now the revisionist Khrushchov clique are damaging the socialist fruits of the Soviet people and taking away their right to go forward to communism. In the circumstances, the issue confronting the Soviet people is not how to build communism but rather how to resist and oppose Khrushchov's effort to restore capitalism.

* * *

23. CHINESE EDITORIAL: DOWN WITH THE NEW TSAR (March, 1969)*

This is the Chinese response to the first of more than 400 military border skirmishes in 1969 between China and the Soviet Union. Chinese Chenpao Island, described in this article, is, in fact, Russian's Damansky Island in the Ussuri River. This editorial was written jointly by the Jen-min Jih-pao *and* Jie-fan Jun-pao (Liberation Army Daily) *on March 4, 1969.*

On March 2, the Soviet revisionist renegade clique sent armed soldiers to flagrantly intrude into Chenpao Island on the Wusuli River, Heilungkiang Province, China, and killed and wounded many frontier guards of the Chinese People's Liberation Army by opening up with cannon and gun fire on them. This is an extremely grave armed border provocation carried out by the Soviet revisionists, a frantic anti-China incident created by them and another big exposure of the rapacious nature of Soviet revisionism as social-imperialism. The Chinese people and the Chinese People's Liberation Army express the greatest indignation at this towering crime committed by the Soviet revisionist renegade clique and voice the strongest protest against it.

This grave border incident of armed provocation was completely premeditated and deliberately engineered by the Soviet revisionist renegade clique. Chenpao Island on the Wusuli River is Chinese territory. It is our sacred right to have our frontier guards patrol our own territory. However, the Soviet revisionist authorities sent large numbers of armed soldiers, armoured vehicles and cars to intrude into China's territory and attack our patrol unit. Our frontier guards repeatedly warned the Soviet revisionists' frontier troops. But it produced no

*From *Peking Review* (March 7, 1969), p. 6.

effect. Only when they were driven to the end of their forbearance were our frontier guards compelled to fight back in self-defence, giving the intruders who carried out the provocations well-deserved punishment and triumphantly safeguarding China's sacred territory. The armymen and civilians throughout China pledge their most resolute support for the just action of the heroic frontier guards in defence of the territorial integrity and sovereignty of the motherland.

After creating this grave incident of border provocation, the Soviet revisionist renegade clique had the audacity to make false charges and send China a so-called "note of protest". It shamelessly described Chenpao Island as its territory, alleging that Chinese frontier guards "crossed the Soviet state frontier" and carried out a "provocative attack" on the Soviet revisionists' frontier troops "protecting" the area of Chenpao Island. This is sheer nonsense! It is an indisputable, iron-clad fact that Chenpao Island is Chinese territory. Even according to the "Sino-Russian Treaty of Peking", an unequal treaty imposed on the Chinese people by tsarist Russian imperialism in 1860, the area of Chenpao Island belongs to China. It has always been under China's jurisdiction and patrolled by Chinese frontier guards since long ago. How is it that the area of Chenpao Island suddenly ran over to the side within "the Soviet state frontier"? How is it that this part of Chinese territory became an area "protected" by the Soviet revisionists' frontier troops? The fact is that the Soviet revisionists' troops invaded China's territory Chenpao Island and launched frenzied attacks on Chinese frontier guards, but you Soviet revisionists made false charges that Chinese frontier guards launched a "provocative attack". You can never succeed in your attempt to cover up your crime of aggression by the old tricks of turning facts upside down and of thief crying "stop thief".

The Soviet revisionist renegade clique has consistently been hostile towards the Chinese people. Filled with hatred and fear, it has redoubled its efforts to carry out anti-China activities especially since China launched the great proletarian cultural revolution and won great and decisive victories. The Soviet revisionist renegade clique has not only wantonly maligned and slandered China and unscrupulously conducted subversive and disruptive activities against her, but has also massed on the Sino-Mongolian and Sino-Soviet borders troops who repeatedly intruded into China's territory and air space, creating border incidents and posing military threats against our country. The Soviet revisionist renegade clique has also done its utmost to collaborate with U.S. imperialism and the reactionaries of all countries in an attempt to form a so-called ring of encirclement against China. The recent intrusion into China's Chenpao Island engineered by the Soviet revisionist renegade clique for armed provocations is obviously a new move to step up its anti-China activities.

The fact that the Soviet revisionist renegade clique has repeatedly carried out armed intrusions into China's territory to create border incidents has once again enabled the people throughout the world to see clearly that this handful of renegades are out-and-out social-imperialists and new tsars pure and simple. They have ruthlessly plundered and brutally oppressed the people of some East European countries at will, and even sent several hundred thousand troops to occupy Czechoslovakia and turned a vast expanse of land in East Europe into their sphere of influence in an attempt to set up a tsarist-type colonial empire. At the same time, they are pushing the same line in Asia. They have not only turned the Mongolian People's Republic into their colony, but are also trying vainly to go further and invade and occupy China's territory. They regard those areas the tsars occupied as theirs and are stretching their hands into areas the tsars did not occupy. They are even more voracious than the tsars. What is the difference between the gangsterism of the Soviet revisionist renegade clique and U.S. imperialism which occupies other countries' territory and encroaches upon their sovereignty at will and rides roughshod everywhere?

In 1900, Lenin, in his essay "The War in China", indignantly condemned the crimes of the tsars in invading China "like savage beasts". He pointed out: "The policy of the tsarist government in China is a criminal policy". "And in this case, as always, the autocratic tsarist government has proved itself to be a government of irresponsible bureaucrats servilely cringing before the capitalist magnates and nobles". These words of Lenin's can be used in their entirety today to portray the shameless features of the Soviet revisionist renegade clique which has taken over the mantle of the tsars.

The Soviet revisionist renegade clique's armed provocation against our country is a frenzied action that has been taken out of the need of its domestic and foreign policies at a time when it is beset with difficulties at home and abroad and has landed in an impasse. In doing so, it tries to whip up anti-China sentiments for the purpose of diverting the attention of the Soviet people whose resentment and resistance against its reactionary bourgeois fascist rule are growing daily and, at the same time, to please U.S. imperialism and curry favour with the newly installed Nixon Administration so that the United States and the Soviet Union may enter into further counter-revolutionary deals on a global scale. The Soviet revisionist renegade clique thought that it would get out of its predicament by creating a new anti-China incident. But the result is just the opposite. There is a profound revolutionary friendship between the peoples of China and the Soviet Union and all the anti-China schemes of the Soviet revisionist renegade clique are bound to go bankrupt completely. This perverse action of the Soviet revisionist renegade clique only serves to reveal its counter-revolutionary features still more clearly and arouse even stronger opposition from the Soviet people and the people all over the world. In lifting a rock only to drop it on its own feet, the Soviet revisionist renegade clique will only hasten its own destruction.

Our great leader Chairman Mao points out: "Historically, all reactionary forces on the verge of extinction invariably conduct a last desperate struggle against the revolutionary forces". This is what the Soviet revisionist renegade clique is doing. Its recent military provocation against China is precisely an expression of its inherent weakness.

We warn the Soviet revisionist renegade clique: We will never allow anybody to encroach upon China's territorial integrity and sovereignty. We will not attack unless we are attacked; if we are attacked, we will certainly counter-attack. Gone for ever are the days when the Chinese people were bullied by others. You are utterly blind and day-dreaming if you think you can deal with the great Chinese people by resorting to the same old tricks used by tsarist Russia. If you continue making military provocations, you will certainly receive severe punishment. No matter in what strength and with whom you come, we will wipe you out resolutely, thoroughly, wholly and completely. The 700 million Chinese people and the Chinese People's Liberation Army who are armed with Mao Tsetung Thought and have been tempered in the great proletarian cultural revolution are more powerful than ever before. Whoever dares to invade our great socialist motherland will inevitably be badly battered and smashed!

Down with the new tsars! Down with the Soviet revisionists' social-imperialism!

24. CHINESE EMBASSY: NOTE OF PROTEST (March, 1969)*

This is an illustration of the serious consequences of the Sino-Soviet border confrontations of 1969-70. After the first Chenpao Island incident in March, 1969, the mood in the two countries resulted in massive demonstrations against each other. Only after the American invasion of Cambodia in May, 1970, was there an improvement of the Sino-Soviet relations, with the resumption of ambassadorial exchange in July.

Ministry of Foreign Affairs of the U.S.S.R.:

After creating the grave incident of armed provocation on Chinese territory Chenpao Island, the Soviet authorities went still farther and organized a despicable anti-China demonstration before the Embassy of the People's Republic of China at 13:30 hours on March 7. The Soviet authorities collected a group of ruffians who grossly insulted and abused the great leader of the Chinese people Chairman Mao Tsetung and the Chinese people, barbarously damaged the buildings of the Chinese Embassy, wrecked its news photo display cases and threw iron objects and fired air-guns at Embassy personnel, thus seriously hampering the normal functioning of the Embassy and seriously menacing the personal safety of its personnel. The Embassy of the People's Republic of China hereby lodges a strong protest against the new anti-China provocation made by the Soviet authorities before the Chinese Embassy and demands that they immediately stop this anti-China farce solely stage-managed by them and compensate for all the losses of the Chinese Embassy caused by the ruffians' sabotaging activities.

*From *Down with the New Tsars* (Peking, Foreign Language Press, 1969), pp. 31-32.

It must be pointed out that the above grave new anti-China provocation engineered by the Soviet authorities is a continuation of the armed provocation against China on the Sino-Soviet border which they plotted single-handedly. The Soviet authorities must be held fully responsible for their anti-China crime which has further worsened Sino-Soviet relations.

Embassy of the People's Republic
of China in the Soviet Union
Moscow, March 7, 1969

25. *CHINESE EDITORIAL: THE BREZHNEV DOCTRINE IS AN OUTRIGHT DOCTRINE OF HEGEMONY (April, 1970)**

While the Soviet invasion of Czechoslovakia on August 21, 1968, seemed to strengthen China's opportunity to damage the Soviet image in East Europe, it also inserted a new element in the Sino-Soviet disputes. For if the Soviet Union could send an army to occupy Czechoslovakia in the name of defending "Socialist unity," who could say that the USSR would not send its troops against China? The following is a most important propaganda statement by China's three leading official papers: Jen-min Jih-pao, Jie-fan Jun-pao, and Hongqi, published on April 22, 1970

In order to press on with its social-imperialist policy of expansion and aggression, the Brezhnev renegade clique has developed Khrushchov revisionism and concocted an assortment of fascist "theories" called the "Brezhnev doctrine."

Now let us examine what stuff this "Brezhnev doctrine" is made of.

First, the theory of "limited sovereignty." Brezhnev and company say that safeguarding their so-called interests of socialism means safeguarding "supreme sovereignty." They flagrantly declare that Soviet revisionism has the right to determine the destiny of another country "including the destiny of its sovereignty."

*From *Peking Review* (April 24, 1970), pp. 10-12 (extract; footnotes omitted).

What "interests of socialism"! It is you who have subverted the socialist system in the Soviet Union and pushed your revisionist line of restoring capitalism in a number of East European countries and the Mongolian People's Republic. What you call the "interests of socialism" are actually the interests of Soviet revisionist social-imperialism, the interests of colonialism. You have imposed your all-highest "supreme sovereignty" on the people of other countries, which means that the sovereignty of other countries is "limited," whereas your own power of dominating other countries is "unlimited." In other words, you have the right to order other countries about, whereas they have no right to oppose you; you have the right to ravage other countries, but they have no right to resist you. Hitler once raved about "the right to rule." Dulles and his ilk also preached that the concepts of national sovereignty "have become obsolete" and that "single state sovereignty" should give place to "joint sovereignty." So it is clear that Brezhnev's theory of "limited sovereignty" is nothing but an echo of imperialist ravings.

Secondly, the theory of "international dictatorship." Brezhnev and company assert that they have the right to "render military aid to a fraternal country to do away with the threat to the socialist system." They declare: "Lenin had foreseen" that historical development would "transform the dictatorship of the proletariat from a national into an international one, capable of decisively influencing the entire world politics."

This bunch of renegades has completely distorted Lenin's ideas.

In his article "Preliminary Draft of Theses on the National and Colonial Questions," Lenin wrote of "transforming the dictatorship of the proletariat from a national one (i.e., existing in one country and incapable of determining world politics) into an international one (i.e., a dictatorship of the proletariat covering at least several advanced countries and capable of exercising decisive influence upon the whole of world politics)." Lenin meant here to uphold proletarian internationalism and propagate proletarian world revolution. But the Soviet revisionist renegade clique has emasculated the proletarian revolutionary spirit embodied in this passage of Lenin's and concocted the theory of "international dictatorship" as the "theoretical basis" for military intervention in or military occupation of a number of East European countries and the Mongolian People's Republic. The "international dictatorship" you refer to simply means the subjection of other countries to the new tsars' rule and enslavement. Do you think that by putting up the signboard of "aid to a fraternal country" you are entitled to use your military force to bully another country, or send your troops to overrun another country as you please? Flying the flag of "unified armed forces," you invaded Czechoslovakia. What difference is there between this and the invasion of China by the allied forces of eight powers in 1900, the 14-nation armed intervention in the Soviet Union and the "16-nation" aggression organized by U.S. imperialism against Korea!

Thirdly, the theory of "socialist community." Brezhnev and company shout that "the community of socialist states is an inseparable whole" and that the "united action" of "the socialist community" must be strengthened.

A "socialist community" indeed! It is nothing but a synonym for a colonial empire with you as the metropolitan state. The relationship between genuine socialist countries, big or small, should be built on the basis of Marxism-Leninism, on the basis of the principles of complete equality, respect for territorial integrity, respect for state sovereignty and independence and of non-interference in each other's internal affairs, and on the basis of the proletarian internationalist principle of mutual support and mutual assistance. But you have trampled other countries underfoot and made them your subordinates and dependencies. By "united action" you mean to unify under your control the politics, economies and military affairs of other countries. By "inseparable" you mean to forbid other countries to free themselves from your control and enslavement. Are you not brazenly trying to enslave the people of other countries?

Fourthly, the theory of "international division of labour." Brezhnev and company have greatly developed this nonsense spread by Khrushchov long ago. They have not only applied "international division of labour" to a number of East European countries and the Mongolian People's Republic as mentioned above, but have extended it to other countries in Asia, Africa and Latin America. They allege that the Asian, African and Latin American countries cannot "secure the establishment of an independent national economy," unless they "co-operate" with Soviet revisionism. "This co-operation enables the Soviet Union to make better use of the international division of labour. We shall be able to purchase in these countries increasing quantities of their traditional export commodities—cotton, wool, skins and hides, dressed non-ferrous ores, vegetable oil, fruit, coffee, cocoa beans, tea and other raw materials, and a variety of manufactured goods."

What a list of "traditional export commodities!"

It is a pity that this list is not complete. To it must be added petroleum, rubber, meat, vegetables, rice, jute, cane sugar, etc.

In the eyes of the handful of Soviet revisionist oligarchs, the people of the Asian, African and Latin American countries are destined to provide them with these "traditional export commodities" from generation to generation. What kind of "theory" is this? The colonialists and imperialists have long advocated that it is they who are to determine what each country is to produce in the light of its natural conditions, and they have forcibly turned Asian, African and Latin American countries into sources of raw materials and kept them in a state of backwardness so that industrial capitalist countries can carry on the most savage colonial exploitation at their convenience. The Soviet revisionist clique has taken over this colonial policy from imperialism. Its theory of "international division of labour" boils down to "industrial Soviet Union, agricultural Asia, Africa and Latin America" or "industrial Soviet Union, subsidiary processing workshop Asia, Africa and Latin America."

Mutual and complementary exchange of goods and mutual assistance on the basis of equality and mutual benefit between genuine socialist countries and Asian, African and Latin American countries are conducted for the purpose of promoting the growth of an independent national economy in these countries keeping the initiative in their own hands. However, the theory of "international division of labour" is preached by the handful of Soviet revisionist oligarchs for the sole purpose of infiltrating, controlling and plundering the Asian, African and Latin American countries, broadening their own spheres of influence and putting these countries under the new yoke of Soviet revisionist colonialism.

Fifthly, the theory that "our interests are involved." Brezhnev and company clamour that "the Soviet Union which, as a major world power, has extensive international contacts, cannot regard passively events that, though they might be territorially remote, nevertheless have a bearing on our security and the security of our friends." They arrogantly declare: "Ships of the Soviet Navy" will "sail . . . wherever it is required by the interests of our country's security"!

Can a country regard all parts of the world as areas involving its interests and lay its hands on the whole globe because it is a "major power"? Can a country send its gunboats everywhere to carry out intimidation and aggression because it "has extensive international contacts"? This theory that "our interests are involved" is a typical argument used by the imperialists for their global policy of aggression. When the old tsars engaged in foreign expansion, they did it under the banner of "Russian interests." The U.S. imperialists too have time and again shouted that the United States bears responsibility "not only for our own security but for the security of all free nations," and that it will "defend freedom wherever necessary." How strikingly similar are the utterances of the Soviet revisionists to those of the old tsars and the U.S. imperialists!

The Soviet revisionist renegade clique which has long gone backrupt ideologically, theoretically and politically cannot produce anything presentable at all; it can only pick up some trash from imperialism and, after refurbishing, come out with "Brezhnevism." This "Brezhnevism" is imperialism with a "socialist" label, it is outright hegemonism, naked neo-colonialism.

* * *

CHAPTER FOUR:
Chinese Strategies in Developing Nations

The People's Republic of China has been increasingly involved in the underdeveloped "Third World," politically, economically, and emotionally. However, her foreign policy goals with respect to these countries in Asia, Africa, and Latin America have undergone many important changes.

In the first phase, from 1949 to 1954, Chinese foreign policy was unequivocally "revolutionary" and "nationalistic militant," under the direct influence of the Russians. The Chinese Communists encouraged open armed struggle and subversion beyond China's borders. And China had joined the Soviet-initiated program of coordinated military action in Korea and also had embarked upon a policy of direct attack in Tibet (see Document 49). Her involvement in the Indochina conflict from the 1950's to the 1960's continues to demand that her people make tremendous political and economic sacrifices at home and abroad (see Document 15).

Fortunately, with the death of Stalin and the convening of the Geneva Conference of 1954 to discuss the Indochina conflict, China began to embark on a new policy of "mutual assistance and nonaggression." In an interlude during the Geneva Conference in June, 1954, Chou En-lai visited in both New Delhi and Rangoon, joining the Indian and Burmese leaders to issue a policy statement of Five Principles of Peaceful Coexistence, which then had become a dominant theme in China's diplomacy with respect to countries in the Third World. These five principles are:

1. Mutual respect for each's territorial integrity and sovereignty
2. Nonaggression

160

3. Noninterference in each other's international affairs
4. Equality and mutual benefit
5. Peaceful coexistence (see Document 26)

China also had hoped that this new change of attitude would corrode the U.S.-sponsored anti-Communist alignment in Asia and offset the pull of SEATO, which was then under active consideration (see Document 29).

When twenty-nine Asian and African nations met in April, 1955, in Bandung, Indonesia, Chou En-lai took advantage of the opportunity to use his diplomatic skills to create a new image of China in the eyes of the developing nations (see Document 27). He visited Afghanistan, Pakistan, India, Burma, Nepal, Ceylon, Cambodia, and North Vietnam and signed more than 100 cultural, trade, and technical treaties and agreements during the autumn and early winter of 1956-57[1] (see Document 39).

During the Bandung Conference, Chou En-lai also met Gamal Nasser of Egypt, and full diplomatic relations between the two countries were established little more than a year later.

As a domestic counterpart to the Bandung strategy in international relations, China also began to promote a thaw in her domestic intellectual life with Mao's famous speech "Let a Hundred Flowers Bloom, and a Hundred Schools of Thought Contend."[2] Meanwhile, Peking's propaganda began to attack the Chinese chauvinism that had been characteristic of attitudes toward non-Chinese in centuries past.

By 1957, a new Afro-Asian People's Solidarity Conference was convened in Cairo, which offered the Chinese an excellent opportunity to win friends and influence people in the Middle East and Africa. According to Zbigniew Brzezinski, "Riding the tide of such recent events as the winning of independence by Morocco, Tunisia, and Ghana, the Suez war, and Algerian rising, this Conference became the first great continent-wide rally of awakening anti-Western nationalism and pan-Africanism of various types."[3]

[1] Douglas M. Johnston and Hungdah Chiu, *Agreements of the People's Republic of China, 1949-1967: A Calendar* (Cambridge, Mass., Harvard University Press, 1968), p. 218.
[2] Mu Fu-sheng, *The Wilting of the Hundred Flowers* (New York, Praeger, 1962).
[3] Zbigniew Brzezinski, *Africa and the Communist World* (Stanford, Stanford University Press, 1963), pp. 150-51.

From Cairo, the Chinese began to extend their influence into other countries in the Middle East and Africa. And the first successful trip to that part of the world was made by Chou En-lai in 1963-64 when he visited the UAR, Algeria, Morocco, Tunisia, Ghana, Mali, Guinea, the Sudan, Ethiopia, and Somalia (see Documents 31, 32).

China has since declared itself to be the friend of "anti-imperialism" in the Middle East and Africa. It supported the Arab countries against the state of Israel in the June, 1967, war, for example (see Document 34). China also shipped small amounts of weapons to the Palestine Liberation Organization. Because of its geographical position several thousand miles distant from the Middle East, China's involvement remains necessarily a limited one with a foreign policy goal for the self-reliance and unity of Arab people themselves (see Document 38).

Chinese ventures into African affairs have not been without setbacks and reverses, however. Peking was unable to persuade the Afro-Asian states to accept its position in subsequent conferences of excluding the USSR as a non-Asian state. In fact, as a result of Sino-Soviet rivalries, a proposed second Bandung Conference was canceled.

In addition, because of the internal instability of many of the newly independent African states, Peking has moved in and out of position of influence with a number of African countries:[1] Cameroon, Mali, Dahomey, Guinea, Burundi, the Congo, Ghana, Kenya, and the Central African Republic. The greatest disappointment to China came in 1966 during President Kwame Nkrumah's official visit to Peking when his government was overthrown in Ghana. China's recognition of the revolutionary splinter government of Antoine Gizenga in Stanleyville (now Kisangani) in the Congo was short-lived when the Gizenga regime collapsed.

Moreover, China's later efforts to support the Congo rebel movement from its embassy in bordering Burundi failed and its embassy was ordered to close. In Kenya when the government suspected the Chinese of supplying money to the dissident

1 Ambassador Olcott H. Deming's speech at the Marshall-Wythe Symposium, edited by Chongban Kim, The College of William and Mary in Virginia, 1967.

vice-president, Oginga Odinga, President Jomo Kenyatta expelled all the personnel of the Chinese Embassy, although diplomatic relations were not suspended.

China also suffered setbacks in her Asian policies. In Indonesia, for instance, the pro-Peking Communists assassinated six Indonesian generals in an attempted *coup d'etat* in October, 1965, which failed. The Indonesian Communist Party (PKI) itself was then decimated, and an estimated 250,000 Indonesian-Chinese were either killed or imprisoned by the new military regime. And, of course, the Liu Shao-chi (then China's chief of state) and Sukarno proposed "Peking-Djakarta Axis" came to an abrupt end.

China's relations with both India and Burma have also deteriorated since the Bandung days as the result of border clashes with India in 1959 and again in 1962, as well as China's propaganda campaign to overthrow General Ne Win's military government in Burma in 1967. The Chinese accused Ne Win of inciting bloody anti-Chinese riots in Rangoon. However, the Chinese had not delivered any direct aid to the Burmese Communist Party, although the Chinese could supply weapons through easily accessible routes in the Kachin State (Burma). Because of China's dispute with India and Burma, Pakistan has now emerged as China's strongest ally in Asia, in spite of the fact that Pakistan is a member of SEATO.

Peking's relations with the two other major Communist nations in Asia, Korea and Vietnam, have fluctuated but have improved considerably since the late 1960's. China signed a treaty of cooperation and mutual assistance with North Korea on July 11, 1961, and continues to give a substantial amount of support to North Vietnam, although the details of her aid have never been made public (see Documents 28, 30).

The Indochina War proves to be costly to both sides. And the conflict has gradually expanded from South Vietnam to Cambodia to Laos. In addition to assuming huge technical and economic costs for the war, the Chinese lost Cambodia politically when Prince Sihanouk was unexpectedly ousted in March, 1970. China's response to the Cambodian situation was characteristically cautious. Almost two and a half weeks after the prince's arrival in Peking, Chou announced his support of Sihanouk's government-in-exile, well after similar expressions of support had been issued by North Vietnam, the NLF of South

Vietnam, and the Pathet Lao. However, China did finally sponsor a Summit Conference of the "Three Indochinese People" and promised "powerful backing for the three Indochinese peoples in their War" (see Document 35).

However, according to estimates made by the U.S. Bureau of Intelligence and Research of the Department of State in 1968, as indicated in the table below, China dominates very few of the Communist parties in her perimeter countries.

Country	CP Membership	Legal Status	Sino-Soviet Dispute
Afghanistan	200 est.		Pro-Soviet
Australia	5,000		Open split
Burma	White Flag 5,000 est.	Both proscribed	Pro-China
	Red Flag 500 est.	10/63	Pro-Soviet
Cambodia	100		Position unknown
Ceylon	1,900		Open split
China, Communist	17,000,000	In power	
China, Rep. of	Negligible	Proscribed 7/47	
Hong Kong	Part of CCP	Proscribed 1949	Pro-China
India	125,000		Open split
Indonesia	150,000	Proscribed 3/66	Position unknown
Japan	250,000		Independent
Korea, North	1,600,000	In power	Independent
Korea, South	Negligible	Proscribed 12/48	
Laos	Unknown		Neutral
Malaysia	2,000	Proscribed 7/48	Pro-Chinese
Mongolia, Outer	48,570	In power	Pro-Soviet
Nepal	8,000	All parties proscribed 1960	Internal factions
New Zealand	400		Open split
Pakistan	1,450	Proscribed 7/54	Unknown
Philippines	1,750	Proscribed 6/57	Neutral
Singapore	200	Proscribed 1948	Pro-Chinese
Thailand	1,450	Proscribed	Pro-Chinese
Vietnam, North	760,000	In power	Neutral
Vietnam, South	No estimate available	Proscribed 10/56	Neutral

Source: Department of State Publication 8499 (December, 1969).

In several states the Communist Party simply split into two opposing factions as a result of the Sino-Soviet disputes. The Communist Party of India, for example, in 1964 split into the "Right" pro-Soviet and the "Marxist" pro-Chinese factions. In the election of 1967 the Right received 7,053,037 votes with 23 seats in the Indian Parliament, while the Marxists gained 6,502,608 votes and 19 seats in the 520-member lower house. In 1966, the Japanese Communist Party broke away from a pro-Peking stand, causing many Japanese Communist-front organizations to split into smaller and less effective pro- and anti-Peking groups.

Underlying China's varying positions in Asia and Africa as governments rise and fall are consistent Chinese programs of economic assistance and cultural exchange which have achieved considerable success. These programs are manifested through the donations and construction of important economic projects, such as the perfect example of the construction of the Tanzania-Zambia Railway, or through participation in trade fairs, visiting cultural displays, and hospitality in China to visiting delegations, as well as student exchanges with foreign countries (see Chapter Five).

As far as China's political and diplomatic influence in Latin American countries, little concrete information is available,[1] except in the area of trade and cultural relations. In April, 1971, Chile provided Peking with its first major diplomatic inroad into the Western Hemisphere since Cuba extended China diplomatic recognition in 1960. Chinese media, however, have yet to note that Chile's President Salvador Allende is an avowed Marxist. To the Chinese Communists, the most important aspects of the Chilean development are the new government's recognition of Peking and Chile's Socialist economic policies.[2]

We do notice, however, that there is a significant shift in Chinese propaganda treatment of Latin American affairs. In 1970, for example, Chinese editorials emphasized "revolutionary struggle" and "mass movement" aimed at overthrowing "reactionary rule." In 1971 Peking began to show her interest in any Latin American government which was willing to resist U. S. domination or to safeguard its national sovereignty, including the issue of upholding territorial sea rights, an emotionally dominated political dispute between the U.S. and several Latin American countries (see Document 37).

Again, judging from Chinese editorials, Peking believes that her most promising policy with respect to Latin America lies in her anti-imperialist foreign policy theme, stressing: (1) the national sovereignty question, (2) questions of the national-

1 In a recent book review of the only comprehensive study available— Cecil Johnson, *Communist China and Latin America, 1959-1967* (New York, Columbia University Press, 1970)—Professor James Petras wrote, "Cecil Johnson's book reflects the outdated cold war thinking which assumes that during the period of his study, 1959-67, the Chinese Communists made a major effort to penetrate and subvert Latin American societies which are simply without proof."—*WAR/Peace* (June/July, 1971), p. 18.

2 *Current Scene*, Vol. IX, No. 4 (April 7, 1971), p. 3.

ization of U.S.-owned enterprises, (3) criticism of U.S. trade
policies, and (4) future status of the Panama Canal. In return
for backing Latin American governments on these issues, China
hopes for political recognition and gain in the years ahead.

26. *JOINT COMMUNIQUÉ OF CHOU EN-LAI AND JAWAHARLAL NEHRU (June, 1954)* *

> *China's relations with Asian countries were consider-*
> *ably improved because of visits by Chou En-lai to*
> *New Delhi in June, 1954, which resulted in the*
> *following joint communiqué of Chinese and Indian*
> *leaders on June 28, 1954. India promised to maintain*
> *"neutrality" in the Cold War and the Chinese not to*
> *commit aggression. A separate but identical an-*
> *nouncement was made by Chinese and Burmese*
> *leaders later, on December 12, 1954.*

His Excellency Chou En-lai, Prime Minister and Foreign
Minister of the People's Republic of China, came to Delhi at the
invitation of His Excellency Jawaharlal Nehru, Prime Minister
and Foreign Minister of the Republic of India. He stayed here
for three days. During this period the two Prime Ministers
discussed many matters of common concern to India and China.
In particular they discussed the prospects of peace in South
East Asia and the developments that had taken place in the
Geneva Conference in regard to Indo-China. The situation in
Indo-China was of vital importance to the peace of Asia and the
world and the Prime Ministers were anxious that the efforts that
were being made at Geneva should succeed. They noted with
satisfaction that some progress had been made in the talks at
Geneva in regard to an armistice. They earnestly hoped that
these efforts will meet with success in the near future and that
they would result in a political settlement of the problems of
that area.

2. The talks between the Prime Ministers aimed at helping, in
such ways as were possible, the efforts at peaceful settlement
that were being made in Geneva and elsewhere. Their main
purpose was to arrive at a clearer understanding of each other's

*From *Foreign Policy of India, Texts of Documents 1947-58* (New
Delhi, India, 1958), pp. 97-98.

point of view in order to help the maintenance of peace, both in co-operation with each other and with other countries.

3. Recently India and China have come to an agreement in which they laid down certain principles which should guide the relations between the two countries. These principles are:

1. Mutual respect for each other's territorial integrity and sovereignty;
2. Non-aggression;
3. Non-interference in each other's internal affairs;
4. Equality and mutual benefit; and
5. Peaceful co-existence.

The Prime Ministers reaffirmed these principles and felt that they should be applied in their relations with other countries in Asia as well as in other parts of the world. If these principles are applied not only between various countries but also in international relations generally, they would form a solid foundation for peace and security and the fears and apprehensions that exist today would give place to a feeling of confidence.

4. The Prime Ministers recognised that different social and political systems exist in various parts of Asia and the world. If, however, the above-mentioned principles are accepted and acted upon and there is no interference by any one country with another, these differences should not come in the way of peace or create conflicts. With the assurance of territorial integrity and sovereignty of each country and of non-aggression, there would be peaceful co-existence and friendly relations between the countries concerned. This would lessen the tension that exists in the world today and help in creating a climate of peace.

5. In particular, the Prime Ministers hoped that these principles would be applied to the solution of the problems in Indo-China where the political settlement should aim at the creation of free, democratic, unified and independent States, which should not be used for aggressive purposes or be subjected to foreign intervention. This will lead to a growth of self-confidence in these countries as well as to friendly relations between them and their neighbours. The adoption of the principles referred to above will also help in creating an area of

peace which, as circumstances permit, can be enlarged, thus lessening the chances of war and strengthening the cause of peace all over the world.

6. The Prime Ministers expressed their confidence in the friendship between India and China which would help the cause of world peace and the peaceful development of their respective countries as well as the other countries of Asia.

7. These conversations were held with a view to help in bringing about a greater understanding of the problems of Asia and to further a peaceful and co-operative effort, in common with the other countries of the world, in solving these and like problems.

The Prime Ministers agreed that their respective countries should maintain close contacts so that there should continue to be full understanding between them. They appreciated greatly the present opportunity of meeting together and having a full exchange of ideas leading to a clearer understanding and co-operation in the cause of peace.

27. CHOU EN-LAI: SPEECH AT BANDUNG CONFERENCE (April, 1955)*

Chou En-lai announced a major change of China's foreign policy at the second day of the first Asian-African Conference, held at Bandung, Java (Indonesia) from April 18-24, 1955. The conference was convened by the five Colombo Powers—India, Burma, Indonesia, Pakistan, and Ceylon—and attended by twenty-four additional nations, including SEATO's three Asian members—the Philippines, Thailand, and Pakistan. At the conclusion of the conference, the twenty-nine nations set forth ten principles designed to promote world peace and cooperation.

Mr. Chairman, fellow delegates:

My main speech has been mimeographed and is being distributed to you. After listening to the speeches delivered by the heads of many delegations, I would like to make some supplementary remarks.

From Asian-African Conferences, Bandung, Indonesia, 18th-24th April 1955: Speeches and Communiques (Djakarta, Indonesia Ministry of Information, May, 1955) (footnotes omitted).

The Chinese Delegation has come here to seek unity and not to quarrel. We Communists do not hide the fact that we believe in communism and that we consider the socialist system a good system. There is no need at this Conference to publicize one's ideology and the political system of one's country, although differences do exist among us.

The Chinese Delegation has come here to seek common ground, and not to create divergence. Is there any basis for seeking common ground among us? Yes, there is. The overwhelming majority of the Asian and African countries and peoples have suffered and are still suffering from the calamities of colonialism. This is acknowledged by all of us. If we seek common ground in doing away with the sufferings and calamities under colonialism, it will be very easy for us to have mutual understanding and respect, mutual sympathy and support, instead of mutual suspicion and fear, mutual exclusion and antagonism. That is why we agree to the four purposes of the Asian-African Conference declared by the Prime Ministers of the five countries at the Bogor Conference, and do not make any other proposal.

As for the tension created solely by the United States of America in the area of Taiwan, we could have submitted for deliberation by the Conference an item such as the proposal made by the Soviet Union for seeking a settlement through an international conference. The will of the Chinese people to liberate their own territory (of) Taiwan and the coastal islands is a just one. It is entirely a matter of our internal affairs and the exercise of our sovereignty. This will of ours has won the support of many countries.

Again, we could have submitted for deliberation by the Conference the question of recognizing and restoring the legitimate status of the People's Republic of China in the United Nations. The Bogor Conference held by the Prime Ministers of the five Colombo Powers last year supported the restoration of the legitimate status of the People's Republic of China in the United Nations. And so did other countries of Asia and Africa. Besides, we could have also made criticisms here as regards the unfair treatment of China by the United Nations. But we did not do all this, because otherwise our Conference would be dragged into disputes about all these problems without any solution.

In our Conference we should seek common ground among us, while keeping our differences. As to our common ground, the Conference should affirm all our common desires and demands. This is our main task here. As to our differences, none of us is asked to give up his own views, because difference in viewpoints is an objective reality. But we should not let our differences hinder us from achieving agreement as far as our main task is concerned. On the basis of our common points, we should try to understand and appreciate the different views that we hold.

Now first of all I would like to talk about the question of different ideologies and social systems. We have to admit that among our Asian and African countries, we do have different ideologies and different social systems. But this does not prevent us from seeking common ground and being united. Many independent countries have appeared since the Second World War. One group of them are countries led by the Communist Parties; another group of them are countries led by nationalists. There are not many countries in the first group. But what some people dislike is the fact that the 600 million Chinese people have chosen a political system which is socialist in nature and led by the Chinese Communist Party and that the Chinese people are no longer under the rule of imperialism. The countries in the second group are greater in number, such as India, Burma, Indonesia and many other countries in Asia and Africa. Out of the colonial rule both of these groups of countries have become independent and are still continuing their struggle for complete independence. Is there any reason why we cannot understand and respect each other and give support and sympathy to each other? There is every reason to make the five principles the basis for establishing friendly co-operation and good neighbourly relations among us. We Asian and African countries, with China included, are all backward economically and culturally. If our Asian-African Conference does not exclude anybody, why couldn't we understand each other and enter into friendly co-operation?

Secondly, I would like to talk about the question as to whether there is freedom of religious belief. Freedom of religious belief is a principle recognized by all modern nations. We Communists are atheists, but we respect all those who have religious belief. We hope that those who have religious belief will also respect those without. China is a country where there is freedom of religious belief. There are in China, not only seven million Communists, but also tens of millions of Islamists and Buddhists and millions of Christians and Catholics. Here in the Chinese Delegation, there is a pious Imam of the Islamic faith. Such a situation is no obstacle to the internal unity of China. Why should it be impossible in the community of Asian and African countries to unite those with religious belief and those without? The days of instigating religious strife should have passed, because those who profit from instigating such strife are not those among us.

Thirdly, I would like to talk about the question of the so-called subversive activities. The struggle of the Chinese people against colonialism lasted for more than a hundred years. The national and democratic revolutionary struggles led by the Chinese Communist Party finally achieved success only after a strenuous and difficult course of thirty years. It is impossible to relate all the sufferings of the Chinese people under the rule of imperialism, feudalism and Chiang Kai-shek. At last, the Chinese people have chosen their state system and the present government. It is by the efforts of the Chinese people that the Chinese revolution has won its victory. It is certainly not imported from without. This point cannot be denied even by those who do not like the victory of the Chinese revolution. As a Chinese proverb says: 'Do not do unto others what you yourself do not desire.' We are against outside interference; how could we want to interfere in the internal affairs of others? Some people say: There are more than ten million overseas Chinese whose dual nationality might be taken advantage of to carry out subversive activities. But the problem of dual nationality is something left behind by old China. Up to date, Chiang Kai-shek is still using some very few overseas Chinese to carry out subversive activities against the country where the overseas Chinese are residing. The People's Government of new China, however, is ready to solve the problem of dual nationality of overseas Chinese with the governments of countries concerned. Some other people say that the autonomous region of Thai people in China is a threat to others. There are in China more than forty million national minorities of scores of nationalities. The Thai people and the Chuang people, who are of the same stock as the Thai people, number more than ten million. Since they do exist we must grant them the right of autonomy, just as there is an autonomous state for Shan people in Burma. In China every national minority has its autonomous region. The national minorities in China exercise their right of autonomy within China, how could that be said to be a threat to our neighbours?

On the basis of the strict adherence to the five principles, now we are prepared to establish normal relations with all the Asian and African countries, with all the countries in the world, and first of all, with our neighbouring countries. The problem at present is not that we are carrying out subversive activities against the governments of other countries, but that there are people who are establishing bases around China in order to carry out subversive activities against the Chinese Government. For instance, on the border between China and Burma, there are in fact remnant armed elements of the Chiang Kai-shek clique who are carrying out destructive activities against both China and Burma. Because of the friendly relations between China and Burma, and because we have always respected the sovereignty of Burma, we have confidence in the Government of Burma for the solution of this problem.

The Chinese people have chosen and support their own government. There is freedom of religious belief in China. China has no intention whatsoever to subvert the governments of its neighbouring countries. On the contrary, it is China that is suffering from the subversive activities which are openly carried out by the United States of America without any disguise. If you do not believe in this you can come personally or send representatives to China to take a look. We allow people to have doubts who do not yet know the truth. There is a saying in China: 'To hear a hundred times cannot be compared with seeing once.' We welcome the delegates of all the participating countries in this Conference to visit China at any time you like. We have no bamboo curtain, but there are people who are spreading a smokescreen between us.

The 1,600 million people of Asia and Africa wish our Conference success. All the countries and peoples of the world who desire peace are looking forward to the contribution which the Conference will make towards the extension of the area of peace and the establishment of collective peace.

Let us, the Asian and African countries, be united and do our utmost to make the Asian-African Conference a success.

28. JOINT COMMUNIQUÉ OF CHOU EN-LAI AND PHAM VAN DONG (November, 1956)*

Many of the important documents concerning China's role with respect to North Vietnam are still unavailable. Although the 1954 Geneva Agreement provided for the all-Vietnam elections to be held on July 20, 1956, to reunify the country, Ngo Dinh Diem refused to carry out the provisions after proclaiming his own republic in the south on October 26, 1955. To offer continued support for the North Vietnamese, Chou visited Hanoi from November 18 to November 22, 1956, and issued the following public communiqué with the North Vietnamese premier, although details of Chinese aid were never published.

On the invitation of the Government of the Democratic Republic of Viet-Nam, Chou En-lai, Premier of the State Council of the People's Republic of China, visited the Democratic Republic of Viet-Nam from the 18th to the 22nd of November 1956. During this visit, Premier Chou En-lai was received by President Ho-chi-Minh of the Democratic Republic of Viet-Nam.

Premier Chou En-lai and Premier Pham-van-Dong of the Democratic Republic of Viet-Nam had cordial talks on international issues of common interest to both countries and on problems relating to the further consolidation and development of friendly co-operation between the two countries.

Participating in the talks on the side of the Democratic Republic of Viet-Nam were Vice-Premier Phan-ke-Toai and Vice-Premier Vo-nguyen-Giap. Participating in the talks on the side of the People's Republic of China was Vice-Premier Ho-Lung.

The two Prime Ministers expressed deep concern over a number of events, recently causing international tension and brought about by the imperialists' aggressive acts and provocative activities. The two Prime Ministers also noted with

*From *Speeches and Joint Statements, 1956* (Hanoi, Ministry of Information, 1956) (extract).

satisfaction that peace-loving countries and peoples throughout the world have strongly urged relaxation of international tension and have made great efforts to this end. The two Prime Ministers strongly condemned the armed invasion of Egypt by Britain, France and their agent, Israel. The two Prime Ministers were of the same opinion that the anti-colonialist forces which had further developed since the Bandung Conference were determined not to allow the colonialists to carry out their plots to reimpose their colonialist rule. Britain, France and Israel should immediately and unconditionally withdraw their troops from Egyptian territory. There should be no further delay. The International Police Force of the United Nations should in no case be used to infringe upon Egypt's sacred sovereignty over the Suez Canal. The two Prime Ministers reiterated that the Democratic Republic of Viet-Nam and the People's Republic of China would resolutely support Egypt's just struggle against aggression and colonialism until Egypt's national independence and sovereignty were completely restored. The two Prime Ministers were convinced that with the active support of Asian-African countries and of peace-loving countries throughout the world, the Egyptian people would triumph in their heroic struggle to defend their national independence and territorial integrity. The two Prime Ministers considered it necessary to resolutely defeat the imperialists' plots and activities aimed at subverting the socialist states. These plots and activities are doomed to failure. The imperialists are trying with these plots and activities to divert the attention of world peoples from their aggression against Egypt, but they will certainly meet with ignominious defeat. The two Prime Ministers deemed it necessary to continue to support the Revolutionary Workers and Peasants Government of Hungary and firmly believed that the forces of the Hungarian labouring people would grow in their unswerving struggle to protect the achievements of the people's democratic system.

* * *

The two Prime Ministers have paid particular attention to the problem of further consolidating and developing friendship between the two countries. They noted with satisfaction that the relations between the Democratic Republic of Viet-Nam and the People's Republic of China have become closer and closer, that the economic and cultural exchanges and contacts under various forms have been expanding with each passing day. During the talks, Premier Pham-van-Dong clearly pointed out the importance of China's technical aid to Viet-Nam. Premier Chou En-lai expressed the opinion that the Chinese experts, who have come to Viet-Nam under agreement must learn from the industriousness and modesty of the Vietnamese people, share the latter's joys and hardships and do their best to help the Vietnamese people push forward their reconstruction work. The Vietnamese and Chinese peoples are pursuing a common ideal. The peoples of the two countries stand resolutely and closely together in order to oppose all plots of the colonialists and defend peace in Asia and the world. China will as before fully support the economic reconstruction of Viet Nam. The unshakable friendship and fraternal co-operation between Viet-Nam and China are important factors guaranteeing the fulfilment of the Geneva Agreements and the maintenance of security of the two countries.

* * *

29. GOVERNMENT STATEMENT: ON SEATO (March, 1958)*

Secretary of State Dulles, in spite of Chinese objec tions, organized the Southeast Asia Collective Defense Treaty (SEATO). The treaty, with its protocol covering South Vietnam, Cambodia, and Laos, went into effect on February 19, 1955. The following is one of the many Chinese reactions issued in response to the varied activities of SEATO.

A Council session of the South-east Asia Treaty Organization will begin in Manila on March 11. Through this session the Western colonial powers headed by the United States attempt to interfere further in the internal affairs of the South-east Asian countries, step up arms expansion and war preparations, set up U.S. bases for nuclear and rocket weapons on the

*From *Peking Review* (March 18, 1958), pp. 22-23.

territories of the Asian member states of this bloc, expand the sphere of activity of this aggressive bloc, and aggravate tension in Asia and the Pacific region. These aggressive designs of the United States are diametrically opposed to the present fervent desire of the peace-loving countries and people throughout the world and, first of all, those in Asia for an end to the cold war and for a further relaxation of international tension.

Making use of the aggressive Manila bloc, the United States has all along been interfering in the internal affairs of many South-east Asian countries under the pretext of combating so-called Communist subversive activities, and recently it has directed its spearhead against Indonesia in particular. Not long ago, U.S. Secretary of State Dulles made statements against the President and Government of Indonesia, crudely intervening in the domestic affairs of a sovereign state. At the same time, as everybody knows, Manila and Singapore have become the main bases through which the rebel elements of Indonesia get their supplies and contact others. The United States Seventh Fleet made a show of force and posed a threat by moving to the vicinity of the territorial waters of Indonesia under the pretext of manoeuvres. At the current Manila meeting the United States is attempting to muster more countries to interfere further in the internal affairs of Indonesia. This cannot but attract the serious attention of all countries and peoples who love peace and treasure their own sovereignty. The Chinese Government and people fully support the Government and people of Indonesia in their just struggle to safeguard their national independence and sovereignty against outside intervention and subversive plots, and are firmly convinced that this struggle will triumph ultimately. The Chinese Government holds that the Asian member states of the Manila bloc should honour the obligations they undertook at the Bandung Asian-African Conference and refuse to follow the United States in interfering in the internal affairs of another Asian country; they should know that it will bring them no good to pull chestnuts out of the fire for the United States. The Chinese Government deems it necessary to point out that the U.S. interference in Indonesia has already aroused ever-mounting censure and opposition from the people of Indonesia and Asia, and that any further action will certainly lead to serious consequences. The United States must immediately stop its interference in the internal affairs of

Indonesia, or else bear full responsibility for all consequences arising therefrom.

As it did at the NATO Paris conference and the Bagdad treaty Ankara meeting held not long ago, the United States also attempts at the present Manila meeting to enlarge its network of bases for nuclear and rocket weapons in Asia and the Pacific region. The setting up by the United States of bases for launching rockets with nuclear warheads on China's territory of Taiwan which it occupies, and in South Korea and Japan has aggravated tension in the Far East and has already met with the strong opposition of the Chinese people and the peoples of other Asian countries. The setting up of such bases in more countries not only will tighten U.S. control over these countries and increase the danger of war, but will bring incalculable disaster upon these countries first of all should war be started by the United States. The Chinese Government and people are firmly opposed to the deployment by the United States of nuclear and rocket weapons in any part of Asia, and are all out for the establishment throughout Asia of an area of peace free from atomic weapons and the conclusion of a treaty of collective peace. We believe these to be in full accord with the vital interests of the peoples of all Asian countries. But in the Asian member states of the Manila bloc there are actually certain leaders who, in disregard of the interests of their own countries and in defiance of the opposition of the people all over the world, have openly welcomed the setting up of bases for nuclear and rocket weapons on the territories of their countries by the United States. Itself an Asian country, China and these countries have the common duty to observe the resolution of the Bandung Asian-African Conference on the ten principles of peaceful co-existence. As a neighbour of these countries, the Chinese Government cannot but express serious concern over the establishment of U.S. bases for nuclear and rocket weapons on their territories.

The people of the whole world are eager for peace and ardently desire negotiations between the Eastern and the Western countries, prohibition of atomic and nuclear weapons, and peaceful co-existence among all peoples. To realize these desires, the Soviet Union, China and other peace-loving countries have put forward a series of peace proposals and took the initiative in measures which have met with universal welcome and support. However, the United States ruling circles have tried hard to obstruct the development of this mainstream in the international situation, press on with arms expansion and war preparations, and bolster up their aggressive blocs which are finding themselves in an increasingly critical situation. The present Manila meeting is precisely part of this struggle put up by the United States. This perverse line of action of the United States will only make it more isolated, and will by no means be able to stem the advance of the powerful current of peace throughout the world. So long as the people of the Asian countries strengthen their unity, heighten their vigilance and persist in their struggle, all conspiratorial activities carried out by the United States and other Western colonial powers through the Manila bloc are doomed to failure.

30. TREATY OF FRIENDSHIP, COOPERATION, AND MUTUAL ASSISTANCE BETWEEN CHINA AND KOREA (July, 1961)*

> *North Korea emerged from the Korean War (1950-53) a proud and militantly nationalistic country. China needs North Korea not only for her support in the Sino-Soviet disputes but as an ally against an emerging Japan. In spite of the Treaty of Friendship signed on July, 1961, Sino-North Korean relations were temporarily strained as a result of China's Cultural Revolution (1966-68). By 1969 Peking made a major effort to repair her relations with North Korea, resulting for the first time in four years in North Korea's sending a delegation to China's National Day celebration. Chou En-lai's latest trip to Pyongyang, in April, 1970, signaled renewed closer cooperation between the two countries.*

The Chairman of the People's Republic of China and the Presidium of the Supreme People's Assembly of the Democratic People's Republic of Korea, determined, in accordance with Marxism-Leninism and the principle of proletarian internationalism and on the basis of mutual respect for state sovereignty and territorial integrity, mutual non-aggression,

*From *China Today*, Vol. VI, No. 29, p. 3.

non-interference in each other's internal affairs, equality and mutual benefit, and mutual assistance and support, to make every effort to further strengthen and develop the fraternal relations of friendship, co-operation and mutual assistance between the People's Republic of China and the Democratic People's Republic of Korea, to jointly guard the security of the two peoples, and to safeguard and consolidate the peace of Asia and the world, and deeply convinced that the development and strengthening of the relations of friendship, co-operation and mutual assistance between the two countries accord not only the fundamental interests of the two peoples but also with the interests of the peoples all over the world, have decided for this purpose to conclude the present treaty and appointed as their respective plenipotentiaries:

The Chairman of the People's Republic of China: Chou En-lai, Premier of the State Council of the People's Republic of China,

The Presidium of the Supreme People's Assembly of the Democratic People's Republic of Korea: Kim Il Sung, Premier of the Cabinet of the Democratic People's Republic of Korea,

Who, having examined each other's full powers and found them in good and due form, have agreed upon the following:

Article I

The Contracting Parties will continue to make every effort to safeguard the peace of Asia and the world and the security of all peoples.

Article II

The Contracting Parties undertake jointly to adopt all measures to prevent aggression against either of the Contracting Parties by any state. In the event of one of the Contracting Parties being subjected to the armed attack by any state or several states jointly and thus being involved in a state of war, the other Contracting Party shall immediately render military and other assistance by all means at its disposal.

Article III

Neither Contracting Party shall conclude any alliance directed against the other Contracting Party or take part in any bloc or in any action or measure directed against the other Contracting Party.

Article IV

The Contracting Parties will continue to consult with each other on all important international questions of common interests to the two countries.

Article V

The Contracting Parties, on the principles of mutual respect for sovereignty, non-interference in each other's internal affairs, equality and mutual benefit and in the spirit of friendly co-operation, will continue to render each other every possible economic and technical aid in the cause of socialist construction of the two countries and will continue to consolidate and develop economic, cultural, and scientific and technical co-operation between the two countries.

Article VI

The Contracting Parties hold that the unification of Korea must be realised along peaceful and democratic lines and that such a solution accords exactly with the national interests of the Korean people and the aim of preserving peace in the Far East.

Article VII

The present treaty is subject to ratification and shall come into force on the day of exchange of instruments of ratification, which will take place in Pyongyang.

The present treaty will remain in force until the Contracting Parties agree on its amendment or termination.

Done in duplicate in Peking on the eleventh day of July, 1961, in the Chinese and Korean languages, both texts being equally authentic.

[Signatures]

31. CHOU EN-LAI'S PRESS CONFERENCE IN CAIRO (December, 1963)*

> *The UAR became one of the first countries in the Middle East to recognize China, and the pace of Chinese interaction with the Middle East quickened in 1958 with the establishment of the Permanent Organization of the Afro-Asian People's Solidarity Conference, of which China is a member. In the Arab world, Chinese ability to make a direct political impact on the domestic scene is also related to the degree of local needs. China's support of the Arab cause in Palestine, for example, had kept the UAR's relations with Peking very strong. The following news conference in Cairo on December 20, 1963, was made by Chou En-lai during his first trip to the Arab-African countries in 1963-64. It dealt with a variety of China's foreign policies.*

Premier Chou En-lai held a press conference in the Republican Palace, Cairo, on the afternoon of December 20. He answered the questions of reporters from the United Arab Republic and other countries.

On his impressions and the results of his visit to the U.A.R., the Premier said: I and Vice-Premier Chen Yi, as well as my other colleagues, are deeply impressed with our visit to the United Arab Republic, the first stop in our first African tour. Here in the U.A.R., we have been welcomed by a warm-hearted and courageous people and seen an industrious and wise people at work in building their new country with enthusiasm. The U.A.R. has an able leader in His Excellency President Nasser and enjoys the strength of unity. That is why an atmosphere of a new emerging country has appeared in the U.A.R. in so short a time.

He said: During the visit, we have held three sincere and friendly talks with President Nasser and other U.A.R. leaders. Today I saw President Nasser again. The main results of our talks will be published in a joint communiqué.

*From *Afro-Asian Solidarity Against Imperialism* (Peking, Foreign Language Press, 1964), pp. 16-25.

On the plans for his current visits abroad, he said: New China is already 14 years old. We have established diplomatic relations with many African countries; leaders, ministers, and delegates of popular organizations of many African countries have made numerous visits to China. This is our first visit to Africa. We have not come too early, rather too late. Soon after our visit to the U.A.R. we will visit Algeria and Morocco. We will also visit Ghana, Mali, Guinea, and the Sudan. The purpose of our African trip is to seek friendship and co-operation, to understand more, and to learn more. According to the ten principles of the Bandung Conference, we Asian and African countries should regularly exchange visits.

Premier Chou En-lai also announced that at the invitation of the People's Republic of Albania he will visit Albania after concluding his North African tour. On his return trip from Africa, he will also visit some friendly countries in South Asia.

Premier Chou En-lai said: One of the main contents of the foreign policy of the Chinese Government is active support for the national democratic movements in Asia, Africa and Latin America. China is a country that has been liberated from the colonial shackles of imperialism. We shared the same lot as the peoples of Asia, Africa and Latin America. Naturally we sympathize with and support each other. Moreover, since China has won its own victory, it has the obligation to support countries which have not yet won victory or are about to win it.

In reply to a question from an American correspondent, Premier Chou En-lai said: People in the southern part of Viet Nam are oppressed by foreign imperialists and the reactionaries at home. Under the leadership of the South Viet Nam National Liberation Front, the people have risen in revolt. Their struggle is entirely based on their own strength. They have achieved victory after victory under incomparably hard conditions. When a people is subjected to foreign oppression, forces of resistance must emerge and grow and must be victorious. How bravely did George Washington lead the American people in resisting foreign aggressors! This is now being repeated in south Viet Nam. It has given many headaches to the White House, the Pentagon, and the U.S. State Department, while we, the people who are now independent, undoubtedly rejoice over, sympathize with, and resolutely support the heroic struggle of the south Vietnamese just as the French at that time supported the Americans then fighting for their independence.

Premier Chou En-lai said: The Chinese people have always stood firmly behind the Arabs in Palestine in their just struggle for their legitimate rights. Our diplomatic actions have testified to this. We have also backed the efforts made by the people of the Arab countries to achieve unification and association by means they themselves have chosen.

Premier Chou En-lai stated: A possibility exists of holding a Second Asian-African Conference. Both President Nasser and myself agreed that good preparations for this conference should be made. Only when good preparations have been made can a meeting be successful. More than eight years have passed since the First Asian-African Conference whose influence has become ever broader and deeper. In the past eight years and more, over 30 countries have achieved independence in Asia and Africa and this trend continues. The ten principles of the Bandung Conference still apply to the countries in Asia, Africa, and Latin America today and they remain worth fighting for.

Reviewing the great achievements of the First Asian-African Conference, Premier Chou En-lai pointed out that the two methods which made the First Asian-African Conference a success would also apply to the Second Asian-African Conference.

He said: The first method is seeking common ground among us while retaining our differences. There are many major problems common to us Asian and African countries which have to be resolved. They are: to combat imperialism and old and new colonialism; to oppose aggression and intervention; to demand the withdrawal of foreign troops and the removal of foreign military bases; to support the national liberation movement; to defend world peace; and to live in friendship in accordance with the principles of respect for each other's sovereignty and territorial integrity, mutual non-aggression, non-interference in each other's internal affairs, equality, and mutual benefit. Individual disputes between us can be put aside. It was because of the adoption of this method that the First Asian-African Conference was crowned with success. In spite of the different political systems of the countries participating in that conference and their divergent views, we finally succeeded in finding common ground and in formulating the well-known ten principles.

He continued: The second method is to let the Asian and African countries settle their own problems without intervention by imperialism. The First Asian-African Conference was an important international conference held by the countries of Asia and Africa without the participation of the imperialist and colonialist countries. Japan was the only exception. Being a vanquished country under the occupation of foreign troops, Japan was also a country under foreign domination and went through the same trials as the other Asian and African countries. We, the Asian and African countries, share common historical experience, have common problems to be worked out, and common goals for which to strive. We ought to, and we can, settle our own problems. This is also the spirit to which the Second Asian-African Conference should adhere.

Referring to the conference of the non-aligned countries, Premier Chou En-lai said: China is a committed country and thus cannot participate in the conference of the non-aligned countries. It is common knowledge that the first conference of non-aligned countries held high the banner of combating imperialism and old and new colonialism, supporting the national independence movement, and defending world peace. It is my belief that the second conference of the non-aligned countries will also follow this line. Otherwise, it will no longer be a conference of non-aligned countries.

Dealing with the efforts made by the U.A.R. and other Colombo Conference countries to promote Sino-Indian reconciliation, Premier Chou En-lai stated: Since the Colombo Conference, China has appreciated and supported the efforts made by the U.A.R. and other Colombo Conference countries to mediate in the Sino-Indian border dispute and bring about direct negotiations between China and India. China backs their continued efforts to bring about direct talks between China and India at an early date and to settle the border dispute peacefully.

A correspondent of an Indian paper asked whether China was ready to renounce its reservations about the Columbo proposals. Premier Chou En-lai replied that he did not think there was any question of renouncing reservations in this matter. This was because the Colombo proposals were recommendations put forward by the mediating countries and not an award given by arbitrating powers. This was what all the government heads of the six Colombo Conference countries had told him. He said that the attitude of the Chinese Government is that in principle it accepts the Colombo proposals as the basis for direct Sino-Indian negotiations, and that China and India should come to the conference table to settle the border question peacefully without advancing any preconditions.

Premier Chou En-lai said: The measures taken by China on its own initiative since November last year have far exceeded the requirements set forth in the Colombo proposals. For instance, the proposals asked China to withdraw 20 kilometres from the western sector of the Sino-Indian boundary, while China, acting in accordance with its own statement, withdrew 20 kilometres along the whole line, in the western sector, the middle sector, and the eastern sector. This has enabled the Chinese frontier guards and civilian administrative personnel to disengage from the Indian side and to avoid further border clashes. That is why, generally speaking, the Sino-Indian border situation has been quiet in the past year and the tension has been eased.

He added: Another example is the further step taken by China in vacating the areas on the Chinese side of the 1959 line of actual control which had been occupied by India and also other areas disputed by the two sides in their ceasefire arrrangements, without even setting up any civilian check-posts there, pending a negotiated settlement with India. These initiatives were taken to create a favourable atmosphere for direct negotiations between the two countries, to bring about a peaceful solution of the boundary question. In taking these steps, China has taken into consideration the dignity and prestige of both sides. China suggests that both sides sit down at the conference table without setting any preconditions, that during the negotiations either side may put forward any proposals, and that the two sides may also discuss the specific details of the Colombo proposals as well as their interpretations of these proposals.

Answering the question why China opposes the tripartite treaty of the United States, Britain and the Soviet Union on a partial nuclear test ban, Premier Chou En-lai said: The three countries concluded this treaty with a view to monopolizing nuclear weapons, hence our stand against it. We stand for the complete prohibition and thorough destruction of nuclear weapons and the prevention of nuclear war. Should such a war break out, mankind would suffer a tremendous catastrophe. On this account, all the countries of the world should have a share in the discussion of the question of complete prohibition and thorough destruction of nuclear weapons and the prevention of nuclear war. Politically all the countries of the world, big or small, strong or weak, are equals. Questions related to the destiny of all mankind should be discussed by all parties together. Such discussions should not be monopolized by a few countries, nor, even worse, should any decision favourable to these few be imposed upon the countries which are not represented in the discussions. This is one aspect of the question. The other aspect is that after the signing of the tripartite treaty, the United States has repeatedly conducted underground nuclear tests. The President and government officials of the United States have time and again declared the intention of the United States to continue its testing, production, and stockpiling of nuclear weapons, and its intention to continue to deliver nuclear weapons to its allies, while refusing to commit itself to a renunciation of the use of nuclear weapons. The U.S. Government has increased its budget expenditure for the testing and manufacture of nuclear weapons. While testifying in Congress, U.S. generals have stressed the need to continue the development of new-type nuclear weapons, tactical nuclear weapons in particular. All this shows that the conclusion of the tripartite treaty has increased the danger of nuclear war, far from lessening it. In face of such a fraudulent treaty, the Chinese Government has no alternative but to expose it, and this is our sacred duty to safeguard the destiny of mankind

Premier Chou En-lai said: There are also well-intentioned people who are so naive as to think that the danger of nuclear war has been reduced as a result of the conclusion of the tripartite treaty. These people might take a look at the course of events to see whether this danger has actually increased or lessened. Even in less than five months since the signing of the treaty, world public opinion has already become less interested in it. Time will give the final verdict.

When the reporter of a U.S. magazine asked why China opposed peaceful consultations between East and West, Premier Chou En-lai asked him to say on what occasion had China made such a statement. The reporter took refuge in silence. Premier Chou En-lai then said: If China is opposed to the settlement of international disputes through peaceful consultations between

East and West, why then should it have held talks with the United States at the ambassadorial level for the past eight years and more? Chinese and American ambassadors have held 118 talks and there is no precedent in modern history for talks to have lasted so long. The United States remains in occupation of the Chinese territory of Taiwan, and its 7th Fleet remains in the Taiwan Straits, threatening China. Under these circumstances, China still continues its ambassadorial talks with the United States and refrains from a recourse to armed force. How can it be said that China rejects peaceful consultations?

Premier Chou En-lai then gave his regards to the American people, and said: The Chinese people want friendship with the American people. But it is the policies of aggression and war pursued by the U.S. Government against China that China must fight unflinchingly to the end. A clear distinction must be made between these two aspects.

Replying to a question on Sino-Soviet differences, Premier Chou En-lai said: We do have serious differences with the leaders of the Communist Party of the Soviet Union on questions of principle of Marxism-Leninism. It is our belief, however, that these disputes will be resolved in the end on the basis of Marxism-Leninism and of the revolutionary principles of the 1957 Declaration and the 1960 Statement. Some countries want to profit by these differences; they are doomed to failure. China and the Soviet Union, the two big powers, are both in the socialist camp. They have between them a Treaty of Friendship, Alliance and Mutual Assistance. In the event of emergency, the Chinese and Soviet peoples will without fail stand by each other, shoulder to shoulder, hand in hand.

Premier Chou En-lai's press conference lasted one and a half hours.

32. CHOU EN-LAI'S RADIO MESSAGE TO GUINEAN PEOPLE (January, 1964)*

> *In the 1960's, the People's Republic of China tried to forge close relations with Guinea, Ghana, and Mali, three of the most "radical" states in Africa. In June, 1959, Peking sent a shipment of 5,000 tons of rice to*

*From *Afro-Asian Solidarity Against Imperialism* (Peking, Foreign Language Press, 1964), pp. 205-9.

Guinea; four months later, on October 4, the two countries established formal diplomatic relations; and in the year following, President Sékou Touré made a five-day state visit (September 10-15) to Peking. The following was the farewell message by Chou En-lai, broadcast by the Guinean radio station during Chou's first visit to that country, in January, 1964.

His Excellency, Esteemed President Sékou Touré,
Dear Friends,

We are concluding our unforgettable visit to the Republic of Guinea and are about to start our journey to East Africa. Geographically speaking, we shall be going further and further away from you every day, but our hearts will grow closer to each other and our friendship will be deeper every day.

The sincere friendship of the Guinean people for the Chinese people has left a deep imprint on our hearts. Everywhere we went in the past few days, from Conakry to Kindia and Labe and from the cities to the countryside, we have received the most considerate hospitality as well as a warm and magnificent welcome. Colourful gardens of friendship were formed by Guinean brothers and sisters who, dressed in their best, lined the streets to welcome us. The whirlwind-like Guinean national dances demonstrated the most ardent friendship of the Guinean people for the Chinese people. At this moment of parting, in the name of Vice-Premier Chen Yi and myself, I wish to express once again my hearty thanks to President Sékou Touré, the Guinean Government and people. We will certainly take home to the 650 million Chinese people the deep affection and profound friendship of the Guinean people which we have received personally.

Beautiful Guinea has left an indelible impression on our minds. We have seen with our own eyes that a republic bubbling with vitality has risen on the Atlantic coast.

After long years of courageous struggle, the Guinean people have freed themselves from slavery and humiliation and become the masters of their own land. Holding your head high, you despise the enemy, slight all the old-time oppressors, and hold in contempt all the new oppressors who seek to enslave the Guinean people again. Such dauntless courage and heroism is essential to the growth of all the new emerging countries. We, as Asians who have long suffered from imperialist aggression and oppression, fully appreciate and warmly acclaim this revolutionary spirit of the Guinean people.

The Guinean people are an industrious, talented people full of enthusiasm and courage. Since their achievement of independence, they have boldly acted as the master of their own country, courageously taking state affairs into their own hands, and have achieved brilliant successes in enforcing the progressive measure of decolonialization. We wish the Guinean Democratic Party headed by President Sékou Touré ever more new successes in leading the Guinean people in the cause of the national democratic revolution.

Under the leadership of President Sékou Touré and the Guinean Democratic Party, the Guinean people vigorously support and promote the African peoples' struggle against imperialism, and old and new colonialism. We appreciate the national songs and dances of Guinea, which not only vividly portray the long, courageous struggle waged by the Guinean people against imperialism, but also extol from various aspects the other African peoples' struggle for national liberation. The name of Lumumba, the national hero of the Congo, is revered and cherished in the memory of the Guinean people like that of Samori Touré and of Alpha Yaya, the national heroes of Guinea. The popularization of the revolutionary songs of Guinea, which brim with militant contents, furthers the national awakening of the African people and enhances their aspirations for the unity and solidarity of the African countries.

In the past month or more, we have visited many friendly countries in North and West Africa. We have keenly felt that a great, earth-shaking change is taking place on the African continent, which for centuries was ravaged and trampled underfoot by the colonialists. The storm of revolution is sweeping over the whole continent, and the yoke of colonial rule is being cast off in one country after another. On this vast expanse of land which covers 30 million square kilometres, the former slaves have stood up and resolved to take their destiny into their own hands. This is a mighty historical tide which no force on earth can stem. The African people have boundless potential, and the African continent has inexhaustible natural resources. The peoples of Africa will assuredly win complete victory in their national liberation struggle, provided that under a correct leadership, they are united and organized for an unswerving struggle against imperialism, and colonialism and neo-colonialism, and build their country by relying on their own efforts. Using their own hands the African people can surely create the most beautiful pictures and the most magnificent poems on the vast, rich continent of Africa. A new, independent Africa free of imperialism and old and new colonialism will undoubtedly emerge. A new, powerful and prosperous Africa with an advanced economy and an advanced culture will emerge without fail.

In accordance with the Five Principles of Peaceful Coexistence and the ten principles of the Bandung Conference, China has consistently taken the following stand in its relations with African countries: 1. It supports the African peoples in their struggle to fight imperialism and old and new colonialism and to win and safeguard national independence. 2. It supports the pursuance of a policy of peace, neutrality and non-alignment by the governments of African countries. 3. It supports the desire of the African peoples to achieve unity and solidarity in the manner of their own choice. 4. It supports the African countries in their efforts to settle their disputes through peaceful consultation. 5. It holds that the sovereignty of African countries should be respected by all other countries and that encroachment and interference from any quarters should be opposed. During our current visit in Africa, we have come to realize more deeply that this stand conforms with the reality of Africa, and with the common interests of the African and Chinese peoples.

We, peoples of Asia, Africa and Latin America, have had the common experience of suffering from imperialist and colonialist aggression and oppression, and have the common militant task of combating imperialism and old and new colonialism. World peace and human progress will certainly be won if the people of Asia, Africa and Latin America, if the people of all continents, become united in a resolute and unremitting struggle against the imperialist policies of aggression and war.

Dear friends, during our visit, we had brotherly, sincere and cordial talks with President Sékou Touré and other Guinean leaders; we had a full exchange of opinions and arrived at identical views on the further development of the friendship and co-operation between our two countries and on international questions of common interest, and we shall issue a joint communiqué. This is a further development in the Sino-Guinean relations of friendship and co-operation since President Sékou Touré's visit to China in 1960. We fervently hail the constant growth of Sino-Guinean friendship. In the years to come, the Chinese people and their fraternal Guinean people will forever support each other and march forward hand in hand in their common struggle against imperialism and old and new colonialism, in the construction of their respective countries and in the development of their national economy and culture.

May Sino-Guinean friendship last eternally!

Long live Afro-Asian solidarity!

Long live world peace!

33. GOVERNMENT STATEMENT: ON U.S. AGGRESSION AGAINST DOMINICAN REPUBLIC (May, 1965)*

This was a major propaganda statement, since China had only limited political and economic involvement in Latin America during the 1960's. However, China was fully aware of the deep sentiments of nationalism and anti-American imperialism of the Latin American people.

A coup d'etat against the traitorous dictatorial regime of Reid Cabral broke out in the Dominican Republic on April 24. The United States has been sending its marines and airborne troops to suppress the coup there since April 28. So far, more than 14,000 U.S. troops have been sent. The patriotic Dominican people are waging a brave anti-U.S. struggle.

The dispatch by the U.S. Johnson Administration of large contingents of armed forces to invade the Dominican Republic and interfere in its internal affairs while frantically carrying on aggression in Viet Nam adds one more shameless and sanguinary instance to the innumerable crimes committed by U.S. imperialism in its aggression against the Latin American countries. The Chinese Government and people strongly condemn the U.S. Government's barbarous intervention and aggression against the

*From *Peking Review* (May 7, 1965), pp. 12-13.

Dominican Republic and express their firm support for the Dominican people in their patriotic and just anti-U.S. struggle.

It is the inviolable, sacred right of the Dominican people, oppressed and plundered beyond endurance by the stooges of U.S. imperialism, to rise and overthrow the traitorous dictatorial regime in their country. The United States has no justification whatsoever to interfere. The assertion by the Johnson Administration that troops have been sent to the Dominican Republic to "protect the lives and ensure the safety of American nationals," to "preserve law and order" and to "establish an international zone of refuge" is nothing but a pretext habitually used by imperialist gangsters. This only serves to reveal once again that U.S. imperialism is the common enemy of the people of the Dominican Republic and other Latin American countries as well as all people of the world who cherish peace, independence and freedom. The sanguinary intervention and aggression against the Dominican Republic by U.S. imperialism show once more that there can be no peaceful coexistence between the countries subjected to U.S. imperialist aggression and the U.S. gangsters.

Having audaciously dispatched thousands of troops to the Dominican Republic, the Johnson Administration sanctimoniously notified the United Nations of it. The United States has acted in the same way as it did when committing aggression in Korea a dozen or more years ago. This was obviously a U.S. attempt to legalize its bloody crime of aggression against the Dominican Republic and to ward off direct condemnation of the U.S. Government by the people throughout the world. But this is not all to the U.S. scheme. In turning the plain fact of its aggression against the Dominican Republic into a topic for endless discussion in the United Nations, the United States hopes that while such discussions go on indefinitely it can carry on its intervention and aggression against the Dominican Republic unhampered. The United Nations has long been an instrument of the United States for aggression. It seems that there will be no exception this time. If the United Nations does want to do some good, it must condemn the United States as an outright aggressor, halt the bloody U.S. intervention and aggression against the Dominican people, call on all nations that love peace and oppose aggression to apply effective sanctions against the United States, and it must compel the U.S.

aggressors to withdraw immediately and completely from the Dominican Republic. Otherwise, it can only reveal itself once again as a pliant tool of the U.S. aggressors.

In hastily sending such large numbers of troops to the Dominican Republic, the Johnson Administration revealed itself to be weak rather than strong. The 3 million and more Dominican people are by no means alone in their patriotic anti-U.S. struggle. The other Latin American peoples support you. The 650 million Chinese people support you. The other peoples in the socialist camp support you. The heroic Vietnamese people are hitting the U.S. imperialists hard. The new campaign of anti-U.S. revolutionary struggles being unfolded in Asia is a support to you. The Arab people support you with their struggle against Israel, the U.S. tool for aggression. The African people support you. And so do all peoples engaged in anti-U.S. struggles. U.S. imperialism is heavily besieged by the people of the world, and no struggle however desperate can save it from ultimate defeat.

U.S. imperialism will surely fail!

The people of the Dominican Republic and other Latin American countries will surely win!

34. CHINESE EDITORIAL: ARAB PEOPLE, UNITE, MAKE SUSTAINED EFFORTS, AND FIGHT IMPERIALISM TO THE END (June, 1967)*

Although China supports the Arabs in their struggles against Israel, its foreign policy operates under a serious handicap due to geographical location, inaccessibility to that region, and limited military and economic involvement. However, China does offer full moral support, as demonstrated in this editorial during the disastrous June War.

As a result of the large-scale armed aggression suddenly unleashed by the U.S.-Israeli aggressors and the pressure being exerted on the Arab countries by the United States, Britain and the Soviet Union working in collusion, the Governments of the United Arab Republic, Syria and Jordan have been compelled

*From *Jen-min Jih-pao*(June 11, 1967).

to announce their acceptance of the U.N. Security Council's "ceasefire resolution". But under cover of the U.N. "ceasefire", U.S. imperialism's lackey, Israel, continues to launch large-scale attacks against Syria. The Arab people's struggle of resistance to U.S. imperialism and its lackey is now at a critical stage.

The struggle of the Arab people against U.S. imperialism and its lackey has merely suffered a temporary setback; the flames of the struggle have not been extinguished and they never will be.

Ever since the war of aggression was launched by the United States and Israel, a wave of extensive mass struggle against the United States has been sweeping through the Arab world. This is an expression of the unprecedented awakening of the Arab people. Although a "ceasefire" has been announced, the spirit of the Arab people remains high and they continue to strike at U.S. imperialism and its lackey in various ways; they are determined to fight the aggressors to the end.

For many years, the Arab people have waged heroic struggles to win and safeguard national independence. Despite repeated setbacks in their struggles, they have nonetheless achieved tremendous successes. Neither the setback in the Arab-Israeli war of 1948, nor the 1950 "tripartite declaration", in which the United States, Britain and France jointly interfered in Arab affairs, have been able to halt the development of the Arab national-liberation struggles. The imperialists were quite arrogant for a while after forming the 1955 Baghdad military bloc, but the Arab people continued to forge ahead. When the Suez war of aggression was launched by the imperialists in 1956, the Arab people closed their ranks and firmly countered the imperialist aggressors. The Arab people were not intimidated when the imperialists plotted aggression against Syria in 1957 or when U.S. imperialism landed its troops in Lebanon and staged armed intervention in the Iraqi revolution in 1958. Facts have demonstrated that the great Arab people have a dauntless fighting spirit and that temporary setbacks only serve to boost their fighting will.

The great leader of the Chinese people Chairman Mao Tse-tung has said: "Fight, fail, fight again, fail again, fight again . . . till their victory; that is the logic of the people." This is a law of Marxism-Leninism, Mao Tse-tung's thought. The Chinese people's revolution has followed this law. The national-liberation struggles of the Asian, African and Latin American peoples have followed this law. The Arab people's struggle against imperialism and its lackey will also inevitably follow this law.

All the political forces in the world have undergone a test through the developments in the Middle East, especially in the face of the Arab people's just war against aggression. Imperialism, headed by the United States, Soviet modern revisionism and the reactionaries of all countries have in a thousand and one ways instigated and encouraged the Israeli aggression, and tried to suppress the Arab people's struggle against aggression. The Chinese people and the peoples of the world have stood firmly by the Arab people, fully exposed the U.S.-British-Soviet big counter-revolutionary conspiracy and extended their all-out support to the Arab people in their struggle against aggression. This is the clear line of demarcation between the two camps. This is a fact which has opened wide the eyes of the Arab people. It is a deep education to them and enables them to recognize even more clearly who are their sinister enemies and who their loyal, reliable comrades-in-arms.

The ferocious features of U.S. imperialism have been completely revealed. Cold facts have proved that U.S. imperialism is the chief culprit in the staging of this war of aggression, the arch-criminal suppressing the Arab people, the biggest aggressor pushing ahead with neo-colonialism in the Arab world, and the No. 1 sworn enemy of the 100 million Arab people.

The aggressive features of British imperialism have also been thoroughly exposed. It was Britain which joined the United States in engineering and supporting Israel's armed attacks on the Arab countries and which engaged in all sorts of cunning political manoeuvres to bring pressure to bear on them. This senile, decrepit old-style imperialism has gone utterly mad in promoting its neo-colonialism in an attempt to maintain its shaky colonialist position in Asia and Africa.

French imperialism, which claimed to be "neutral" during these events, has actually played "big power politics" along with the United States, Britain and the Soviet Union and shown itself as standing on the side of the U.S.-Israeli aggressors.

Through the recent developments in the Middle East, the Arab people have learnt an important lesson. They have come to gradually recognize the sinister features of the Soviet revisionist clique as those of a false and treacherous friend. Israel's armed aggression against the Arab people was in essence a frantic attack jointly plotted by the United States and the Soviet Union. It was also a joint U.S.-Soviet political manoeuvre to trap the Arab countries. Examine the facts! The Soviet revisionist clique on the one hand "guaranteed" that Israel would not attack and on the other, working hand in glove with the United States, instigated Israel to launch a surprise attack on the Arab countries and catch them unawares. One day it voiced "support" for the Arab people and the next day it engaged in behind-the-scenes dealings with the United States and cooked up a so-called "cease-fire" resolution in the U.N. Security Council, a most shameless betrayal of the Arab people. It publicly issues one statement after another, one note after another, in "condemnation" of Israel, while secretly flirting with Israel. When Israel took over control of the Tiran Strait, a Soviet vessel was the first ship to pass the Gulf of Aqaba. The Soviet revisionist clique is a heinous swindler specializing in double-dealings, a big traitor to the Arab people and, in collusion with U.S. and British imperialism, a butcher suppressing the Arab people's struggle against aggression.

The Arab people's struggle against imperialist aggression will be a protracted one. Looked at in essence and from a long-term point of view, it is the Arab people who are really powerful. U.S. imperialism, British imperialism, Soviet revisionism, Israel—all are paper tigers. It is only a temporary phenomenon that Israel, by relying on the assistance of U.S. and British imperialism and Soviet revisionism, has been able to occupy some Arab territory by force of arms. The Arab people will sooner or later liberate all their territory now under forcible occupation by imperialism and its lackey. Without fail the debt owed by imperialism to them will be repaid. No force on earth can stop the Arab people from exercising their sacred right!

An excellent revolutionary situation now prevails throughout the whole world. Struggles against U.S. imperialism are growing vigorously everywhere. The heroic Vietnamese people, giving full play to the infinite power of people's war, have badly mauled the nearly 500,000 U.S. aggressor troops. Over the vast expanses of Asia, Africa and Latin America the people are more awakened than ever before and the flames of anti-imperialist revolution burn ever higher. The imperialist bloc is heading towards disintegration, and the modern revisionist clique is beset with difficulties. The world situation is extremely favourable to the revolutionary people of all countries and most unfavourable to imperialism. It is favourable to the Arab people for persistence in their fight against aggression. Whatever desperate struggles imperialism, headed by the United States, may make and whatever despicable treacherous activities the Soviet modern revisionists may conduct, this general trend of the world situation can never be changed. The zigzags which the Arab people encounter in the course of their anti-imperialist struggle can under no circumstances halt their continuous advance.

Chairman Mao has said: "The people, and the people alone, are the motive force in the making of world history." The Arab people are the makers of Arab history. No encroachment on or violation of Arab land by imperialism and its lackey will be tolerated. So long as the 100 million Arab people raise their political consciousness, adopt correct policies and persevere in struggle, they will certainly be able to drive away the old and new colonialists, headed by the United States, and to wipe out all aggressor bandits!

Arab people, unite, make sustained efforts and plunge into long-term fierce struggles! The 700 million Chinese people support you. So do all the revolutionary people the world over. Final victory will surely belong to the heroic Arab people!

35. *CHOU EN-LAI: SUMMIT CONFERENCE OF THE INDO-CHINESE PEOPLE (April, 1970)**

This is Chou En-lai's speech at the banquet celebrating the conclusion of the Summit Conference of the Three Indochinese Peoples. The conference, hosted by the Chinese, was attended by Prince Sihanouk (Cambodia), Prince Souphanouvong (Pathet Lao), Premier Pham Van Dong (North Vietnam), and President Nguyen Huu Tho (National Liberation Front of South Vietnam) in late April, 1970, somewhere in southwest China. Although Chou pledged "the 700 million Chinese people provide a powerful

*From *Peking Review* (May 8, 1970), pp. 34-35.

backing for the three Indo-Chinese peoples and the vast expanse of China's territory is their reliable rear area [against U.S. invasion]," he did not include active combat support.

The Summit Conference of the Indo-Chinese Peoples attended by the highest leaders of the four parties of three countries, Cambodia, Laos, the Republic of South Viet Nam and the Democratic Republic of Viet Nam has come to a victorious conclusion. We are very happy today to gather with the highest leaders of the four parties of the three countries and all the other distinguished guests attending the conference in celebrating together the complete success of the conference. On behalf of the Chinese people's great leader Chairman Mao Tsetung and his close comrade-in-arms Vice-Chairman Lin Piao and on behalf of the Chinese Government and people, I extend the most cordial greetings and the highest respects to you and, through you, to the fraternal peoples of Cambodia, Laos and Viet Nam.

In celebrating the success of the conference, I have brought you a gift from the Chinese people, and that is, China successfully launched its first man-made earth satellite yesterday. The launching into space of China's man-made earth satellite is a victory of the Chinese people and also a victory for all of us.

The Summit Conference of the Indo-Chinese Peoples was held at an important juncture when U.S. imperialism is stepping up the expansion of its war of aggression in Indo-China. Through this conference, the highest leaders of the four parties of the three Indo-Chinese countries have reached identical views on the present situation in Indo-China and the common tasks confronting this region, and a Joint Declaration will soon be issued. This is a conference of great significance in the history of the anti-imperialist revolution of the three Indo-Chinese peoples. The Chinese Government and people express the warmest congratulations on the tremendous achievements scored at the conference.

At present, the international situation is excellent. Under the heavy blows of the three Indo-Chinese peoples and the people of the rest of the world, U.S. imperialism, beset with difficulties both at home and abroad and driven into an impasse, is finding the going tougher and tougher. However, U.S. imperialism is not reconciled to its defeat and is putting up a last-ditch struggle.

In Indo-China, the Nixon government has resorted to still more cunning and sinister counter-revolutionary tactics. While talking glibly about "a negotiated settlement of the Viet Nam question," "troop withdrawal from south Viet Nam" and "pledge of respect for the peace and neutrality of Cambodia and Laos," etc., it is frantically expanding its war of aggression. In south Viet Nam, it is energetically carrying out the "Vietnamization" of its war of aggression against Viet Nam; it is stepping up its wanton bombing of Laos and has flagrantly brought the Thai accomplice troops into the battlefield of Laos in a feverish effort to expand its war of aggression against Viet Nam and Laos. At the same time, it is intensifying its aggression, intervention and subversion against the Kingdom of Cambodia. The reactionary coup d'etat staged on March 18 by the Lon Nol-Sirik Matak Rightist traitorous clique of Cambodia against Head of State Samdech Norodom Sihanouk is an important component part of the U.S. imperialists' plan to further expand their war of aggression in Indo-China.

U.S. imperialism had thought that by staging a reactionary coup d'etat through the instrumentality of its lackey the Lon Nol-Sirik Matak Rightist traitorous clique, it could control Cambodia at will and stamp out the Vietnamese people's war against U.S. aggression and for national salvation so as further to realize its wild ambition of forcibly occupying Indo-China. However, the development of the objective situation diametrically runs counter to the wishes of U.S. imperialism. On the international arena, the aggressive acts of U.S. imperialism and the brutal rule of the Cambodian Rightist traitorous clique have been condemned with one voice by the people throughout the world, and U.S. imperialism and the Cambodian Rightist traitorous clique are very much isolated; within Cambodia they have evoked the boundless indignation and strong resistance of the Cambodian people. In the last month and more, in response to the call of Head of State Samdech Norodom Sihanouk, the Cambodian people, weapons in hand, have risen up and are waging valiant and tenacious struggles against U.S. imperialism and its lackeys throughout the country, dealing telling blows at the reactionary rule of the Rightist traitorous clique.

In Viet Nam and Laos, U.S. imperialism has long been badly battered by the heroic Vietnamese and Laotian peoples, and now, further stretching its aggressive claws into Cambodia, it has put a new noose round its own neck, thus finding itself besieged ring upon ring by the three Indo-Chinese peoples and hastening its own defeat in this region.

The three Indo-Chinese peoples have a glorious tradition of unity against imperialism. In order to realize their sacred goal of national independence and liberation of their fatherland, the peoples of Cambodia, Laos and Viet Nam, going together through thick and thin and sharing difficulties and hardships, had fought shoulder to shoulder in the long struggle against French colonialism and Japanese imperialism. And now the common struggle against U.S. imperialist aggression has united the three Indo-Chinese peoples even more closely. We believe that the victorious convocation of this Summit Conference of the Indo-Chinese Peoples attended by the highest leaders of the four parties of the three countries will surely further strengthen the militant unity of the three peoples and push the struggle against U.S. aggression and for national salvation to a new stage.

The Chinese Government and people are deeply convinced that with the support of the people of the whole world, the heroic peoples of Cambodia, Laos and Viet Nam will surely win final victory in their struggle against U.S. aggression and for national salvation. No matter how U.S. imperialism and its accomplices try to undermine the Cambodian and other Indo-Chinese peoples' struggle against U.S. aggression and for national salvation by utilizing the United Nations or any other international organization or conference, they can never save themselves from their fate of complete defeat.

The three Indo-Chinese countries are China's close neighbours. The Chinese people and the three Indo-Chinese peoples have forged a profound militant friendship through protracted struggles against imperialism. The Chinese Government and people firmly support the five-point declaration solemnly made on March 23 by Cambodian Head of State Samdech Norodom Sihanouk, firmly support the Cambodian people in taking up arms and waging a patriotic just struggle to drive out U.S. imperialism and overthrow the traitors, firmly support the Laotian people in their valiant struggle against U.S. imperialist aggression and firmly support the Vietnamese people in their just struggle against U.S. aggression and for national salvation.

The Chinese people's great leader Chairman Mao has pointed out: "The 700 million Chinese people provide a powerful backing for the Vietnamese people; the vast expanse of China's territory is their reliable rear area." Likewise, the 700 million Chinese people provide a powerful backing for the three Indo-Chinese peoples and the vast expanse of China's territory is their reliable rear area. The three fraternal Indo-Chinese peoples may rest assured that in the common struggle against U.S. imperialism, the Chinese people will always stand by their side. Together we unite, together we fight and together we will win victory.

In conclusion, I propose a toast to the complete success of the Summit Conference of the Indo-Chinese Peoples. . . .

36. CHINESE EDITORIAL: PEOPLE OF ASIA, AFRICA, AND LATIN AMERICA WILL CERTAINLY WIN IN THEIR CAUSE OF UNITY AGAINST IMPERIALISM (September, 1970)*

The underdeveloped countries of Asia, Africa, and Latin America are of special interest to the People's Republic of China, which regards itself as the "champion of the anti-imperialistic front." This is a major propaganda statement commenting on the Third Conference of Non-Aligned Countries attended by more than fifty nations in September, 1970.

The Third Conference of the Heads of State and Government of Non-Aligned Countries in which more than 50 countries attended closed triumphantly on September 10 in Lusaka, capital of the Republic of Zambia. The speeches by the delegates of many countries and the declarations and resolutions adopted at the conference have reflected the common aspirations of the Asian, African and Latin American people for unity against imperialism and have made positive contribution to the struggles of the people of various countries against imperialism, colonialism and neo-colonialism, against racial discrimination and against domination of the world by the "superpowers." The Chinese people extend heartfelt congratulations on the successes achieved by the conference.

The recent Conference of the Heads of State and Government of Non-Aligned Countries was held in an excellent

*From *Jen-min Jih-pao* (September 14, 1970).

situation when a new high tide had emerged in the struggle of the people throughout the world against U.S. imperialism. The people of the three countries of Viet Nam, Laos and Cambodia are winning one victory after another in the war against U.S. aggression and for national salvation. The flames of struggle of the people of Korea, Japan, the Southeast Asian countries and other countries in Asia against U.S. imperialism and against the revival of Japanese militarism by the U.S. and Japanese reactionaries are raging more and more fiercely. The Palestinian and other Arab people are indomitably persisting in their armed struggle against the U.S.-Israeli aggressors. From Asia, Africa, Latin America to North America, Europe and Oceania, the storm of revolutionary struggles of the people of various countries is raging furiously. The current world situation has become still more favourable to the revolutionary struggles of the people of various countries and unfavourable to U.S.-led imperialism and colonialism, old and new.

At the conference the delegates of many countries sternly condemned U.S. imperialism for its aggression against the countries in Indo-China and the Middle East, and other Asian, African and Latin American countries and for its support to and connivance at Israeli Zionism, the colonial authorities of South Africa and Southern Rhodesia and the Portuguese colonialists. In their speeches they demanded the immediate, complete and unconditional withdrawal of the troops of the United States and those of its accomplices from south Viet Nam, and the recognition of the Provisional Revolutionary Government of the Republic of South Viet Nam. They expressed support for the Royal Government of National Union of Cambodia under the leadership of Samdech Norodom Sihanouk, Head of State of Cambodia, for the struggle of the three Indo-Chinese peoples against U.S. aggression and for national salvation, for the just struggle of the Palestinian and other Arab people against the U.S.-Israeli aggressors, and for the anti-imperialist and anti-colonialist struggles of the people of Angola, Mozambique, Guinea (Bissau), Zimbabwe, Azania (South Africa) and South West Africa. These just demands and positions have been reflected in the declarations and resolutions adopted by the conference. All this demonstrates the strong will of the Asian, African and Latin American peoples to oppose U.S. imperialism, colonialism, neo-colonialism, racial discrimination and national oppression.

At the conference, the delegates of many countries voiced their opposition to interference by the big powers and their opposition to power politics. Kenneth David Kaunda, President of the Republic of Zambia, the host country, pointed out that "the danger of weak nations being bullied by the more powerful ones still exists." A declaration adopted by the conference accused certain big powers of trying "to monopolize decision-making on world issues which are of vital concern to all countries." All this expresses the will and aspirations of all the countries and people cherishing national independence in Asia, Africa, Latin America and the rest of the world.

In the world today, there are one or two "superpowers" which are everywhere browbeating people with their power, bullying the weak and the small, and carrying out penetration, expansion and control in the countries of Asia, Africa, Latin America and the rest of the world in a vain attempt to dominate and divide the world. However, gone for ever are the days when a strong nation can bully a weak and a big nation can dictate the destiny of a small at will. So long as the Asian, African and Latin American countries and all countries and people in the world cherishing national independence rely on their own efforts, dare to fight and strengthen their unity, they can surely defeat the schemes of interference and aggression by the "superpowers," shake off the latter's control and grasp their destiny tightly in their own hands. Today, the struggle of the Asian, African and Latin American peoples against imperialism, colonialism and power politics and for winning and safeguarding national independence has become an irresistible historical current.

In their speeches at the Lusaka Conference, the delegates of many countries pointed out that the legitimate rights in the United Nations of the People's Republic of China must be restored. The Chinese people express their heartfelt thanks for the just stand taken by these countries. This is another indication that the Chinese people have friends all over the world. U.S. imperialism's criminal policy of hostility towards the Chinese people can only land itself in deeper isolation.

Our great leader Chairman Mao has pointed out: "The Chinese people regard victory in the anti-imperialist struggle of the people of Asia, Africa and Latin America as their own victory and give warm sympathy and support to all their anti-imperialist and anti-colonialist struggles."

The Chinese people who are armed with Mao Tsetung Thought firmly support the people of the Asian, African and Latin American countries and all the countries and people in the world that cherish national independence in their just struggle against imperialist aggression, oppression and interference, against colonialism and racial discrimination. We are firmly convinced that the people of the Asian, African and Latin American countries will surely march forward valiantly along the road of unity against imperialism and will win still greater victories while imperialism, colonialism and neo-colonialism will be dealt still heavier blows by the people of all countries and will meet with more bitter defeats.

37. CHINESE EDITORIAL: SUPPORT LATIN AMERICAN COUNTRIES STRUGGLING TO DEFEND THEIR TERRITORIAL SEA RIGHTS (November, 1970)*

This illustrates the new Chinese propaganda theme with respect to Latin America in the 1970's. China has changed from emphasizing revolutionary struggle aimed at overthrowing reactionary rule to a new tone in defense of the rights of territorial seas, among other popular nationalistic themes.

A new upsurge has recently emerged in the struggle of the Latin American countries and people against U.S. imperialist aggression and in defence of their rights of territorial seas. This marks a further decline of U.S. imperialism as the overlord in Latin America.

In defiance of the protests of the Latin American countries, U.S. imperialism has for a long time been sending its fishing fleets to intrude into the fishing grounds along the coasts of these countries to wantonly plunder their resources, behaving just like pirates on the high seas. To achieve the purpose of aggression and plunder, U.S. imperialism has unreasonably insisted that the limit of territorial waters should not extend beyond three nautical miles. The Latin American countries have waged a head-on struggle against U.S. imperialism in defence of their national interests and state sovereignty. Earlier in 1947, Chile and Peru took the lead in declaring that the limits of their

*From *Jen-min Jih-pao* (November 20, 1970).

territorial waters extend to 200 nautical miles. Later, similar action was taken by El Salvador and Ecuador. Up to last March, Nicaragua, Argentina, Panama, Uruguay and Brazil had one after another declared 200 nautical miles as the limit of their territorial waters. At the meeting on problems related to the law of the sea held by 21 Latin American countries last August, Mexico, Guatemala, Honduras, Costa Rica and Colombia, together with nine other countries which had declared the 200 nautical mile territorial limit, signed a joint declaration reaffirming that the Latin American countries have the right to fix the limits of their own territorial waters. Thus, altogether 14 Latin American countries have taken a unanimous principled stand on the rights of territorial seas. The fact that so many Latin American countries have joined together to take common action against U.S. imperialism is a significant development in the Latin American people's struggle against U.S. imperialism.

Our great leader Chairman Mao pointed out long ago: "The peoples of Latin America are not slaves obedient to U.S. imperialism." This wise thesis has been fully borne out by the daily mounting national-liberation movement in Latin America.

U.S. imperialism has always ridden roughshod over Latin America. It has never cared a straw for the sovereign rights of the Latin American countries. The fact that it is blustering and impervious to reason is fully exposed over the question of the rights of territorial seas. At first, it tried hard to impose the three nautical mile "limit" on the Latin American countries. But when the Latin American countries rose in force against this and when the situation went beyond its control, U.S. imperialism colluded and worked out jointly with social-imperialism a 12 nautical mile territorial limit, vainly trying to force this on the Latin American countries. In other words, when it insisted on a three nautical mile limit, others had to accept it and when it insists on a 12 nautical mile limit now, others must also act accordingly. But when many Latin American countries declared a 200 nautical mile territorial limit in accordance with their geographical, geological and biological characteristics and to meet the needs of using their own resources rationally, U.S. imperialism raved loudly against it. U.S. imperialism takes the resources of other countries as its own property, and regards the territorial waters of other countries as its "inland lakes." This is out-and-out gangster logic and pure imperialist power politics.

Tailing behind U.S. imperialism, social-imperialism has in recent years plotted a series of schemes over the question of the rights of territorial seas. It made secret deals with U.S. imperialism, or talked in a haughty tone about jointly "exploiting" oceanic resources at an international conference trying hard to cash in on the dirty game of plundering the Latin American countries. This despicable action has further revealed its aggressive and expansionist features.

However, the day has gone for ever when imperialism could do as it pleases in Latin America. On the question of the rights of territorial seas, U.S. imperialism has taken various measures to bring pressure to bear on the Latin American countries. It lodged "protests" at one time and threatened to terminate "aid" at another. But the result has turned out to be just the opposite. The more U.S. imperialism exerts pressure on them, the more numerous are the countries opposing it, and the more resolutely they fight back. They detained the fishing vessels which intruded into their territorial waters no matter to whom they belonged and dared to fire on them. Facts have shown that if only the weak and small countries dare to resist and struggle, U.S. imperialism can in no way coerce them into submission. Abetment by social-imperialism can only arouse strong opposition from the Latin American countries and people. One overlord or two overlords in league with each other cannot shake the just stand of the Latin American countries and people to defend their national sovereignty. The scheme of U.S. imperialism and social-imperialism to divide the oceans and the world by colluding with each other can never succeed.

In a talk with Latin American friends, Chairman Mao pointed out: "U.S. imperialism is our common enemy, and we all stand on the same front and need to unite with and support each other."

The countries and people of Latin America share the same fate with those of Asia and Africa as well as all others suffering from U.S. imperialist aggression. The common struggle against U.S. imperialism has naturally bound them together. The struggle of the Latin American countries and people in defence of their national sovereignty has won wide sympathy and support from many countries and people in Asia, Africa and other parts of the world. What U.S. imperialism fears is precisely the political consciousness and the unity of the people of all countries. So long as the people of various countries of the world unite and fight together, they will drive U.S. imperialism out of Asia, Africa and Latin America, and all other places occupied by it.

The Chinese people regard the struggle of the Latin American countries and people against U.S. imperialist aggression as their own struggle. They express firm support for the Latin American countries and people in their struggle against U.S. imperialist aggression and in defence of the rights of territorial seas. They are convinced that the Latin American countries and people will win new and greater victories so long as they strengthen unity and persist in their struggle.

38. COMMENTATOR: A GREAT EVENT IN THE ARAB COUNTRIES' CAUSE OF UNITY AGAINST IMPERIALISM (April, 1971)*

Although the USSR was the major ally of the UAR, Chinese support of the Arab cause in Palestine had kept the UAR's relations with Peking very strong. This authoritative statement made by a ranking Chinese official outlines China's approval of the formation of a new Federation of the Arab Republic.

The Heads of State of the United Arab Republic, Libya and Syria reached an agreement recently and declared that the three states would unite to form the Federation of Arab Republics. This is a great event in the Arab countries' cause of unity against imperialism.

The declaration on the setting up of the Federation of Arab Republics states solemnly "that there will be no negotiations and reconciliation with Israel; that not an inch of the Arab land is to be given up; that there will be no doing away with the Palestinian question or compromise over it." This solemn stand reflects the militant will of the Arab and Palestinian people to carry their struggle against the U.S.-Israeli aggressors through to the end, as well as their determination to recover their territories and to return to their homeland.

Israeli Zionism is a tool of aggression fostered by U.S. imperialism and a dagger thrust into the heart of the Arab

*From *Jen-min Jih-pao* (April 25, 1971).

countries. For more than 20 years it has committed heinous crimes against the Arab people by launching three large-scale wars of aggression. With the instigation and support of U.S. imperialism, the Israeli aggressors are today still very arrogant and they constantly threaten the security of the Arab countries. In an effort to safeguard the independence of the Arab nation and to recover the occupied territories, the Arab people will never cease their struggle against the Israeli aggressors. The principled stand against negotiations and reconciliation with Israel as laid down in the declaration conforms with the common aspirations of the broad masses of the Arab people and it is a blow to the plot for a Middle East Munich being hatched by U.S. imperialism and its accomplices.

Over the past 20 years and more, the Israeli Zionists occupied large tracts of Arab territories through wars of aggression. The Arab people's demand for the recovery of their lost land is entirely just and nobody has the right to stand in their way and undermine their demand. U.S. imperialism, however, has always supported Israel's acts of aggression; it flagrantly announced not long ago that it has "never said that Israel had to withdraw from all territory." This is an outrageous infringement upon the sovereignty of the Arab countries and a rabid provocation to the Arab people. Every inch of the Arab territories the Israeli aggressors have occupied must be recovered. The plots which U.S. imperialism and its accomplices are playing with in this respect will never be tolerated by the broad masses of the Arab and Palestinian people.

Through their protracted and arduous struggle, the Palestinian guerrillas have grown into an important force of the Arab people for opposing the U.S.-Israeli aggressors. While repeatedly instigating the Jordanian reactionaries to suppress the Palestinian guerrillas, U.S. imperialism is resorting to such political schemes as that for a "Palestinian state." By employing such counter-revolutionary dual tactics, it is attempting to ultimately liquidate the Palestinian revolution. The Palestinian people have waged a tit-for-tat struggle against the U.S. imperialists' counter-revolutionary dual tactics. Their just struggle is winning increasingly great support from the people in Asia, Africa and the rest of the world. Victory certainly belongs to the Palestinian and other Arab people.

Our great leader Chairman Mao pointed out: "The Chinese people regard victory in the anti-imperialist struggle of the people of Asia, Africa and Latin America as their own victory and give warm sympathy and support to all their anti-imperialist and anti-colonialist struggles."

The Chinese people resolutely support the people of Arab countries in their struggle against U.S. imperialism and Israeli Zionism, and support their desire to achieve unity and solidarity in a way of their own choice. We are convinced that the Arab countries and people will continuously push forward their cause of unity against imperialism by overcoming all kinds of obstacles and difficulties on their way ahead.

CHAPTER FIVE:
Policies on Economic Aid, Trade, and Cultural Relations

The Chinese Communists place tremendous importance not only on economic aid but on trade and cultural relations as well in their dealings with foreign countries. Yeh Chi-chuang, Minister of Foreign Trade, once stated that "foreign trade is one of the component parts of our national economy . . . and serves our industrial and agricultural production as well as socialist construction of our country."[1]

In the formative years of the People's Republic, because of her foreign policy "lean to one side," China was ready to become dependent on Soviet aid in spite of the leadership's hopes to avoid any further dependence on foreign powers. And the initial Soviet aid to China was indeed impressive, as we have noted in our study of Sino-Soviet relations in Chapter Three.

However, contrary to the norms of international trade relations, prices of imported commodities from the USSR (as noted in the Introduction) were generally much higher than prices of similar goods produced in the People's Republic of China. China also discovered that the Soviet Union used trade and aid to implement her political goals of subduing China into a subservient position. Because of these major dissatisfactions, China switched her trade to non-Soviet-bloc countries, resulting in seventy-five percent of Peking's trade being transacted with non-Communist countries in the 1960's.

This new practice displeased the Russians, especially in view of statistics indicating that China's international trade steadily grew from $1.2 billion in 1950 to $4.3 billion in 1959. Because of her domestic difficulties China's trade suffered somewhat, most noticeably during the Cultural Revolution (1966-68). The following table indicates, however, a new upward trend with at least the thirty-six non-Communist states.

1 Hsin Hua News Release (Canton), September 2, 1959.

China's Trade 1967-69[1]

(36 non-communist trading partners)

US$ million

	Imports			Exports		
	1969	1968	1967	1969	1968	1967
Argentina	0.32	0.58	6.45	0.76	0.29	0.30
Australia	119.01	89.30	194.94	34.75	39.48	27.92
Austria	4.09	6.80	13.72	9.39	8.25	8.40
Belgium	16.35	19.96	22.67	12.40	11.83	13.04
Canada	113.24	151.01	84.46	25.36	21.68	23.19
Ceylon	40.37	32.68	31.52	47.36	41.23	38.42
Denmark	1.30	2.11	5.97	9.13	8.27	8.88
Finland	5.70	11.52	12.00	7.43	6.97	9.41
France	44.41	87.68	93.22	75.99	53.34	48.11
Ghana	1.12	0.56	0.70	4.27	1.62	0.79
Greece	0.02	—	—	0.39	0.13	1.07
Hong Kong	6.15	7.36	8.37	445.50	400.89	397.25
Iran	0.86	1.54	3.66	1.79	2.29	5.88
Italy	56.33	61.08	73.58	64.17	48.01	57.76
Japan	390.83	325.44	288.32	234.56	224.20	269.46
Jordan	0.60	0.50	0.02	4.90	4.59	3.97
Kenya	1.34	1.23	3.06	3.22	4.47	2.45
Morocco	6.82	7.28	8.31	13.16	11.96	13.17
Netherlands	23.00	28.87	12.25	27.87	27.15	27.78
New Zealand	4.59	5.75	10.70	5.65	4.55	4.08
Norway	4.76	6.44	7.49	5.94	5.42	5.16
Pakistan	28.88	25.49	34.69	26.42	29.62	33.66
Peru	—	0.10	—	4.10	4.19	—
Portugal	0.01	—	0.03	0.26	0.13	0.19
Singapore	57.10	26.53	31.32	136.72	150.30	124.73
Spain	0.81	1.35	0.36	1.11	0.98	1.01
Sudan	18.47	13.89	13.00	14.00	17.21	17.06
Sweden	11.81	23.78	43.94	18.57	18.23	17.01
Switzerland	14.51	19.51	21.35	18.17	16.00	17.43
Tanzania	10.89	7.68	7.72	11.10	12.08	8.68
Tunisia	—	0.78	0.54	0.02	0.52	1.16
Turkey	0.09	1.05	0.62	0.20	0.24	0.14
Uganda	1.24	4.88	3.96	2.51	2.89	2.21
United Kingdom	130.78	69.83	108.00	90.55	82.26	81.60
West Germany	157.92	173.75	206.53	88.24	85.30	76.54
Yugoslavia	0.60	1.00	0.97	1.00	0.20	14.19
TOTAL	1,274.32	1,217.31	1,354.44	1,446.96	1,346.77	1,362.10

1 Source: *1971 Far Eastern Economic Review Yearbook*, p. 141.

China's Trade 1968-70

US$ million

	Imports 1968	Imports 1969	Imports 1970	Exports 1968	Exports 1969	Exports 1970
Australia (7)	60.84	55.74	79.81	16.15	18.62	20.82
Belgium	8.42 (8)	8.07 (6)	8.36 (5)	4.88 (6)	6.04 (6)	3.90 (5)
Canada (7)	93.10	91.53	93.08	11.68	16.51	10.85
France	67.68 (7)	15.10 (6)	45.67 (6)	15.80 (6)	35.00 (6)	42.94 (6)
Germany, West (7)	85.30	92.10	102.50	45.70	45.70	49.90
Hong Kong (9)	5.27	4.33	7.77	277.72	314.91	317.63
Italy (6)	28.50	30.50	27.70	22.10	32.50	34.80
Japan	221.80 (9)	205.90 (8)	391.60 (8)	157.10 (9)	152.80 (8)	151.80 (8)
Netherlands	5.82 (6)	16.44 (6)	3.22 (3)	13.06 (6)	13.27 (6)	7.50 (3)
Singapore (7)	15.10 (7)	40.20 (8)	19.80 (7)	91.70 (7)	96.40 (8)	74.40 (7)
Sweden	13.32 (7)	7.68 (6)	6.56 (6)	10.07 (7)	9.48 (6)	10.17 (6)
UK (8)	41.35	79.97	76.40	54.48	61.25	53.48
TOTAL	646.50	647.56	862.47	720.44	802.48	778.19

(Figures in brackets indicate number of months covered)

We must realize that foreign trade is very much a part of Peking's domestic economic planning, as Alexander Eckstein wrote: "In the absence of these imports [from foreign trade], China's economic growth might possibly have fallen from an average annual rate of 6-7 per cent to 3-5 per cent."[1] And China built up her trade and her aid programs to non-Communist countries to coincide with her own economic development, thus attempting to formulate a coordinated effort for mutual benefit, as illustrated in the following table (see Documents 41, 42):[2]

Year	Most Important Trade Agreements	Most Important Aid Agreements
1952	Ceylon, Japan	
1953	Indonesia	
1954[3]	Burma, India	
1955	– – –	
1956	Cambodia, Egypt, Syria	Cambodia, Nepal
1957	Afghanistan	Ceylon
1958[4]	Yemen, Morocco	Yemen
1959	Iraw, Tunisia	
1960	Mali, Ghana	Burma, Indonesia, Mali, Ghana
1962	Sudan	Laos
1963	Somalia	Syia, Algeria
1964	Congo (B), C.A.R., Algeria, Burundi, Kenya	Tanzania, Congo (B)
1965	Tanzania	Pakistan, Afghanistan, C.A.R.
1966[5]	– – –	
1967	Mauretania, Zambia	Mauretania
1968	– – –	
1969[6]	Pakistan, Singapore, Ceylon, Sudan	Pakistan, Nepal, Tanzania, Zambia, Congo (B), Guinea, Algeria, Mozambique, Mali

1 Alexander Eckstein, *Communist China's Economic Growth and Foreign Trade* (New York, McGraw-Hill, 1966), p. 260.
2 Source: Bernhard Grossman, "Intern'l Economic Relations of the PRC," *Asian Survey* (September, 1970), p. 794, with additions by this author.
3 1953-57—First Five-Year Plan.
4 1958-62—Second Five-Year Plan.
5 1966-68—Cultural Revolution.
6 1969—Post Cultural Revolution.

As a clarification of China's policy of self-reliance, Chou En-lai outlined a program of Eight Principles on Economic and Technical Assistance during his first visits to African countries in 1953-54. They are:

1. The Chinese government always bases itself in the principle of equality and mutual benefit in providing aid to other countries. It never regards such aid as a kind of unilateral alms but as something mutual.
2. In providing aid to other countries, the Chinese government strictly respects the sovereignty of the recipient countries and never asks for any privileges or attaches any conditions.
3. The Chinese government provides economic aid in the form of interest-free or low-interest loans.
4. In providing aid to other countries, the purpose of the Chinese government is not to make the recipient countries dependent on China but to help them embark on the road of self-reliance step by step.
5. The Chinese government tries its best to help the recipient countries build projects which require less investment while yielding quicker results.
6. The Chinese government provides the best-quality equipment and material of its own manufacture at international market prices.
7. In giving any particular technical assistance, the Chinese government will see to it that the personnel are best qualified.
8. Chinese experts will have the same standards of living as those of the recipient country (see Document 40).

Are there any "credibility gaps" in China's publicly announced policies and her actual practices in conducting international aid and trade relations with developing countries?

Complete records still are yet to be analyzed; however, initial statistics are impressive. For example, by the end of 1965 China already made a total $2-billion economic grant to some twenty-five underdeveloped countries, out of which 74.5 percent were interest-free loans, 16.6 percent donations, and only 8.9 percent had a 2.0-2.5 percent interest charge.

In addition, several individual aid projects were very much pointed in her favor. One case was China's relations with Ceylon, a non-Communist state. China concluded a trade agreement with Ceylon in December, 1952. Under the provisions of the agreement, China guaranteed a stable market for Ceylon's rubber, among other commodities, for five years. In 1957, the agreement was renewed and a new aid pact was signed. And China has never attempted to exert direct political influence on Ceylon, in spite of Peking's ability to do so (see Document 39).

Another illustration involves China's agreement to undertake the costly ($340,000,000-$400,000,000) and difficult project of constructing the 1,060-mile Tanzania-Zambia Railway, especially after the project was rejected by the World Bank, the United States, and the USSR, among other powers. China undertook this costly project at considerable self-sacrifice, as George T. Yu wrote: "It has been estimated that China had added only 10,000 miles of railway since 1949 to the mere 12,500 miles which the regime inherited. It could be said that China will be deprived of the 1,060 miles of railway being contributed to Tanzania's and Zambia's development. . . . It (therefore) can be seen as a role response to specific Tanzanian expectations which China felt obligated to perform, even at great self-sacrifice"[1] (see Document 44).

The pattern of Sino-Japanese relations, on the other hand, contrasts considerably with the examples of Sino-Ceylonese or Sino-Tanzania relations. Here China used both the trade and cultural exchanges as a weapon to influence Japanese political attitudes and domestic policies. For instance, China temporarily suspended trade with Japan in 1958 in order "to influence the outcome of the then Japanese general election . . . and to influence Japanese public opinion and to help the Leftist parties."[2] And Chou En-lai himself had also violated his own pledge by giving a new set of policy directives to a Japanese trade delegation in Peking in 1960 strongly injecting political considerations in reaching trade agreements (see Document 43).

Finally, China has always been rather successful in her practice of "people's diplomacy" in cultural exchange programs

---

1 George T. Yu, *China and Tanzania* (Berkeley, University of California Center for Chinese Studies, China Research Monographs Number Five, 1970), p. 58.

2 George P. Jan, "Japan's Trade with Communist China," *Asian Survey* (December, 1969), p. 910.

with foreign countries.[1] Since 1955, the People's Republic has opened her gates to citizen groups from all over the world. Thousands of delegations from the Middle East, Africa, Europe, and Latin America have visited China. Chinese also visited other countries with their opera companies and acrobatic or sports teams. Bookstores in the third world were flooded with inexpensive Chinese literature.[2] China also began broadcasting daily foreign language news and cultural programs in 1956 with worldwide services. Radio Peking's daily English-language transmissions serve as a good illustration:

East and South Africa, Peking time: 00:00-01:00
West and North Africa: 03:30-05:30
Europe: 04:30-06:30
North America (East Coast): 08:00-21:00
North America (West Coast): 11:00-13:00
Australia and New Zealand: 16:30-18:30
Southeast Asia: 20:00-22:00
South Asia: 02:00-03:00, 22:00-24:00[3]

Cultural relations in the modern sense have an impressive history. In fact, the major Western colonial powers, notably France, Germany, and Great Britain, all came at the turn of the century to rely more and more on cultural influence as an instrument of achieving their foreign policy objectives. [4]

Chinese success in this art of diplomacy can be seen especially in her relations with Latin American countries. Prior to the establishment of the People's Republic in 1949, very few people in Latin America either cared where China was located or knew what was happening there. And by 1965—in only fifteen years—there was "more talk of China than of the Soviet Union,"[5] although no official relations had been established

1 Herbert Passin, *China's Cultural Diplomacy* (New York, Praeger, 1963).

2 The new Constitution of the Chinese Communist Party, adopted on April 14, 1969, has been translated into twenty-nine foreign languages, including Arabic, Hindi, Swahili, Urdu, and Esperanto. See *Peking Review* (July 2, 1971).

3 *Peking Review* (February 5, 1971).

4 See Robert Blum, ed., *Cultural Affairs and Foreign Relations* (Englewood Cliffs, Prentice Hall for the American Assembly, 1963).

5 Victor Alba, "The Chinese in Latin America," *China Quarterly*, No. 5 (January-March, 1961), p. 53.

with any non-Communist Latin American states (only Cuba recognized Peking in 1960).

"Cultural relations" is often synonymous with "subversion" and "propaganda"; they do nevertheless have a sort of dynamism that is far more compelling at times than the planned diplomacy, as illustrated by the reopening of Sino-American relations after twenty-two years of open hostility by a handful of ping-pong players (see Document 45).

39. AGREEMENTS ON ECONOMIC AID, TRADE, AND PAYMENTS BETWEEN CHINA AND CEYLON (September, 1957)*

Ceylon was the first non-Communist country to conclude a successful trade agreement with China, in December, 1952. According to that agreement, China guaranteed a stable market for Ceylon's rubber, among other commodities, for five years. The following are two additional agreements signed on September 19, 1957: (1) a new international aid pact with Ceylon, under which China granted 75 million Ceylon Rupees (about U.S. $15.8 million), and (2) a renewal of the 1952 trade pact.

[I]

For the purpose of promoting friendly co-operation between Ceylon and China and of strengthening the friendship between the two peoples, on the basis of the Resolution on Economic Co-operation adopted at the Bandung Conference, and the five principles of mutual respect for territorial integrity and sovereignty, non-aggression, non-interference in each other's internal affairs, equality and mutual benefit and peaceful co-existence, and animated by the lofty desire of the two countries to give each other mutual support and assistance, the Government of the People's Republic of China has decided, after negotiations between the two Contracting Parties, to grant economic aid without repayment and without any attached conditions to the Government of Ceylon for its Rubber Replanting Subsidy Program. For this purpose, the two Parties have reached agreement as follows:

* From *United Nations Treaty Series*, Vol. CCCXXXVII (1959), No. 4822.

Article I

The Government of the People's Republic of China agrees to grant economic aid to the Government of Ceylon for a period of five years from the date on which this Agreement comes into force of 15,000,000 Ceylon Rupees annually, and with a total value of 75,000,000 Ceylon Rupees for the period of five years.

Article II

The assistance granted to the Government of Ceylon by the Government of China in accordance with the provisions of Article I of this Agreement shall be made in commodities; the specific commodities shall be negotiated separately by representatives of the two Governments.

Article III

The prices of all commodities supplied to Ceylon by China under this Agreement shall be quoted in Ceylon Rupees at international market price levels (F. O. B. prices).

Article IV

The organs to carry out this Agreement shall be the Ministry of Foreign Trade of the People's Republic of China and the Ministry of Finance of Ceylon.

Article V

Technical details regarding the maintenance of accounts in connection with the implementation of this Agreement shall be worked out by the People's Bank of China and the Central Bank of Ceylon.

Article VI

This Agreement shall come into force on 1st January, 1958, and remain effective for a period of five years.

Done and signed in Peking this 19th day of September, 1957, in two copies, each in the Chinese and English languages, both texts being equally authentic.

[Signatures]

[II]

The Government of Ceylon and the Government of the People's Republic of China, for the purpose of further developing the friendship between the Governments and the peoples of the two countries and of strengthening the economic and trade relations between the two countries have, on the basis of equality and mutual benefit, reached agreement as follows:

Article I

The two Contracting Parties will take all appropriate measures to develop trade between their two countries and agree to facilitate the exchange of goods between the two countries.

Article II

The trade between the two countries shall be based on the principle of a balance between the values of imports and exports.

Article III

The two annexed Schedules A and B which constitute an integral part of this Agreement show the export commodities of each country. This Agreement shall not preclude trade in commodities not mentioned in the annexed Schedules A and B.

Article IV

The two Contracting Parties shall, before the end of October each year, conclude a protocol of the commodities to be exchanged between the two parties in the following calendar year. This protocol shall specify:

(1) The aggregate value together with the names and approximate quantities of the commodities which the two Contracting Parties will undertake to import and export during the year covered by the protocol and,

(2) The aggregate value together with the names and approximate quantities of the commodities which the two Contracting Parties will endeavour to import and export during the year covered by the protocol.

Article V

The prices of commodities to be imported and exported under this Agreement shall be fixed at international market price levels.

Article VI

The exchange of goods between the two countries shall be carried out in accordance with the import and export and foreign exchange regulations in force from time to time in each country.

Article VII

The two Contracting Parties agree that trade under this Agreement, including trade under the protocols signed in terms of Article IV, may be conducted through the state trading organizations of China and Ceylon as well as through other importers and exporters in the two countries.

Article VIII

The two Contracting Parties will grant to each other most-favoured-nation treatment in respect of the issue of import and export licenses, and the levy of customs duties, taxes, and any other charges imposed on or in connection with the importation, exportation and transshipment of commodities, subject to the following exceptions:

(1) Any special advantages which are accorded or may be accorded in the future by either of the Contracting Parties to contiguous countries in order to facilitate frontier trade and,

(2) Any special advantages which are accorded or may be accorded in the future under any preferential system of which either of the Contracting Parties is or may become a member.

Article IX

The two Contracting Parties agree that the payment arrangements between the two countries under this Agreement shall be in accordance with the following terms:

1. The Government of China shall open two accounts in the Central Bank of Ceylon, Colombo, styled Government of China Account "A" and Government of China Account "B".

The Government of Ceylon shall open two accounts in the People's Bank of China, Peking, styled Government of Ceylon Account "A" and Government of Ceylon Account "B".

The above accounts shall bear no interest and shall be free of charges.

2. Payments for the purchase of commodities which the two Contracting Parties have undertaken to import and export in terms of the yearly protocol referred to in Article IV of this Agreement, and payments for the relative incidental expenses, shall be made through the "A" accounts mentioned in paragraph (1) above.

Payments for other purchases and the relative incidental expenses as well as other payments approved by the Foreign Exchange Control authorities of both countries shall be made through the "B" accounts mentioned in paragraph (1) above.

The phrase "relative incidental expenses" shall mean the expenses of services in connection with the exchange of goods such as transport charges including charter hire of ships and connected expenses, insurance, arbitration awards, warehousing and customs fees, agents' commissions, advertising, brokerage and other such charges.

3. The accounts specified in paragraph (1) above shall be maintained in Ceylon Rupees.

4. Any residual balances in the "A" accounts specified in paragraph (1) above, outstanding on 31st March of the succeeding year, shall be settled by payment in Pound Sterling or any other currency mutually acceptable immediately after the accounts have been reconciled.

Payments in respect of contracts entered into under the annual protocol of any year, which are made after 31st March of the succeeding year shall be brought to account under the "A" account of the succeeding year.

5. The balances in the "B" accounts specified in paragraph (1) above shall be reviewed once every quarter by the two Contracting Parties for the purpose of ensuring that trade between the two countries progresses in balance.

Any balances in the "B" accounts remaining outstanding at the end of each calendar year, shall be settled as far as possible by delivery of goods during the first three months of the succeeding year. Any residual balances in the "B" accounts still remaining outstanding on 31st March of the succeeding year, shall be settled by payment in Pound Sterling or any other currency mutually acceptable immediately after the accounts have been reconciled.

6. The exchange rate for settlement of balances contemplated in paragraphs (4) and (5) above shall be the middle of the Central Bank of Ceylon's buying and selling rates for Pound Sterling or other currency at the time of payment.

7. The People's Bank of China and the Central Bank of Ceylon shall work out the technical details necessary for the implementation of this Article.

Article X

This Agreement shall come into force on 1st January, 1958, and shall remain in force for a period of five years. This Agreement may be extended by negotiation of both parties three months before its expiration.

This Agreement is signed in Peking, this 19th day of September, 1957, in two copies, each written in the Chinese and English languages, and both texts being equally authentic.

[Signatures]

SCHEDULE "A"

List of Export Commodities from Ceylon to China

1.	Cardamom.	8.	Pepper.
2.	Cinnamon.	9.	Rubber.
3.	Citronella oil.	10.	Handicrafts.
4.	Copra.	11.	Precious and semi-precious
5.	Coconut oil.		stones.
6.	Other coconut products	12.	Others.
7.	Cocoa beans.		

40. CHOU EN-LAI'S INTERVIEW WITH REPORTERS OF THE GHANA NEWS AGENCY (January, 1964)*

This is a major policy announcement with respect to countries of the Third World made by Chou En-lai in his first trip to Africa in 1963-64, before reporters of the Ghana News Agency in Accra, January 15, 1965.

Question one. May we know the purpose of this tour of African countries?

Answer: The purpose of our present visit to Africa is to enhance the mutual understanding between China and friendly African countries, strengthen the traditional friendship between the Chinese people and the African people, further develop the relations of friendship and co-operation between China and the African countries, increase our knowledge and learn useful things from the African people.

The Chinese people and the African people share the same experience of suffering from imperialist and colonialist aggression and oppression and have before them the common fighting task of opposing imperialism and old and new colonialism. China and the independent countries of Africa can support and closely co-operate with each other in consolidating national independence, safeguarding state sovereignty, developing national economy, promoting Asian-African solidarity and defending world peace.

Question two. What are your impressions of your visit to the Republic of Ghana?

Answer: We have spent five pleasant days in the Republic of Ghana which made a good impression on us.

We have seen that the people of Ghana who have won independence are a warm-hearted people, courageous and firm, vigorous and dynamic. With such a people the Republic of Ghana will certainly march victoriously along the path of independent development by relying on their own strength.

We have seen that the Republic of Ghana has made marked progress in economic and cultural development under the leadership of President Kwame Nkrumah. I believe that by

* From *Afro-Asian Solidarity Against Imperialism* (Peking, Foreign Language Press, 1964), pp. 146-50.

consolidating independence politically and relying on its own efforts economically the Republic of Ghana will certainly be able to build itself into a prosperous and strong country step by step.

We are deeply moved by the most sincere and warm welcome accorded us by the Ghanaian people. This is a manifestation of the profound friendship of the Ghanaian people for the Chinese people. With the passage of time, the friendship between the Chinese and the Ghanaian peoples will certainly develop continuously.

Question three. What in your opinion are the prospects for the developing countries of Africa?

Answer: The African people have suffered from the darkest rule and the most cruel oppression of the Western colonialists. The African people have waged and are waging heroic struggles against imperialism and old and new colonialism. Now the banners of independence and freedom are being raised one after another on the African continent. The future of the African people is infinitely bright. By closely relying on the strength of their own people, strengthening unity and heightening vigilance, the new emerging independent African countries will surely be able to smash all intrigues and plots of the imperialists and reactionaries and preserve their independence and sovereignty.

By bringing into full play the boundless potentialities of their people and making full use of their rich natural resources, the new emerging independent African countries will certainly be able to wipe out step by step the poverty and backwardness caused by prolonged colonial domination and continuously score new success in developing their national economy, culture and language.

By assisting each other and striving for common development, strengthening their solidarity and promoting unity, the African countries will be able to augment their strength in a concerted fight against imperialsim and in the reconstruction of their respective countries.

The African people are marching forward with gallant strides. The imperialists and old and new colonialists can never turn back the trend of African history. An independent, united and unified, prosperous, rich and strong new Africa is bound to emerge on earth and make great contributions towards the cause of human progress.

Question four. Do you think the establishment of Chinese industries in Ghana will be some of the results of your visit?

Answer: The aid China offers to all friendly new emerging countries is based on socialist principles and the principle of respecting the sovereignty of the countries concerned. It never takes the form of the export of capital, direct investment and profit-seeking. It consists of providing economic and technical assistance to the governments of these countries and helping these countries develop their own independent national economies.

In providing economic and technical aid to other countries, the Chinese Government strictly observes the following eight principles:

First, the Chinese Government always bases itself on the principle of equality and mutual benefit in providing aid to other countries. It never regards such aid as a kind of unilateral alms but as something mutual. Through such aid the friendly new emerging countries gradually develop their own national economy, free themselves from colonial control and strengthen the anti-imperialist forces in the world. This is in itself a tremendous support to China.

Second, in providing aid to other countries, the Chinese Government strictly respects the sovereignty of the recipient countries, and never asks for any privileges or attaches any conditions.

Third, the Chinese Government provides economic aid in the form of interest-free or low-interest loans and extends the time limit for the repayment so as to lighten the burden of the recipient countries as far as possible.

Fourth, in providing aid to other countries, the purpose of the Chinese Government is not to make the recipient countries dependent on China but to help them embark on the road of self-reliance step by step.

Fifth, the Chinese Government tries its best to help the recipient countries build projects which require less investment while yielding quicker results, so that the recipient governments may increase their income and accumulate capital.

Sixth, the Chinese Government provides the best-quality equipment and material of its own manufacture at international market prices. If the equipment and material provided by the Chinese Government are not up to the agreed specifications and quality, the Chinese Government undertakes to replace them.

Seventh, in giving any particular technical assistance, the Chinese Government will see to it that the personnel of the recipient country fully master such technique.

Eighth, the experts dispatched by the Chinese Government to help in construction in the recipient countries will have the same standard of living as the experts of the recipient country. The Chinese experts are not allowed to make any special demands or enjoy any special amenities.

41. TSENG YUN: HOW CHINA CARRIES OUT THE POLICY OF SELF-RELIANCE (June, 1965)*

This is a major position paper outlining China's important policy of self-reliance especially for the benefit of readers of the underdeveloped countries by a Chinese economist.

The Chinese people have adhered to the policy of self-reliance both in revolution and in construction. It is a policy of key importance.

Marxist-Leninists see the people as the makers of history and the peoples of the various countries as the makers of the histories of their countries. Revolution cannot be exported. The revolution in a country can only be made by its own people. In line with this principle, the Chinese people, led by the Chinese Communist Party, relied mainly on themselves in their protracted and arduous struggle to overthrow the reactionary rule of imperialism, feudalism and bureaucrat-capitalism and carry the democratic revolution to victory.

After the founding of the People's Republic of China, the Chinese people continued to follow the policy of self-reliance in socialist construction. Relying mainly on their own efforts, they rapidly restored the run-down, war-ravaged economy left by the reactionary Kuomintang regime, started large-scale planned economic construction, developed agriculture and laid a preliminary and solid foundation for an independent industry.

The practical experience of the Chinese people has fully testified to the correctness of the view set forth by the Central Committee of the Chinese Communist Party in the *Proposal*

---

* From *Peking Review* (June 18, 1965), pp. 12-15.

Concerning the General Line of the International Communist Movement that "every socialist country must rely mainly on itself in construction."

Main Aspects of the Policy

What are the main aspects of the policy of self-reliance during the period of socialist revolution and socialist construction?

First, self-reliance means to rely on the strength and diligent labour of our people to carry on economic construction.

Man is the most valuable asset of society and the leading factor in the social productive forces. After the victory of the democratic revolution, China immediately took steps to carry out the socialist revolution and free all the working people in the country from the system of exploitation. Our working people have thus become the real masters of their country. They show boundless enthusiasm for socialist construction, in which their vital interests lie. This enthusiasm has proved to be a great dynamic force in our socialist construction and the decisive factor in the high-speed development of our national economy. In undertaking any task and considering any problem, we always take full account of the fact that China has 650 million hard-working and courageous people.

In addition to the socialist system, it is essential to have a Marxist-Leninist line in order to mobilize the initiative of the broad masses of the people fully and make steady progress in socialist construction.

In 1958, the Central Committee of the Chinese Communist Party and Comrade Mao Tse-tung, summing up experience in China's socialist construction on the basis of the fundamental principles of Marxism-Leninism, put forward the general line of going all out, aiming high and achieving greater, quicker, better and more economical results in building socialism. This is a Marxist-Leninist general line—a general line that brings all positive factors into play for the building of socialism.

The achievements of the Taching Oilfield and the Tachai Agricultural Production Brigade clearly demonstrate what power the Chinese people can display under the guidance of the general line of socialist construction.

Relying on their own efforts and working under most difficult conditions, the Taching oil workers got a full knowledge of the size and reserves of a big oilfield in a little over a year and built a modern oil enterprise in the short span of three years. Displaying a similar spirit of self-reliance, the Tachai peasants built up their farm with industry and thrift. By a collective effort they terraced seven ravines and scores of gullies and turned them into fertile land. Thus, in a relatively short period, they succeeded in transforming a poor hilly region into an area giving high yields of grain and other crops.

We Chinese people used to be looked down upon by the imperialists. Even when we had won our basic victory in the revolution, the imperialists did not believe that we would be able to undertake construction. Dean Acheson, former Secretary of State of the United States, and his like predicted that the Chinese Communist Party would never be able to solve the problem of feeding the people. They calculated that we would inevitably have to beg the U.S. imperialists for help. But Comrade Mao Tse-tung, on behalf of the Chinese people, solemnly declared: "Once China's destiny is in the hands of the people, China, like the sun rising in the east, will illuminate every corner of the land with a brilliant flame, swiftly clean up the mire left by the reactionary government, heal the wounds of war and build a new, powerful and prosperous people's republic worthy of the name." This prediction of Comrade Mao Tse-tung has become a living reality: A powerful and prosperous People's Republic of China now stands towering in the East.

Secondly, to build socialism self-reliantly means to make full use of all available resources in our country.

China has an area of 9,600,000 square kilometres and rich natural resources. Before the liberation, because of imperialist aggression and the reactionary rule of landlords and bureaucrat-capitalists, the rich natural resources of our country were far from being explored and developed; those resources that had been opened up were recklessly plundered by the foreign imperialists and the reactionary rulers at home and suffered great damage and waste. Thus, when China began her socialist construction, certain natural resources were found to be lacking. In most cases, however, it was not that these things were really lacking but that they had not yet been discovered or extensively exploited due to scientific and technological backwardness or other causes. With the establishment of our socialist system and progress in our science and technology, our ability to know and change nature has grown tremendously. With soaring revolutionary spirit, our people have forged steadily ahead in the conquest of nature and in the endeavour to explore and develop the natural resources of our country.

The imperialists have in the past spread all kinds of lies about China lacking the natural resources necessary for industrial development. During the 1930s, James Arthur Salter, a British bourgeois economist who was previously on the staff of the imperialist-controlled League of Nations, came to China to make an economic survey of the country. After this survey, it was declared that China did not have the necessary natural resources at home to develop heavy industry and thus could only develop agriculture and industries to process farm products. China was also considered an "oil-poor" country by some imperialist know-alls and bourgeois experts. The liberated Chinese people, however, have worked miracles in their land: They have found various natural resources and built new branches of heavy industry one after the other. They have also exploded the myth that China is oil-poor. Rich oil deposits have been found. An oil industry has been swiftly developed and China is now basically self-sufficient in oil.

Thirdly, to build socialism self-reliantly means to get the necessary funds for construction through internal accumulation. Being a socialist country led by a Marxist-Leninist party, China cannot procure funds for construction by contracting enslaving foreign loans at the expense of her sovereignty and independence, by resorting to imperialist methods of seizing colonies and grabbing the fruits of labour of other countries, or by launching wars of aggression and extorting war indemnities from the defeated countries. All this is incompatible with our socialist system. Our only source of funds for construction is our people's efforts to increase production and practise economy.

Before the liberation, as a result of ruthless exploitation by imperialism, feudalism and bureaucrat-capitalism, our industrial and agricultural level was low, our national income was small, and a considerable portion of this income, small as it was, was taken by our domestic and foreign exploiters. After the liberation, we abolished all privileges enjoyed by the imperialists in old China, confiscated the bureaucrat-capitalist enterprises and turned them into enterprises owned by the people's state. We also carried out land reform throughout the country, distributed to the landless and land-poor peasants a total of 700 million *mu* of land formerly owned by the landlords, and thus relieved the peasants of the burden of an annual rent of over 30 million tons of grain paid to the landlords. Immediately after land reform we took steps to realize agricultural collectivization step by step. At the same time, we brought about the socialist transformation of capitalist industry and commerce owned by the national bourgeoisie. With the means of production transferred to ownership by the whole people or collective ownership by the working people, the material wealth created by the working people is no longer turned into profits for the imperialists or capitalists or land rent paid to the landlords. Apart from that part allocated for raising the living standards of the working people and aiding other countries, it can now all be used as funds for construction.

In order to accumulate more funds for construction, while on the one hand endeavouring to increase production, we have resolutely followed the policy of building our country with industry and frugality and of running all our enterprises industriously and thriftily. We have advocated the practice of economy and opposed waste and extravagance in construction. A small sum saved by an enterprise or organization may seem negligible by itself, but, as China is a big country, a surprisingly big sum will be saved up if each enterprise and organization in the country does its bit of saving.

Our is a planned economy. All construction funds are concentrated and used according to plan. In making our plans for capital construction, we apply the principle of "concentrating forces to fight a war of annihilation." In order to ensure the most rational use of funds and get the maximum economic results from them, we concentrate our funds on the most urgently needed projects so that they can be completed and commissioned as quickly as possible and refrain from building or postpone the building of those projects which are not necessary or not urgently needed. This constitutes the greatest economy in the use of funds.

In undertaking large-scale socialist construction, we have not borrowed a penny in loans from the capitalist countries. We have also completely paid off all our debts (including interest) to the Government of the Soviet Union to the total amount of 1,406 million new rubles. We rely solely on internal accumulation of funds for large-scale construction.

Fourthly, self-reliance in building socialism also means that we must gain and accumulate our own experience in building socialism and get to know the laws of socialist construction through our own efforts instead of copying the experience of other countries.

A country must rely mainly on itself to accumulate and sum up its experience in construction. It should also learn from the good experience of other countries, but not copy it mechanically without considering its own conditions. It must not regard the experience of other countries as a "golden rule" and so bind itself hand and foot. It is all the more impermissible to have a blind faith in foreign countries. A nation must think independently and dare to create something original and to develop and assimilate the useful experience of other countries and integrate it with its own practice in construction.

All roads are made by man and all experience is accumulated in the course of practice. By summing up our experience in construction, we have formulated our general line for socialist construction, a general line which conforms to the actual conditions of our country, as well as a number of specific policies necessary for the implementation of this general line. We have also gained fairly rich experience now in overcoming various kinds of difficulties. We are still constantly summing up our experience in order to understand the objective laws of construction better and amass more experience in building socialism.

For an Independent, Comprehensive and Modern Economic System

In building socialism self-reliantly our goal is to establish an independent, comprehensive and modern national economic system in accordance with the conditions and needs of our country.

Agriculture and industry are the main branches of material production in the national economy. In building our national economic system, we have followed the general policy of taking agriculture as the foundation and industry as the leading factor in developing the national economy, arranged our plan for economic development in the order of priority of agriculture, light industry and heavy industry and correctly handled the relations between agriculture, light industry and heavy industry.

Agriculture is the foundation for the development of the national economy. It supplies food and other basic means of livelihood to the people, provides raw materials and a market for industry and accumulates funds for national construction. The labour power needed for economic development comes mainly from the countryside. Therefore, we have always paid great attention to the growth of agriculture and made vigorous efforts to develop it in accordance with the policy of diversification with grain production as the key link. We have also enlisted the efforts of all trades and professions in giving support to agriculture so that it can develop at a fairly rapid rate.

Industry is the leading factor in the development of the national economy. As the producer of means of production, and primarily the instruments of production, industry, particularly heavy industry, supplies agriculture and other branches of the national economy with modern technical equipment to promote the modernization of the entire economy. In old China, industry was extremely backward. Modern industry accounted for only 10 per cent of the total value of industrial and agricultural output. The few industries that did exist were in the service of imperialism. They were mainly processing plants and plants doing repairs and assembly. They could not even make simple machines and equipment. They depended on foreign countries for their supply of raw materials and technical guidance. Hence, an important task that confronted us at the beginning of our socialist construction was the socialist industrialization of our country.

Starting from a weak industrial base, we have met many difficulties in building new branches of industry and manufacturing products which we had never made before. But we Chinese people have the determination and means to overcome difficulties. Consequently, one difficulty after another has been surmounted. Today, we are able to rely entirely on ourselves in designing and building many important modern industrial enterprises, designing and making various large, complicated and high-precision machines and equipment and producing large quantities of high-quality raw and other materials and fuels of a fairly complete range of types and specifications. The number of complete sets of equipment we are manufacturing has also increased. Beginning from last October, we have successfully exploded two atomic bombs which we made ourselves.

In industrializing our country, we do not place a one-sided emphasis on heavy industry and develop it in isolation. On the contrary, we have developed heavy industry step by step on the basis of ensuring a comparatively bigger growth of agriculture and light industry in order to speed up industrialization. Facts have proved that this is the correct road to China's industrialization.

Our experience in construction over the last 15 years shows that there can be no real political independence in the absence of economic independence. It is the implementation of the policy of self-reliance that has enabled us to withstand the pressures of imperialism, old and new colonialism and modern revisionism and preserve our national independence and sovereignty.

As soon as New China was founded, U.S. imperialism, along with other imperialist countries, took piratical measures to impose an economic blockade on us in an attempt to strangle the newborn People's Republic. In recent years, when our country was struck by serious natural calamities for three consecutive years, the Khrushchov modern revisionists employed unprecedentedly perfidious means to put pressure on us, such as the withdrawal of Soviet experts working in China and the scrapping of contracts and agreements, in an attempt to make us submit to their revisionist line. But neither blockade nor pressure can intimidate the Chinese people who have maintained the glorious tradition of self-reliance. On the contrary, these only served to stimulate our revolutionary spirit of self-reliance, enterprise, hard struggle and building the country by diligence and thrift, and thus helped quicken the tempo of our socialist construction. Far from submitting to the pressures of imperialism and modern revisionism, we have consistently held aloft the banner of struggle against imperialism, the reactionaries of all countries and modern revisionism and continued to contribute to the revolutionary cause of the world's people.

Self-Reliance and International Aid

As a result of our implementation of the policy of self-reliance and the smooth development of our national economy, we are now in a better position to fulfil our internationalist duty. Our increased capacity for building socialism self-reliantly has directly strengthened the might of the whole socialist camp.

Through the successful advance of our national construction, we have not only lightened the burden on the fraternal socialist countries but gained greater strength to assist them. We have also been able to give strong support to those countries which have just freed themselves from imperialist rule and won their national independence and to those peoples who are still engaged in revolutionary struggles.

While adhering to the policy of self-reliance in our socialist construction, we have highly valued and welcomed international assistance. But life has taught us the lesson that it is important to discern the real nature of foreign aid before accepting it. The foreign "aid" provided by imperialism and old and new colonialism is nothing but an instrument of aggression. We Chinese people do not want such "aid." We welcome and accept aid given on the basis of proletarian internationalism, aid coming from socialist countries which uphold Marxism-Leninism as well as aid provided by the revolutionary people all over the world.

Acting in the spirit of proletarian internationalism, the Chinese people have always endeavoured to develop economic co-operation and trade relations with the socialist countries and other friendly countries. We are not in the least harmed no matter how certain people, because of our adherence to the policy of self-reliance, slander us for "maintaining a policy of exclusion," "going it alone" and "building an autarkic national economy." We will continue to persist in our policy of self-reliance—a policy that is making itself felt ever more strongly in the socialist construction of our country.

42. KUO WEN: IMPERIALIST PLUNDER—BIGGEST OBSTACLE TO THE ECONOMIC GROWTH OF "UNDERDEVELOPED COUNTRIES" (June, 1965)*

> *This is another major position paper further explaining China's policy of self-reliance as compared with U.S. and Soviet practices.*

The imperialists in recent years have tried to spread the false idea that "colonialism is dead" and that economic differences between the "developed" and "underdeveloped" countries are

* From *Peking Review* (June 18 and 25, 1965) (footnotes omitted).

the sole question that separates them today. Their aim is to cover up the basic contradictions between the oppressors and the oppressed, the exploiters and the exploited, which mark the relations between the imperialist countries and many Asian, African and Latin American countries.

Imperialist oppression and exploitation is the main reason for the retarded economic development of many Asian, African and Latin American countries. The only way they can build independent and prosperous national economies is to make a clean sweep of colonialist economic relationships and to oppose vigorously the political and military measures used to support them.

Investment Overseas—Basis of Imperialist Exploitation

The huge capital invested by the imperialist monopolies abroad is, as Lenin pointed out, "a sound basis for the imperialist oppression and exploitation of most of the countries and nations of the world." In the vast "underdeveloped" areas of Asia, Africa and Latin America, this basis has not yet been destroyed, but it must be destroyed.

The end of World War II saw the nationalization of some imperialist enterprises in a number of "underdeveloped" countries. But this has not been followed by a fall in the investments of the imperialist monopolies; on the contrary they have increased. By these investments, imperialism has seized more and more sources of raw materials in the "underdeveloped" countries, exploited an increasing number of local workers and raked in bigger and bigger profits. As a result, despite their hard-working people and rich resources, the "underdeveloped" countries find it difficult to accumulate national capital and develop independent national economies.

Take, for example, the United States, the biggest colonialist of our times. According to U.S. Department of Commerce statistics, the book value of direct investments by U.S. monopolies in the "underdeveloped" areas in Asia, Africa and Latin America more than doubled from about $5,700 million in 1950 to $13,340 million in 1963. The real value of these investments, however, should be $26,680 million as the department itself admitted that the book value roughly represented only half the actual worth.

These large investments have enabled U.S. monopolies to control countless important sources of raw materials in the "underdeveloped" countries. For instance, more than half the production of crude oil in these countries is now under the control of U.S. monopolies. They also exploit large numbers of local workers. In Latin America, 2 million people are directly employed by enterprises controlled by American capital. Because the mines in these countries are extraordinarily rich and the wages of local workers are extremely low, the rate of profit on U.S. investment there is very high. In 1963, even according to official U.S. figures the return from direct U.S. private investments in the "underdeveloped" countries was 17.1 per cent, approximately twice as much as from direct U.S. private investments in the "developed" countries. It was as high as 76.7 per cent from the oil industry in the Middle East.

Staggering profits. The large increase in the amount of capital invested in "underdeveloped" countries, with its high rate of profit, has brought bigger and bigger profits to the U.S. monopolies. According to the U.S. Department of Commerce, in 1950 U.S. monopolies earned $970 million in profits from their direct investments in the "underdeveloped" countries. By 1963 these had increased to $2,280 million. These figures were, of course, greatly minimized. It has been estimated that the profit concealed would amount to about 75 per cent of the official figures. Calculated on this basis, the U.S. monopolies in 1963 grabbed $4,000 million in profits from their direct investments in the "underdeveloped" countries, or $2,300 million more than what they actually were in 1950.

The imperialist monopolies remitted home a portion of their profits, issued generous dividends to shareholders and paid their directors handsomely. In addition to feeding this pack of parasites at home, they also reinvested part of their profits in the "underdeveloped" countries. In 1961-63, profits ploughed back for reinvestment made up about one half of the U.S. monopolies' newly increased direct investments in these countries.

If this process is allowed to continue, imperialist monopolies will be able to use their earnings to exploit still larger numbers of local wage labourers, lay hold of still more resources and reap still bigger profits.

Latin America—a case in point. This is best illustrated by investments in Latin America where U.S. monopoly capital has a long history of infiltration and exploitation. The U.S. Department of Commerce gave the book value of the total increase in direct U.S. private investments in Latin America from 1946 to 1962 as $6,600 million. If calculated on the basis that the actual value is double the book value, the total increase was $13,200 million. And it is legitimate to say that the new investment was made possible entirely by exploiting local wage labour because capital outflow of new direct U.S. private investment to Latin America in that period was about $6,000 million less than the profits remitted back to the United States. With the steep increase in investment, the profits which U.S. financial oligarchies had secured doubled during the same period.

The above-mentioned $13,200 million plus $6,000 million roughly equalled the aggregate profits from direct U.S. private investments in Latin America in that period—$19,200 million. These figures were three times the total postwar U.S. economic "aid" to Latin American countries up to fiscal 1962, and about $10,000 million more than the total foreign debts incurred by the "underdeveloped" countries on that continent up to the end of 1962.

This shows that if "underdeveloped" countries in Latin America had taken over all the U.S. capital-controlled enterprises in postwar years, and had used them to accumulate national capital instead of allowing them to be used by the U.S. monopolies to extort profits, it would have been entirely possible for these countries to free themselves from foreign "aid" and foreign loans and to create favourable conditions for the development of their national economies.

"Political guarantees." It is pertinent to point out that the imperialist monopolies have to rely not only on their own economic power for investment and profit grabbing abroad but also on the backing of their governments, not excluding the use of supra-economic means.

"Political guarantees," as is well known, are more needed for investments than for trade. After the end of World War II, the imperialists have had to use some neo-colonialist tricks to cope with the surging tide of the national-liberation movements, and in certain circumstances they have recognized the independence of their former colonies. But when the newly independent countries "infringe" upon the colonial interests of the financial oligarchies, it is not unusual for the imperialists to retaliate by every possible means, including the use of violence. An example of this is the Anglo-French war against Egypt over the latter's nationalization of the Suez Canal Company.

U.S. imperialism has an even worse record in this respect.

In 1953, the United States engineered a military coup d'etat in Iran and overthrew the Mossadegh government which nationalized the oil industry. U.S. oil magnates then secured from the pro-U.S. Zahedi regime 40 per cent of the shares in the reconstituted International Petroleum Company.

In 1954, the United States subverted Guatemala's popularly elected Arbenz government because it expropriated land held by the U.S. United Fruit Company and started building a state power station to break the monopoly of the U.S.-owned Empresa Electrica de Guatemala. Then Carlos Castillo Armas, a placeman of U.S. imperialism, became President, Carlos Salazar Gatica, a United Fruit Company lawyer, was appointed Foreign Minister, and Jorje Arenales Catalan, a lawyer for the Empresa Electrica de Guatemala, Minister of Economic Affairs. The Armas government gave back the expropriated land to United Fruit. Work on the state power station was stopped.

In April last year the United States engineered a military coup d'etat in Brazil because the Goulart government not only opposed intervention in Cuba but also took some steps to restrict foreign capital and protect the interests of the national economy. These measures included abrogation of the mining rights of the U.S. Hanna Corporation, restriction of the outflow of profits mulcted from the people by foreign capital and plans to take over oil refineries controlled by American capital. The new Brazilian authorities have ordered the repeal of the law restricting the remittance of profits abroad.

Unequal treaties. Another way of providing "political guarantees" for investments is to coerce the "underdeveloped" countries into signing unequal treaties. Today the old-type unequal treaties which provided only for naked colonialist investment prerogatives, are gradually being replaced by unequal treaties of a new type which, on the face of it, seem to be "reciprocal" but are actually advantageous to the imperialist investors only. In this category are those treaties which the imperialists concluded with their former colonies when the latter obtained independence, and which included "national treatment" granted by one party to investors of the other. The 1946 U.S.-Philippine "Treaties of General Relations" specifically stipulated that the property rights enjoyed by citizens or legal persons of one party should be respected and protected in the same way as those of citizens or legal persons of the other. The "treaties of friendship, commerce and navigation" which the United States concluded with the Chiang Kai-shek clique, the south Korean puppet authorities and the reactionary regime in south Viet Nam also incorporated clauses of "national treatment."

The facts mentioned above demonstrate that in order to cut off the tentacles of the imperialist monopolies which suck their life blood in the form of capital export, the "underdeveloped" countries must fight staunchly against the various means of colonialist oppression the imperialists use to protect their investments.

Exploitation Through Unequal Terms of Trade

Imperialist exploitation by means of investment is accompanied by exploitation in the form of unequal terms of trade with the "underdeveloped" countries which are exporters of primary products.

During the period of industrial capitalism the "advanced" capitalist countries in Europe and North America, backed by gunboat diplomacy, had already begun the large-scale export of commodities to Asia, Africa and Latin America. This led to the destruction of the handicrafts of the colonial and semi-colonial countries and the throttling of their national industries, thereby turning them into suppliers of raw materials. In the period of imperialism, by means of capital exports, the monopolies took a direct part in developing the production of primary products in the "underdeveloped" countries, which they needed themselves, particularly mineral raw materials. At the same time they established more factories there. As a result, the national industries suffered both from competition from imported goods and directly from local factories operated by foreign capital. The economies of the "underdeveloped" countries thus became more lopsided.

After the end of World War II, many "underdeveloped

countries tried to develop a number of national industries so as to extricate themselves from their position as mere appendages supplying agricultural and mineral products to the imperialists. All kinds of imperialist obstruction, however, barred their path.

Imperialist trade privileges. Even today a number of "underdeveloped" countries are still compelled to grant the imperialists many colonialist trade privileges including immunity from import quotas, reduction in or exemption from tariff rates. Foreign industrial goods hit hard at local industries. Take the Philippines for instance. Its markets are flooded with American goods, protected by various kinds of trade privileges. Its national industries, especially the textile industry, are facing great difficulties. In a report presented prior to his resignation, former Chairman of the Philippine National Economic Commission Sixto Roxas charged the United States with squeezing Filipino industrial goods out of the local markets by means of immunity from taxation, low taxes and smuggling, with the result that local industry operated below capacity, some branches working at only 28 per cent of it.

In recent years, the imperialists have stepped up their efforts to establish factories in the "underdeveloped" countries in order to rob the latter of their markets for industrial goods in a more direct way. Even such old commercial monopolies as the British United Africa Company are busy with setting up new factories in the African countries. Certain major U.S. industrial branches also put emphasis on building and extending local factories as a means of cornering the Latin American markets. According to a report of the U.S. Department of Commerce, in 1962, the sales of goods made by the factories set up in Latin America by U.S. machine-building, electric equipment, communications, chemical, rubber and paper-making industries doubled the figure for 1957. Whereas in 1957 the value of these sales was about 50 per cent less than that of the goods exported by these industries to Latin America, by 1962, the former was 30 per cent more than the latter.

In addition to seizing the "underdeveloped" countries' domestic markets and thus hampering those sections of the national industries which supply them, the imperialists have also prevented the "underdeveloped" countries from exporting manufactures into their own domestic markets and are thus crippling the growth of those national industries which depend on foreign markets.

It is common knowledge that a big number of the tropical agricultural products of the "underdeveloped" countries are dependent to a large extent on foreign markets, especially the markets of the imperialist countries. If the "underdeveloped" countries can process these agricultural products first before exporting them, which does not in any case require large capital, then they have the opportunity to develop an important aspect of their national industries. But, as a rule, the imperialists only want to buy their unprocessed farm products, and charge progressive import duties on processed ones. This poses serious problems to the "underdeveloped" countries in developing their agricultural products processing industry. As the former Ghanaian Foreign Minister Kojo Botsio aptly said: "In Ghana we know that the processing of cocoa and other raw materials could be an important factor in our industrialization programme. Yet it is impossible for us to embark upon such an enterprise because the industrialized countries have arranged their tariffs in such a way as to prevent us from so doing."

"Underdeveloped" countries remain suppliers of primary products. Up till now the "underdeveloped" countries have not been able to get rid of their position as suppliers of primary products to the imperialist countries. This is shown by the following:

1. The national industries of the new emerging countries are very weak. According to the August 1964 issue of the *U.N. Monthly Bulletin of Statistics*, the share of the manufacturing industries of the "less-industrialized countries"—even if those factories owned by the imperialists are counted in—made up only 9 per cent of the capitalist world's manufacturing industries in 1963. It was only 4.4 per cent in so far as the metal products manufacturing industry was concerned.

2. The "underdeveloped" countries must, through the channel of foreign trade, export large quantities of agricultural and mineral products in exchange for a certain amount of manufactures, including machinery and equipment which are needed for the development of their national economies but of which they can produce only a little or none at all. In recent years, generally speaking, six-sevenths of their exports have been primary products while two-thirds of their imports have been manufactures. Moreover, more than half of the exports of many "underdeveloped" countries comprise only one or two kinds of

agricultural and mineral products. The results of an analysis of 1960-61 foreign trade statistics made by the British National Institute of Economic and Social Research are revealing: 55 "underdeveloped" countries or regions depend for more than half of their exports on one kind of agricultural or mineral product, 33 on two, and five "underdeveloped" countries on three.

3. The "underdeveloped" countries export primary products mainly to the imperialist countries in exchange for their manufactured goods. In 1961, according to recent U.N. statistics, 95 per cent of the foreign trade of "underdeveloped" countries was conducted within the capitalist world economic system, 70 per cent of their primary products were exported to six major imperialist countries (the United States, Britain, France, West Germany, Italy and Japan) and 80 per cent of their manufactures were imported from these same countries.

Prices of primary products forced down. The imperialists, with their monopoly position on the capitalist world market, also intensify their exploitation of the "underdeveloped" countries through non-equivalent exchange, namely, forcing down the prices of primary products while boosting those of manufactures.

The mineral products exported by "underdeveloped" countries are almost entirely owned by foreign monopolies while the exported farm products, generally speaking, are grown mainly by their own people. The prices these agricultural products fetch on foreign markets have a direct bearing on the ability of the "underdeveloped" countries to accumulate national capital from the farming economy, on the amount of foreign exchange earnings to import machinery and equipment needed by the national economy and on the incomes and purchasing power of the peasants who form the overwhelming majority of the population.

But it was precisely these tropical agricultural products which suffered the most drastic fall in prices on the postwar capitalist world market as a result of imperialist monopolies' manipulation, and this brought enormous losses to the "underdeveloped" countries. In the eight years from 1955 to 1962, foreign exchange earnings of the "underdeveloped" countries in Asia, Africa and Latin America were down by $14,850 million, or an average of $1,860 million a year, through the price falls of coffee, cocoa and tea alone.

Coupled with the sharp fall of prices in farm produce exported by the "underdeveloped" countries there has been a big rise in the prices of machinery and equipment bought from the imperialist countries. The *U.N. Monthly Bulletin of Statistics* in its January 1965 issue revealed that from 1951 to 1962 the fall of prices in food and drink exported by the "underdeveloped" countries to the imperialist countries averaged 20 per cent and the prices of raw materials fell by 42 per cent while the prices of machinery and equipment imported from the imperialist countries rose by 32.5 per cent.

This means that the "underdeveloped" countries now must export an increased amount of agricultural products in order to buy the same amount of machinery and equipment. At a meeting of the U.N. Conference on Trade and Development in Geneva on March 25, 1964, Ernesto Che Guevara, leader of the Cuban delegation, presented some relevant data. He showed that, compared with 1955, the percentage increase in the quantities of primary commodities needed to be exported to buy a 30-39 h.p. tractor in 1962 was as follows:

Commodity	Country	Percentage Increase
Cocoa	Ghana	133
Coffee	Brazil	101
Cotton	United Arab Republic	61
Natural Rubber	Malaya	70
Tea	Ceylon	55

It is clear that the widening gap between the prices of exported farm produce and imported machinery and equipment has done great harm to the national economies of the "underdeveloped" countries, particularly their efforts to increase the fixed assets of their national enterprises.

The Way Out. In order to get rid of their position as mere providers of primary products and to oppose imperialist exploitation in the form of non-equivalent exchange, the "underdeveloped" countries need diversified economies and particularly the development of national industries. In the era of monopoly capitalism, owing to the vast differences between the productivity of the imperialist enterprises and the national enterprises in the "underdeveloped" countries, the latter require an even greater degree of protection from the state. They will find it difficult to develop these national enterprises unless they keep intact their national sovereignty, liquidate the colonialist trade privileges still in imperialist hands, and prevent foreign monopolies from building local factories to seize the markets for their own industrial goods.

There is also the need for the "underdeveloped" countries to develop trade among themselves and with the anti-imperialist and anti-colonialist countries on a basis of equality and mutual benefit. This will help to alter step by step the present state of affairs in which over 70 per cent of their trade is conducted with the imperialist powers. To this end the "underdeveloped" countries have no alternative but to fight resolutely against all the measures the imperialists take to control the direction of their trade.

Furthermore, if the exploitation through non-equivalent exchange is to be ended, the imperialist monopolies must not be allowed to control market prices. Countries exporting the same kinds of primary products, by united efforts, can have a say in the prices of primary commodities. In recent years, a number of organizations comprising countries exporting the same products have been founded. The reactions to their activities show that strengthened unity and persevering struggle on the part of the exporting countries concerned will make their influence felt on the prices of primary products in the capitalist world market.

Imperialist "Aid" and Colonialist Plunder

Imperialism, U.S. imperialism in particular, is now spreading the idea in Asia, Africa and Latin America that its "aid" to the "underdeveloped" countries is to provide them with capital for national construction and help them to tide over their balance of payments difficulties. And the imperialists are passing themselves off as alms-givers so that they may not be seen as the exploiters that they are.

The truth of the matter is that brutal imperialist plunder is one of the main causes for the shortage of capital and the balance of payments difficulties experienced by the "underdeveloped" countries. The imperialist countries' "aid" is aimed precisely at helping their domestic monopolies to continue fleecing the "underdeveloped" countries already weakened through long years of colonialist oppression. At the same time, even though "aid" may temporarily make good a part of their balance of payments deficits it will not be long before the recipients find themselves in a still more critical payments crisis as their debts pile up day by day.

"Aid"—instrument to protect private investment. The imperialists actually make no bones about the fact that one of the purposes in giving "aid" to the "underdeveloped" countries is to further the interests of private investors there. In the United States in particular, not one of its presidents in the postwar years has failed to emphasize that "aid" to the "underdeveloped" countries was intended to open a way for the export of private capital.

Investment, as we have already mentioned above, cannot do without political guarantees. Imperialist "aid"—a measure of state monopoly capitalism—is precisely one of the weapons the imperialists have been using in the postwar years in their search for such guarantees.

The imperialists, especially the U.S. imperialists, are doing all they can to use "aid" as a means to buy over influential politicians, support reactionary regimes, foster financial dependence, maintain and supply satellite troops, "rent" military bases and try to suppress the people's revolution, etc., in the "aid" recipient countries. One of the main aims in doing this is to maintain colonialist political control and influence in these countries, thus providing general political guarantees for investment.

Hunting for specific "political guarantees," the imperialists also use "aid" as an instrument to interfere in the financial and economic policies of the recipient countries. U.S. conduct is particularly striking in this respect. Using "aid" as a bait, it urges them to adopt measures that will be conducive to the interests of U.S. investors and to refrain from taking such actions as nationalization of enterprises controlled by U.S. capital. Failing this they are threatened with the stoppage of "aid."

A report by the U.S. Senate Committee on Foreign Aid made it quite clear that one of the chief advantages in "aid" was that while a private enterprise would find it difficult to press a foreign government to adjust its exchange rate and ease its controls over foreign enterprises, U.S. foreign "aid" agencies and such international financial institutions as the World Bank could do so. In 1957, advisers on foreign "aid" told the then

President Eisenhower: "In cases where private investors cannot act alone because of restrictions imposed by foreign governments, and where a few reasonable changes in policy by the foreign government concerned would make the private investment possible, the U.S. should administer its assistance in a manner designed to overcome the obstacles to private investment." The 1963 U.S. Foreign Aid Bill stressed that those who have not signed "agreements relating to investment guarantees" before the end of 1965 would not be given "aid."

In addition to political guarantees, large-scale export of private capital requires certain material conditions. Imperialist "aid" to "underdeveloped" countries precisely aims at creating or improving these conditions for private investment. A very large portion of imperialist "aid," bilateral or multilateral, is used in basic public works. This is because with poor power supply and communications it is difficult to make investments, especially in the exploitation of mineral resources. Kennedy, while still a senator, admitted that the reason why the U.S. Government put stress on "aiding" "underdeveloped" countries to develop transport, fuel and power was because "they are essential to the creation of a setting in which efficient and profitable private operations can grow."

Another major item in imperialist "aid" to "underdeveloped" countries is "technical aid" such as surveys of resources, the operation of health services, education, and so on. In his message on the "Point Four Program" presented to Congress on June 24, 1949, Truman said: "Technical surveys of resources and of the possibilities of economic development must precede substantial capital investment. Furthermore, in many of the areas concerned, technical assistance in improving sanitation, communications, or education is required to create conditions in which capital investment can be fruitful."

"Aid" for promoting sales of high-priced goods. It is a general practice for the imperialist countries to stipulate that "aid" funds must be used for making purchases in the "aid" giving countries. Former President of the World Bank Eugene Black admitted that one of the main contents of the "aid" given by the "developed" countries was a race for markets "with the lending government allied with their own export industries to outbid or outsell all rivals."

In addition to boosting its sales abroad, the United States also uses "aid" as a means of compelling the recipient countries to buy high-priced American goods and services. A report released by the U.S. Department of Commerce in 1963 revealed that for many categories of capital goods, U.S. prices were substantially higher, sometimes by as much as 40 per cent, than those of competing suppliers. Without the "buy American" provision, sales of these goods would be impossible. At the same time American law stipulates that at least half of the "aid" materials must be carried in U.S. vessels. U.S. freight charges are sometimes double those of other maritime countries.

Loans with high interest rates. Loans make up an increasingly large proportion of imperialist "aid" to the "underdeveloped" countries and the annual rate of interest for many of these loans is over 5 per cent. At the United Nations Conference on Trade and Development last year many "underdeveloped" countries bitterly attacked the imperialists for making loans at high rates of interest, and demanded that the annual rate should not exceed 3 per cent. This demand however was turned down.

The "underdeveloped" countries have incurred foreign debts to the tune of U.S. $30,000 million. It is estimated that about 40 per cent of these is owned to the United States. According to a recent estimate by the U.S. Agency of International Development, by 1957, foreign debts owned by the "underdeveloped" countries in Asia, Africa and Latin America will have reached $90,000 million.

The service of foreign debts cost the "underdeveloped" countries $5,000 million in 1964. Even U.S. President Johnson admitted in his foreign aid message to Congress on January 14, 1965 that foreign debts had become a heavy burden for the "underdeveloped" countries.

India is the largest client for foreign "aid" among the "underdeveloped" countries in Asia, Africa and Latin America. In 1951, its foreign debts were below U.S. $100 million, but now they exceed $5,000 million. In the fiscal year 1965-1966, debt services will cost India close to $400 million, about 20 per cent of its export earnings.

In Latin America, Argentina, Brazil and Chile are in debt to the imperialists only to a lesser extent than India. According to a recent report of the U.N. Economic Commission for Latin

America, the foreign debts of these three major Latin American countries are $4,000 million, $4,400 million and $3,000 million respectively. On January 10, AP reported from Buenos Aires that Argentina's foreign debts maturing in 1965 amount to $600-700 million. This is almost one half of its annual export revenue in recent years.

The *London Financial Times* reported in July 1964 that in 1964 and 1965 Brazil had to use 40 per cent of its foreign exchange earnings to service its foreign debts (including amortization and interest). Chile's foreign debts due in 1964 amounted to $343 million while the total value of its exports per year do not exceed $550 million.

Foreign debts are usually repaid through trade surpluses. But in the postwar period, trade deficits have appeared frequently in the "underdeveloped" countries, the more so when their trade with the imperialists is conducted on a basis of growing inequality. As export surpluses are not available for debt repayment, the only way left is to raise new loans on a still larger scale. A part of these new loans is used to make good trade deficits and another part to repay old debts. The *Wall Street Journal* of January 15, 1964, reported that in 1962, 40 per cent of the loans to the "underdeveloped" countries was returned to the lending countries.

To avoid the trap of imperialist "aid," the "underdeveloped" countries are increasingly aware that they must rely on their own efforts to develop their national economies and at the same time strengthen co-operation and mutual assistance among themselves and with all others who are opposed to imperialism and colonialism.

Only when they are determined to take the road of self-reliance in developing their national economies and not count on imperialist, especially U.S. imperialist "aid," will they be able to fight imperialism and colonialism without hindrance. On the other hand, only when they persevere in the anti-imperialist struggle and put an end to colonialist oppression can they make the best use of their manpower, materials and financial resources to build independent national economies.

Two Diametrically Opposed Views

There are now two diametrically opposed views on how the "underdeveloped" countries can overcome their economic backwardness, and these represent two different roads.

One view is that the anti-imperialist and anti-colonialist tasks of these countries come to an end with the declaration of independence, and that they should be well satisfied with their present position and need only rely on "aid" of "developed" countries for national construction. This is the prescription of the imperialists and their agents.

If the "underdeveloped" countries take this road, they can never break the fetters of the colonialist economy, liquidate the imperialist forces in the country, or stop the outflow of their national wealth. On the contrary they will have to lean more heavily on the imperialists. Not only will they find it difficult to develop their national economies and consolidate the independence they have already achieved but there is also the danger that that independence may be again lost.

Another view is that having become independent the "underdeveloped" countries in Asia, Africa and Latin America should carry on their struggle against imperialism and colonialism, exercise their national sovereignty to liquidate the imperialist economic forces in their countries and resolutely fight against all the political and military means used by the imperialists to uphold colonialist economic relationships. At the same time they have to rely mainly on the strength of their own people, on their internal resources and accumulation so as to build and develop independent national economies.

Self reliance, however, by no means excludes international economic co-operation on the basis of equality and mutual benefit. In combating imperialism and colonialism and developing independent national economies, it is necessary for the Asian, African and Latin American peoples to strengthen their militant unity and relations of mutual help.

In order to successfully carry on the struggle against imperialism and colonialism and implement the policy of self-reliance effectively, democratic reforms, especially land reform are necessary. These reforms will hit at the reactionary forces which collaborate with imperialism and colonialism and hamstring the domestic productive forces; they will also enhance the initiative and creativeness of the people in national revolution and economic development.

This is the road of pushing ahead the national-democratic revolution uninterruptedly, the road of self-reliance. It is the only one which will enable the "underdeveloped" countries to become strong and prosperous.

43. COMMUNIQUÉ ON TALKS BETWEEN CHINA AND JAPAN TRADE OFFICES (March, 1971) and CHOU EN-LAI'S STATEMENT ON CHINA'S TRADE WITH JAPAN (August, 1960)*

The following two documents should be read together to understand the different Chinese trade policies with respect to Japan: the new attitudes of 1971, and the old policy of the 1960's. The latter document is the minutes of Chou En-lai's statement before Kazuo Suzuki, managing director of the Japan-China Trade Promotion Association, on August 27, 1960.

I

The representatives of the Memorandum Trade Offices of China and Japan held talks in Peking from February 15 to March 1, 1971. Participating in the talks on the Chinese side were Liu Hsi-wen, Hsu Ming, Wu Shu-tung, Lin Po and Ting Min. Participating in the talks on the Japanese side were Kaheita Okazaki, Yoshimi Furui, Seiichi Tagawa, Shunichi Matsumoto, Ryoichi Kawai, Yaeiji Watanabe, Tomoharu Okubo, Seiichi Kataoka and Yoshizo Yasuda.

During this period, Premier Chou En-Lai and Vice-Chairman of the Standing Committee of the National People's Congress Kuo Mo-jo met all the members of the Delegation of the Japan-China Memorandum Trade. The delegation visited factories and a people's commune in Peking.

The two sides unanimously hold that the communiqué on talks they signed on April 19, 1970 is entirely correct, and that facts over the past year have further confirmed this.

The two sides unanimously condemn the Japanese reactionaries for intensifying collusion with U.S. imperialism in reviving Japanese militarism and joining U.S. imperialism's aggression and expansion in Asia. Actively following the line of the Japan-U.S. joint communique, the Sato government has in the past year gone further in turning Japan into a base of U.S. imperialist aggression against Asia. The Sato government has not only propagandized militarism in a big way, but has "auto-

* From *Peking Review* (March 12, 1971), pp. 24-25; and *China Today*, Vol. V., No. 43, pp. 7-8, respectively.

matically extended" the Japan-U.S. "security treaty," put forward the "draft outline of the fourth national defence build-up programme" and the "national defence white paper," and stepped up armaments expansion. Furthermore, it has worked in coordination with the U.S. policy of aggression against Asia and helped U.S. imperialism expand its war of aggression against Viet Nam, Laos and Cambodia. All this shows that the revival of Japanese militarism is already a reality. The Japanese side states that it is determined to make still greater efforts to denounce and smash the revival of Japanese militarism.

The Chinese side strongly condemns the Japanese reactionaries for their intensified collusion with the Chiang Kai-shek and Pak Jung Hi puppet cliques in rigging up a new military alliance in Northeast Asia and for directing the spearhead of their aggression against China and the Democratic People's Republic of Korea. The newly established Japan-Chiang-Pak "liaison committee" has gone so far as to decide on the "joint exploitation" of the resources of the shallow seas adjacent to China's coasts. This is a flagrant encroachment on China's sovereignty. The Chinese people absolutely will not tolerate this.

The Japanese side states that it understands this solemn stand of the Chinese side. It holds that the Japan-Chiang-Pak "liaison committee" is a reactionary organization formed by the Japanese reactionaries in following the line of the Japan-U.S. joint communiqué. The decision of this "liaison committee" to exploit the resources of the shallow seas adjacent to China's coasts is an encroachment on China's sovereignty. The Japanese side states that it will resolutely struggle against all these reactionary activities.

The Chinese side solemnly states: The Chinese people are determined to liberate their sacred territory Taiwan Province. It is absolutely China's internal affair to liberate its Taiwan Province and no country whatsoever has the right to interfere with it. By clinging desperately to the illegal Japan-Chiang "peace treaty" and emphasizing what it called "keeping faith in international affairs," the Sato government has fully revealed its persistent hostility towards the Chinese people and its vain attempt to obstruct the Chinese people from liberating Taiwan and to realize its ambition of occupying it permanently.

The Japanese side agrees completely with the stand of the Chinese side and, once again, explicitly states: The Government of the People's Republic of China is the sole legal government representing the Chinese people; Taiwan Province is an inseparable part of the territory of China; the plot to create "two Chinas" or "one China and one Taiwan" in any form is intolerable; and the Japan-Chiang "peace treaty" is itself illegal, null and void and should be abolished.

Both sides reiterate and affirm once again that the three political principles and the principle that politics and economics are inseparable must be adhered to in the relations between China and Japan, and they are the political basis of the relations between our two sides. To promote Sino-Japanese trade on this basis, the Chinese side puts forward four conditions in its trade with Japan, namely: The Chinese side will not have trade exchanges with factories, firms and enterprises belonging to any of the following categories:

First, factories and firms helping the Chiang Kai-shek gang stage a come-back to the mainland or helping the Pak Jung Hi clique intrude into the Democratic People's Republic of Korea;

Second, factories and firms with large investments in Taiwan or south Korea;

Third, enterprises supplying arms and ammunition to U.S. imperialism for aggression against Viet Nam or Laos or Cambodia; and

Fourth, U.S.-Japan joint enterprises or subsidiaries of U.S. companies in Japan.

The Japanese side agrees to the stand of the Chinese side and holds that the above-mentioned four conditions are important for the development of Japan-China trade on the basis of the three political principles and the principle that politics and economics are inseparable, and states that it is willing to make efforts to ensure faithful compliance with the four conditions.

The two sides seriously point out in unanimity: The Sato government has redoubled its efforts to tail after U.S. imperialism and has obstinately pursued a policy of hostility towards China, thus placing new serious obstacles in the way of normalizing the relations between China and Japan. The Japanese side resolutely opposes the Sato government's policy of hostility towards China, and is determined to make new efforts to remove the obstacles placed by the Sato government and promote the normalization of Japan-China relations and the restoration of diplomatic relations between the two countries.

The two sides are unanimous of the opinion that China and Japan are close neighbours and there exists a traditional friendship between the two peoples; the desire of the Chinese and Japanese peoples for peace and friendship represents the general trend of events and popular feelings. A mass movement for Japan-China friendship and promoting the restoration of Japan-China diplomatic relations is developing vigorously in Japan. No one can hold back this torrent of the times and the prospects of China-Japan friendship are bright. Both sides maintain that promoting friendship between the two peoples and normal relations between the two countries conforms to the common desire of the Chinese and Japanese peoples and is in the interests of safeguarding peace in Asia and the world.

The two sides reached agreement on 1971 memorandum trade matters, etc.

Representatives of the China-Japan
Memorandum Trade Office of China

Liu Hsi-wen
Hsu Ming
Wu Shu-tung
Lin Po
Ting Min

Representatives of the Japan-China
Memorandum Trade Office of Japan

Kaheita Okazaki
Yoshimi Furui
Seiichi Tagawa
Shunichi Matsumoto
Yaeiji Watanabe
Tomoharu Okubo

II

Premier Chou En-lai said: "You have spoken at length, and I will now tell you a bit about China's trade policy toward Japan. Japanese people like using three principles and I, too, will now

state three principles, that is, three Sino-Japanese trade principles, which have grown up out of the developments in the
struggle with Nobusuke Kishi's hostile policy to China.

In the past, China and Japan made mutual agreement
between private organizations, thinking that such agreements
would serve to develop Sino-Japanese trade. During the period
of the Nobusuke Kishi government, this method proved
unworkable. Nobusuke Kishi would not recognize, would not
guarantee the implementation of private agreements and,
furthermore, torpedoed it by his policy of hostility to China.
We could not tolerate this behaviour and had to suspend
Sino-Japanese trade interflow for two and a half years.

If according to the wishes of the Chinese and Japanese
people, Sino-Japanese trade could be gradually resumed, this
would be a good thing for the people of both countries.
However, we still have to wait a while and see what the attitude
of the new Japanese Government really is.

Now we put forward three principles, namely, one, government agreement; two, private contracts; three, special consideration in individual cases.

First of all, all agreements from now on must be concluded
between the governments on both sides and only so are they
guaranteed, because before with the private agreements the
Japanese Government did not want to guarantee them. And as
regards a government agreement it can only be signed in
conditions when the relations of the governments of the two
countries are developing in a friendly direction and, in fact,
when normal relations are established; otherwise, it cannot be
signed.

As regards the relations between the two governments,
Comrade Liu Ning-yi made it very clear when he was in Tokyo
that we still maintain the three political principles we stated
formerly. The three principles stated formerly do not place a
heavy demand on the Japanese Government; they are very fair.
They are: Firstly, the Japanese Government must not be hostile
to China. For the Chinese Government is not hostile to Japan; it
recognises Japan's existence and is glad to see the advances of
the Japanese people; and if the two sides were to conduct
negotiations, the Japanese Government would naturally be
taken as the other party to the negotiations.

But the Japanese Government's attitude to China has not
been the same—they have not recognized the existence of new

China; on the contrary, they have been hostile to new China and have recognized Taiwan, saying it represents China. Also, they have not taken the Government of new China as the other party to negotiations.

Secondly, Japan must not follow the United States in the 'two Chinas' plot. The United States will carry on the 'two Chinas' intrigue whether the Democratic Party or the Republican Party has the presidency. Taiwan-paid newspapers in Hong Kong say that the Republican Party is passive about 'two Chinas' and taking its time, while if the Democratic Party takes office, it will pursue the 'two Chinas' business actively and display initiative. I believe there is some truth in this kind of remark. If the United States does this sort of thing and Japan follows of course we oppose.

Thirdly, Japan must not obstruct the development of Sino-Japanese relations in the direction of normalization.

These three principles of ours are very equitable. If we put them the other way round you will understand. Firstly, the Chinese Government is not hostile to Japan but wants to be friendly with Japan; secondly, the Chinese Government recognizes only one Japan and does not create two Japans, and moreover, in any negotiations, would invariably take the Japanese Government as the other party; thirdly, it invariably encourages, supports and helps Sino-Japanese relations to develop towards normalisation. Why should the Japanese Government not do the same?

The new Japanese Government, both Prime Minister Ikeda and Foreign Minister Kosaka, have recently made some statements which are not good. We still have to wait and see. I was Foreign Minister in 1957 and Vice-Premier Chen Yi became Foreign Minister in 1958. Both of us condemned the Nobusuke Kishi government's policy towards China, all entirely on the basis of the numerous hostile activities of the Nobusuke Kishi government to China. Therefore, we now have to wait and see with regard to the Ikeda government.

In view of all this, we draw the conclusion that any agreement between the two countries must be concluded by the governments; there is no guarantee for private agreements. This applies to trade, fishery, postal service, navigation, etc.

Then, is it impossible to do business between the two countries in the absence of agreements? No. Business can be done and private contracts can be concluded whenever conditions are mature. For instance, a certain Japanese enterprise and a certain Chinese company may negotiate and sign contracts and make a deal for a fixed term, if they want to be friendly to each other and proceed from the requirements of both parties. If the contract is fulfilled well, if both parties are on good terms and if the political environment of the two countries turns for the better, the short-term contracts may be converted into relatively longer-term ones. This is thinking of the future.

Further, there is special consideration in specific cases, which has been going on for two years. It is correct for the General Council of Trade Unions of Japan and the All China Federation of Trade Unions to mediate in the interests of the labouring people when the medium and small enterprises of Japan have special difficulties. Special consideration for this kind of trade may be continued in the future and the volume may even be expanded a bit in accordance with the needs. This has already been explained by Comrade Liu Ning-yi in Tokyo.

Your Japan-China Trade Promotion Association, in accordance with the three principles for Sino-Japanese trade mentioned above, may recommend such business which you hold to be friendly, possible and beneficial to both sides. You may contact the Council for the Promotion of International Trade of our country. They know this principle. The All China Federation of Trade Unions also knows this principle of special consideration in specific cases, and you may also talk with them. After Mr. Suzuki returns, you may talk it over with friends belonging to firms connected with the Japan-China Trade Promotion Association.

I want to add one more thing. We continue to oppose the new Japan-U.S. 'security treaty' because it regards China and the Soviet Union as enemies, poses a menace to Southeast Asia, and jeopardises peace in the Far East and Asia. We support the Japanese people's struggle against the new Japan-U.S. 'security treaty' and for the building up of an independent, peaceful, democratic and neutral Japan. Mr. Suzuki, please convey the Chinese people's respect and support for the Japanese people."

44. NEWS COMMENTARY: TANZANIAN AND ZAMBIAN DELEGATIONS VISIT CHINA (July, 1970) and THE SINO-TANZANIAN TREATY OF FRIENDSHIP (February, 1965)*

* From *Peking Review* (July 17, 1970), pp. 16-17, and (February 26, 1965), p. 9.

Chinese-Tanzanian and Chinese-Zambian relations provide an excellent model of China's cooperative international role. First, the relationship was formalized with the conclusion of the Sino-Tanzanian Treaty of 1965, signed during President Julius Nyerere's first state visit to Peking. Later in the same year Chou En-lai paid a return visit to Tanzania and established an extensive economic and technical assistance program for Tanzania. And the cooperative relations flourished, marked by new governmental delegations from Tanzania as well as from Zambia to celebrate China's formal commitment to finance and construct the important Tanzania-Zambia Railway in 1970.

I

The Tanzanian Government Delegation led by Amir Habib Jamal, Minister for Finance, and the Zambian Government Delegation led by E. H. K. Mudenda, Minister of Development and Finance, arrived in Peking on July 5 for a friendly visit to China. The two delegations were given a warm welcome by several thousand revolutionary people in the capital. Vice-Premier Li Hsien-nien was among those who greeted the distinguished guests at the airport.

On July 9, Premier Chou En-lai met all the members of the two government delegations and had a cordial and friendly talk with them. Vice-Premier Li Hsien-nien held talks with the delegations of the two governments. The talks proceeded in a cordial and friendly atmosphere.

On July 6, Vice-Premier Li Hsien-nien gave a banquet warmly welcoming the Tanzanian Government Delegation and the Zambian Government Delegation. Vice-Premier Li Hsien-nien and Minister Mudenda spoke at the banquet which was filled with an atmosphere of unity and friendship between the people of China, Tanzania and Zambia.

In his speech, Vice-Premier Li Hsien-nien said: "In international affairs, the Tanzanian Government and the Zambian Government have always upheld justice, opposed the imperialist policies of aggression and war and supported the national-liberation movements in Asia and Africa, thus making positive contributions to the cause of the Afro-Asian people's unity against imperialism and winning the praise and admiration of the Afro-Asian countries and peoples."

The Vice-Premier added: "Tempered through the Great Proletarian Cultural Revolution and armed with Mao Tsetung Thought, the 700 million Chinese people, in warm response to the call of our great leader Chairman Mao, are determined to build our socialist motherland into a still more consolidated and stronger state and to make still greater contributions in supporting the three Indo-Chinese peoples and the peoples of Asia, Africa, Latin America and the rest of the world in their revolutionary struggle against U.S. imperialism and its running dogs and in supporting the oppressed peoples and nations in their just struggle to win national liberation and safeguard national independence, thus fulfilling our proletarian internationalist duty."

Vice-Premier Li Hsien-nien spoke highly of the all-round and satisfactory development of the friendly relations and co-operation between China and Tanzania and Zambia on the basis of the Five Principles of Peaceful Coexistence. He said: "Our Tanzanian and Zambian friends may rest assured that, in the common struggle against imperialism, colonialism and neo-colonialism, the Chinese people will remain for ever the reliable friends of the Tanzanian and Zambian peoples."

Minister Mudenda said in his speech that there existed a deep-rooted friendship between the people of Tanzania, Zambia and China. This friendship confounded the exploiters and oppressors of people. He warmly praised the role played by the Chinese people in supporting the struggle for the total liberation of all the oppressed peoples the world over. He pointed out that on the African continent large areas were still occupied by fascists and imperialists. He said: Our commitment in this regard is the same as yours—to eliminate the oppressor from our continent. He added: "We strongly support similar efforts which are now under way in Asia and Latin America. We uphold the heroic struggle that is going on in Asia today. We feel that it will not be long before the people of North America and Europe realize the truth and also join us in stamping out exploitation, imperialism and colonialism."

Minister Mudenda went on to say: "In our common struggle against these enemies, your country, Party and people have resolved to assist us build the railway. We strongly appreciated the friendly thinking behind this decision and we are extremely thankful to the great leader Chairman Mao Tsetung, the people and the Party of the People's Republic of China." He pointed out that the dedication to duty shown by the Chinese people in building the project was unparalleled.

Protocols and minutes of the talks concerning the construction of the Tanzania-Zambia railway were signed between the Government of China and the Governments of Tanzania and Zambia in Peking on July 12.

They are the Protocol Between the Government of the People's Republic of China and the Governments of the United Republic of Tanzania and the Republic of Zambia Concerning the Amount of the Loan for the Construction of the Tanzania-Zambia Railway and the Method of Its Repayment, the Protocol Between the Government of the People's Republic of China and the Governments of the United Republic of Tanzania and the Republic of Zambia Concerning the "Report on the Survey and Design for the Tanzania-Zambia Railway," and the Minutes of Talks on the Construction of the Tanzania-Zambia Railway.

Premier Chou En-lai and Vice-Premier Li Hsien-nien were present at the signing ceremony. The protocols and the minutes of the talks were signed by Fang Yi, Minister of the Chinese Commission for Economic Relations With Foreign Countries, Amir Habib Jamal, leader of the Tanzanian Government Delegation and Minister for Finance, and E. H. K. Mudenda, leader of the Zambian Government Delegation and Minister of Development and Finance, on behalf of their respective governments.

E. H. K. Mudenda, leader of the Zambian Government Delegation and Minister of Development and Finance, and Amir Habib Jamal, leader of the Tanzanian Government Delegation and Minister for Finance, gave a farewell banquet on July 12. Vice-Premier Li Hsien-nien and leading members of the departments concerned attended the banquet on invitation.

Minister Jamal and Vice-Premier Li Hsien-nien made speeches at the banquet.

In his speech, Minister Jamal expressed his deep appreciation for the very warm hospitality extended to the two delegations by the Government and the people of China. "We feel particularly honoured that Chairman Mao Tsetung and his close comrade-in-arms Vice-Chairman Lin Piao were able to spare their most precious time to receive us," he said.

Jamal said that a protocol was concluded in 1967 between the People's Republic of China, the Republic of Zambia and the United Republic of Tanzania in which the People's Republic of China, at the request of the Zambian and Tanzanian Governments, agreed to assist in the construction of a railway linking Tanzania with Zambia, and at the same time provide Tanzania's sister state Zambia with an unfettered outlet to the sea at the port of Dar-es-Salaam.

He praised the technical staff sent by the Chinese Government who worked arduously day and night under a wide range of difficult conditions, in a strange and exacting environment, and completed the survey and designing work.

"Inspired by the unqualified successes already achieved," he said, "the Government Delegations of the People's Republic of China, of Zambia and of Tanzania have met once again in Peking and discussed important matters connected with the railway project. Our deliberations have been brought to a most gratifyingly successful conclusion."

He said: "Your massive assistance to the cause of developing countries, while engaged in a much needed reconstruction at home, is a clear demonstration of the commitment of the Chinese people to international solidarity in the struggle for the construction of a just and peaceful world order in which imperialism, fascism and colonialism will have been banished for ever."

He added: "In assisting us to achieve our cherished aim of close communications with each other, thus serving the needs of our national economy, the Government and the people of the People's Republic of China are making a most positive and significant contribution towards total liberation of Africa. We salute and thank sincerely the Chinese people and their great leader Chairman Mao for this magnificent act of international solidarity."

In his speech, Vice-Premier Li Hsien-nien said: The two government delegations have come to our country for a friendly visit and have achieved positive results during their short stay of a few days. "Your present visit has not only pushed to a new stage the construction of the Tanzania-Zambia railway through the co-operative efforts of our three countries, but has also made new contributions to the further strengthening of the friendship between the peoples of China, Zambia and Tanzania and the development of friendly relations and co-operation between our three countries," he said.

Li Hsien-nien said: Three years ago, thanks to the direct concern of Chairman Mao, President Kaunda and President Nyerere, our three countries decided to co-operate in building the Tanzania-Zambia railway. Since then, with our joint efforts we have victoriously made survey, designing and preparations for the railway construction. The rapid progress of this grand yet difficult project within a relatively short period forcefully testifies to the great vitality and broad prospects for the development of the cause of friendly co-operation between the peoples of China, Zambia and Tanzania and between the Afro-Asian peoples on the basis of the common struggle against imperialism and colonialism.

He continued: Chairman Mao teaches us: "China ought to make a greater contribution to humanity." What we have done is far from adequate. "We are determined," he said, "to give stronger support to the just struggles of the Afro-Asian peoples and the peoples of the world against U.S. imperialism and all its lackeys, and stronger assistance to friendly countries in their cause of national construction. 'The just struggles of the people of all countries support each other.' We are sincerely grateful to the Governments and peoples of Zambia and Tanzania for their support to China in international affairs."

Li Hsien-nien pointed out: "The road of advance before us Afro-Asian countries is definitely not a straight and smooth one. In eliminating the imperialist and colonialist forces and in building our respective countries, we shall yet encounter all kinds of hardships and obstacles, including natural barriers and disruptive schemes by imperialism and its lackeys. But so long as we firmly rely on the unity and struggle of our own peoples and continuously strengthen the anti-imperialist unity and mutual assistance and co-operation among the Afro-Asian peoples, we will certainly overcome every difficulty and advance from victory to victory."

On July 13, the two delegations left Peking for the southern part of China on a visit.

II

The Chairman of the People's Republic of China and the President of the United Republic of Tanzania,

Desiring to consolidate and further develop the profound friendship between the People's Republic of China and the United Republic of Tanzania, and

Being convinced that the strengthening of friendly cooperation between the People's Republic of China and the United Republic of Tanzania conforms to the fundamental interests of the peoples of the two countries, helps promote the solidarity between them as well as among Asian and African peoples and the common struggle against imperialism, and conduces to peace in Asia, Africa and the world,

Have decided for this purpose to conclude the present Treaty, the articles of which are as follows:

Article I

The Contracting Parties will maintain and develop the relations of peace and friendship between the People's Republic of China and the United Republic of Tanzania.

Article II

The Contracting Parties pledge to take the Five Principles of mutual respect for sovereignty and territorial integrity, mutual non-aggression, non-interference in each other's internal affairs, equality and mutual benefit, and peaceful coexistence as the principles guiding the relations between the two countries.

Article III

The Contracting Parties agree to develop economic and cultural relations between the two countries in the spirit of equality, mutual benefit and friendly cooperation.

Article IV

The Contracting Parties undertake to settle through peaceful consultations any issue that may arise between them.

Article V

The present Treaty is subject to ratification, and the instruments of ratification shall be exchanged in Dar es Salaam as soon as possible.

The present Treaty shall come into force on the date of exchange of the instruments of ratification and shall remain in force for a period of ten years. Unless either of the Contracting Parties gives to the other notice in writing to terminate the present Treaty one year before the expiration of this period, the present Treaty shall be automatically prolonged for another period of ten years, and shall thereafter be renewable accordingly.

Done in duplicate in Peking on February 20, 1965, in the Chinese, Swahili, and English languages, all three texts being equally authentic.

[Signatures]

45. NEWS COMMENTARY: THIRTY-FIRST WORLD TABLE TENNIS CHAMPIONSHIP (April, 1971)*

Although these are routine news announcements about sports by New China News Agency, the Thirty-first World Table Tennis Championship held in Nagoya, Japan, from March 28 to April 5, 1971, became a turning point in the Sino-American relationship. It was during this competition that China invited the thirteen-member table tennis team from the United States to take part in matches in Peking and Shanghai and permitted U.S. journalists for the first time in twenty-two years to visit China.

According to eyewitness account,[1] the main table tennis contest in the Peking sports stadium, which the Chinese won with ease, was an impressive display of courage and hospitality. Banners hailed the friendliness of the world's peoples, and the 18,000 spectators enthusiastically applauded each time a member of the American team made a point. And at the end of the match between American and Chinese teams, the crowd rose and clapped slowly in unison for a solid twenty minutes.

* From Hsin Hua News Release, April 5 and 11, 1971, translated by *Peking Review* (April 9 and 16, 1971) (extract).
1 *Life* (April 20, 1971), p. 28.

Finally, in the Great Hall of the People in Peking Chou En-lai greeted members of the American table tennis team and the three U.S. journalists and said: "You have opened a new page in the relations of the Chinese and American people."

I

[Hsin Hua News Agency Release, April 11, 1971] —

On April 9, the Canadian Table Tennis Delegation led by Margaret Walden, Secretary-General of Canadian Table Tennis Association, and on April 10, the Colombia Table Tennis Delegation led by Pedro Garcia, leading member of the Colombian Table Tennis Federation, and the U.S. Table Tennis Delegation led by Graham Steenhoven, President of the U.S. Table Tennis Association, arrived in Peking for friendship visits to China after participating in the 31st World Table Tennis Championships.

At the airport to welcome these delegations were leading members of the All-China Sports Federation and the Chinese People's Association for Friendship with Foreign Countries as well as coaches and players of the Chinese Table Tennis Team. When the visitors stepped down from the planes, their Chinese hosts went forward to shake hands with them in welcome.

The Chinese sportsmen and their friends had warm and friendly talks in the airport's waiting room during which the guests said they were very glad to come and to visit China. They also expressed the belief that their visits would surely further promote friendship with the Chinese people.

II

[Hsin Hua News Agency Release, April 5, 1971] —

The opening ceremony of the 31st World Table Tennis Championship took place in Nagoya, Japan on the afternoon of March 28. It was attended by players from more than 50 countries and regions.

After H. Roy Evans, President of the International Table Tennis Federation, made the opening speech, Koji Goto, chairman of the organizing committee of the championships and President of the Japan Table Tennis Association, delivered a welcoming speech, extending high respects and thanks to the players taking part in the tournament. He expressed the wish that the present World Table Tennis Championships would help strengthen friendship between the sportsmen of various countries and the Japanese people and promote friendship among participating sportsmen.

More players from the Democratic People's Republic of Korea, Nepal, the United Arab Republic, Mexico, Colombia and other Asian, African and Latin American countries and regions were at the present championships than at the previous two.

Many well-known European teams such as from Romania, Yugoslavia, Hungary, Sweden and England took part in the tournament.

Japan, whose players had done well at the world championships for years, was represented by 32 men and women players, the largest participating team.

Tempered in the Great Proletarian Cultural Revolution, Chinese players sent their representatives to the world championships for the first time in six years. Among them were veterans as well as newcomers to the world championships.

After the ceremony Chuang Tse-tung told Hsinhua: "We are very glad to enjoy the enthusiastic help and support of our Japanese friends in coming to participate in the 31st World Table Tennis Championships in Nagoya and to have the opportunity to learn from players of various countries and exchange experience with them. Players from various countries have shown the most friendly feeling for China. This makes us deeply aware that 'we have friends all over the world,' as our great leader Chairman Mao has said."

Lin Hui-ching, playing vice-captain of the Chinese women's team, said: "We are at the championships to promote friendship among the sportsmen and people of various countries. We place friendship above competition. We believe that our wish will certainly come true through the tournament and what we learn from players of other countries will be of value."

* * *

CHAPTER SIX:

Policies on Overseas Chinese, Boundaries, and Disputed Territories

Peking today continues to face two complicated foreign policy problems in her relations with neighboring countries: the problem of overseas Chinese, and the problem of boundaries and disputed territories.

The Chinese have been vague about the precise number of overseas Chinese that they claim as Chinese. There appear to be between 10,000,000 and 12,000,000[1] not including those on Taiwan, Hong Kong, or Macao, who still have relatives living in mainland China and who are maintaining some sort of contact.

The bulk of overseas Chinese are living in Southeast Asia, however, and based upon earlier estimates made by G. William Skinner,[2] the distributions may be classified as follows:[3]

	Overseas Chinese	% of native pop.
Malaya	2,365,000	37.8
Singapore	965,000	76.6
Thailand	2,360,000	11.3
Borneo	270,000	27.0
Cambodia	230,000	5.5
S. Viet.	780,000	6.2
N. Viet.	50,000	0.4
Laos	10,000	0.6
Indonesia	2,250,000[4]	2.7
Burma	320,000	1.6
Philippines	270,000	1.2

1 *Jen-min Jih-pao* (October 6, 1964; April 15, 1960).

2 Quoted in A. Doak Barnett, *Communist China and Asia* (New York, Council on Foreign Relations, 1960), p. 176.

3 Source: *The Annals of the American Academy of Political and Social Science*, Vol. 321 (January, 1959), p. 133.

4 Before 1965 coup in Indonesia.

Over ninety percent of these overseas Chinese came from China's provinces of Kwantung (Canton) and Fukien several generations ago, and yet they do not as a rule acknowledge that they are different from their cousins on the mainland, although many perhaps have never set foot in China. They have also traditionally avoided becoming involved in local politics and being assimilated into the local cultures or societies. During the colonial days they frequently achieved a measure of autonomy as separate communities and increasingly organized themselves into clan groups, occupational guilds, secret societies, and dialect associations.

Because of their alleged primary loyalties to China as well as their newly acquired economic wealth, they have become a problem as the Southeast Asian countries gain their independence and gradually develop their own economy and nationalism. And throughout Southeast Asia, steps have been taken to restrict Chinese immigration, education, economic power, and citizenship [1] (see Document 19).

The Chinese Communist government, like all Chinese governments, regards the overseas Chinese as a useful instrument, especially since they are a steady source of enormous foreign exchange for China. Between 1929 and 1941, for example, remittance from the overseas Chinese ranged between $80,000,000 and $200,000,000 annually under the Nationalist regime.[2]

Some branches of Chinese government, such as China's intelligence and propaganda agencies, had also attempted to use the overseas Chinese to gather information and to influence the politics and policies of local Southeast Asian countries. As resentments and hostility toward the Chinese grew among the local population there was a gradual shift of Peking's subversive policy, with a new moderate effort to promote friendship between the overseas Chinese and their countries of residence.[3] The first clear indication of the implementation of Peking's new

---

1 A. Doak Barnett, *Communist China and Asia, op. cit.*, p. 186.
2 Stephen Fitzgerald, "China and the Overseas Chinese: perceptions and policies," *China Quarterly*, No. 44 (October—December, 1970), p. 12.
3 There were renewed efforts to encourage subversive activities of the overseas Chinese in their host countries during the Cultural Revolution (1966-68). See Klaus Mehnert, *Peking and the New Left: At Home and Abroad* (Berkeley, University of California Center for Chinese Studies, Research Monographs #4, 1969).

policy was the complete revision of the earlier position on nationality, as evidenced by the conclusion with Indonesia of a "dual nationality" pact (see Document 47).

On the other hand, there remained those overseas Chinese who refused to think of themselves as anything but Chinese and those who were deported for a variety of reasons by their host countries. China then adopted a policy of resettlement on the Chinese motherland. However, the People's Republic, because of its own domestic population pressure, did not make any particular effort to encourage large numbers of overseas Chinese to leave their countries of residence and resettle in China [1] (see Document 48).

With the ever-growing nationalism in Asia, there are continuing frictions, conflict, and fear among the more affluent overseas Chinese and the indigenous native population. However, the People's Republic has adopted a policy based on "a high degree of sensitivity to the attitudes and emotions of indigenous South East Asians, and a well-informed and realistic appraisal of the situation in these countries."[2] But at times Peking's new official policy was not carried out by the local, more radical revolutionary groups.

For instance, the disturbances of the local Chinese leftists during the Cultural Revolution in Hong Kong were certainly in opposition to the Peking policy. During the Cultural Revolution the local leftists began to take policies into their own hands, including the use of Macao Radio to urge Chinese policemen to desert their posts and a call on the Chinese masses for revolution. In fact, at times the Chinese People's Liberation Army had to restrain the overenthusiastic Chinese villagers from crossing the border to "liberate" Hong Kong.[3]

Another illustration involves a small group of American overseas Chinese who organized themselves as pro-Maoists in Chinatowns throughout the United States, allied themselves with the new radical left movement, and continued to denounce the United States and the establishment in spite of the desire of the Peking leadership to relax international tensions and normalize relations with Washington.[4]

1 Stephen Fitzgerald, "China and the Overseas Chinese . . .," *op. cit.*, p. 24.

2 Washington *Post* (August 25, 1967).

3 *Ibid.*

4 *Getting Together* (San Francisco and New York, I Wor Kuen), Vol. 2., No. 6 (July/ August, 1971).

Chinese territorial disputes with its neighbors largely stem from China's humiliating defeat after the Opium War which resulted in the signing of a number of unequal treaties (see Introduction and Document 53).

A Chinese history handbook published in Peking in 1954 includes a map showing China's frontier as claimed in 1840 and in 1919 which captioned "The Past Democratic Revolutionary Era (1840-1919)—Imperialist Encroachments of Chinese Territory."[1] It specifies nineteen individual losses of Chinese territories:

1. The Great Northwest [Soviet Kazakhstan, Kirghizstan and Tadzhikistan in Central Asia]: seized by Imperial Russia under the Treaty of Chunguchak, 1864;

2. Pamirs [Kashmir]: secretly divided between England and Russia in 1896;

3. Nepal: went to England after "independence" in 1898;

4. Sikkim: occupied by England in 1889;

5. Bhutan: went to England after "independence" in 1865;

6. Assam: given to England by Burma in 1826;

7. Burma: became part of the British Empire in 1886;

8. Andaman Archipelago: went to England;

9. Malaya: occupied by England in 1895;

10. Thailand: declared "independent" under joint Anglo-French control in 1904;

11. Annam [Indochina]: occupied by France in 1885;

12. Taiwan and Penghu Archipelago [Pescadores]: relinquished to Japan by the treaty of Shimonoseki, 1895;

13. Sulu Archipelago (between the Philippines and North Borneo): went to England;

14. Region [North Burma] where the British crossed the border and committed aggression (against China);

15. Ryukyu Archipelago: occupied by Japan in 1879;

16. Korea: "independent" in 1895 and annexed by Japan in 1910;

17-18. The Great Northeast (the Amur River Basin): seized by imperial Russia under the Treaties of Aigun, 1858, and the Treaty of Peking, 1860;

1 Liu Pei-hua, ed., *Chung-kuo Chin-tai Chieh-shih* (Peking, I Chang Shu Chu, 1954), following page 253, as quoted in Dennis J. Doolin, *Territorial Claims in the Sino-Soviet Conflict* (Stanford, Hoover Institution Studies #7, 1965), pp. 16-17. Nationalist China published a similar book in 1946 entitled *General Geography of China* (Shanghai, 1946).

19. Sakhalin: divided between Russia and Japan.

Of course not all of these territories are in dispute. No Chinese now or in the past has been taught that countries such as Korea, Indochina, Malaya, Burma, Thailand, Nepal, or Bhutan are part of China. In addition, the Chinese signed a number of new agreements or treaties to guarantee or reaffirm the permanence of these boundaries: Burma (1960), Nepal (1961), Pakistan (1962), Afghanistan (1963), and Mongolia (1963) (see Appendix Map E).

However, there are still some very serious boundary disputes with India (see Document 51), the USSR (see Documents 50, 54), and the United States (see Documents 50, 54). China's dispute with the United States is primarily concerning Taiwan, the Vietnam War, and such minor points as the United States' refusal to recognize China's extension of territorial waters to twelve miles (instead of three to six miles, as practiced by the United States.)

The claims of the Chinese government, according to Robert C. North, "have not been translated into active policy,"[1] although the Chinese did move quickly to reintegrate Tibet into her national territory (see Document 49). And China was "less aggressive in its lateral expansion than many outside observers had expected."[2]

Specific Chinese Communist foreign goals, in the opinion of many observers, seem to be motivated primarily by the maintenance of the security and integrity of the Chinese People's Republic rather than by acquisition of new territories. As China moves into a more conciliatory diplomacy in the 1970's, it will undoubtedly be "working for the settlement of boundary questions with its neighboring countries through negotiations and for the maintenance of the status quo of the boundary pending a settlement" (see Document 53).

46. GOVERNMENT STATEMENT: PROTEST AGAINST HONG KONG RESTRICTIONS ON CHINESE (May, 1950)*

Hong Kong, as a British Crown Colony comprised of a portion of the Chinese mainland and 236 islands,

1 Robert C. North, *The Foreign Relations of China, op. cit.*, p. 73.
2 *Ibid.*
* From *China Monthly Review*, Vol. CXIX, No. 2-Supplement (October, 1950), p. 9.

lies on the eastern side of the Pearl River estuary. The main Hong Kong Island and its adjacent islets were ceded to the British by China in 1841 after the Opium War; and Kowloon Peninsula and Stonecutters Island were ceded in 1860. However, the remaining islands and the mainland, stretching from Boundary Street Kowloon northward to the Sham Chun River, are known as the New Territories and were leased to the British in 1898 for ninety-nine years.

Although the colony has a total land area of only 398 square miles, the British have always practiced an "open door" policy with respect to the admission of Chinese. Only after the establishment of the People's Republic did the British chargé d'affaires ad interim in Peking (J. C. Hutchinson) send an official letter to the Chinese government stating that the Hong Kong authorities found it necessary to restrict the hitherto free passage of the Chinese by subjecting them to the same measures of control as were other foreign nationals. The following is a protest note from Chang Han-fu, the Chinese Vice-Foreign Minister. The Peking government has never made any direct threats to take over Hong Kong, however.

My Dear Mr. Hutchinson,

With reference to your letter No. 23 dated 27th April 1950, which was received on 28th April, stating briefly that the British authorities in Hong Kong will remove, on 28th April of this year, the special exemptions as provided by regulations under Section 34 of the Hong Kong Immigration Control Ordinance of 1949, by which Chinese nationals entering or leaving Hong Kong are exempted from Sections 18, 24 and 25, concerning travel documents, of the said ordinance; and that, in the future, Chinese nationals will be subject to the same measures of control as other nationals, I have the honor to inform you the following:

For more than 100 years, Chinese nationals entering or leaving Hong Kong have never been treated as foreign immigrants; nor have the British authorities in Hong Kong any justification whatsoever to treat Chinese nationals as other foreign immigrants. Hence, with regard to the regulations controlling Chinese nationals entering or leaving Hong Kong as have been promulgated recently by the British authorities in Hong Kong, the Central People's Government of the People's Republic of China cannot but regard them as an unreasonable and unfriendly act towards the People's Republic of China and her people, and hereby protest to the British government.

The Central People's Government considers that the British government should undertake necessary measures to remove immediately all restrictions upon Chinese nationals entering or leaving Hong Kong.

I avail of this opportunity to express my respects.

[Signature]

47. TREATY ON DUAL NATIONALITY BETWEEN CHINA AND INDONESIA (April, 1955)*

In international law, nationality may be acquired through jus sanguinis *(law of blood), or* jus soli *(law of soil or place), or through naturalization. Because of the divergent practices of* jus sanguinis *and* jus soli, *a person may be born of dual nationality. For example, a Chinese who was born in the United States of Chinese parents may be both a Chinese and an American citizen. Millions of Chinese face this problem abroad. The following is the first treaty concluded by the People's Republic and Indonesia on April 22, 1955. Because it favors Indonesia, many other countries have moved to conclude similar pacts.*

The Government of the People's Republic of China and the Government of the Republic of Indonesia,

In order to achieve a reasonable solution of the question of the nationality of persons who hold simultaneously the nationality of the People's Republic of China and the nationality of the Republic of Indonesia,

Have agreed to conclude the present treaty in accordance with the principles of equality and mutual benefit and non-interference in each other's internal affairs and on the basis of friendly co-operation, and

* From Hsin Hua News Release, April 29, 1955.

Have appointed as their respective plenipotentiaries: the Government of the People's Republic of China, Minister for Foreign Affairs of the People's Republic of China, Chou En-lai; the Government of the Republic of Indonesia, Minister for Foreign Affairs of the Republic of Indonesia, Sunarjo.

The plenipotentiaries of both parties, after having examined each other's credentials and found them in good and due order, have agreed upon the following provisions:

Article I

The high contracting parties agree that all persons who hold simultaneously the nationality of the People's Republic of China and the nationality of the Republic of Indonesia shall choose, in accordance with their own will, between the nationality of the People's Republic of China and the nationality of the Republic of Indonesia. All married women who hold the above-mentioned two nationalities shall also choose, in accordance with their own will, between the two nationalities.

Article II

All persons who hold the two nationalities mentioned in Article I and who have come of age when the present treaty comes into effect, shall choose their nationality within two years of the coming into effect of the present treaty. For the purpose of this treaty, persons who have come of age are understood to be persons who have attained the age of 18 years and married persons under the age of 18 years.

Article III

Any person holding the two nationalities mentioned in Article I desiring to retain the nationality of the People's Republic of China must declare before the appropriate authorities of the People's Republic of China that he or she renounces the nationality of the Republic of Indonesia, and shall, after such declaration, be considered as having chosen voluntarily the nationality of the People's Republic of China. Any person holding the two nationalities mentioned in Article I desiring to retain the nationality of the Republic of Indonesia must declare before the appropriate authorities of the Republic of Indonesia that he or she renounces the nationality of the People's Republic of China, and shall, after such declaration, be considered as having chosen voluntarily the nationality of the Republic of Indonesia. The above-mentioned appropriate authorities of the People's Republic of China are as follows: in the People's Republic of China, government organs designated by the Government of the People's Republic of China; in the Republic of Indonesia, the Embassy of the People's Republic of China in the Republic of Indonesia, the Consulates of the People's Republic of China in the Republic of Indonesia, and such temporary offices established by the above-mentioned embassy or consulates as necessary and with the consent of the Government of the Republic of Indonesia. The above-mentioned appropriate authorities of the Republic of Indonesia are as follows: in the Republic of Indonesia, government organs designated by the Government of the Republic of Indonesia; in the People's Republic of China, the Embassy of the Republic of Indonesia in the People's Republic of China, the Consulates of the Republic of Indonesia in the People's Republic of China, if there be any, and such temporary offices established by the above-mentioned embassy or consulates as necessary and with the consent of the Government of the People's Republic of China.

In order to facilitate the choosing of their nationality by persons holding the two nationalities mentioned in Article I, the high contracting parties agree to adopt a convenient method for the said declaration. The method of choosing nationalities as stipulated in this article also applies in principle to those persons who reside in places outside the territories of the People's Republic of China and the Republic of Indonesia and who hold the two nationalities mentioned in Article I.

Article IV

The high contracting parties agree that any person holding the two nationalities mentioned in Article I shall automatically lose the nationality of the Republic of Indonesia upon choosing, in accordance with the provisions of this treaty, the nationality of the People's Republic of China; and that any person holding the two nationalities mentioned in Article I shall automatically lose the nationality of the People's Republic of

China upon choosing, in accordance with the provisions of this treaty, the nationality of the Republic of Indonesia.

Article V

The high contracting parties agree that the nationality of those persons who hold the two nationalities mentioned in Article I and who fail to choose their nationality within the period of two years prescribed in Article II shall be determined in the following manner: if their fathers are of Chinese origin, they shall be considered as having chosen the nationality of the People's Republic of China; if their fathers are of Indonesian origin, they shall be considered as having chosen the nationality of the Republic of Indonesia. The nationality of those of the above-mentioned persons who fail to choose their nationality within the prescribed period and who have no legal relationship with their fathers or whose father's nationality is unascertainable, shall be determined in the following manner: if their mothers are of Chinese origin, they shall be considered as having chosen the nationality of the People's Republic of China; if their mothers are of Indonesian origin, they shall be considered as having chosen the nationality of the Republic of Indonesia.

Article VI

All those persons who hold the two nationalities mentioned in Article I and who have not come of age when the present treaty comes into effect shall choose their nationality within a year of their coming of age. Pending their coming of age, they shall be considered as only holding the nationality chosen by their parents or their fathers in accordance with the provisions of the present treaty. In case they have no legal relationship with their fathers or their fathers have died without choosing a nationality or their father's nationality is unascertainable, those persons shall, pending their coming of age, be considered as only holding the nationality chosen by their mothers in accordance with the provisions of the present treaty. If they fail to choose their nationality within the period prescribed in this article after their coming of age, they shall be considered as having chosen voluntarily the nationality held by them before they come of age.

Article VII

All those persons holding the two nationalities mentioned in Article I who, after having chosen the nationality of the Republic of Indonesia and lost the nationality of the People's Republic of China, leave the Republic of Indonesia and take up permanent residence outside its territory shall automatically lose the nationality of the Republic of Indonesia if they regain, in accordance with their own will, the nationality of the People's Republic of China. All those persons holding the two nationalities mentioned in Article I who, after having chosen the nationality of the People's Republic of China and lost the nationality of the Republic of Indonesia, leave the People's Republic of China and take up permanent residence outside its territory shall automatically lose the nationality of the People's Republic of China if they regain, in accordance with their own will, the nationality of the Republic of Indonesia.

Article VIII

All children born in the Republic of Indonesia acquire, upon their birth, the nationality of the People's Republic of China if both their parents or only their fathers hold the nationality of the People's Republic of China; all children born in the People's Republic of China, acquire, upon their birth, the nationality of the Republic of Indonesia if both their parents or only their fathers hold the nationality of the Republic of Indonesia.

Article IX

Any child holding the nationality of the People's Republic of China, if legally adopted by a citizen of the Republic of Indonesia before attaining five years of age, acquires the nationality of the Republic of Indonesia and automatically loses the nationality of the People's Republic of China; any child holding the nationality of the Republic of Indonesia, if legally adopted by a citizen of the People's Republic of China before attaining five years of age, acquires the nationality of the People's Republic of China and automatically loses the nationality of the Republic of Indonesia.

Article X

In the case of a citizen of the People's Republic of China marrying a citizen of the Republic of Indonesia, each party retains after their marriage his or her original nationality. However, if one party applies for and acquires the nationality of the other party in accordance with his or her own will, he or she shall automatically lose his or her original nationality upon acquiring the nationality of the other party. The said applications shall be made to the appropriate authorities of the country concerned.

Article XI

With a view to improving the conditions under which citizens of one country reside in the other, each high contracting party agrees to encourage its own citizens residing in the other country, that is citizens of the Republic of Indonesia residing in the People's Republic of China and citizens of the People's Republic of China residing in the Republic of Indonesia, to respect the laws and social customs of the country in which they reside and not to take part in political activities of that country. Each high contracting party affirms its willingness to protect according to its laws the proper rights and interests of the citizens of the other party residing in its territory.

Article XII

The high contracting parties agree that matters relating to the implementation of the present treaty which are not provided for in this treaty may be decided upon through negotiations between the two parties.

Article XIII

Should disputes arise between the high contracting parties over the interpretation or implementation of the present treaty, the two parties will settle such disputes through negotiations.

Article XIV

The present treaty shall be ratified by the high contracting parties in accordance with their respective constitutional procedures and shall come into effect upon the date of the exchange of ratifications, which shall take place in Peking. The present treaty shall be valid for 20 years and shall remain in force thereafter. If, after the expiration of the period of 20 years, one party requests its termination, it must so notify the other party one year in advance and in written form; and the present treaty shall be terminated one year after the tendering of such notification.

In faith whereof, the plenipotentiaries of the high contracting parties put seals and signatures thereon. Done in Bandung on the 22nd day of April, 1955, in duplicate in the Chinese and Indonesian languages, both texts being equally authentic.

[Signatures]

48. STATE COUNCIL: DIRECTIVE ON RECEPTION AND RESETTLEMENT OF RETURNED OVERSEAS CHINESE (February, 1960)*

Since 1949 several hundred thousand overseas Chinese have returned to China, either on a permanent or a temporary basis. These returned Chinese may be divided into two major categories; students and residents, and both of them have presented the government with some problems of management. The following is an important government directive especially promulgated in 1960 in order to meet the sizable influx of repatriates from Indonesia in that year.

There are tens of millions of overseas Chinese residing in foreign countries. In the old days, large numbers of Chinese made their way to foreign lands to make a living. They labored together with the people of their host countries and made lasting contributions to the economic and cultural developments of these countries. They also fought shoulder to shoulder with the local people, shedding their sweat and blood, in the struggles for the national independence of their host countries. For this reason, the overseas Chinese have not only

*From *Survey of China Mainland Press*, No. 2192 (February 9, 1960), pp. 23-24.

established close friendship with the local people, but also played a good role in developing friendly relations between the Chinese people and the people of the host countries concerned.

Since the founding of the new China, many of the overseas Chinese have returned to China. They have received proper treatment and settled down in their fatherland. They are playing an active role in the socialist construction of their fatherland.

Our government has always been willing, on the basis of the five principles of peaceful co-existence, to negotiate with foreign countries concerned for the settlement of all questions concerning overseas Chinese, including the dual nationality question. The Chinese government is happy to see the overseas Chinese residing in foreign countries choose the nationality of their host countries according to the principle of voluntary willingness. With regard to the overseas Chinese who voluntarily want to preserve their Chinese nationality, the Chinese Government has consistently encouraged them to abide by the laws and decrees of their host countries, and to contribute to the economic and cultural development of these countries. Their legitimate rights and interests should also be given realistic protection. This has been the consistent policy of the Chinese Government. It will not be changed in the future.

It is regrettable that anti-Chinese activities have recently broken out in some south-eastern Asian countries. Large numbers of overseas Chinese have been subjected to persecution without any reason. In view of this development, the Chinese Government decides to receive and resettle in China the overseas Chinese who have become displaced in foreign countries, who are unable to make a living there, or who are unwilling to continue their living in foreign countries, so that they may live and participate in construction in China according to their wish.

The socialist construction program is now progressing by leaps and bounds in China. China is having a shortage, not a surplus, of manpower. For this reason, we warmly welcome the return not only of the overseas Chinese under persecution, but also of all overseas Chinese who are willing to return, so that they may contribute to the socialist construction of the fatherland.

To carry out properly the work of receiving and resettling the returning overseas Chinese, the following directive is hereby promulgated:

(1) It is hereby decided to establish a "Committee of the People's Republic of China for Receiving and Resettling Returned Overseas Chinese" which will assume over-all responsibility for receiving and resettling returned overseas Chinese. Liao Ch'engchih is appointed chairman, and T'ao Chu, Yeh Fei, Liu Chien-hsun, Yen Hung-yan, Tan Kah-kee, and Wang Chen Vice-Chairmen of the Committee;

Fang Fang, Chuang-Hsi ch'uan, Mao Ch'i-hua, Ch'en Ch'i-yuan, Tung Ch'un-ts'ai, Sun Ta-kuang, Chang Chu-kuo, Ch'in Li-chen, Chang Hsia-ping, Hu Jen-k'uei, Min I-min, Shen Tzu-chiu, Chang Ch'ao, Yu Yang-tzu, Wang Yuan-hsing, Huang Chieh, Wu I-hsiu, and Li Mai, are appointed members of the Committee.

(2) Reception offices will be established at the ports of Canton, Swatow, Changchiang (Tsamkong) and Haikou to receive returning overseas Chinese.

(3) To resettle the returned overseas Chinese properly in order to enable them to actively participate in the socialist construction program in the fatherland, the People's Councils of Kwangtung, Fukien, Kwangsi, and Yunnan will be charged with the responsibility for resettling the returned overseas Chinese.

(4) With regard to the expenditure for receiving and resettling returned overseas Chinese, the People's Councils of the provinces and autonomous region concerned will draw up separate budgets for the study of the "Committee of the People's Republic of China for Receiving and Resettling Returned Overseas Chinese", which will submit, after giving its approval, the budgets to the State Council with a request for allocation of funds.

(5) The following are the principles governing the resettlement of returned overseas Chinese:

(a) The returned overseas Chinese shall be resettled properly according to the needs of the state as well as the wishes of persons concerned.

(b) Arrangements shall be made for returned overseas Chinese students and ex-student youth who are qualified for further schooling to enroll in educational institutions. Those who have financial difficulty shall receive subsidies from the state.

(c) Returned overseas Chinese who want to return to their native places to reunite with thier kinsfolk shall be resettled properly by the People's Councils concerned in conjunction with the people's communes concerned.

(d) The various localities shall give suitable favourable consideration to the livelihood of returned overseas Chinese.

(6) The following are provisions governing the property brought back by overseas Chinese:

(a) All baggage and articles brought back by returning overseas Chinese shall be exempted from Customs duties.

(b) All money and materials brought back by returning overseas Chinese shall forever be their private property.

49. AGREEMENT WITH LOCAL GOVERNMENT OF TIBET (May, 1951) and ORDER TO DISSOLVE THE LOCAL GOVERNMENT OF TIBET (March, 1959)*

Both the Nationalist and Communist Chinese are very emotional about Tibet, which they regard as Chinese territory in spite of the fact that the Tibetans have always had the opposite conviction. Communist China's invasion of Tibet took place simultaneously with the first stage of its intervention in Korea in October, 1950. An appeal by the Tibetans themselves and by San Salvador to the United Nations led to no action. Finally, a Tibetan delegation appeared in Peking on April 22, 1951, just before the pro-Chinese Pan-chen Lama to negotiate with the Chinese, resulting in the following agreement signed on May 23, 1951 (I). To consolidate the Chinese legal position over Tibet, China signed another important agreement with India on April 29, 1954, in which India formally recognized Chinese claims to Tibet.[1]

However, the Tibetans, led by the pro-Indian Dalai Lama, continued to resist Chinese domination, leading to a number of open revolts in Tibet against

*From Hsin Hua News Release, May 28, 1951; and *Concerning the Question of Tibet* (Peking, Foreign Language Press, 1969), pp. 1-3.

1 Harold C. Hinton, *Communist China in World Politics* (Boston, Houghton Mifflin, 1966), p. 28.

the Chinese. The final struggle by the Tibetans lasted until March, 1959, when the Chinese Liberation Army crushed the revolt and the Dalai Lama fled to India, requesting political asylum. Tibet today is under Chinese military rule (II).

I

The Tibetan nationality is one of the nationalities with a long history within the boundaries of China and, like many other nationalities, it has done its glorious duty in the course of the creation and development of the great Motherland. But, over the last 100 years or more, imperialist forces penetrated into China and in consequence also penetrated into the Tibetan region and carried out all kinds of deceptions and provocations. Like previous reactionary Governments, the Kuomintang reactionary Government continued to carry out a policy of oppression and sowing dissension among the nationalities, causing division and disunity among the Tibetan people. The local government of Tibet did not oppose the imperialist deception and provocation and adopted an unpatriotic attitude towards the great Motherland. Under such conditions the Tibetan nationality and people were plunged into the depths of enslavement and sufferings. In 1949 basic victory was achieved on a nation-wide scale in the Chinese people's war of liberation; the common domestic enemy of all nationalities—the Kuomintang reactionary Government—was overthrown and the common foreign enemy of all nationalities—the aggressive imperialist forces—was driven out. On this basis the founding of the People's Republic of China (CPR) and of the Central People's Government (CPG) was announced.

In accordance with the Common Programme passed by the Chinese People's Political Consultative Conference (CPPCC), the CPG declared that all nationalities within the boundaries of the CPR are equal and that they shall establish unity and mutual aid and oppose imperialism and their own public enemies, so that the CPR will become a big family of fraternity and co-operation, composed of all its nationalities. Within the big family of all nationalities of the CPR, national regional autonomy shall be exercised in areas where national minorities are concentrated and all national minorities shall have freedom to develop their spoken and written languages and to preserve or reform their customs, habits and religious beliefs, and the CPG shall assist all national minorities to develop their political, economic, cultural, and educational construction work. Since then, all nationalities within the country—with the exception of those in the areas of Tibet and Taiwan—have gained liberation. Under the unified leadership of the CPG and the direct leadership of higher levels of people's governments, all national minorities have fully enjoyed the right of national equality and have exercised, or are exercising, national regional autonomy.

In order that the influences of aggressive imperialist forces in Tibet might be successfully eliminated, the unification of the territory and sovereignty of the CPR accomplished, and national defence safeguarded; in order that the Tibetan nationality and people might be freed and return to the big family of the CPR to enjoy the same rights of national equality as all other nationalities in the country and develop their political, economic, cultural and educational work, the CPG, when it ordered the People's Liberation Army (PLA) to march into Tibet, notified the local government of Tibet to send delegates to the central authorities to conduct talks for the conclusion of an agreement on measures for the peaceful liberation of Tibet. At the latter part of April 1951 the delegates with full powers of the local government of Tibet arrived in Peking. The CPG appointed representatives with full powers to conduct talks on a friendly basis with the delegates with full powers of the local government of Tibet. As a result of the talks both parties agreed to establish this agreement and ensure that it be carried into effect.

(1) The Tibetan people shall unite and drive out imperialist aggressive forces from Tibet; the Tibetan people shall return to the big family of the Motherland—the People's Republic of China.

(2) The local government of Tibet shall actively assist the PLA to enter Tibet and consolidate the national defences.

(3) In accordance with the policy towards nationalities laid down in the Common Programme of the CPPCC, the Tibetan people have the right of exercising national regional autonomy under the unified leadership of the CPG.

(4) The central authorities will not alter the existing political system in Tibet. The central authorities also will not alter the

established status, functions and powers of the Dalai Lama. Officials of various ranks shall hold office as usual.

(5) The established status, functions and powers of the Panchen Ngoerhtehni (Lama) shall be maintained.

(6) By the established status, functions and powers of the Dalai Lama and the Panchen Ngoerhtehni are meant the status, functions and powers of the thirteenth Dalai Lama and of the ninth Panchen Ngoerhtehni when they were in friendly and amicable relations with each other.

(7) The policy of freedom of religious belief laid down in the Common Programme of the CPPCC shall be carried out. The religious beliefs, customs and habits of the Tibetan people shall be respected and lama monasteries shall be protected. The central authorities will not effect a change in the income of the monasteries.

(8) Tibetan troops shall be reorganized step by step into the PLA and become a part of the national defence forces of CPR.

(9) The spoken and written language and school education of the Tibetan nationality shall be developed step by step in accordance with the actual condition in Tibet.

(10) Tibetan agriculture, livestock-raising, industry and commerce shall be developed step by step and the people's livelihood shall be improved step by step in accordance with the actual condition in Tibet.

(11) In matters related to various reforms in Tibet, there will be no compulsion on the part of the central authorities. The local government of Tibet should carry out reforms of its own accord, and, when the people raise demands for reform, they shall be settled by means of consultation with the leading personnel of Tibet.

(12) In so far as former pro-imperialist and pro-Kuomintang officials resolutely sever relations with imperialism and the Kuomintang and do not engage in sabotage or resistance, they may continue to hold office irrespective of their past.

(13) The PLA entering Tibet shall abide by all the above-mentioned policies and shall also be fair in all buying and selling and shall not arbitrarily take a needle or thread from the people.

(14) The CPG shall have centralised handling of all external affairs of the area of Tibet; and there will be peaceful co-existence with neighbouring countries and establishment and

development of fair commercial and trading relations with them on the basis of equality, mutual benefit and mutual respect for territory and sovereignty.

(15) In order to ensure the implementation of this agreement, the CPG shall set up a Military and Administrative Committee and a Military Area HQ in Tibet and—apart from the personnel sent there by the CPG—shall absorb as many local Tibetan personnel as possible to take part in the work. Local Tibetan personnel taking part in the Military and Administrative Committee may include patriotic elements from the local government of Tibet, various districts and various principal monasteries; the name-list shall be set forth after consultation between the representatives designated by the CPG and various quarters concerned and shall be submitted to the CPG for appointment.

(16) Funds needed by the Military and Administrative Committee, the Military Area HQ and the PLA entering Tibet shall be provided by the CPG. The local government of Tibet should assist the PLA in the purchase and transport of food, fodder and other daily necessities.

(17) This agreement shall come into force immediately after signatures and seals are affixed to it.

Signed and sealed by delegates of the CPG with full powers: Chief Delegate—Li Wei-Han (Chairman of the Commission of Nationalities Affairs); Delegates—Chang Ching-wu, Chang Kuo-hua, Sun Chih-yuan. Delegates with full powers of the local government of Tibet: Chief Delegate—Kaloon Ngabou Ngawang Jugme (Ngabo Shape); Delegates—Dizasak Khemey Sonam Wangdi, Khentrung Thupten Tenthar, Khenchung Thupten Lekmuun, Rimshi Samposey Tenzin Thundup.

Peking, 23rd May, 1951.

II

The following order is herewith proclaimed:

Most of the Kaloons of the Tibet Local Government and the upper-strata reactionary clique colluded with imperialism, assembled rebellious bandits, carried out rebellion, ravaged the people, put the Dalai Lama under duress, tore up the 17-Article Agreement on Measures for the Peaceful Liberation of Tibet and, on the night of March 19, directed the Tibetan local army and rebellious elements to launch a general offensive against the People's Liberation Army garrison in Lhasa. Such acts which betray the motherland and disrupt unification are not allowed by law. In order to safeguard the unification of the country and national unity, in addition to enjoining the Tibet Military Area Command of the Chinese People's Liberation Army to put down the rebellion thoroughly, the decision is that from this day the Tibet Local Government is dissolved and the Preparatory Committee for the Tibet Autonomous Region shall exercise the functions and powers of the Tibet Local Government. During the time when the Dalai Lama Dantzen-Jaltso, Chairman of the Preparatory Committee for the Tibet Autonomous Region, is under duress by the rebels, Panchen Erdeni Chuji-Geltseng, Vice-Chairman of the Preparatory Committee will act as the Chairman. Pebala Cholichnamje, Member of the Standing Committee of the Preparatory Committee for the Tibet Autonomous Region, is appointed Vice-Chairman of the Preparatory Committee; Ngapo Ngawang Jigme, Member of the Standing Committee and Secretary-General of the Preparatory Committee is appointed Vice-Chairman and Secretary-General of the Preparatory Committee. Eighteen traitorous elements, Surkong Wongching-Galei, Neusha Thubten-Tarpa, Hsinka Jigmedorje (Shasu), Yuto Chahsidongchu, Tsrijong Lozong-Yiehsi, Kachang Lozong-Rentzen, Dala Lozongsungdin, Khemey Sonamwongdui, Rongnamse Thubtan-Norzong, Pala Thubtenwenten, Nongshi Thubtan-Zongchu, Namselin Panchun Jigme, Menjelin Jalyanggeltseng, Karihpen Tsewong-Dorje, Pengchu, Weisegeltseng (Kundelinchasa), Gungalama, and Tsupugamapa Rihpeidorje, are relieved of their posts as members of the Preparatory Committee for the Tibet Autonomous Region and of all their other posts and are to be punished individually under law. Sixteen persons, Teng Shao-tung, Chan Hua-yu, Hui-Yi-jan, Liang Hsuan-hsien, Tsuiko Dongchutseren, Chantung Lozongnamje, Gahdehitsripa Thubtn Kunga, Chienpaitzuli, Ngapo Tsirtenchoga, Dorjetsirten, Shirou Dungchu, Geltsengpintso, Lozong Tzucheng, Chunjae, Pintsowongchiu, and Wang Pei-sheng are appointed members of the Preparatory Committee for the Tibet Autonomous Region. It is to be hoped that the Preparatory Committee for the Tibet Autonomous Region will lead all the people of Tibet, ecclesiastical and secular, to unite as one and make common efforts to assist the People's Liberation Army to put down the rebellion quickly, consolidate national defence, protect the interests of the people of all nationalities, secure social order and strive for the building of a new democratic and socialist Tibet.

[Signature]

50. CHOU EN-LAI: SPEECH ON THE LIBERATION OF TAIWAN (June, 1956)*

Taiwan, 90 miles off the southeast coast of the Chinese mainland, comprises 13 islands in the Taiwan group and 64 in the Pescadores group (Penghu). In addition, the Nationalist government on Taiwan also controls the Quemoy (Kinmen) and Matsu islands, adjacent to two major Communist ports, Amoy and Foochow.

The population in Taiwan according to the 1970 estimates is 14,320,000, of whom 150,000 are aborigine and the remaining Chinese. However, the eighty percent of the population settled there before the Nationalists came from the mainland in 1949 regard themselves as Taiwanese, a unique part of the Chinese family.

Taiwan remains as one of the most critical problems with respect to Sino-American relations, as illustrated by the following speech by Chou En-lai delivered as a policy statement at the Third Session of the First National People's Congress on June 28, 1956. On the other hand, the United States is committed to defend Taiwan by treaty agreement with the Nationalists, who, as illustrated by Premier C. K. Yen's response to Nixon's proposed visit, further complicate the problem:

*From *Oppose U.S. Occupation of Taiwan* (Peking, Foreign Language Press, 1958), pp. 40-51 (extract). Title is editor's.

"We are greatly surprised at President Nixon's announcement that he will visit the Chinese mainland by May of next year. ... The tragic loss of the Chinese mainland has led to afflictions of war in Korea, Vietnam and the rest of the Indochina Peninsula, and to violence and unrest throughout the world. How can the United States now go even further in paving the way for additional aggression by Peiping [Peking] and thereby make possible an even more disastrous catastrophe? ... We have the faith and determination to recover the Chinese mainland and to resist any external adverse tide. Under no circumstance shall we relax or weaken our stand. We shall never yield to any pressure or to any violences or might."[1] (See also Document 66.)

During the past seven years, the Chinese people have achieved tremendous successes in the peaceful construction of their country. Our motherland is being transformed step by step from a poverty-stricken, backward agricultural country into a prosperous and powerful socialist industrial country. At the same time, China's international position has risen to unprecedented heights. China is playing an ever more important role in promoting the development of the entire international situation. It has become more and more difficult to ignore China's views in the settlement of many major international issues.

At present, 26 countries with an aggregate population in excess of one thousand million have already established diplomatic relations with our country. Still more countries and broader mass of people are maintaining trade and cultural relations with us. Clearly, it is already impossible for anyone to deny the reality that the People's Republic of China exists and that it is growing ever stronger.

True, the United States is up to now still attempting to deny the Chinese people's right to choose their own state system, refusing to recognize the People's Republic of China and trying hard to exclude New China from participation in international

1 *The Central Daily News* (Taipei) (July 17, 1971). See also Jerome Alan Cohen *et al., Taiwan and American Policy* (New York, Praeger, 1971).

affairs. However, as history has proved, budding forces which have broken through the old system will eventually grow mighty in spite of all obstructions. This was the case with the American War of Independence against colonial rule, with the French bourgeois revolution which overthrew feudal rule, and also with the Russian October Socialist Revolution which wiped out capitalist rule from one-sixth of the earth's surface. Those who today refuse to recognize New China had better review these historical facts.

Actually, although the United States does not recognize the People's Republic of China, a representative of the United States Government is nevertheless holding talks at Geneva with a representative of the Chinese Government. It is not difficult to see from this apparent contradiction that the real aim of the United States in refusing to recognize the People's Republic of China is to profit by using the Chiang Kai-shek clique in bargaining with China and in creating tension.

The strenuous efforts of the United States to exclude New China from participation in international affairs have not caused China any harm. On the contrary, by obstructing the restoration to the People's Republic of China of its legitimate position and rights in the United Nations, the United States has damaged the prestige of the United Nations and made it impossible for that organization to play effectively the role envisaged by its Charter. The United States has also aroused the dissatisfaction of many countries by forcing them to refrain from establishing diplomatic relations with China, and accelerated their tendency to fall away from the United States. As for China, regardless of recognition or non-recognition by the United States, it will all the same exist and develop with growing strength, its contacts with other countries will further increase, and its international position will further rise.

In the face of such undeniable and powerful facts, certain people are hatching a plot to create "two Chinas." They are vainly attempting to describe Taiwan as another China or as a separate independent state. But these vain attempts can only be interpreted as a sign of losing one's senses in the face of powerful facts. Taiwan has always been a part of China. Solemn international agreements have also long affirmed that Taiwan belongs to China. Even the Chiang Kai-shek clique also admits that Taiwan belongs to China. All Chinese people, including those on Taiwan, will never tolerate the detachment of Taiwan from their motherland.

Those who vainly seek to create "two Chinas" recognize that it is becoming more and more difficult to continue to exclude the People's Republic of China from international organizations and conferences. Therefore, they are attempting to create beforehand a state of "two Chinas" in international organizations and conferences. The Chinese people long ago saw through this plot. It is futile to hope that China will fall into this trap. International organizations and conferences are only one means of effecting international exchanges and contacts. China will not find it any more difficult to expand its contacts and connections with other countries because of its being excluded from international organizations and conferences. Only one China exists in the world. Only the Government of the People's Republic of China can represent the Chinese people. We believe that sooner or later this fact will receive general recognition in the world. The sooner this day arrives, the sooner will normal international relations be restored.

Now, I should like to report to the Congress on the situation in the Sino-American talks.

After agreement was reached on the return of civilians of both sides at the Sino-American ambassadorial talks in Geneva on September 10, 1955, the two sides entered into discussions on the question of renunciation of force. Up to now, nearly ten months have elapsed, but no agreement has yet been reached.

The Chinese side is not against the issuance jointly with the United States of an announcement on mutual renunciation of the use and threat of force in Sino-American relations. In fact, as early as during the Bandung Conference, China declared that the Chinese people do not want war with the United States and that the Chinese Government is willing to sit down and enter into negotiations with the United States Government on the question of easing and eliminating the tension in the Taiwan area. However, it must be pointed out that the tension in the Taiwan area was entirely created by the U.S. occupation by force of China's territory of Taiwan. Therefore, any announcement concerning the renunciation of the use of force between China and the United States must be capable of leading to the relaxation and elimination of the tension, and must not imply acceptance of the U.S. occupation of Taiwan. At the same time, the question as to what means will be used by China to liberate Taiwan is entirely a matter of China's sovereignty and internal affairs, in which no outside interference will be tolerated. Therefore, a Sino-American announcement should in no way allow interference in this matter.

On the basis of the foregoing principles, the Chinese side has proposed two different forms for the announcement. If a statement is to be specifically included in the Sino-American announcement that the disputes between the two countries in the Taiwan area will be settled through peaceful negotiations without resorting to force, then it must also be explicitly provided that a Sino-American conference of the foreign ministers be held so as to implement this statement. Such is the draft put forward by the Chinese side on October 27, 1955. Alternately, China and the United States may first issue an announcement of principle that the disputes between the two countries will be settled by peaceful means without resorting to force, and then the ambassadors of the two countries would continue their talks to seek concrete means of realizing this common desire of the two sides. Such is the December 1, 1955 draft of the Chinese side. Recently, taking into consideration the view of the American side, the Chinese side again proposed on May 11, 1956 that while declaring in the announcement that the disputes between the two countries in the Taiwan area would be settled peacefully without resorting to force, the two countries should also lay down the provision that, within a definite period of the issuance of the announcement, they must seek and ascertain the means for the realization of this desire, including the holding of a Sino-American conference of the foreign ministers. However, in spite of these proposals, the American side is still unwilling to come to an agreement.

Although the United States suggested that the principle of renunciation of force should be made specifically applicable to the Taiwan area, yet it is against providing for the holding of a Sino-American conference of the foreign ministers to realize this principle, and even refuses to agree to seek and ascertain, within a definite period of time, the means of settling peacefully the disputes between China and the United States. In addition, the United States even insists that it has a so-called "right of individual or collective self-defence" on China's territory of Taiwan. All this indicates that the United States is attempting to secure an announcement of sole advantage to itself, so that it could, on the one hand, maintain the present state of its occupation of Taiwan and, on the other hand, continue to interfere with the liberation of Taiwan by the Chinese people. If it could not secure such an announcement, the United States would then attempt to drag out indefinitely the Sino-American ambassadorial talks in order to attain the same objective of freezing the status quo in the Taiwan area.

These attempts of the United States are precisely what block an agreement in the Sino-American talks up to now. China cannot agree to issue an announcement of sole advantage to one side; nor can it tolerate the use of the Sino-American talks by one side as a tool to achieve its unilateral aims. China maintains that any joint announcement must be advantageous to both sides, and that continuance of the Sino-American talks is possible only on condition that it is advantageous to both sides. Finally, I wish to say something on the question of the liberation of Taiwan, about which we are all concerned.

The Chinese people are determined to liberate Taiwan. This is the unshakable common will of the 600 million people of China.

The Chinese Government has repeatedly pointed out that there are two ways for the Chinese people to liberate Taiwan, that is, by war or by peaceful means, and that the Chinese people would seek to liberate Taiwan by peaceful means so far as it is possible. There is no doubt that if Taiwan can be liberated peacefully, it would be best for our country, for all the Chinese people and for Asian and world peace.

At present, the possibility of peacefully liberating Taiwan is increasing. This is first of all because the international situation is now definitely tending towards relaxation, and the United States armed occupation of Taiwan and interference in China's internal affairs are opposed by more and more peace-loving countries and peoples. As regards our internal situation, our great motherland has grown even stronger and become even more consolidated. It is inspiring more pride in all patriotic Chinese than ever before. At present, our compatriots on Taiwan, who have a revolutionary tradition, are unwilling to suffer any longer their bitter life of slavery, and want to return as soon as possible to the embrace of the motherland; and even among the Kuomintang military and political personnel who have fled to Taiwan from the mainland, more and more people have come to realize that their only future lies in the peaceful reunification of their motherland. Since we issued the call to strive for peaceful liberation of Taiwan, many Kuomintang military and political personnel in Taiwan and abroad have expressed their patriotic aspirations. We believe that those who wish to bring about the peaceful liberation of Taiwan and the complete unification of our motherland will certainly grow in number from day to day. This will be an inexorable trend.

The trends are very clear. The situation of the Taiwan authorities maintaining a feeble existence by following the behest of the United States cannot possibly last long. The foreign forces on which they depend are by no means reliable. On the contrary, by inviting the wolf into the house, they would not only lose everything they have, but also be in constant danger of being treacherously bitten in the back or abandoned. An important lesson can be drawn from a comparison of the contrasting attitudes taken by China and the United States in the Geneva talks. The Chinese Government has consistently maintained that only the international dispute between China and the United States in the Taiwan area can be discussed and settled by China and the United States; as for the question of the return of Taiwan to the motherland, regardless of the means by which it is realized, this is a question which can only be settled and definitely can be settled by us Chinese people, and no foreign interference will be tolerated. The United States, however, has adopted a totally different attitude in the talks. It regards Taiwan as its colony and makes use of it to bargain with China. It can also be seen that the United States has not only occupied Taiwan and extended its control into every sphere in Taiwan—political, military, economic and cultural, but is also playing its usual splitting tactics to create suspicion and feuds inside Taiwan, attempting thus to strengthen its control and to profit thereby. However, these tactics of the U.S. aggressive forces to make fools of the Chinese people, interfere in China's internal affairs and disrupt China's national unity have aroused ever stronger dissatisfaction among the Kuomintang military and political personnel on Taiwan. Many of them have indicated that they will suffer no longer their life of abject dependence, at the beck and call of others. They want to enhance national self-respect, defend national dignity, free themselves from U.S. control and handle domestic matters in an independent spirit. We welcome this patriotic stand of theirs.

We have consistently stood for national solidarity and united resistance against external enemies. In the interest of our great motherland and our people, the Chinese Communists and the Kuomintang members have twice fought shoulder to shoulder against imperialism. After the conclusion of the War of Resistance to Japanese Aggression, we also made efforts to bring about internal peace. Even during the Chinese War of Liberation when the Chinese people were forced to take up arms, and even after the mainland was liberated, we have never given up our efforts for peaceful negotiations. Although in the past few years, owing the U.S. armed intervention, we and the Kuomintang military and political personnel on Taiwan have taken different paths, yet so long as we all hold supreme the interests of our nation and motherland, we can still link arms again and unite. We believe that our great nation, which experienced long years of suffering, will certainly be able through our own efforts to accomplish the complete unity of our motherland.

Now, on behalf of the Government, I formally state: We are willing to negotiate with the Taiwan authorities on specific steps and terms for the peaceful liberation of Taiwan, and we hope that the Taiwan authorities will send their representatives to Peking or other appropriate places, at a time which they consider appropriate, to begin these talks with us.

In order to unite all patriotic forces to realize at an early date the complete unification of our motherland, I wish here to declare once again that all patriotic people, regardless of whether they joined the patriotic ranks earlier or later, and regardless of how great the crimes they committed in the past may have been, will be treated in accordance with the principle that "patriots belong to one family" and the policy of no punishment for past misdeeds; they are all welcome to perform meritorious service for the peaceful liberation of Taiwan, and will be duly rewarded according to the degree of their merit and provided with appropriate jobs.

Our compatriots in Taiwan have always been an inseparable part of the Chinese people. We not only have constant concern for them and support them in various ways in their struggle against foreign rule, but also stand ready to welcome them at any time to participate in the socialist construction of the motherland and to share the glory of our nation.

We appreciate the situation in which all the Kuomintang military and political personnel on Taiwan whose homes are on the mainland find themselves, and we hope that they may soon realize their desire of reuniting with their families. They can communicate with their relatives and friends on the mainland; they can also return to the mainland for short visits to their relatives and friends. We are prepared to give them all kinds of convenience and assistance.

We hope the responsible Kuomintang military and political personages on Taiwan will play an important role in the cause of the peaceful liberation of Taiwan. So long as they work in this direction, their future position will be definitely assured. If they still harbour doubts, they can obtain clarification through their relatives and friends on the mainland or send people to the mainland to ascertain what the situation is. We guarantee the latter's freedom of movement in coming and going.

We hope the Kuomintang military personnel on Taiwan will actively expedite the peaceful liberation of Taiwan. If they do so, they will surely earn the confidence and care of the motherland and the people. The treatment accorded to those commanders and soldiers who came over peacefully on the mainland is a precedent.

We also hope that all Kuomintang military and political personnel who are abroad will work for the peaceful liberation of Taiwan. Only thus can they escape the fate of leading the life of exiles in foreign lands, looked down upon by others.

We attach great importance to the positive role played by the broad mass of patriotic overseas Chinese in promoting the cause of the peaceful liberation of Taiwan. We hope that those few overseas Chinese who used to maintain or still maintain a hostile attitude towards the motherland will distinguish between right and wrong, see the direction in which events are moving, and, together with the broad mass of patriotic overseas Chinese, contribute towards the patriotic cause of the peaceful liberation of Taiwan.

The gate of the motherland is always wide open for all

patriots. Every Chinese has both the right and the duty to make his contribution to the sacred cause of the unification of the motherland. With the unity of the entire nation and the efforts of all our people, the liberation of Taiwan will certainly be consummated.

51. CHOU EN-LAI'S LETTER TO JAWAHARLAL NEHRU (September, 1959)*

Although Sino-Indian relations were friendly in the 1950's, potential for conflict was present because of differences with respect to India's special interest in China's infiltration of Nepal, Chinese friendly attitudes toward Pakistan, and Sino-Indian border disputes which resulted in two border wars in 1959 and 1962. However, in the views of an experienced China scholar, "China emerged from the crisis with minor territorial gains and uncontested leadership in the third world."[1]

Dear Mr. Prime Minister,

I have carefully read Your Excellency's letter dated March 22, 1959. I find from your letter that there is a fundamental difference between the positions of our two Governments on the Sino-Indian boundary question. This has made me somewhat surprised and also made it necessary for me to take a longer period of time to consider how to reply to your letter.

The Sino-Indian boundary question is a complicated question left over by history. In tackling this question, one cannot but, first of all, take into account the historical background of British aggression on China when India was under British rule. From the early days, Britain harboured aggressive ambition towards China's Tibet region. It continuously instigated Tibet to separate from China, in an attempt to put under its control a nominally independent Tibet. When this design failed, it applied all sorts of pressures on China, intending to make Tibet a British sphere of influence while allowing China to maintain so-called suzerainty over Tibet. In the meantime, using India as its base,

*From *Report of the Chinese and Indian Officials on the Boundary Question* (New Delhi, Ministry of External Affairs, 1961), pp. 27-33.

1 Robert C. North, *The Foreign Relations of China* (Belmont, Calif., Dickenson Publishing Co., 1969), p. 94.

Britain conducted extensive territorial expansion into China's Tibet region, and even the Sinkiang region. All this constitutes the fundamental reason for the long term disputes over and non-settlement of the Sino-Indian boundary question.

China and India are both countries which were long subjected to imperialist aggression. This common experience should have naturally caused China and India to hold an identical view of the above-said historical background and to adopt an attitude of mutual sympathy, mutual understanding and fairness and reasonableness in dealing with the boundary question. The Chinese Government originally thought the Indian Government would take such an attitude. Unexpectedly to the Chinese Government, however, the Indian Government demanded that the Chinese Government give formal recognition to the situation created by the application of the British policy of aggression against China's Tibet region as the foundation for the settlement of the Sino-Indian boundary question. What is more serious, the Indian Government has applied all sorts of pressures on the Chinese Government, not even scrupling the use of force to support this demand. At this the Chinese Government cannot but feel a deep regret.

The Chinese Government has consistently held that an overall settlement of the boundary question should be sought by both sides, taking into account the historical background and existing actualities and adhering to the Five Principles, through friendly negotiations conducted in a well-prepared way step by step. Pending this, as a provisional measure, the two sides should maintain the long-existing *status quo* of the border, and not seek to change it by unilateral action, even less by force. As to some of the disputes, provisional agreements concerning isolated places could be reached through negotiations to ensure the tranquillity of the border areas and uphold the friendship of the two countries. This is exactly the basic idea expressed in my January 23, 1959 letter to you. The Chinese Government still considers this to be the way that should be followed by our two countries in settling the boundary question. Judging from Your Excellency's letter of March 22, 1959, it seems you are not completely against this principle.

I would like now to further explain the position of the Chinese Government in connection with the questions raised in Your Excellency's letter and in conjunction with the recent situation along the Sino-Indian border.

1. In my letter to Your Excellency dated January 23, 1959, I pointed out that the Sino-Indian boundary has never been formally delimited. In your letter of March 22, 1959, Your Excellency expressed disagreement to this and tried energetically to prove that most parts of the Sino-Indian boundary had the sanction of specific international agreements between the past Government of India and the Central Government of China. In order to prove that the Sino-Indian boundary has never been formally delimited, I would like to furnish the following facts:

(i) *Concerning the boundary separating China's Sinkiang and Tibet regions from Ladakh.* In 1842, a peace treaty was indeed concluded between the local authorities of China's Tibet and the Kashmir authorities. However, the then Chinese Central Government did not send anybody to participate in the conclusion of this treaty, nor did it ratify the treaty afterwards. Moreover, this treaty only mentioned in general terms that Ladakh and Tibet would each abide by its borders, and did not make any specific provisions or explanations regarding the location of this section of the boundary. It is clear that this treaty cannot be used to prove that this section of the boundary has been formally delimited by the two sides, even less can it be used as the foundation to ask the Chinese Government to accept the unilateral claim of the Indian Government regarding this section of the boundary. As to the Chinese Government official's statement made in 1847 to the British representative that this section of the boundary was clear, it can only show that the then Chinese Government had its own clear view regarding this section of the boundary and cannot be taken as the proof that the boundary between the two sides had already been formally delimited. As a matter of fact, down to 1899, the British Government still proposed to formally delimit this section of the boundary with the Chinese Government, but the Chinese Government did not agree. Your Excellency also said on August 28 this year in India's Lok Sabha: "This was the boundary of the old Kashmir State with Tibet and Chinese Turkestan. Nobody had marked it." It can thus be seen that this section of the boundary has never been delimited. Between China and Ladakh, however, there does exist a customary line derived from historical traditions, and Chinese maps have always drawn the boundary between China and Ladakh in accordance with this line. The marking of this section of the boundary on the map of "Punjab, Western Himalaya and Adjoining Parts of Tibet" compiled by the British John Walker by order of the Court of Directors of East India Company (which was attached to the British Major Alexander Cunningham's book "Ladakh" published in 1854) corresponded fairly close to the Chinese maps. Later British and Indian maps included large tracts of Chinese territory into Ladakh. This was without any legal grounds, nor in conformity with the actual situation of administration by each side all the time.

(ii) *Concerning the section of the boundary between the Ari Area of China's Tibet and India.* It can be seen from your letter that you also agree that this section of the boundary has not been formally delimited by the two countries. Not only so, there have in fact been historical disputes between the two sides over the right to many places in this area. For example, the area of Sang and Tsungsha, southwest of Tsaparang Dzong in Tibet, which had always belonged to China, was thirty to forty years back gradually invaded and occupied by the British. The local authorities of China's Tibet took up this matter several times with Britain, without any results. It has thus become an outstanding issue left over by history.

(iii) *Concerning the Sino-Indian boundary east of Bhutan.* The Indian Government insists that this section of the boundary has long been clearly delimited, citing as its grounds that the so-called MacMahon Line was jointly delineated by the representatives of the Chinese Government, the Tibet local authorities and the British Government at the 1913-1914 Simla Conference. As I have repeatedly made clear to Your Excellency, the Simla Conference was an important step taken by Britain in its design to detach Tibet from China. At the Conference were discussed the so-called boundary between Outer and Inner Tibet and that between Tibet and the rest of China. Contrary to what was said in your letter, the so-called MacMahon Line was never discussed at the Simla Conference, but was determined by the British representative and the representative of the Tibet local authorities behind the back of the representative of the Chinese Central Government through an exchange of secret notes at Delhi on March 24, 1914, that is, prior to the signing of the Simla treaty. This line was marked on the map attached to the Simla treaty as part of the boundary between Tibet and the rest of China. The so-called MacMahon Line was a product of the British policy of aggression against the Tibet Region of China and has never been recognised by any Chinese Central Government and is therefore decidedly illegal. As to the Simla treaty, it was not formally signed by the representative of the then Chinese Central Government, and this is explicitly noted in the treaty. For quite a long time after the exchange of secret notes between Britain and the Tibet local authorities, Britain dared not make public the related documents, nor change the traditional way of drawing this section of the boundary on maps. This illegal line aroused the great indignation of the Chinese people. The Tibet local authorities themselves later also expressed their dissatisfaction with this line, and, following the independence of India in 1947, cabled Your Excellency asking India to return all the territory of the Tibet region of China south of this illegal line. This piece of territory corresponds in size to the Chekiang Province of China and is as big as ninety thousand square kilometres. Mr. Prime Minister, how could China agree to accept under coercion such an illegal line which would have it relinquish its rights and disgrace itself by selling out its territory—and such a large piece of territory as that? The delineation of the Sino-Indian boundary east of Bhutan in all traditional Chinese maps is a true reflection of the actual situation of the customary boundary before the appearance of the so-called MacMahon Line. Both the map of "Tibet and Adjacent Countries" published by the Indian Survey in 1917 and the map attached to the 1929 edition of the Encyclopaedia Britannica drew this section of the boundary in the same way as the Chinese maps. And it was only in the period around the peaceful liberation of China's Tibet region in 1951 that Indian troops advanced on a large scale into the area south of the so-called MacMahon Line. Therefore, the assertion that this section of the boundary has long been clearly delimited is obviously untenable.

In Your Excellency's letter, you also referred to the boundary between China and Sikkim. Like the boundary between China and Bhutan, this question does not fall within the scope of our present discussion. I would like, however, to take this opportunity to make clear once again that China is willing to live together in friendship with Sikkim and Bhutan, without committing aggression against each other, and has always respected the proper relations between them and India.

It can be seen from the above that the way the Sino-Indian boundary has always been drawn in maps published in China is not without grounds and that at first British and Indian maps also drew the Sino-Indian boundary roughly in the same way as the Chinese maps. As a matter of fact, it was not Chinese maps, but British and Indian maps that later unilaterally altered the way the Sino-Indian boundary was drawn. Nevertheless, since China and India have not delimited their mutual boundary through friendly negotiations and joint surveys, China has not asked India to revise its maps. In 1954, I explained to Your Excellency for the same reason that it would be inappropriate for the Chinese Government to revise the old map right now. Some people in India, however, are raising a big uproar about the maps published in China, attempting to create a pressure of public opinion to force China to accept India's unilateral claims concerning the Sino-Indian boundary. Needless to say, this is neither wise nor worthy.

2. As stated above, the Chinese Government has all along adhered to a clear-cut policy on the Sino-Indian border question: on the one hand, it affirms the fact that the entire Sino Indian boundary has not been delimited, while on the other, it also faces reality, and, taking specially into consideration the friendly relationship between China and India, actively seeks for a settlement fair and reasonable to both sides, and never tries unilaterally to change the long-existing state of the border between the two countries pending the settlement of the boundary question.

Regarding the eastern section of the Sino-Indian boundary, as I have stated above, the Chinese Government absolutely does not recognise the so-called MacMahon Line, but Chinese troops have never crossed that line. This is for the sake of maintaining amity along the border to facilitate negotiations and settlement of the boundary question, and in no way implies that the Chinese Government has recognised that line. In view of the fact that my former explanation of this point to Your Excellency is obviously misunderstood in Your Excellency's latest two letters to me, I have deemed it necessary once again to make the above explanation clearly.

Regarding the western section of the Sino-Indian boundary,

China has strictly abided by the traditional customary line and, with regard to Indian troops' repeated intrusions into or occupation of Chinese territory, the Chinese Government, acting always in a friendly manner, has dealt with each case in a way befitting it. For example, regarding the invasion of Wu-je by Indian troops and administrative personnel, the Chinese Government has tried its best to seek a settlement of the question with the Indian Government through negotiations and to avoid a clash. Regarding the Indian troops who invaded the southwestern part of China's Sinkiang and the area of Lake Pankong in the Tibet Region of China, the Chinese frontier guards, after disarming them according to international practice, adopted an attitude of reasoning, asking them to leave Chinese territory and returning to them their arms. Regarding the Indian troops' successive invasion and occupation of the areas of Shipki Pass, Parigas, Sang, Tsungsha, Puling-sumdo, Chuva, Chuje, Sangcha and Lapthal, the Chinese Government, after discovering these happenings, invariably conducted thorough and detailed investigations rather than laying charges against the Indian Government immediately and temperamentally. These measures prove that the Chinese Government is exerting its greatest effort to uphold Sino-Indian friendship.

Despite the above-mentioned border incidents caused wholly by the trespassing of Indian troops, until the beginning of this year, the atmosphere along the Sino-Indian border had on the whole been fairly good. The fact that no armed clashes had ever occurred along the 2,000 or so kilometres of the Sino-Indian boundary, which is wholly undelimited, is in itself a powerful proof that, given a friendly and reasonable attitude on both sides, amity can be maintained in the border areas and tension ruled out pending the delimitation of the boundary between the two countries.

3. Since the outbreak of the rebellion in Tibet, however, the border situation has become increasingly tense owing to reasons for which the Chinese side cannot be held responsible. Immediately after the fleeting of a large number of Tibetan rebels into India, Indian troops started pressing forward steadily across the eastern section of the Sino-Indian boundary. Changing unilaterally the long-existing state of the border between the two countries, they not only overstepped the so-called MacMahon Line as indicated in the map attached to

the secret notes exchanged between Britain and the Tibet local authorities, but also exceeded the boundary drawn in current Indian maps which is alleged to represent the so-called MacMahon Line, but which in many places actually cuts even deeper into Chinese territory than the MacMahon Line. Indian troops invaded and occupied Longju, intruded into Yashar, and are still in occupation of Shatze, Khinzemane and Tamaden—all of which are Chinese territory—shielding armed Tibetan rebel bandits in this area. Indian aircraft have also time and again violated China's territorial air near the Sino-Indian border. What is especially regrettable is that, not long ago, the Indian troops unlawfully occupying Longju launched armed attacks on the Chinese frontier guards stationed at Migyitun, leaving no room for the Chinese frontier guards but fire back in self-defence. This was the first instance of armed clash along the Sino-Indian border. It can be seen from the above that the tense situation recently arising on the Sino-Indian border was all caused by trespassing and provocations by Indian troops, and that for this the Indian side should be held fully responsible. Nevertheless, the Indian Government has directed all sorts of groundless charges against the Chinese Government, clamouring that China has committed aggression against India and describing the Chinese frontier guards' act of self-defence in the Migyitun areas as armed provocation. Many political figures and propaganda organs in India have seized the occasion to make a great deal of anti-Chinese utterances, some even openly advocating provocative actions of an even larger scale such as bombarding Chinese territory. Thus a second anti-Chinese campaign has been launched in India in six months' time. The fact that India does not recognise the undelimited state of the Sino-Indian boundary and steps up bringing pressure to bear on China militarily, diplomatically and through public opinion cannot but make one suspect that it is the attempt of India to impose upon China its one-sided claims on the boundary question. It must be pointed out that this attempt will never succeed and such action cannot possibly yield any results other than impairing the friendship of the two countries, further complicating the boundary question and making it more difficult to settle.

4. The friendly relations between China and India are based on the Five Principles of peaceful co-existence. The Chinese

Government has consistently held that all differences between our two countries must and certainly can be resolved through peaceful consultations and should not be allowed to affect the friendly relationship between the two countries. China looks upon its southwestern border as a border of peace and friendship. I can assure Your Excellency that it is merely for the purpose of preventing remnant armed Tibetan rebels from crossing the border back and forth to carry out harassing activities that the Chinese Government has in recent months dispatched guard units to be stationed in the south-eastern part of the Tibet Region of China. This is obviously in the interest of ensuring the tranquillity of the border and will in no way constitute a threat to India. Your Excellency is one of the initiators of the Five Principles and has made significant contributions to the consolidation and development of Sino-Indian friendship and constantly stressed the importance of this friendship. This has deeply impressed the Chinese Government and people. I have therefore given Your Excellency a systematic explanation of the whole picture of the Sino-Indian boundary. I hope that Your Excellency and the Indian Government will, in accordance with the Chinese Government's request, immediately adopt measures to withdraw the trespassing Indian troops and administrative personnel and restore the long existing state of the boundary between the two countries. Through this, the temporary tension on the Sino-Indian border would be eased at once and the dark clouds hanging over the relations between our two countries would be speedily dispelled, setting at ease our friends who are concerned for the Sino-Indian friendly relations and dealing a blow to those who are sowing discord in the Sino-Indian relations and creating tension.

With cordial regards,

[Signature]

52. *AGREEMENT ON BOUNDARY BETWEEN CHINA AND PAKISTAN (March, 1963)**

> *Because of common enmity toward India, China and Pakistan began to develop closer relations, in spite of*

*From Hsin Hua News Release, March 2, 1963.

the fact that Pakistan is a member of SEATO and that often SEATO military exercises were held at Karachi. Pakistan is particularly interested in cultivating Chinese friendship in order to gain support for her claim to Kashmir.

After the Sino-Indian border clashes, delegations went back and forth between China and Pakistan and a number of mutually beneficial agreements were made, such as that concerning a direct air link between the two countries (1963) and the following boundary agreement signed on March 2, 1963.

The Government of the People's Republic of China and the Government of Pakistan,

Having agreed, with a view to ensuring the prevailing peace and tranquillity on the border, to formally delimit and demarcate the boundary between China's Sinkiang and the contiguous areas the defence of which is under the actual control of Pakistan, in a spirit of fairness, reasonableness, mutual understanding and mutual accommodation, and on the basis of the ten principles as enunciated in the Bandung conference;

Being convinced that this would not only give full expression to the desire of the peoples of China and Pakistan for the development of good-neighbourly and friendly relations, but also safeguard Asian and world peace;

Have resolved for this purpose to conclude the present agreement and have appointed as their respective plenipotentiaries the following:

For the Government of the People's Republic of China: Chen Yi, Minister of Foreign Affairs;

For the Government of Pakistan: Zulfikar Ali Bhutto, Minister of External Affairs;

Who, having mutually examined their full powers and found them to be in good and due form, have agreed upon the following:

Article I

In view of the fact that the boundary between China's Sinkiang and the contiguous areas the defence of which is under the actual control of Pakistan has never been formally delimited, the two parties agree to delimit it on the basis of the traditional customary boundary line, including natural features, and in a spirit of equality, mutual benefit and friendly co-operation.

Article II

In accordance with the principle expounded in Article I of the present agreement, the two parties have fixed, as follows, the alignment of the entire boundary line between China's Sinkiang and the contiguous areas the defence of which is under the actual control of Pakistan:

(1) Commencing from its north-western extremity at height 5630 meters (a peak, the reference co-ordinates of which are approximately longitude 74 degrees 34 minutes E. and latitude 37 degrees 03 minutes N.) the boundary line runs generally eastward and then south-eastward strictly along the main watershed between the tributaries of the Tashkurgan river of the Tarim River system on the one hand, and the tributaries of the Hunza River of the Indus River system on the other hand, passing through the Kilik Daban, the Mintaka Daban (pass), the Kharchanai Daban (named on the Chinese map only), the Mutsjilga Daban (named on the Chinese map only), and the Parpik Pass (named on the Pakistani map only), and reaches the Khunjerab (Yutr) Daban (pass).

(2) After passing through the Khunjerab (Yutr) Daban (pass), the boundary line runs generally southward along the above-mentioned main watershed up to a mountain-top south of this Daban (pass), where it leaves the main watershed to follow the crest of a spur lying generally in a south-easterly direction, which is the watershed between the Akjilga River (a nameless corresponding river on the Pakistani map) on the one hand, and the Taghumbash (Oprang) River and the Keliman Su (Oprang Jilga) on the other hand.

According to the map of the Chinese side, the boundary line, after leaving the south-eastern extremity of this spur, runs along a small section of the middle line of the bed of the Keliman Su to reach its confluence with the Kelechin River. According to the map of the Pakistani side, the boundary line after leaving the south-eastern extremity of this spur, reaches the sharp bend of the Shakasgam or Muztagh River.

(3) From the aforesaid point, the boundary line runs up the Kelechin River (Shaksgam or Muztagh River) along the middle line of its bed to its confluence (reference co-ordinates approximately longitude 76 degrees 02 minutes E. and latitude 36 degrees 26 minutes N.) with the Shorbulak Daria (Shimshal River or Braldu River).

(4) From the confluence of the aforesaid two rivers, the boundary line, according to the map of the Chinese side, ascends the crest of a spur and runs along it to join the Karakoram range main watershed at a mountain-top (reference co-ordinates approximately longitude 75 degrees 54 minutes E. and latitude 36 degrees 15 minutes N.), which on this map is shown as belonging to the Shorbulak mountain.

According to the map of the Pakistani side, the boundary line from the confluence of the above-mentioned two rivers ascends the crest of a corresponding spur and runs along it, passing through height 6,520 meters (21,390 feet) till it joins the Karakoram range main watershed at a peak (reference co-ordinates approximately longitude 75 degrees 57 minutes E. and latitude 36 degrees 03 minutes N.).

(5) Thence, the boundary line, running generally southward and then eastward, strictly follows the Karakoram range main watershed which separates the Tarim River drainage system from the Indus River drainage system, passing through the east Mustagh Pass (Muztagh Pass), the top of the Chogri Peak (K2), the top of the Broad Peak, the top of the Gasherbrum mountain (8,068), the Indirakoli Pass (names on the Chinese map only) and the top of the Teram Kangri Peak, and reaches its south-eastern extremity at the Karakoram Pass.

Two. The alignment of the entire boundary line, as described in Section 1 of this Article, has been drawn on the 1/1,000,000 scale map of the Chinese side in Chinese and the 1/1,000,000 scale map of the Pakistani side in English, which are signed and attached to the present agreement.

Three. In view of the fact that maps of the two sides are not fully identical in their representation of topographical features, the two parties have agreed that the actual features on the ground shall prevail so far as the location and alignment of the boundary described in Section I is concerned; and that they will be determined as far as possible by a joint survey on the ground.

Article III

The two parties have agreed that:

One. Wherever the boundary follows a river, the middle line of the river-bed shall be the boundary line; and that,

Two. Wherever the boundary passes through a daban (pass), the water-parting line thereof shall be the boundary line.

Article IV

One. The two parties have agreed to set up, as soon as possible, a joint boundary demarcation commission. Each side will appoint a chairman, one or more members and a certain number of advisers and technical staff. The commission is charged with the responsibility, in accordance with the provisions of the present agreement, to hold concrete discussions on and carry out the following tasks jointly:

(1) To conduct necessary surveys of the boundary area on the ground as stated in Article 2 of the present agreement, so as to set up boundary markers at places considered to be appropriate by the two parties and to delineate the boundary line of the jointly-prepared accurate maps.

(2) To draft a protocol setting forth in detail the alignment of the entire boundary line and the location of all the boundary markers and prepare and get printed detailed maps, to be attached to the protocol, with the boundary line and the location of the boundary-markers shown on them.

Two. The aforesaid protocol, upon being signed by the representatives of the Governments of the two countries, shall become an annexe to the present agreement, and the detailed maps shall replace the maps attached to the present agreement.

Three. Upon the conclusions of the above-mentioned protocol, the tasks of the joint boundary demarcation commission shall be terminated.

Article V

The two parties have agreed that any dispute concerning the boundary which may arise after the delimitation of the boundary line actually existing between the two countries shall be settled peacefully by the two parties through friendly consultations.

Article VI

The two parties have agreed that, after the settlement of the Kashmir dispute between Pakistan and India, the sovereign authority concerned will reopen negotiations with the Government of the People's Republic of China on the boundary, as described in Article 2 of the present agreement, so as to sign a formal boundary treaty to replace the present agreement, provided that, in the event of that sovereign authority being Pakistan, the provisions of the present agreement and of the aforesaid protocol shall be maintained in the formal boundary treaty to be signed between the People's Republic of China and Pakistan.

Article VII

The present agreement shall come into force on the date of its signature.

[Signatures]

53. *GOVERNMENT STATEMENT: SINO-SOVIET BORDER DISPUTES (May, 1969)**

After the establishment of the People's Republic in 1949, the territorial questions were not formally raised with the Soviet Union. Mao Tse-tung, however, attempted to discuss the status of Outer Mongolia with Soviet leaders in 1954; he dropped it after receiving no response. In January, 1957, Chou En-lai privately raised the territorial issue with Khrushchev, but again without success. Finally, in March, 1963, the Chinese for the first time made public references to Sino-Soviet boundary questions in angry response to Khrushchev's remark about the "colonial vestige of Hong Kong and Macao."

Since then there have been many unpublicized minor border skirmishes between the two countries. In

*From Peking Review (May 30, 1969), pp. 3-9 (footnotes omitted).

1969, after repeated failures of Sino-Soviet negotiations, China used the Chenpao Island clashes as an occasion to open the issue to world public opinion.

The reason for this unusual move is perhaps attributable to China's fear of a direct nuclear attack from the Soviet Union. In the same month of the Chenpao Island clashes, the Soviet Defense Ministry newspaper published a warning that "military force would be used if necessary."[1] Over broadcasts monitored in London, the Soviet Union also issued two direct threats of using force against China, including the statement that the "Soviet forces are equipped with nuclear missiles."[2]

In response to these threats, China issued this most important policy statement on May 24, 1969, which includes a call for "peaceful negotiations and against the resort to use force."

On March 29, 1969, the Soviet Government issued a statement on the Sino-Soviet boundary question. On April 1, 1969, Vice-Chairman Lin Piao of the Central Committee of the Communist Party of China pointed out in his report to the Ninth National Congress of the Communist Party of China: In its statement, the Soviet Government was "still clinging to its obstinate aggressor stand, while expressing willingness to resume 'consultations'. Our Government is still considering its reply to this."

The Communist Party of China and the Chinese Government have always held that boundary questions should be settled by negotiations through diplomatic channels and that, pending a settlement, the status quo of the boundary should be maintained and conflicts averted. This was our stand in the past and remains our stand at present. The development of the Sino-Soviet boundary question to its present state is wholly the responsibility of the Soviet side. The Chinese Government

1 New York *Times* (March 9, 1969).
2 New York *Times* (March 21, 1969).

hereby states the truth about the Sino-Soviet boundary question and its consistent position as follows:

I

Chenpao Island has always been China's territory. Before 1860, the Wusuli River where Chenpao Island is situated was still an inland river of China. It was only after the Opium War in the 19th century when the capitalist powers, one after another, imposed unequal treaties on China that the Wusuli River was stipulated as forming part of the boundary between China and Russia in the "Sino-Russian Treaty of Peking" of 1860. According to established principles of international law, in the case of navigable boundary rivers, the central line of the main channel shall form the boundary line and determine the ownership of islands. Situated on the Chinese side of the central line of the main channel of the Wusuli River, Chenpao Island indisputably belongs to China and has always been under China's jurisdiction.

The Soviet Government invoked the map attached to the "Sino-Russian Treaty of Peking", asserting that in the area of Chenpao Island the demarcation line shown on this map "passes directly along the Chinese bank of the Ussuri River" and vainly attempting to prove thereby that Chenpao Island belongs to the Soviet Union. But this attached map can in no way help it out of its present predicament.

The map attached to the "Sino-Russian Treaty of Peking" was drawn unilaterally by tsarist Russia before the boundary was surveyed in 1861. And in 1861, China and Russia surveyed and marked only the land boundary south of the Hsingkai Lake but not the river boundary on the Wusuli and Heilung Rivers, and a red line was drawn on the attached map on a scale smaller than 1:1,000,000 only to indicate that the two rivers form the boundary between the two countries. The red line on this attached map does not, and cannot possibly, show the precise location of the boundary line in the rivers, still less is it intended to determine the ownership of islands. Hence, it can in no way prove that Chenpao Island belongs to the Soviet Union.

In fact, after the conclusion of the "Sino-Russian Treaty of Peking", the two sides always took the central line of the main channel for determining the ownership of islands and exercised jurisdiction accordingly. This was also repeatedly borne out by letters from the frontier officials of tsarist Russia to the Chinese side. For instance, in his letter of May 8, 1908 to a Chinese official, the frontier commissar of the Amur Region of tsarist Russia Kuzmin made it clear: "If countries are divided by a river, then the line running along the middle of the river should be taken as the boundary line between them. On navigable rivers, this line should be drawn along the channel." Again, in his letter of September 6 of the same year to the Chinese official, Kuzmin stated: "Islands in the rivers are divided by the river channel."

During the Sino-Soviet boundary negotiations in 1964, the Soviet representative also had to admit that the red line on the map attached to the "Sino-Russian Treaty of Peking" cannot show the precise alignment of the boundary line in the rivers, nor can it possibly determine the ownership of islands; he could not but agree that the central line of the main channel should be taken for determining the boundary line on the rivers and the ownership of islands.

It should also be pointed out that Chenpao Island was originally not an island, but a part of the bank on the Chinese side of the Wusuli River, which later became an island as a result of erosion by the river water. To this day, Chenpao Island still connects with the Chinese bank at low water, and the river-arm to the west of the Island has never become a waterway.

The Chenpao Island incident was deliberately provoked by the Soviet side. In recent years, Soviet troops have repeatedly been sent in helicopters, armoured cars and vehicles to intrude into China's territory Chenpao Island for provocations. During the first two months of this year alone, they intruded into the Island as many as eight times. They kidnapped Chinese inhabitants, assaulted and wounded Chinese frontier guards and seized arms and ammunition. With regard to the provocations by the Soviet side, the Chinese side all along exercised the utmost forbearance, persisting in reasoning things out on the basis of the facts and demanding that the Soviet side stop its intrusions and provocations. However, thinking that China was weak and could be bullied, the Soviet side became ever more unbridled. When they intruded into China's Chenpao Island on February 16, the Soviet troops flagrantly clamoured that they would use force of arms should the Chinese frontier guards go there for patrols again. Following that, the Soviet Far Eastern frontier troops entered into No. 1 combat readiness. On March 2, large numbers of Soviet troops in armoured cars and vehicles intruded into China's territory the Chenpao Island area simultaneously from Nizhne-Mikhailovka and Kulebyakinye, launched a sudden attack on the Chinese frontier guards on normal patrol duty and were the first to open fire with guns and cannons, killing and wounding many Chinese frontier guards on the spot. Driven beyond the limits of forbearance, the Chinese frontier guards were compelled to fight back in self-defence. On March 15, Soviet troops again intruded into Chenpao Island and shelled areas deep within Chinese territory on the Chinese side of the river, thus creating a new incident of bloodshed. Such is the truth about the Chenpao Island incident. No amount of lies will help the Soviet Government escape the responsibility for its crimes.

II

Tsarist Russia, a European country, was originally not contiguous to China. Tsarist Russia began to expand eastwards in the 16th century, and it was not until the latter half of the 17th century that there arose the question of a boundary with China. In 1689, China and Russia concluded their first boundary treaty, the "Treaty of Nipchu", which defined the eastern sector of the Sino-Russian boundary. In 1727, China and Russia concluded the "Burinsky Treaty", which defined the middle sector of the Sino-Russian boundary (the larger part of this sector of the boundary has now become Mongolian-Soviet boundary). As for the western frontier of China, it was then at the Balkhash Lake, a great distance from the boundary of tsarist Russia.

After the Opium War of 1840, China was gradually reduced to a semi-colony, while Russia was gradually becoming a military-feudal imperialist country. Beginning from the fifties of the 19th century, tsarist Russia colluded with the Western imperialist countries in pursuing the aggressive policy of carving up China. Within the short space of half a century, it forced China to sign a series of unequal treaties, by which it annexed more than 1.5 million square kilometres of Chinese territory, an area three times that of France or twelve times that of Czechoslovakia.

While the allied Anglo-French imperialist forces were attacking Tientsin and threatening Peking in their aggression against China, tsarist Russian imperialism seized the opportunity to compel the authorities of the Ching Dynasty by force of arms to sign the "Sino-Russian Treaty of Aigun" on May 28, 1858, by which it annexed more than 600,000 square kilometres of Chinese territory north of the Heilung River and south of the Outer Khingan Mountains and placed the Chinese territory east of the Wusuli River under the joint possession of China and Russia.

Taking advantage of the military pressure brought about by the occupation of Peking by the allied Anglo-French forces invading China, alleging that it had made contributions in mediation and threatening that "it is not difficult to renew the war", tsarist Russia forced the Ching Dynasty Government, to sign the "Sino-Russian Treaty of Peking" on November 14, 1860, by which it forcibly incorporated some 400,000 square kilometres of Chinese territory east of the Wusuli River into Russia.

By the "Sino-Russian Treaty of Peking" and by the "Tahcheng Protocol on the Delimitation of Sino-Russian Boundary" which tsarist Russia forced the Ching Dynasty Government to sign on October 7, 1864, tsarist Russia further annexed more than 440,000 square kilometres of territory in the western part of China.

In 1871, tsarist Russia sent troops to forcibly occupy China's Ili area, who entrenched themselves there for as long as ten years; on February 24, 1881, it forced the Ching Dynasty Government to sign the "Sino-Russian Ili Treaty". By the "Sino-Russian Ili Treaty" and the subsequent protocols on boundary delimitation, tsarist Russia further incorporated more than 70,000 square kilometres of Chinese territory into the territory of tsarist Russia.

The great teachers of the world proletariat Marx, Engels and Lenin had long made brilliant conclusions on the unequal nature of these treaties. Commenting on the "Sino-Russian Treaty of Aigun" in 1858, Marx said that ". . . by his second opium-war he [John Bull] has helped her [Russia] to the invaluable tract lying between the Gulf of Tartary and Lake Baikal, a region so much coveted by Russia that from Czar Alexey Michaelowitch down to Nicolaus, she has always attempted to get it". Engels also pointed out in the same year that Russia despoiled "China of a country as large as France and Germany put together, and of a river as large as the Danube" and that "Not satisfied with this, she has obtained the establishment of a Russo-Chinese Commission to fix the boundaries. Now, we all know what such a commission is in the hands of Russia. We have seen them at work on the Asiatic frontiers of Turkey, where they kept slicing away piece after piece from that country, for more than twenty years." Things turned out to be exactly as Engels had wisely foreseen. After 1858, tsarist Russia was "slicing away piece after piece" of Chinese territory with the signing of each treaty and with every survey of the boundary. Lenin also bitterly denounced tsarist Russia more than once for its crimes of aggression against China. Lenin pointed out that ". . . the European governments (the Russian Government among the very first) have already started to partition China. However, they have not begun this partitioning openly, but stealthily, like thieves" and that "The policy of the tsarist government in China is a criminal policy."

While glibly talking about being "true to Lenin's behests" in its statement of March 29, the Soviet Government in the very same statement directly opposed the brilliant conclusions made by Marx, Engels and Lenin and thoroughly betrayed their teachings.

In order to suit the needs of its social-imperialist policy, the Soviet Government even described tsarist Russian imperialist aggression against semi-colonial China after the mid-19th century as "disputes" between "Chinese emperors and tsars", in which there was no question of who was the aggressor and who the victim of aggression, nor was there any question of whether the treaties concluded between them are equal or not. This is a gangster logic in defence of tsarist Russian imperialist aggression.

In his time the great Lenin warmly supported China and all other oppressed countries in opposing aggression by tsarist Russian imperialism and all other imperialists. He said that ". . . if tomorrow, Morocco were to declare war on France, or India on Britain, or Persia or China on Russia, and so on, these would be 'just', and 'defensive' wars, irrespective of who would be the first to attack; any socialist would wish the oppressed, dependent and unequal states victory over the oppressor, slave-holding and predatory 'Great' Powers". Today when people review these teachings of Lenin's, they can only come to one conclusion: Such energetic propagation of the imperialist gangster logic by the Soviet Government is not only "alien to the Leninist policy", but is also a most shameless betrayal of Leninism.

III

There exists a boundary question between China and the Soviet Union not only because tsarist Russia annexed more than 1.5 million square kilometres of Chinese territory by the unequal treaties it imposed on China, but also because it crossed in many places the boundary line stipulated by the unequal treaties and further occupied vast expanses of Chinese territory. Even tracts of Chinese territory which have always been under the Chinese Government's jurisdiction have been drawn as Soviet territory. For instance, in the Pamir area, tsarist Russia occupied more than 20,000 square kilometres of Chinese territory in violation of the stipulations of the "Protocol on Sino-Russian Boundary in the Kashgar Region" of 1884. Again for instance, in the sector of the Wusuli and Heilung Rivers, the Soviet Government, in violation of the "Sino-Russian Treaty of Aigun", the "Sino-Russian Treaty of Peking" and the established principles of international law, has gone so far as to draw the boundary line almost entirely along the Chinese bank and in some places even on China's inland rivers and islands, marking as Soviet territory over 600 of the 700 and more Chinese islands on the Chinese side of the central line of the main channel, which cover an area of more than 1,000 square kilometres. With regard to the unequal treaties imposed on China by tsarist Russia, the great Lenin always stood for their annulment.

On September 27, 1920, the Government of Soviets led by Lenin solemnly proclaimed: It "declares null and void all the treaties concluded with China by the former Governments of Russia, renounces all seizure of Chinese territory and all Russian concessions in China and restores to China, without any compensation and for ever, all that had been predatorily seized from her by the Tsar's Government and the Russian bourgeoisie".

Furthermore, the "Agreement on General Principles for the Settlement of the Questions Between China and the Soviet Union" signed on May 31, 1924 stipulates that at the conference agreed upon by both sides, they are to "annul all Conventions, Treaties, Agreements, Protocols, Contracts, etcetera, concluded between the Government of China and the Tsarist Government and to replace them with new treaties, agreements, etcetera, on the basis of equality, reciprocity and justice, as well as the spirit of the Declarations of the Soviet Government of the years of 1919 and 1920" and "to re-demarcate their national boundaries . . . , and pending such re-demarcation, to maintain the present boundaries".

In pursuance of the 1924 Agreement, China and the Soviet Union held talks in 1926 to discuss the redemarcation of the boundary and the conclusion of a new treaty. Owing to the historical conditions at the time, no agreement was reached by the two sides on the boundary question, no re-demarcation of the boundary between the two countries was made and no new equal treaty was concluded by the two countries, and thus this proletarian policy of Lenin's failed to come true.

The above facts fully show that the treaties relating to the present Sino-Soviet boundary are all unequal treaties, that they should all be annulled and that the Sino-Soviet boundary question remains an outstanding issue. In its statement, the Soviet Government did not even say a single word about the fact that under the above-mentioned Declarations and Agreement, it is "all" the treaties concluded with China that are to be annulled and it is "all" the seized Chinese territory that is to be renounced, but uttered the nonsense that the 1924 Agreement did not "consider" the boundary treaties "as being among the unequal treaties" and that "there was no talk of their being annulled". This is indeed a "juggling with history, adapting it to its territorial claims".

Chairman Mao spoke highly of the declaration of the annulment of the unequal treaties between China and Russia made by the Government of Soviets led by Lenin. However, from Chairman Mao's words no conclusion whatsoever can be drawn that there does not exist a boundary question between China and the Soviet Union. The same is true of Dr. Sun Yat-sen's remarks. As for the "Sino-Soviet Treaty of Friendship, Alliance and Mutual Assistance" and the "Sino-Soviet

Agreement on Navigation on Boundary Rivers", they are in no sense a treaty or agreement for the settlement of the boundary question, still less can they prove that there does not exist a boundary question between China and the Soviet Union.

IV

It is understandable that the boundary question existing between China and the Soviet Union was not settled when China was under reactionary rule. The founding of the People's Republic of China created all the necessary conditions for a reasonable settlement of the Sino-Soviet boundary question. Owing to various reasons, no start was made to settle the question of the time, yet the Sino-Soviet border was all along tranquil.

Since 1960, the Soviet Government has gone farther and farther down the road of betraying Marxism-Leninism. It restores capitalism at home and pursues a social-imperialist policy abroad, it allies with U.S. imperialism and opposes socialist China, and it has incessantly violated the status quo of the boundary and tried to occupy Chinese territory which has always been under the Chinese Government's jurisdiction, thus aggravating the Sino-Soviet boundary question. The Soviet Government directed Soviet frontier troops to push their patrol routes into Chinese territory, build military installations within Chinese territory, assault and kidnap Chinese border inhabitants, sabotage their production and carry out all sorts of provocative and subversive activities. In 1962, the Soviet Government incited and coerced more than 60,000 Chinese citizens in the Ili and Tahcheng areas of Sinkiang, China into going to the Soviet Union, and it has up to now refused to send them back.

Since 1964, the Soviet Government has sent large reinforcements to the Sino-Soviet border, stepped up its violation of the status quo of the boundary, carried out armed provocations and created incidents of bloodshed. From October 15, 1964 to March 15 this year, the Soviet side provoked as many as 4,189 border incidents, two and a half times the number of those it provoked from 1960 to 1964, with its tactics getting even more vicious and its behaviour even more unbridled. Soviet troops intruded into Chinese territory, indulging in murder and arson, killing barehanded Chinese fishermen and peasants by beating and running armoured cars over them or even throwing them alive into the river. Lenin indignantly condemned the Russian government for its atrocities of slaughtering peaceable Chinese inhabitants in these words: ". . . they flung themselves upon it [China] like savage beasts, burning down whole villages, shooting, bayonetting, and drowning in the Amur River unarmed inhabitants, their wives, and their children". What difference is there between the present-day atrocities committed by the Soviet Government against Chinese inhabitants on the Wusuli and Heilung Rivers and the atrocities by the tsarist Russian government which were bitterly denounced by Lenin in those days!?

The Chenpao Island incident is the inevitable result of the Soviet Government's violation of the status quo of the Sino-Soviet boundary and pursuance of its social-imperialist policy over a long period of time. The sanguinary conflicts on Chenpao Island were deliberately engineered by the Soviet Government in order to cover up its capitulation on the Berlin question and curry favour with U.S. imperialism, so that it can further ally with U.S. imperialism against China. By this action, the Soviet Government tells the United States that China is the common enemy of the United States and the Soviet Union.

V

In its statement, the Soviet Government slanderously asserted that China "queries the present boundaries of the countries neighbouring on China" and that "claims are being advanced on neighbouring territories", vainly attempting to show that the Chinese Government pursues a policy of expansion. Such clumsy tactics are indeed both ridiculous and pitiable! The whole world knows that since the founding of the People's Republic of China, the Chinese Government has satisfactorily settled complicated boundary questions left over by history and concluded boundary treaties with neighbouring countries such as Burma, Nepal, Pakistan, the People's Republic of Mongolia and Afghanistan, with the exception of the Soviet Union and India. China does not have a single soldier stationed in any foreign country. China has no territorial claims against any of her neighbouring countries, and has not invaded or occupied a single inch of territory of any foreign country.

Today, the Soviet Government is not only forcibly occupying the territories of other countries and refuses to return them, but has under new conditions advanced new theories for aggression—the theories of "limited sovereignty", of "international dictatorship" and of the "socialist community". It has already turned some East European countries and the People's Republic of Mongolia into its colonies and military bases. It flagrantly sent several hundred thousand troops to occupy Czechoslovakia and brutally suppress the Czechoslovak people. It regards heroic Albania as a thorn in its flesh. It menaces Rumania and Yugoslavia. It has dispatched its fleet to the Mediterranean Sea, trying hard to control the Arab countries by taking advantage of their difficulties. Its aggressive designs are even more ambitious, and its claws have stretched out even farther, than those of tsarist Russia.

Harbouring ulterior motives, the Soviet Government, moreover, talked glibly about Soviet assistance to China in its statement. It is true that under the leadership of the great Lenin and Stalin, the Soviet people rendered assistance to the Chinese people, which the Chinese people will never forget. In turn, the Chinese people led by their great leader Chairman Mao also rendered assistance to the Soviet people, which the Soviet people will never forget either. Such mutual support and assistance between the Chinese and Soviet peoples in revolutionary struggles will certainly continue in the future. However, it must be pointed out that in the past decade the Soviet Government has completely betrayed the internationalist foreign policy of Lenin and Stalin, done all evils against China and committed towering crimes against the Chinese people. It is not qualified at all to talk about assistance rendered to the Chinese people at the time of Lenin and Stalin. At present, the Soviet Government is everywhere perpetrating acts of aggression and plunder against the people of other countries under the signboard of "assistance". Such practice of the Soviet Government is exactly the same as that of U.S. imperialism.

VI

The Chinese Government has consistently stood and worked for the settlement of boundary questions with its neighbouring countries through negotiations and for the maintenance of the status quo of the boundary pending a settlement. As early as August 22 and September 21, 1960, the Chinese Government twice took the initiative in proposing to the Soviet Government that negotiations be held. Furthermore, on August 23, 1963, the Chinese Government put forward to the Soviet Government a six-point proposal for maintaining the status quo of the boundary and averting conflicts. Sino-Soviet boundary negotiations finally took place in Peking in 1964. During the negotiations, the Chinese side took the reasonable stand that the treaties relating to the present Sino-Soviet boundary should be taken as the basis for settling the boundary question, and it made the maximum efforts and showed the greatest sincerity for the settlement of the Sino-Soviet boundary question. If the Soviet Government had the slightest sincerity, it would not have been difficult to settle the Sino-Soviet boundary question. What Premier Chou En-lai said in answering the provocative question of an American correspondent at a press conference held in Kathmandu on April 28, 1960 precisely expressed this idea of the Chinese Government. However, the Soviet Government clung to its big-power chauvinist and territorial expansionist stand; it not only wanted to keep under its forcible occupation of the Chinese territory which tsarist Russia had seized by means of the unequal treaties, but also insisted that China recognize as belonging to the Soviet Union all the Chinese territory which it had occupied or attempted to occupy in violation of the treaties, and as a result the negotiations were disrupted. Hence, while China has now settled boundary questions with many of her neighbouring countries, only the boundary questions between China and the Soviet Union and between China and India remain unsettled.

While expressing willingness to resume "consultations" in its statement of March 29, the Soviet Government tried hard to deny the existence of a boundary question between China and the Soviet Union, which actually amounts to saying that there is nothing to discuss at all.

While indicating in its statement that "urgent practical measures should be taken to normalize the situation on the Soviet-Chinese border", the Soviet Government has continued to direct Soviet troops to open fire with light and heavy machine-guns and heavy artillery on China's Chenpao Island and areas deep within Chinese territory, and to this day the firing has not ceased; at the same time, it is carrying out provocations in other sectors of the Sino-Soviet boundary. Reading from a prepared text, the Soviet frontier representative even brazenly threatened on April 3: "The Soviet Union will not cease fire unless the Chinese Government holds negotiations with the Soviet Government, nor will it cease fire unless the Chinese withdraw from Damansky Island" (N.B. China's Chenpao Island). Furthermore, the Soviet Government has canvassed among the imperialist countries headed by the United States, begging for their support. Meanwhile, setting in motion all its propaganda machines, it has done its utmost to spread lies and slanders, tried to fan up national chauvinist sentiments, made war clamours and brandished nuclear weapons at China. The above series of facts show that it is highly doubtful as to how much sincerity the Soviet Government has, after all, for negotiations.

The development of the Sino-Soviet boundary question to its present state is not the responsibility of the Chinese side. Nevertheless, the Chinese Government is still ready to seek an overall settlement of the Sino-Soviet boundary question through peaceful negotiations and is against resort to the use of force.

The Chinese Government holds that it must be confirmed that the treaties relating to the present Sino-Soviet boundary are all unequal treaties imposed on China by tsarist Russian imperialism. But taking into consideration the fact that it was tsarist Russian imperialism which compelled China to sign these treaties when power was in the hands of neither the Chinese people nor the Russian people and the Soviet people bear no responsibility and that large numbers of Soviet labouring people have lived on the land over a long period of time, the Chinese Government, out of the desire to safeguard the revolutionary friendship between the Chinese and Soviet peoples, is still ready to take these unequal treaties as the basis for determining the entire alignment of the boundary line between the two countries and for settling all existing questions relating to the boundary. Any side which occupies the territory of the other side in violation of the treaties must, in principle, return it wholly and unconditionally to the other side, and this brooks no ambiguity. The Chinese Government maintains that what should be done is to hold negotiations for the overall settlement of the Sino-Soviet boundary question and the conclusion of a new equal treaty to replace the old unequal ones, and not to hold "consultations" for "clarification on individual sectors of the Soviet-Chinese state border line".

Of course, on the premise that the treaties relating to the present Sino-Soviet boundary are taken as the basis, necessary adjustments at individual places on the boundary can be made in accordance with the principles of consultation on an equal footing and of mutual understanding and mutual accommodation. But it is absolutely impermissible to take such a truculent attitude: What the tsars occupied is yours, and what you want to occupy is yours, too.

In order to bring about a peaceful settlement of the Sino-Soviet boundary question, the Soviet Government must stop all its provocations and armed threats on the Sino-Soviet border. Neither a small war, nor a big war, nor a nuclear war can ever intimidate the Chinese people. The Chinese Government once again proposes: Each side ensures that it shall maintain the status quo of the boundary and not push forward by any means the line of actual control on the border, and that in sectors where a river forms the boundary, the frontier guards of its side shall not cross the central line of the main channel and of the main waterway; each side ensures that it shall avert conflicts and that under no circumstances shall the frontier guards of its side fire at the other side; there should be no interference in the normal productive activities carried out by the border inhabitants of both sides according to habitual practice.

The Chinese Government holds that negotiations are intended for settling questions and not for deceiving the people. To make serious negotiations possible, it is essential to adopt an honest attitude, and not a hypocritical attitude. In its note of April 11 to the Chinese Government, the Soviet Government suggested that "consultations" start right on April 15 in Moscow and, without waiting for a reply from the Chinese Government, it published the note on the following day. This attitude of the Soviet Government's is far from being serious, to say the least. The Chinese Government proposes that the date and place for the Sino-Soviet boundary negotiations be discussed and decided upon by both sides through diplomatic channels.

The Chinese Government hopes that the Soviet Government will make a positive response to the above proposals.

The Soviet Government will have completely miscalculated if it should take the Chinese Government's stand for a peaceful settlement of the boundary question as a sign that China is weak and can be bullied, thinking that the Chinese people can be cowed by its policy of nuclear blackmail and that it can realize its territorial claims against China by means of war. Armed with Mao Tsetung Thought and tempered through the Great Proletarian Cultural Revolution, the 700 million Chinese people are not to be bullied. The Chinese people's great leader Chairman Mao has taught us: "We will not attack unless we are attacked; if we are attacked, we will certainly counter-attack." "As far as our own desire is concerned, we don't want to fight even for a single day. But if circumstances force us to fight, we can fight to the finish." This is the answer of the Chinese Government and people to the Soviet Government's policies of war and nuclear blackmail.

54. COMMENTATOR: ON CHINA'S SEABED AND SUBSOIL RESOURCES (December, 1970) and GOVERNMENT'S STATEMENT ON THE EXTENSION OF TERRITORIAL WATERS OF CHINA (September, 1958)*

As land resources become increasingly scarce, man's attention is directed to space and the oceans. China, seeking to protect her own interests and looking toward the future, issued two policy papers. The extension of territorial waters to 12 nautical miles was rejected by the United States but accepted by all other countries in the Soviet bloc and the Third World. There is, however, under international law no uniform limit of territorial waters at present.

I

In disregard of the strong opposition and warning of the Chinese and Korean people, the Japanese reactionaries, ganging up with the Chiang Kai-shek bandit gang and the Pak Jung Hi [Chung Hee Park] clique, are stepping up their scheme to plunder, together with U.S. imperialism, the sea-bed and subsoil

*From *Jen-min Jih-pao* (December 29, 1970); and Hsin Hua News Release, September 4, 1958.

resources of China and Korea. On December 21, the "joint committee for ocean development research" of the so-called Japan-Chiang-Pak "liaison committee" held a meeting in Tokyo which brazenly decided to carry out "investigation, research and development" of the oil and other mineral resources of the sea-bed and subsoil of the seas around China's Taiwan Province and the islands appertaining thereto and of the shallow seas adjacent to other parts of China and to Korea. This is a flagrant encroachment by the U.S. and Japanese reactionaries upon the sovereignty of China and the Democratic People's Republic of Korea, and another towering crime perpetrated by the Chiang Kai-shek gang in selling out the sovereignty and resources of our country.

The U.S. and Japanese reactionaries have long been casting a covetous eye on China's sea-bed and subsoil resources. In recent years, they have been colluding with the Chiang Kai-shek gang in conducting frequent and large-scale "surveys" of the sea-bed and subsoil resources of the seas around China's Taiwan Province and the islands appertaining thereto and of the shallow seas adjacent to other parts of China. Furthermore, U.S. imperialism has concluded contracts with the Chiang Kai-shek gang, delimiting mining areas in preparation for oil exploitation in the sea-bed and subsoil of the seas to the west of the northern part of Taiwan. Now, the U.S. and Japanese reactionaries are making one more attempt to wilfully plunder the sea-bed and subsoil resources of our country by feverishly engaging in so-called "joint development" through the establishment of a Japan-Chiang-Pak "joint ocean development company." The Chinese people hereby express their utmost indignation at these naked piratical acts of the U.S. imperialists and the Japanese reactionaries.

Taiwan Province and the islands appertaining thereto, including the Tiaoyu [Tiao-Yu Tai], Huangwei, Chihwei, Nanhsiao, Peihsiao and other islands, are China's sacred territories. The resources of the sea-bed and subsoil of the seas around these islands and of the shallow seas adjacent to other parts of China all belong to China, their owner, and we will never permit others to lay their hands on them. The People's Republic of China alone has the right to explore and exploit the resources of the sea-bed and subsoil of these areas. The Chiang Kai-shek gang is a political mummy spurned long ago by the Chinese people. All agreements and contracts concerning the exploration and exploitation of China's sea-bed and subsoil resources that gang concluded with any country, any international organization or any foreign public or private enterprise under the signboard of "joint development" or anything else are illegal and null and void.

Not only have the Japanese reactionaries deliberately tried to plunder China's sea-bed and subsoil resources, they are vainly attempting to incorporate into Japan's territory the Tiaoyu and other islands and the seas which belong to China. Of late, Kiichi Aichi, Foreign Minister of the reactionary Sato government, has repeatedly made the outcry that Japan has its "title" to these islands. "Director-General" of Japan's "Defence Agency" Yasuhiro Nakasone has gone so far as to openly list these islands in the scope of "defence" in Japan's fourth military build-up programme. This fully reveals the aggressive ambitions of Japanese militarism. Like Taiwan, the Tiaoyu, Huangwei, Chihwei, Nanhsiao, Peihsiao and other islands have been China's territories since ancient times. This is a historical fact no one can change. No matter what pretext they may create and what tricks they may play, the Japanese reactionaries will never succeed in their scheme to forcibly occupy China's sacred territories.

Our great leader Chairman Mao has pointed out: "The Chinese people will defend their territory and sovereignty and absolutely will not permit encroachment by foreign governments." The U.S. imperialists and the Japanese reactionaries must immediately stop their criminal acts of encroaching upon China's territory and sovereignty and plundering her sea-bed and subsoil resources, they must withdraw their claws of aggression. The U.S. and Japanese reactionaries will lift a rock only to drop it on their own feet if they cling to their obdurate course.

(December 29, 1970)

II

The Government of the People's Republic of China declares:
(1) The breadth of the territorial sea of the People's

Republic of China shall be twelve nautical miles. This provision applies to all territories of the People's Republic of China, including the Chinese mainland and its coastal islands, as well as Taiwan and its surrounding islands, the Penghu Islands, the Tungsha Islands, the Hsisha Islands, the Chungsha Islands, the Nansha Islands and all other islands belonging to China which are separated from the mainland and its coastal islands by the high seas.

(2) China's territorial sea along the mainland and its coastal islands takes as its baseline the line composed of the straight lines connecting base-points on the mainland coast and on the outermost of the coastal islands; the water area extending twelve nautical miles outwards from this baseline is China's territorial sea. The water areas inside the baseline, including Pohai Bay and the Chiungchow Straits, are Chinese inland waters. The islands inside the baseline, including Tungyin Island, Kaoteng Island, the Matsu Islands, the Paichuan Islands, Wuchiu Island, the Greater and Lesser Quemoy Islands, Tatan Island, Erhtan Island and Tungting Island, are islands of the Chinese inland waters.

(3) No foreign vessels for military use and no foreign aircraft may enter China's territorial sea and the air space above it without the permission of the Government of the People's Republic of China.

While navigating Chinese territorial sea, every foreign vessel must observe the relevant laws and regulations laid down by the Government of the People's Republic of China.

(4) The principles provided in paragraphs (2) and (3) likewise apply to Taiwan and its surrounding islands, the Penghu Islands, the Tungsha Islands, the Hsisha Islands, the Chungsha Islands, the Nansha Islands, and all other islands belonging to China.

The Taiwan and Penghu areas are still occupied by the United States by armed force. This is an unlawful encroachment on the territorial integrity and sovereignty of the People's Republic of China. Taiwan, Penghu and such other areas are yet to be recovered, and the Government of the People's Republic of China has the right to recover these areas by all suitable means at a suitable time. This is China's internal affair, in which no foreign interference is tolerated.

55. COMMENTATOR: ON OKINAWA "REVERSION" AND TIAO-YU-TAI ISLANDS (May, 1971)*

During 1970-71, several thousand overseas-Chinese students in the United States for the first time in recent history were suddenly organized to protest the "violation of Chinese sovereignty" over the Tiao-Yu-Tai Islands by the Japanese and Ryukyu governments in several major cities of the United States.[1]

The so-called Tiao-Yu-Tai Islands (or Senkaku Islands, in Japanese) are a group of eight islands located about 120 miles northeast of Taiwan on the continental shelf of China. Because of the recent discovery of potential oil reserves in these islands, they have become a focal point of dispute among the Japanese, mainland Chinese, and Taiwan Chinese.

The following statement issued on May 1, 1971, by a ranking Chinese official not only reiterates the Chinese claim over Tiao-Yu-Tai Island (the Communists use the name Tiaoyu Island) but also expresses China's opposition to the reversion of Okinawa to Japan. Ironically, the Nationalists on Taiwan who oppose the Communists on the mainland are in complete agreement on these two nationalistic and emotional issues. The United States, on the other hand, maintains complete "neutrality."

In setting up their recent Okinawa "reversion" fraud, the U.S. and Japanese reactionaries even included the Tiaoyu [Tiao-Yu-Tai] and other islands in the so-called "areas of reversion." Ignoring the Chinese people's warning, Eisaku Sato and Kiichi Aichi and their ilk continue to clamour that the Tiaoyu and other islands are the "territory of Japan," and that "there is no need to hold talks with any country about the question of territorial rights." The Chinese people express their boundless indignation at and protest vehemently against the

---

*From *Jen-min Jih-pao* (May 1, 1971). The title is editor's.
1 New York *Times* (May 23, 1971).

criminal activities of the U.S. and Japanese reactionaries in flagrantly plotting to annex China's territory.

Like Taiwan, the Tiaoyu, Huangwei, Chihwei, Nanhsiao, Peihsiao and other islands located in the waters northeast of China's Taiwan Province have from time immemorial been part of the sacred territory of China and the ownership of these islands is indisputable. However, the Japanese reactionaries have resorted to all kinds of despicable ruses in order to occupy China's Tiaoyu and other islands. They even dug up the Japanese emperor's "imperial edict" of 1896 as a "basis." This alleged that after Japan's annexation of Taiwan from China following the 1894 Sino-Japanese War, a "cabinet meeting [of Japan] decided that this archipelago [Tiaoyu and other islands] is Japanese territory." This kind of "basis" is absolutely absurd. Can a state, wilfully, unilaterally and illegally, incorporate into its own original territory the territory of another country which was annexed for a time? In an attempt to create a fait accompli in occupying China's territory, the Japanese reactionary government authorities have repeatedly and stealthily sent people to Tiaoyu and other islands to carry out criminal activities in violation of China's territory and sovereignty. But all these attempts are futile. No matter how they refuse to talk reason and invent stories, the Japanese reactionaries cannot turn China's territory into Japan's.

It is worth noting that the U.S. imperialists even openly support the scheme of the Japanese reactionaries to occupy China's territory. They have asserted that according to their "peace treaty" with Japan, they enjoyed so-called "administrative rights" over the Tiaoyu and other islands of China and that they will return these islands together with Okinawa to Japan. How ridiculous! The Tiaoyu and other islands are China's territory, over which China has inviolable sovereignty. The question of U.S. imperialism having so-called "administrative rights" over these islands which belong to China simply does not exist. What right has U.S. imperialism to clandestinely offer China's territory to the Japanese reactionaries? It is obvious that U.S. imperialism's aim in doing so is to connive at and encourage Japanese militarism to carry out expansion abroad and use the Japanese reactionaries as an instrument for pushing the "Nixon doctrine" in Asia. This is a fresh crime in U.S. imperialism's hostility towards the Chinese people. But this clumsy trick of U.S. imperialism can neither help the Japanese reactionaries nor save the "Nixon doctrine" from complete failure in Asia. The Chinese people have always maintained that U.S. imperialism should return Okinawa, which it has occupied by force, to the Japanese people. But we will never permit the U.S. and Japanese reactionaries to annex China's sacred territory Tiaoyu and other islands by making use of the "Okinawa reversion" swindle.

The Chiang Kai-shek bandit gang plays a despicable role in the international intrigue to annex China's territory. This gang of political mummies that have been repudiated by the Chinese people are shamelessly selling the territory and sovereignty of China and her resources. On the one hand they cannot but express "disagreement" over the claim that the Tiaoyu and other islands belong to Japan; on the other hand they continue to plot to work in cahoots with Japan and the Pak Jung Hi [Chung Hee Park] clique to "jointly develop" the sea-bed and subsoil resources of this area. They act servilely and humiliatingly towards the arrogant move of the Japanese reactionaries to encroach on China's territory and sovereignty in an effort to win the Japanese reactionaries' support in return. This shows that the Chiang Kai-shek bandit gang's so-called safeguarding the sovereignty of the Tiaoyu island, etc., are nothing but deceitful lies. The Chinese people will definitely not let the Chiang Kai-shek bandit gang go unpunished for its traitorous crimes.

The aggressive scheme of the U.S. and Japanese reactionaries to occupy China's territory and plunder her resources in collusion with the Chiang bandit gang can only arouse the burning anger of every patriotic Chinese. The broad masses of the overseas Chinese are launching a patriotic campaign to safeguard national sovereignty and oppose the annexation of the Tiaoyu and other islands by the U.S. and Japanese reactionaries. Their just action has won resolute support from the people of their motherland.

Our great leader Chairman Mao pointed out long ago: "The People's Republic of China cannot be bullied." "No imperialist will be allowed to invade our territory again." We want to warn the Japanese reactionaries once again: Gone for ever are the days when China was compelled by armed force to cede territory and waive sovereignty. China's sovereignty over the Tiaoyu and other islands brooks no encroachment by anybody. In the face of the great Chinese people, all your intrigues to annex China's territory in collusion with U.S. imperialism are futile and bound to be dashed to pieces.

(May 1)

CHAPTER SEVEN:
Policies on War, Peace, World Order, and Ecology

In the Introduction to this book, the author has already mentioned five major themes dominating China's relations with foreign countries:

1. Maoism as theory and practice in international relations;
2. People's wars as a strategy for the seizure of political power;
3. Self-reliance as a model for Socialist construction in developing nations;
4. Paper-tiger concept as a psychological deterrent to big-power hegemony; and finally,
5. Anti-imperialism as a condition for peaceful coexistence and world peace.

However, there are still many questions left unanswered with respect to Chinese attitudes on war, peace, world order, and ecology. First and foremost, do the Chinese believe in world peace? And will the Chinese live in a world based upon international law and world order? Finally, are the Chinese concerned with the ecological problems of the 1970's, such as overpopulation, pollution, and the harmful effects of industrial wastes, etc.?

The Chinese attitudes on war and peace are definitely conditioned by historical experience, domestic environment, and international politics. In ideological terms, China follows the Marxist-Leninist model of "dialectical materialism"—that the world is a one-directional movement from feudalism to capitalism, to Socialism, etc.[1] During the transition from

1 *Cf.* Tung Chi-ming, *A Short History of China* (Peking, Foreign Language Press, 1965).

capitalism to Socialism, the Chinese believe there are two possibilities: peaceful transition and nonpeaceful transition.[1] Nonpeaceful transition includes the doctrine of the people's wars (see Introduction and Document 58).

The Chinese claim to be disciples of Lenin, and they insist on following Lenin's definition of "peaceful coexistence," which only applies to a relationship between friendly countries and not to the relations between "oppressed and oppressor nations or oppressed and oppressor class."[2]

In practical politics, however, the Chinese have never defined just what are the "oppressed and oppressor nations" beyond the generalizations of colonialism and/or imperialism, and in practice the terms prove to be applied according to simple convenience: "Who is a friend and who is an enemy of the CCP?"[3]

For example, in his policy statement "On People's Democratic Dictatorship" in 1949, Mao Tse-tung wrote, "Who are the people? At the present stage in China, they are the working class, the peasantry, the urban petty bourgeoisie and the national bourgeoisie. These classes, led by the working class and the Communist Party, unite to form their own state and elect their own government; they enforce their dictatorship over the running dogs of imperialism—the landlord class and bureaucrat-bourgeoisie, as well as representatives of those classes, the Kuomintang reactionaries and their accomplices. . . ."[4]

This inclusion of the "national bourgeoisie" allied with the Communist Party would have shocked Lenin, since Lenin's own use of the term "people" excluded the national bourgeoisie in the Soviet state organization.[5]

1 See the Chinese position paper submitted to the 1957 Moscow Meeting of Communist Parties in *The Polemic on the General Line of the International Communist Movement* (Peking, Foreign Language Press, 1965), p. 105.

2 See the Chinese proposal concerning the "General Line of the International Communist Party Movement" in *Ibid.*, pp. 30-31.

3 Arthur A. Cohen, *The Communism of Mao Tse-tung* (Chicago, University of Chicago Press, 1964), p. 82.

4 *Selected Works of Mao Tse-tung*, Vol. IV (Peking, Foreign Language Press, 1965), pp. 417-18.

5 Vladimir I. Lenin, "Two Tactics of the Social Democracy in the Democratic Revolution," as quoted in Arthur A. Cohen, *The Communism of Mao Tse-tung, op. cit.*, p. 83.

But the Chinese, at least the majority of them, are pragmatists, and this is perhaps why, despite the recent Maoist ideology of anti-imperialist revolutionism, the party official report of the Ninth Congress on April 1, 1969, stated that "The foreign policy of our Party and Government is consistent. It is: to develop relations of friendship, mutual assistance and cooperation . . . to support and assist the revolutionary struggle of all the oppressed people and nations; to strive for peaceful coexistence. . . . Our proletarian policy is not based on expediency; it is a policy which we have long persisted." (See Document 59.)

Why, then, does China develop a national nuclear capability? In the opinion of experienced observers, China needs to be an independent nuclear power in order (1) to establish a Chinese sphere of influence in Asia, (2) to become a more credible deterrent against nuclear attack from the USSR or the United States, and (3) to exercise greater power within the world community of nations.[1] And China's nonaggressive intentions can be seen through her various nuclear disarmament proposals submitted after the country's first nuclear explosion on October 16, 1964 (see Documents 56, 57).

In addition, China has on a number of occasions repeated its intention not to be first to use nuclear weapons. China has also protested the manufacture and testing of chemical and biological weapons.[2] Although President Nixon announced on November 25, 1969, that the United States had decided on the "renunciation" of first use of lethal chemical and biological weapons, the Chinese claim that Nixon's stand was invalidated by U.S. troops' continued use of toxic chemicals in Vietnam.[3]

On the other hand, China did not participate in any of the following treaties: (1) 1963 partial nuclear test-ban treaty, (2) 1967 treaty on the peaceful uses of outer space, (3) 1968 treaty on the nonproliferation of nuclear weapons, and (4) 1971 treaty for the prohibition of the emplacement of nuclear weapons on the seabed.

1 *Cf.* Morton H. Halperin and Dwight H. Perkins, *Communist China and Arms Control* (New York, Praeger, 1965), p. 63; and Alice Langley Hsieh, "China's Nuclear-Missile Program," *China Quarterly*, No. 45 (January/March, 1971).

2 Hsin Hua News Release, July 30, 1969.

3 Hsin Hua News Release, December 8, 1969.

China denounced these treaties and the strategic arms limitation talks (SALT) in Helsinki as "a big plot" which revealed that "the U.S. and the Soviet Union are contending with each other, each seeking to maintain its own nuclear superiority by restricting the other, while at the same time both are colluding with each other ... to maintain their nuclear monopoly."[1] When and under what conditions China will participate in the future U.S.-USSR disarmament negotiations is still a question that remains to be answered (see Document 66).

Will China, with one-quarter of the human race, live in a world based on international law and world-order? Chinese Communists, contrary to popular misconceptions, do recognize the usefulness of law and order in theory as well as in practice. This has been demonstrated in several ways in China's conduct of foreign relations in the last twenty-two years and in its policy pronouncements, such as by condemnation of the actions of another state as "violations of international law," by justifying China's own position in terms of international law, and finally, by teaching international law courses in Chinese specialized colleges.[2]

However, Chinese legal scholars do differ considerably with respect to the proper role of international law and its future development from Western writers of law. For instance, some Chinese scholars accept Russian Menzhinsky's view that there does not exist a unified international law but instead there are two separate systems, "the bourgeois and socialist international laws."[3] And there are still other law specialists in China who believe that modern international law is comprised of three different sets of norms and institutions: the first based upon norms and institutions of the capitalist system, the second established by the "socioeconomic" pattern of the new "Socialism," and the third, norms enacted commonly among all countries.[4]

---

1 *Peking Review* (November 14, 1969).

2 See Hungdah Chiu, "Communist China's Attitude Toward International Law," *American Journal of International Law*, Vol. 60, No. 2 (April, 1966), pp. 245-67.

3 *Chinese Law and Government*, Vol. II, No. 1 (Spring, 1969), p. 39.

4 *Ibid.*

In view of the number of treaties and agreements signed with foreign countries—a total of 2,292 from 1949 to 1967[1] —we can be reasonably sure that while there are different interpretations of international law by Chinese scholars, the People's Republic of China has certainly not rejected it.

As to Chinese attitudes with respect to world order, in the sense that world order means the United Nations system China certainly welcomes it (see Document 66). In fact, Mao Tse-tung wrote on the eve of the United Nations San Francisco Conference in 1945 that "in regard to the establishment of an institution to preserve international peace and security, the Chinese Communist Party completely approves of the proposals made at the Dumbarton Oaks Conference.... The Chinese Communist Party has already sent its own representative to join the Chinese delegation at the San Francisco Conference in order to express the will of the Chinese people."[2]

However, after Chinese intervention in Korea in 1950 and United Nations refusal to admit China into the organization for twenty-one years (1950-71), China had become rather bitter and once demanded a "thorough reorganization of the United Nations," as well as the setting up of a new "revolutionary U.N."[3] However, the People's Republic has never once repudiated the Charter of the United Nations.[4]

In the United Nations, China hopes to lead the Third World, continuing to oppose the "imperialistic" policies of the USSR as "international dictatorship" and of the United States as "big-nation hegemony" (see Documents 60-66).

Finally, are the Chinese concerned with the ecological problems such as overpopulation, pollution, industrial wastes, etc., which now threaten the very survival of the earth planet?

Chinese leadership has been extremely conscious of the historical argument of Karl Marx against Thomas Malthus, who first introduced the concept of population explosion. In industrial Europe Marx had attacked Malthus and claimed

---

[1] See Douglas M. Johnston and Hungdah Chiu, *Agreements of the People's Republic of China, 1949-1967: A Calendar* (Cambridge, Mass., Harvard University Press, 1968), p. 222.

[2] *Selected Works of Mao Tse-tung, op.cit.*, III, p. 255.

[3] *Peking Review* (January 29, 1965), pp. 5-6.

[4] See Winberg Chai, "China and the United Nations: Problems of Representation and Alternatives," *Asian Survey*, Vol. X, No. 5 (May, 1970).

victory; but in the urban cities and communes of China, it was Malthus who challenged Marx.

In spring, 1953, the People's Republic began one of the greatest statistical projects in Chinese history—for the first time the population of the world's largest country was to be counted by modern census methods. The total was announced on June 30, 1953: 582,603,417.

The completion of the vital statistics coincided with the opening of a great public debate on population policy resulting in the Ministry of Health's program to "help the masses practice birth control."[1] But the major efforts were directed toward food production because of ideological considerations.

In 1957, the second official population statistics showed an increase to 646,530,000. Party leadership began to relate population growth to China's economic situation. Mao's famous speech "On Contradiction" in February, 1957, included a strongly worded statement that the Chinese people as a whole should begin to control their fertility.[2]

Meanwhile, a new policy was enacted of transferring Chinese population from areas of high density to areas of low density, especially because traditionally over ninety-five percent of China's population is concentrated on about forty percent of the land area from Aigun in Heilungkiang in the northeast to Tengchung in Yunnan in the southwest.[3] However, the expansion of Chinese settlement in less populated border regions—Tibet, Sinkiang, Inner Mongolia, and Manchuria—have caused considerable anxiety on the part of its neighbors.

After the total economic failures of the Great Leap Forward, China made an intensive renewed effort to begin a rather comprehensive nationwide (except minority areas) program of birth control in 1962, and many mobile teams were sent from cities to villages and communes. An English surgeon, Joshua S. Horn, spent the years from 1954 to 1969 in China and gave the following eyewitness account:

1 In fact, the ministry had on its own initiative already begun a small program of "planned parenthood" a year before, in 1952. See John S. Aird, "Population, Planning and Economic Development," *Population Bulletin*, Vol. XIX, No. 5 (August, 1963), pp. 114-35.

2 Quoted in John S. Aird, "Population, Planning and Economic Development,"*op. cit.*

3 See H. Yuan Tien, "The Demographic Significance of Organized Population Transfer in Communist China," *Demography* (November, 1964), pp. 220-26.

I attended an evening lecture on hygiene and birth control illustrated by an old style magic lantern using a pressurized paraffin lamp. The village hall was packed . . . .

After dealing with such mundane subjects as night-soil disposal, fly control and food protection, the speaker, a doctor from the mobile team, described the anatomy and physiology of the male and female organs of reproduction. An animated filmstrip showed the process . . . .

Then, he described various methods of contraception, discussed their advantages and disadvantages and passed round contraceptive appliances for inspection . . . .

He spoke of the advantage of planned parenthood . . . . He urged the women to discuss it among themselves and with their husbands . . . . When he had finished, the barrage of questions showed that the women were deeply interested in the new possibilities opening up for them.[1]

As far as other Chinese ecological problems in the 1950's and 1960's are concerned, they were quite different from those of the highly industrialized nations because of China's own underdeveloped agrarian-oriented economy. In order to increase the productivity of a land that has supported the Chinese civilization for more than three millennia, great efforts were made on afforestation, erosion control, and water conservation. In the twelve-year period since 1949, it is claimed that the Chinese people have built more than 1,000,000 small reservoirs and ponds, dug 9,000,000 wells, and developed new canals and storage basins which increased the irrigated area by 120,000,000 acres. And in 1958 alone a nationwide drive resulted in the afforestation of 69,000,000 acres.[2]

However, as China began to enter into industrialization in the late 1960's, many modern urban centers were built in haste and population there increased dramatically, aggravating the problems of industrial pollution (see Documents 64, 65).

1 Dr. Joshua S. Horn, *Away with all Pests* (New York, Monthly Review Press, 1969), p. 141.

2 Yi-Fu Tuan, *The World's Landscapes: China* (Chicago, Aldine Publishing Co., 1969), pp. 196-97.

56. GOVERNMENT STATEMENT: ON NUCLEAR TEST-BAN TREATY (July, 1963)*

As of 1971, China has been protesting the drafting and conclusion of all international treaties on nuclear and related matter on the grounds that these treaties and agreements are used by the two superpowers, the United States and the USSR, to maintain a nuclear monopoly and in particular to oppose China's own development of nuclear defense capabilities.

During the five years from 1964 to 1969, the Chinese had detonated ten nuclear devices: six were air-dropped, two were detonated on a tower, one was delivered by a missile, and one was detonated underground. And since her launching of an earth satellite on April 24, 1970, China has demonstrated the capability of delivering a payload at ICBM range. However, the current Chinese missile strategy seems to indicate that she is experimenting with the development of tactical nuclear weapons in order to deter both a U.S. and/or Soviet invasion and U.S. introduction of tactical nuclear weapons, should a conflict break out.[1]

A treaty on the partial halting of nuclear tests was initialled by the representatives of the United States, Britain and the Soviet Union in Moscow on July 25.

This is a treaty signed by three nuclear powers. By this treaty they attempt to consolidate their nuclear monopoly and bind the hands of all the peace loving countries subjected to the nuclear threat.

This treaty signed in Moscow is a big fraud to fool the people of the world. It runs diametrically counter to the wishes of the peace-loving people of the world.

The people of the world demand a genuine peace; this treaty provides them with a fake peace.

*From *People of the World Unite for the Complete, Thorough, Total and Resolute Prohibition and Destruction of Nuclear Weapons* (Peking, Foreign Language Press, 1963), pp. 1-6. The title is the editor's.

1 See Alice Langley Hsieh, "China's Nuclear Missile Program," *China Quarterly*, No. 45 (January/March, 1971), p.99.

The people of the world demand general disarmament and a complete ban on nuclear weapons; this treaty completely divorces the cessation of nuclear tests from the total prohibition of nuclear weapons, legalizes the continued manufacture, stockpiling and use of nuclear weapons by the three nuclear powers, and runs counter to disarmament.

The people of the world demand the complete cessation of nuclear tests; this treaty leaves out the prohibition of underground nuclear tests, an omission which is particularly advantageous for the further development of nuclear weapons by U.S. imperialism.

The people of the world demand the defence of world peace and the elimination of the threat of nuclear war; this treaty actually strengthens the position of nuclear powers for nuclear blackmail and increases the danger of imperialism launching a nuclear war and a world war.

If this big fraud is not exposed, it can do even greater harm. It is unthinkable for the Chinese Government to be a party to this dirty fraud. The Chinese Government regards it as its unshirkable and sacred duty to thoroughly expose this fraud.

The Chinese Government is firmly opposed to this treaty which harms the interests of the people of the whole world and the cause of world peace.

Clearly, this treaty has no restraining effect on the U.S. policies of nuclear war preparation and nuclear blackmail. It in no way hinders the United States from proliferating nuclear weapons, expanding nuclear armament or making nuclear threats. The central purpose of this treaty is, through a partial ban on nuclear tests, to prevent all the threatened peace-loving countries, including China, from increasing their defence capability, so that the United States may be more unbridled in threatening and blackmailing these countries.

U.S. President Kennedy, speaking on July 26, laid bare the substance of this treaty. Kennedy pointed out that this treaty did not mean an end to the threat of nuclear war, it did not prevent but permitted continued underground nuclear tests, it would not halt the production of nuclear weapons, it would not reduce nuclear stockpiles and it would not restrict their use in time of war. He further pointed out that this treaty would not hinder the United States from proliferating nuclear weapons among its allies and countries under its control under the name of "assistance," whereas the United States could use it to prevent non-nuclear peace-loving countries from testing and manufacturing nuclear weapons. At the same time, Kennedy formally declared that the United States remains ready to withdraw from the treaty and resume all forms of nuclear testing. This fully shows that U.S. imperialism gains everything and loses nothing by this treaty.

The treaty just signed is a reproduction of the draft treaty on a partial nuclear test ban put forward by the United States and Britain at the meeting of the Disarmament Committee in Geneva on August 27, 1962. On August 29, 1962, the Head of the Soviet Delegation Kuznetsov pointed out that the obvious aim of the United States and Britain in putting forward that draft was to provide the Western powers with one-sided military advantage to the detriment of the interests of the Soviet Union and other socialist countries. He pointed out that the United States had been using underground tests to improve its nuclear weapons for many years already, and that should underground nuclear tests be legalized with a simultaneous prohibition of such tests in the atmosphere, this would mean that the United States could continue improving its nuclear weapons and increase their yield and effectivity. The Head of the Soviet Government Khrushchov also pointed out on September 9, 1961, that "the program of developing new types of nuclear weapons which has been drawn up in the United States now requires precisely underground tests," and that an "agreement on the cessation of one kind of tests only—in the atmosphere— would be a disservice to the cause of peace. It would mean deceiving the peoples."

But now the Soviet Government has made a 180 degree about-face, discarded the correct stand they once persisted in and accepted this reproduction of the U.S.-British draft treaty, willingly allowing U.S. imperialism to gain military superiority. Thus the interests of the Soviet people have been sold out, the interests of the people of the countries in the socialist camp, including the people of China, have been sold out, and the interests of all the peace-loving people of the world have been sold out.

The indisputable facts prove that the policy pursued by the Soviet Government is one of allying with the forces of war to oppose the forces of peace, allying with imperialism to oppose socialism, allying with the United States to oppose China, and allying with the reactionaries of all countries to oppose the people of the world.

Why should the Soviet leaders so anxiously need such a treaty? Is this a proof of what they call victory for the policy of peaceful coexistence? No! This is by no means a victory for the policy of peaceful coexistence. It is capitulation to U.S. imperialism.

The U.S. imperialists and their partners are with one voice advertising everywhere that the signing of a treaty on the partial halting of nuclear tests by them is the first step towards the complete prohibition of nuclear weapons. This is deceitful talk. The United States has already stockpiled large quantities of nuclear weapons, which are scattered in various parts of the world and seriously threaten the security of all peoples. If the United States really will take the first step towards the prohibition of nuclear weapons, why does it not remove its nuclear threat to other countries? Why does it not undertake to refrain from using nuclear weapons against non-nuclear countries and to respect the desire of the people of the world to establish nuclear weapon-free zones? And why does it not undertake in all circumstances to refrain from handing over to its allies its nuclear weapons and the data for their manufacture? On what grounds can the United States and its partners maintain that the United States may use nucelar threat and blackmail against others and pursue policies of aggression and war, while others may not take measures to resist such threat and blackmail and defend their own independence and freedom? To give the aggressors the right to kill while denying the victims of aggression the right to self-defence—is this not like the Chinese saying: "The magistrate may burn down houses but the ordinary people cannot even light their lamps"?

The Chinese Government is firmly opposed to nuclear war and to a world war. It always stands for general disarmament and resolutely stands for the complete prohibition and thorough destruction of nuclear weapons. The Chinese Government and people have never spared their efforts in order to realize this aim step by step. As is known to the whole world, the Chinese Government long ago proposed, and has consistently stood for, the establishment of a zone free from nuclear weapons in the Asian and Pacific region, including the United States.

The Chinese Government holds that the prohibition of nuclear weapons and the prevention of nuclear war are major questions affecting the destiny of the world, which should be discussed and decided on jointly by all the countries of the world, big and small. Manipulation of the destiny of more than one hundred non-nuclear countries by a few nuclear powers will not be tolerated.

The Chinese Government holds that on such important issues as the prohibition of nuclear weapons and the prevention of nuclear war, it is impermissible to adopt the method of deluding the people of the world. It should be affirmed unequivocally that nuclear weapons must be completely banned and thoroughly destroyed and that practical and effective measures must be taken so as to realize step by step the complete prohibition and thorough destruction of nuclear weapons, prevent nuclear war and safeguard world peace.

For these reasons, the Government of the People's Republic of China hereby proposes the following:

(1) All countries in the world, both nuclear and non-nuclear, solemnly declare that they will prohibit and destroy nuclear weapons completely, thoroughly, totally and resolutely. Concretely speaking, they will not use nuclear weapons, nor export, nor import, nor manufacture, nor test, nor stockpile them; and they will destroy all the existing nuclear weapons and their means of delivery in the world, and disband all the existing establishments for the research, testing and manufacture of nuclear weapons in the world.

(2) In order to fulfill the above undertakings step by step, the following measures shall be adopted first:

a. Dismantle all military bases, including nuclear bases, on foreign soil, and withdraw from abroad all nuclear weapons and their means of delivery.

b. Establish a nuclear weapon-free zone of the Asian and Pacific region, including the United States, the Soviet Union, China and Japan; a nuclear weapon-free zone of Central Europe; a nuclear weapon-free zone of Africa; and a nuclear weapon-free zone of Latin America. The countries possessing nuclear weapons shall undertake due obligations with regard to each of the nuclear weapon-free zones.

c. Refrain from exporting and importing in any form nuclear weapons and technical data for their manufacture.

d. Cease all nuclear tests, including underground nuclear tests.

(3) A conference of the government heads of all the countries of the world shall be convened to discuss the question of the complete prohibition and thorough destruction of nuclear weapons and the questions of taking the above-mentioned four measures in order to realize step by step the complete prohibition and thorough destruction of nuclear weapons.

The Chinese Government and people are deeply convinced that nuclear weapons can be prohibited, nuclear war can be prevented and world peace can be preserved. We call upon the countries in the socialist camp and all the peace-loving countries and people of the world to unite and fight unswervingly to the end for the complete, thorough, total and resolute prohibition and destruction of nuclear weapons and for the defence of world peace.

57. *CHOU EN-LAI: PROPOSAL ON DESTRUCTION OF NUCLEAR WEAPONS (October, 1964)**

Chinese policy on disarmament is a matter of considerable controversy. China fears nuclear war coming as a direct preemptive assault either by the United States or the USSR against her nuclear installations. As a result of these fears, China has given top priority to scientific nuclear missile development since the 1960's, while at the same time making a number of proposals for the "complete prohibition and thorough destruction of nuclear weapons." A recent Chinese attempt to initiate action in the field of nuclear disarmament came at the beginning of November, 1970, in a joint statement with delegations of the Japanese Socialist Party.

The following proposal, rejected by the United States as propaganda, was made by Chou En-lai on October 17, 1964, to heads of government for the convocation of a summit conference of all countries to discuss nuclear disarmament.

*From *Break the Nuclear Monopoly. . . .* (Peking, Foreign Language Press, 1965), pp. 9-10. The title is the editor's.

Your Excellency:

On October 16, 1964, China exploded an atom bomb, thus successfully making its first nuclear test. On the same day, the Chinese Government issued a statement on this event, setting forth in detail China's position on the question of nuclear weapons.

The Chinese Government consistently stands for the complete prohibition and thorough destruction of nuclear weapons. China has been compelled to conduct nuclear testing and develop nuclear weapons. China's mastering of nuclear weapons is entirely for defence and for protecting the Chinese people from the U.S. nuclear threat.

The Chinese Government solemnly declares that at no time and in no circumstances will China be the first to use nuclear weapons.

The Chinese Government will continue to work for the complete prohibition and thorough destruction of nuclear weapons through international consultations and, for this purpose, has put forward in its statement the following proposal:

> That a summit conference of all the countries of the world be convened to discuss the question of the complete prohibition and thorough destruction of nuclear weapons, and that as the first step, the summit conference should reach an agreement to the effect that the nuclear powers and those countries which may soon become nuclear powers undertake not to use nuclear weapons, neither to use them against non-nuclear countries and nuclear-free zones, nor against each other.

It is the common aspiration of all peace-loving countries and people of the world to prevent a nuclear war and eliminate nuclear weapons. The Chinese Government sincerely hopes that its proposal will be given favourable consideration and positive response by your Government.

Please accept the assurances of my highest consideration.

CHOU EN-LAI
Premier of the State Council of
the People's Republic of China

58. LIN PIAO: LONG LIVE THE VICTORY OF PEOPLE'S WAR (September, 1965)*

Lin Piao (1907-), a native of Hupei, Minister of National Defense of Communist China, was at one time recognized as heir-designate to Mao Tse-tung. This essay has been widely publicized as "a comprehensive, systematic and profound analysis of Comrade Mao Tse-tung's theory and strategic concept of people's war and provides the revolutionary people of the whole world with a powerful ideological weapon in the fight against imperialism and modern revisionism."

Comrade Mao Tse-tung has said that our fundamental policy should rest on the foundation of our own strength. Only by relying on our own efforts can we in all circumstances remain invincible.

The peoples of the world invariably support each other in their struggles against imperialism and its lackeys. Those countries which have won victory are duty bound to support and aid the peoples who have not yet done so. Nevertheless, foreign aid can only play a supplementary role.

In order to make a revolution and to fight a people's war and be victorious, it is imperative to adhere to the policy of self-reliance, rely on the strength of the masses in one's own country and prepare to carry on the fight independently even when all material aid from outside is cut off. If one does not operate by one's own efforts, does not independently ponder and solve the problems of the revolution in one's own country and does not rely on the strength of the masses, but leans wholly on foreign aid—even though this be aid from socialist countries which persist in revolution—no victory can be won, or be consolidated even if it is won.

The International Significance of Comrade Mao Tse-tung's Theory of People's War

The Chinese revolution is a continuation of the great October Revolution. The road of the October Revolution is the common

---

*From *Long Live the Victory of People's War* (Peking, Foreign Language Press, 1965), pp. 40-52 (extract; footnotes omitted).

road for all people's revolutions. The Chinese revolution and the October Revolution have in common the following basic characteristics: (1) Both were led by the working class with a Marxist-Leninist party as its nucleus. (2) Both were based on the worker-peasant alliance. (3) In both cases state power was seized through violent revolution and the dictatorship of the proletariat was established. (4) In both cases the socialist system was built after victory in the revolution. (5) Both were component parts of the proletarian world revolution.

Naturally, the Chinese revolution had its own peculiar characteristics. The October Revolution took place in imperialist Russia, but the Chinese revolution broke out in a semi-colonial and semi-feudal country. The former was a proletarian socialist revolution, while the latter developed into a socialist revolution after the complete victory of the new democratic revolution. The October Revolution began with armed uprisings in the cities and then spread to the countryside, while the Chinese revolution won nation-wide victory through the encirclement of the cities from the rural areas and the final capture of the cities.

Comrade Mao Tse-tung's great merit lies in the fact that he has succeeded in integrating the universal truth of Marxism-Leninism with the concrete practice of the Chinese revolution and has enriched and developed Marxism-Leninism by his masterly generalization and summation of the experience gained during the Chinese people's protracted revolutionary struggle.

Comrade Mao Tse-tung's theory of people's war has been proved by the long practice of the Chinese revolution to be in accord with the objective laws of such wars and to be invincible. It has not only been valid for China, it is a great contribution to the revolutionary struggles of the oppressed nations and peoples throughout the world.

The people's war led by the Chinese Communist Party, comprising the War of Resistance and the Revolutionary Civil Wars, lasted for twenty-two years. It constitutes the most drawn-out and most complex people's war led by the proletariat in modern history, and it has been the richest in experience.

In the last analysis, the Marxist-Leninist theory of proletarian revolution is the theory of the seizure of state power by revolutionary violence, the theory of countering war against the people by people's war. As Marx so aptly put it, "Force is the midwife of every old society pregnant with a new one."

It was on the basis of the lessons derived from the people's wars in China that Comrade Mao Tse-tung, using the simplest and the most vivid language, advanced the famous thesis that "political power grows out of the barrel of a gun".

He clearly pointed out:

> The seizure of power by armed force, the settlement of the issue by war, is the central task and the highest form of revolution. This Marxist-Leninist principle of revolution holds good universally, for China and for all other countries.

War is the product of imperialism and the system of exploitation of man by man. Lenin said that "war is always and everywhere begun by the exploiters themselves, by the ruling and oppressing classes". So long as imperialism and the system of exploitation of man by man exist, the imperialists and reactionaries will invariably rely on armed force to maintain their reactionary rule and impose war on the oppressed nations and peoples. This is an objective law independent of man's will.

In the world today, all the imperialists headed by the United States and their lackeys, without exception, are strengthening their state machinery, and especially their armed forces. U.S. imperialism, in particular, is carrying out armed aggression and suppression everywhere.

What should the oppressed nations and the oppressed people do in the face of wars of aggression and armed suppression by the imperialists and their lackeys? Should they submit and remain slaves in perpetuity? Or should they rise in resistance and fight for their liberation?

Comrade Mao Tse-tung answered this question in vivid terms. He said that after long investigation and study the Chinese people discovered that all the imperialists and their lackeys "have swords in their hands and are out to kill. The people have come to understand this and so act after the same fashion". This is called doing unto them what they do unto us.

In the last analysis, whether one dares to wage a tit-for-tat struggle against armed aggression and suppression by the imperialists and their lackeys, whether one dares to fight a people's war against them, means whether one dares to embark on revolution. This is the most effective touchstone for distinguishing genuine revolutionaries and Marxist-Leninists from fake ones.

In view of the fact that some people were afflicted with the fear of the imperialists and reactionaries, Comrade Mao Tse-tung put forward his famous thesis that "imperialism and all reactionaries are paper tigers". He said,

> All reactionaries are paper tigers. In appearance, the reactionaries are terrifying, but in reality they are not so powerful. From a long-term point of view, it is not the reactionaries but the people who are really powerful.

The history of people's war in China and other countries provides conclusive evidence that the growth of the people's revolutionary forces from weak and small beginnings into strong and large forces is a universal law of development of class struggle, a universal law of development of people's war. A people's war inevitably meets with many difficulties, with ups and downs and setbacks in the course of its development, but no force can alter its general trend towards inevitable triumph.

Comrade Mao Tse-tung points out that we must despise the enemy strategically and take full account of him tactically.

To despise the enemy strategically is an elementary requirement for a revolutionary. Without the courage to despise the enemy and without daring to win, it will be simply impossible to make revolution and wage a people's war, let alone to achieve victory.

It is also very important for revolutionaries to take full account of the enemy tactically. It is likewise impossible to win victory in a people's war without taking full account of the enemy tactically, and without examining the concrete conditions, without being prudent and giving great attention to the study of the art of struggle, and without adopting appropriate forms of struggle in the concrete practice of the revolution in each country and with regard to each concrete problem of struggle.

Dialectical and historical materialism teaches us that what is important primarily is not that which at the given moment seems to be durable and yet is already beginning to die away, but that which is arising and developing, even though at the given moment it may not appear to be durable, for only that which is arising and developing is invincible.

Why can the apparently weak new-born forces always triumph over the decadent forces which appear so powerful?

The reason is that truth is on their side and that the masses are on their side, while the reactionary classes are always divorced from the masses and set themselves against the masses.

This has been borne out by the victory of the Chinese revolution, by the history of all revolutions, the whole history of class struggle and the entire history of mankind.

The imperialists are extremely afraid of Comrade Mao Tse-tung's thesis that "imperialism and all reactionaries are paper tigers", and the revisionists are extremely hostile to it. They all oppose and attack this thesis and the philistines follow suit by ridiculing it. But all this cannot in the least diminish its importance. The light of truth cannot be dimmed by anybody.

Comrade Mao Tse-tung's theory of people's war solves not only the problem of daring to fight a people's war, but also that of how to wage it.

Comrade Mao Tse-tung is a great statesman and military scientist, proficient at directing war in accordance with its laws. By the line and policies, the strategy and tactics he formulated for the people's war, he led the Chinese people in steering the ship of the people's war past all hidden reefs to the shores of victory in most complicated and difficult conditions.

It must be emphasized that Comrade Mao Tse-tung's theory of the establishment of rural revolutionary base areas and the encirclement of the cities from the countryside is of outstanding and universal practical importance for the present revolutionary struggles of all the oppressed nations and peoples, and particularly for the revolutionary struggles of the oppressed nations and peoples in Asia, Africa and Latin America against imperialism and its lackeys.

Many countries and peoples in Asia, Africa and Latin America are now being subjected to aggression and enslavement on a serious scale by the imperialists headed by the United States and their lackeys. The basic political and economic conditions in many of these countries have many similarities to those that prevailed in old China. As in China, the peasant question is extremely important in these regions. The peasants constitute the main force of the national-democratic revolution against the imperialists and their lackeys. In committing aggression against these countries, the imperialists usually begin by seizing the big cities and the main lines of communication, but they are unable to bring the vast countryside completely under their control. The countryside, and the countryside alone, can provide the broad areas in which the revolutionaries can manoeuvre freely. The countryside, and the countryside alone, can provide the revolutionary bases from which the revolutionaries can go forward to final victory. Precisely for this reason, Comrade Mao Tse-tung's theory of establishing revolutionary base areas in the rural districts and encircling the cities from the countryside is attracting more and more attention among the people in these regions.

Taking the entire globe, if North America and Western Europe can be called "the cities of the world", then Asia, Africa and Latin America constitute "the rural areas of the world". Since World War II, the proletarian revolutionary movement has for various reasons been temporarily held back in the North American and West European capitalist countries, while the people's revolutionary movement in Asia, Africa and Latin America has been growing vigorously. In a sense, the contemporary world revolution also presents a picture of the encirclement of cities by the rural areas. In the final analysis, the whole cause of world revolution hinges on the revolutionary struggles of the Asian, African and Latin American peoples who make up the overwhelming majority of the world's population. The socialist countries should regard it as their internationalist duty to support the people's revolutionary struggles in Asia, Africa and Latin America.

The October Revolution opened up a new era in the revolution of the oppressed nations. The victory of the October Revolution built a bridge between the socialist revolution of the proletariat of the West and the national-democratic revolution of the colonial and semi-colonial countries of the East. The Chinese revolution has successfully solved the problem of how to link up the national-democratic with the socialist revolution in the colonial and semi-colonial countries.

Comrade Mao Tse-tung has pointed out that, in the epoch since the October Revolution, anti-imperialist revolution in any colonial or semi-colonial country is no longer part of the old bourgeois, or capitalist world revolution, but is part of the new world revolution, the proletarian-socialist world revolution.

Comrade Mao Tse-tung has formulated a complete theory of the new-democratic revolution. He indicated that this revolution, which is different from all others, can only be, nay must be, a revolution against imperialism, feudalism and bureaucrat-capitalism waged by the broad masses of the people under the leadership of the proletariat.

This means that the revolution can only be, nay must be, led by the proletariat and the genuinely revolutionary party armed with Marxism-Leninism, and by no other class or party.

This means that the revolution embraces in its ranks not only the workers, peasants and the urban petty bourgeoisie, but also the national bourgeoisie and other patriotic and anti-imperialist democrats.

This means, finally, that the revolution is directed against imperialism, feudalism and bureaucrat-capitalism.

The new-democratic revolution leads to socialism, and not to capitalism.

Comrade Mao Tse-tung's theory of the new-democratic revolution is the Marxist-Leninist theory of revolution by stages as well as the Marxist-Leninist theory of uninterrupted revolution.

Comrade Mao Tse-tung made a correct distinction between the two revolutionary stages, *i.e.*, the national-democratic and the socialist revolutions; at the same time he correctly and closely linked the two. The national-democratic revolution is the necessary preparation for the socialist revolution, and the socialist revolution is the inevitable sequel to the national-democratic revolution. There is no Great Wall between the two revolutionary stages. But the socialist revolution is only possible after the completion of the national-democratic revolution. The more thorough the national-democratic revolution, the better the conditions for the socialist revolution.

The experience of the Chinese revolution shows that the tasks of the national-democratic revolution can be fulfilled only through long and tortuous struggles. In this stage of revolution, imperialism and its lackeys are the principal enemy. In the struggle against imperialism and its lackeys, it is necessary to rally all anti-imperialist patriotic forces, including the national bourgeoisie and all patriotic personages. All those patriotic personages from among the bourgeoisie and other exploiting classes who join the anti-imperialist struggle play a progressive historical role; they are not tolerated by imperialism but welcomed by the proletariat.

It is very harmful to confuse the two stages, that is, the

national-democratic and the socialist revolutions. Comrade Mao Tse-tung criticized the wrong idea of "accomplishing both at one stroke", and pointed out that this utopian idea could only weaken the struggle against imperialism and its lackeys, the most urgent task at that time. The Kuomintang reactionaries and the Trotskyites they hired during the War of Resistance deliberately confused these two stages of the Chinese revolution, proclaiming the "theory of a single revolution" and preaching so-called "socialism" without any Communist Party. With this preposterous theory they attempted to swallow up the Communist Party, wipe out any revolution and prevent the advance of the national-democratic revolution, and they used it as a pretext for their non-resistance and capitulation to imperialism. This reactionary theory was buried long ago by the history of the Chinese revolution.

The Khrushchov revisionists are now actively preaching that socialism can be built without the proletariat and without a genuinely revolutionary party armed with the advanced proletarian ideology, and they have cast the fundamental tenets of Marxism-Leninism to the four winds. The revisionists' purpose is solely to divert the oppressed nations from their struggle against imperialism and sabotage their national-democratic revolution, all in the service of imperialism.

The Chinese revolution provides a successful lesson for making a thoroughgoing national-democratic revolution under the leadership of the proletariat; it likewise provides a successful lesson for the timely transition from the national-democratic revolution to the socialist revolution under the leadership of the proletariat.

Mao Tse-tung's thought has been the guide to the victory of the Chinese revolution. It has integrated the universal truth of Marxism-Leninism with the concrete practice of the Chinese revolution and creatively developed Marxism-Leninism, thus adding new weapons to the arsenal of Marxism-Leninism.

Ours is the epoch in which world capitalism and imperialism are heading for their doom and socialism and communism are marching to victory. Comrade Mao Tse-tung's theory of people's war is not only a product of the Chinese revolution, but has also the characteristics of our epoch. The new experience gained in the people's revolutionary struggles in various countries since World War II has provided continuous evidence that Mao Tse-tung's thought is a common asset of the revolutionary people of the whole world. This is the great international significance of the thought of Mao Tse-tung.

59. PARTY REPORT: ON RELATIONS WITH FOREIGN COUNTRIES (April, 1969)*

This is part of the official report, made by Lin Piao on April 1, 1969, at the party's post-Cultural Revolution Ninth Congress which was adopted by the Chinese Communist Party as the "program of action" for the 1970's.

Now we shall go on specifically to discuss China's relations with foreign countries.

The revolutionary struggles of the proletariat and the oppressed people and nations of the world always support each other. The Albanian Party of Labour and all other genuine fraternal Marxist-Leninist Parties and organizations, the broad masses of the proletariat and revolutionary people throughout the world as well as many friendly countries, organizations and personages have all warmly acclaimed and supported the Great Proletarian Cultural Revolution of our country. On behalf of the great leader Chairman Mao and the Ninth National Congress of the Party, I hereby express our heartfelt thanks to them. We firmly pledge that we the Communist Party of China and the Chinese people are determined to fulfil our proletarian internationalist duty and, together with them, carry through to the end the great struggle against imperialism, modern revisionism and all reaction.

The general trend of the world today is still as Chairman Mao described it: "The enemy rots with every passing day, while for us things are getting better daily." On the one hand, the revolutionary movement of the proletariat of the world and of the people of various countries is vigorously surging forward. The armed struggles of the people of southern Vietnam, Laos, Thailand, Burma, Malaya, Indonesia, India, Palestine and other countries and regions in Asia, Africa and Latin America are steadily growing in strength. The truth that "Political power grows out of the barrel of a gun" is being grasped by ever

*From *Peking Review*, special issue (April 28, 1969), pp. 25-30. Title is the subtitle of the original report.

broader masses of the oppressed people and nations. An unprecedentedly gigantic revolutionary mass movement has broken out in Japan, Western Europe and North America, the "heartlands" of capitalism. More and more people are awakening. The genuine fraternal Marxist-Leninist Parties and organizations are growing steadily in the course of integrating Marxism-Leninism with the concrete practice of revolution in their own countries. On the other hand, U.S. imperialism and Soviet revisionist social-imperialism are bogged down in political and economic crises, beset with difficulties both at home and abroad and find themselves in an impasse. They collude and at the same time contend with each other in a vain attempt to re-divide the world. They act in co-ordination and work hand in glove in opposing China, opposing communism and opposing the people, in suppressing the national liberation movement and in launching wars of aggression. They scheme against each other and get locked in strife for raw materials, markets, dependencies, important strategic points and spheres of influence. They are both stepping up arms expansion and war preparations, each trying to realize its own ambitions.

Lenin pointed out: Imperialism means war. " . . . imperialist wars are absolutely inevitable under *such* an economic system, *as long as* private property in the means of production exists." (Lenin, *Collected Works*, Chinese ed., Vol. 22, p. 182.) Lenin further pointed out: "Imperialist war is the eve of socialist revolution." (Lenin, *Collected Works*, Chinese ed., Vol. 25, p. 349.) These scientific theses of Lenin's are by no means out of date.

Chairman Mao has recently pointed out, "With regard to the question of world war, there are but two possibilities: One is that the war will give rise to revolution and the other is that revolution will prevent war." This is because there are four major contradictions in the world today: The contradiction between the oppressed nations on the one hand and imperialism and social-imperialism on the other; the contradiction between the proletariat and the bourgeoisie in the capitalist and revisionist countries; the contradiction between imperialist and social-imperialist countries and among the imperialist countries; and the contradiction between socialist countries on the one hand and imperialism and social-imperialism on the other. The existence and development of these contradictions are bound to give rise to revolution. According to the historical experience of

World War I and World War II, it can be said with certainty that if the imperialists, revisionists and reactionaries should impose a third world war on the people of the world, it would only greatly accelerate the development of these contradictions and help arouse the people of the world to rise in revolution and send the whole pack of imperialists, revisionists and reactionaries to their graves.

Chairman Mao teaches us: "All reactionaries are paper tigers." "Strategically we should despise all our enemies, but tactically we should take them all seriously." This great truth enunciated by Chairman Mao heightens the revolutionary militancy of the people of the whole world and guides us from victory to victory in the struggle against imperialism, revisionism and all reaction.

The nature of U.S. imperialism as a paper tiger has long since been laid bare by the people throughout the world. U.S. imperialism, the most ferocious enemy of the people of the whole world, is going downhill more and more. Since he took office, Nixon has been confronted with a hopeless mess and an insoluble economic crisis, with the strong resistance of the masses of the people at home and throughout the world and with the predicament in which the imperialist countries are disintegrating and the baton of U.S. imperialism is getting less and less effective. Unable to produce any solution to these problems, Nixon, like his predecessors, cannot but continue to play the counter-revolutionary dual tactics, ostensibly assuming a "peace-loving" appearance while in fact engaging in arms expansion and war preparations on a still larger scale. The military expenditures of the United States have been increasing year by year. To date the U.S. imperialists still occupy our territory Taiwan. They have dispatched aggressor troops to many countries and have also set up hundreds upon hundreds of military bases and military installations in different parts of the world. They have made so many airplanes and guns, so many nuclear bombs and guided missiles. What is all this for? To frighten, suppress and slaughter the people and dominate the world. By doing so they make themselves the enemy of the people everywhere and find themselves besieged and battered by the broad masses of the proletariat and the people all over the world, and this will definitely lead to revolutions throughout the world on a still larger scale.

The Soviet revisionist renegade clique is a paper tiger, too. It has revealed its social-imperialist features more and more clearly. When Khrushchov revisionism was just beginning to emerge, our great leader Chairman Mao foresaw what serious harm modern revisionism would do to the cause of world revolution. Chairman Mao led the whole Party in waging resolute struggles in the ideological, theoretical and political spheres, together with the Albanian Party of Labour headed by the great Marxist-Leninist Comrade Enver Hoxha and with the genuine Marxist-Leninists of the world, against modern revisionism with Soviet revisionism as its centre. This has enabled the people all over the world to learn gradually in struggle how to distinguish genuine Marxism-Leninism from sham Marxism-Leninism and genuine socialism from sham socialism and brought about the bankruptcy of Khrushchov revisionism. At the same time, Chairman Mao led our Party in resolutely criticizing Liu Shao-chi's revisionist line of capitulation to imperialism, revisionism and reaction and of suppression of revolutionary movements in various countries and in destroying Liu Shao-chi's counter-revolutionary revisionist clique. All this has been done in the fulfilment of our Party's proletarian internationalist duty.

Since Brezhnev came to power, with its baton becoming less and less effective and its difficulties at home and abroad growing more and more serious, the Soviet revisionist renegade clique has been practising social-imperialism and social-fascism more frantically than ever. Internally, it has intensified its suppression of the Soviet people and speeded up the all-round restoration of capitalism. Externally, it has stepped up its collusion with U.S. imperialism and its suppression of the revolutionary struggles of the people of various countries, intensified its control over and its exploitation of various East European countries and the People's Republic of Mongolia, intensified its contention with U.S. imperialism over the Middle East and other regions and intensified its threat of aggression against China. Its dispatch of hundreds of thousands of troops to occupy Czechoslovakia and its armed provocations against China on our territory Chenpao Island are two foul performances staged recently by Soviet revisionism. In order to justify its aggression and plunder, the Soviet revisionist renegade clique trumpets the so-called theory of "limited sovereignty", the theory of "international dictatorship" and the theory of "socialist community". What does all this stuff mean? It means that your sovereignty is "limited", while his is unlimited. You won't obey him? He will exercise "international dictatorship" over you—dictatorship over the people of other countries, in order to form the "socialist community" ruled by the new tsars, that is, colonies of social-imperialism, just like the "New Order of Europe" of Hitler, the "Greater East Asia Co-prosperity Sphere" of Japanese militarism and the "Free World Community" of the United States. Lenin denounced the renegades of the Second International: "Socialism in words, imperialism in deeds, *the growth of opportunism into imperialism.*" (Lenin, *Collected Works,* Chinese ed., Vol. 29, p. 458.) This applies perfectly to the Soviet revisionist renegade clique of today which is composed of a handful of capitalist-roaders in power. We firmly believe that the proletariat and the broad masses of the people in the Soviet Union with their glorious revolutionary tradition will surely rise and overthrow this clique consisting of a handful of renegades. As Chairman Mao points out:

> The Soviet Union was the first socialist state and the Communist Party of the Soviet Union was created by Lenin. Although the leadership of the Soviet Party and state has now been usurped by revisionists, I would advise comrades to remain firm in the conviction that the masses of the Soviet people and of Party members and cadres are good, that they desire revolution and that revisionist rule will not last long.

Now that the Soviet government has created the incident of armed encroachment on the Chinese territory Chenpao Island, the Sino-Soviet boundary question has caught the attention of the whole world. Like boundary questions between China and some of her other neighbouring countries, the Sino-Soviet boundary question is also one left over by history. As regards these questions, our Party and Government have consistently stood for negotiations through diplomatic channels to reach a fair and reasonable settlement. Pending a settlement, the status quo of the boundary should be maintained and conflicts avoided. Proceeding from this stand, China has satisfactorily and successively settled boundary questions with neighbouring countries such as Burma, Nepal, Pakistan, the People's Republic of Mongolia and Afghanistan. Only the boundary questions between the Soviet Union and China and between India and China remain unsettled to this day.

The Chinese Government held repeated negotiations with the Indian government on the Sino-Indian boundary question. As the reactionary Indian government had taken over the British imperialist policy of aggression, it insisted that we recognize the illegal "MacMahon line" which even the reactionary governments of different periods in old China had not recognized, and moreover, it went a step further and vainly attempted to occupy the Aksai Chin area, which has always been under Chinese jurisdiction, thereby disrupting the Sino-Indian boundary negotiations. This is known to all.

The Sino-Soviet boundary question is the product of tsarist Russian imperialist aggression against China. In the latter half of the 19th century when power was not in the hands of the Chinese and Russian people, the tsarist government took imperialist acts of aggression to carve up China, imposed a series of unequal treaties on her, annexed vast expanses of her territory and, moreover, crossed the boundary line stipulated by the unequal treaties, in many places, and occupied still more Chinese territory. This gangster behaviour was indignantly condemned by Marx, Engels and Lenin. On September 27, 1920, the Government of Soviets led by the great Lenin solemnly proclaimed: It "declares null and void all the treaties concluded with China by the former Governments of Russia, renounces all seizure of Chinese territory and all Russian concessions in China and restores to China, without any compensation and for ever, all that had been predatorily seized from her by the Tsar's Government and the Russian bourgeoisie." (See *Declaration of the Government of the Russian Socialist Federated Soviet Republic to the Chinese Government.*) Owing to the historical conditions of the time, this proletarian policy of Lenin's was not realized.

As early as August 22 and September 21, 1960, the Chinese Government, proceeding from its consistent stand on boundary questions, twice took the initiative in proposing to the Soviet government that negotiations be held to settle the Sino-Soviet boundary question. In 1964, negotiations between the two sides started in Peking. The treaties relating to the present Sino-Soviet boundary are unequal treaties imposed on the Chinese people by the tsars, but out of the desire to safeguard the revolutionary friendship between the Chinese and Soviet people, we still maintained that these treaties be taken as the basis for the settlement of the boundary question. However, betraying Lenin's proletarian policy and clinging to its new-tsarist social-imperialist stand, the Soviet revisionist renegade clique refused to recognize these treaties as unequal and, moreover, it insisted that China recognize as belonging to the Soviet Union all the Chinese territory which they had occupied or attempted to occupy in violation of the treaties. This great-power chauvinist and social-imperialist stand of the Soviet government led to the disruption of the negotiations.

Since Brezhnev came to power, the Soviet revisionist rene-gade clique has frenziedly stepped up its disruption of the status quo of the boundary and repeatedly provoked border incidents, shooting and killing our unarmed fishermen and peasants and encroaching upon China's sovereignty. Recently it has gone further and made successive armed intrusions into our territory Chenpao Island. Driven beyond the limits of their forbearance, our frontier guards have fought back in self-defence, dealing the aggressors well-deserved blows and triumphantly safeguarding our sacred territory. In an effort to extricate them from their predicament, Kosygin asked on March 21 to communicate with our leaders by telephone. Immediately on March 22, our Government replied with a memorandum, in which it was made clear that, "In view of the present relations between China and the Soviet Union, it is unsuitable to communicate by telephone. If the Soviet government has anything to say, it is asked to put it forward officially to the Chinese Government through diplomatic channels." On March 29, the Soviet government issued a statement still clinging to its obstinate aggressor stand, while expressing willingness to resume "consultations". Our Government is considering its reply to this.

The foreign policy of our Party and Government is con-sistent. It is: To develop relations of friendship, mutual assistance and co-operation with socialist countries on the principle of proletarian internationalism; to support and assist the revolutionary struggles of all the oppressed people and nations; to strive for peaceful coexistence with countries having different social systems on the basis of the Five Principles of mutual respect for territorial integrity and sovereignty, mutual non-aggression, non-interference in each other's internal affairs, equality and mutual benefit, and peaceful coexistence, and to oppose the imperialist policies of aggression and war. Our proletarian foreign policy is not based on expediency; it is a policy in which we have long persisted. This is what we did in the past and we will persist in doing the same in the future.

We have always held that the internal affairs of each country should be settled by its own people. The relations between all countries and between all parties, big or small, must be built on the principles of equality and non-interference in each other's internal affairs. To safeguard these Marxist-Leninist principles, the Communist Party of China has waged a long struggle against the sinister great-power chauvinism of the Soviet revisionist renegade clique. This is a fact known to all. The Soviet revisionist renegade clique glibly talks of "fraternal parties" and "fraternal countries", but in fact it regards itself as the patriarchal party, and as the new tsar, who is free to invade and occupy the territory of other countries. They conduct sabotage and subversion against the Chinese Communist Party, the Albanian Party of Labour and other genuine Marxist-Leninist Parties. Moreover, when any part or any country in their so-called "socialist community" holds a slightly different view, they act ferociously and stop at nothing in suppressing, sabotaging and subverting and even sending troops to invade and occupy their so-called "fraternal countries" and kidnapping members of their so-called "fraternal parties". These fascist piratical acts have sealed their doom.

U.S. imperialism and Soviet revisionism are always trying to "isolate" China; this is China's honour. Their rabid opposition to China cannot do us the slightest harm. On the contrary, it serves to further arouse our people's determination to maintain independence and keep initiative in our own hands, rely on our own efforts and work hard to make our country prosperous and powerful; it serves to prove to the whole world that China has drawn a clear line between herself on the one hand and U.S. imperialism and Soviet revisionism on the other. Today, it is not imperialism, revisionism and reaction but the proletariat and the revolutionary people of all countries that determine the destiny of the world. The genuine Marxist-Leninist Parties and organizations of various countries, which are composed of the advanced elements of the proletariat, are a new rising force that has infinitely broad prospects. The Communist Party of China is determined to unite and fight together with them. We firmly support the Albanian people in their struggle against imperialism and revisionism; we firmly support the Vietnamese people in carrying their war of resistance against U.S. aggression and for national salvation through to the end; we firmly support the revolutionary struggles of the people of Laos, Thailand, Burma, Malaya, Indonesia, India, Palestine and other countries and regions in Asia, Africa and Latin America; we firmly support the proletariat, the students and youth and the masses of the Black people of the United States in their just struggle against the U.S. ruling clique; we firmly support the proletariat and the labouring people of the Soviet Union in their just struggle to overthrow the Soviet revisionist renegade clique; we firmly support the people of Czechoslovakia and other countries in their just struggle against Soviet revisionist social-imperialism; we firmly support the revolutionary struggles of the people of Japan and the West European and Oceanian countries; we firmly support the revolutionary struggles of the people of all countries; and we firmly support all the just struggles of resistance against aggression and oppression by U.S. imperialism and Soviet revisionism. All countries and people subjected to aggression, control, intervention or bullying by U.S. imperialism and Soviet revisionism, unite and form the broadest possible united front and overthrow our common enemies!

On no account must we relax our revolutionary vigilance because of victory or ignore the danger of U.S. imperialism and Soviet revisionism launching a large-scale war of aggression. We must make full preparations, preparations against their launching a big war and against their launching a war at an early date, preparations against their launching a conventional war and against their launching a large-scale nuclear war. **In short, we must be prepared.** Chairman Mao said long ago: **We will not attack unless we are attacked; if we are attacked, we will certainly counter-attack.** If they insist on fighting, we will keep them company and fight to the finish. The Chinese revolution won out on the battlefield. Armed with Mao Tsetung Thought, tempered in the Great Proletarian Cultural Revolution, and with full confidence in victory, the Chinese people in their hundreds of millions, and the Chinese People's Liberation Army are determined to liberate their sacred territory Taiwan and resolutely, thoroughly, wholly and completely wipe out all aggressors who dare to come!

Our great leader Chairman Mao points out:

> Working hand in glove, Soviet revisionism and U.S. imperialism
> have done so many foul and evil things that the revolutionary
> people the world over will not let them go unpunished. The
> people of all countries are rising. A new historical period of
> opposing U.S. imperialism and Soviet revisionism has begun.

Whether the war gives rise to revolution or revolution
prevents the war, U.S. imperialism and Soviet revisionism will
not last long! Workers of all countries, unite! Proletarians and
oppressed people and nations of the world, unite! Bury U.S.
imperialism, Soviet revisionism and their lackeys!

60. KUNG CHUNG-PING: THE THEORY OF "INTER-NATIONAL DICTATORSHIP" IS A GANGSTER THEORY OF SOCIAL-IMPERIALISM (May, 1969)*

*As China enters the 1970's, many of her foreign
policy goals have substantially altered or changed as a
result of new domestic and international environ-
ments. The 1969 border wars with the Russians have
once and for all shattered any attempt to paper over
the cracks and bring the two former allies together
again, as illustrated in the following policy announcement by an official of the Chinese Communist Party.*

In his report to the Ninth National Congress of the
Communist Party of China, Vice-Chairman Lin Piao sharply
exposed the social-imperialist nature of the Soviet revisionist
renegade clique's theory of "international dictatorship."

A thief breaks into someone's home and says he did so to
"protect" that family's "security"—such is the gangster logic
the imperialist and fascists always advocate. U.S. imperialism
always falls back on this gangster "theory" when it is launching
its wars of aggression. The theory of "international dictatorship" that the Soviet revisionist renegade clique has spared no
efforts to publicize is simply a new variation of this same
gangster logic.

*From *Hongqi*, No. 5, 1969; translated in *Peking Review* (May 16,
1969), pp. 4-5.

In his speech at the "5th congress" of the Polish revisionist party on November 12 last year, Soviet revisionist chieftain Brezhnev clamoured that when what Soviet revisionism called "the security of the community" (that is, Soviet revisionist colonialist interests in some East European countries and the People's Republic of Mongolia) is threatened, "this becomes no longer a problem of the people of that country alone" and Soviet revisionism has the right to take military action against this member of the "community." Another Soviet revisionist renegade clique chieftain blatantly said that "historical development" had set the task of turning "national dictatorship" into "international dictatorship." The Soviet revisionist press time and again gave great publicity to the idea that at present, to "protect" the "community" "acquires a more profound international character" and that the members of the "community" must be "protected by the joint efforts" of the "community," etc.

By putting out this theory of "international dictatorship," the Soviet revisionists intend first of all to justify their barefaced social-imperialist aggression and, second, to fabricate a "theoretical" basis for their rapacious expansionist ambitions. We must expose this theory for what it is and lay bare the diabolical features of Soviet revisionist social-imperialism in the broad light of day.

The Soviet revisionist renegade clique glibly talks about "national dictatorship" and "international dictatorship." Let the question be asked: Which class exercises the "dictatorship" you speak of, and which class is subjected to this "dictatorship"?

Our great teacher Chairman Mao has pointed out: "To protect the masses or to repress them—here is the basic distinction between the Communist Party and the Kuomintang, between the proletariat and the bourgeoisie, and between the dictatorship of the proletariat and the dictatorship of the bourgeoisie." The Soviet revisionist renegade clique has established fascist reactionary rule at home, laid down all kinds of counter-revolutionary "laws" and "regulations," deprived the working people of their democratic rights and carried out bloody repression, thus throwing the Soviet working people into the abyss of misery again. This fully confirms that the "dictatorship" exercised by the Soviet revisionist renegade clique at home is an out-and-out bourgeois dictatorship.

Foreign policy is the continuation of domestic policy. By turning "national dictatorship" into "international dictatorship," the Soviet revisionists are out to extend their domestic counter-revolutionary bourgeois dictatorship abroad and, by plunder and aggression, exercise a counter-revolutionary dictatorship over the people of other countries. The Soviet revisionist renegade clique has made use of the "Council for Mutual Economic Assistance" to push its social-imperialist policies in some East European countries and in the People's Republic of Mongolia, ruthlessly exploit and plunder the people of these countries and trample on their sovereignty at will, thus turning them into its dependencies and colonies.

The "specialization of production" and "international division of labour" brayed about and put into operation by the Soviet revisionists have brought about a lopsided development of the economies of those East European countries and turned them into workshops of the Soviet revisionists for processing raw materials and dumping grounds for their goods. Moreover, by "granting credits," Soviet revisionism has savagely plundered these countries and grabbed fabulous profits from them. Such plunder and squeezing have incurred growing resistance from the broad masses in these countries. Soviet revisionism has dispatched hundreds of thousands of troops to hold down the people of these countries, and even carried out, in the case of Czechoslovakia, armed aggression and military occupation. Plunder, aggression, suppression of the people of other countries, and even military occupation—this is the reactionary essence of the Soviet revisionists' so-called theory of "international dictatorship."

Today, under the pretext of "safeguarding the socialist gains," the Soviet revisionist renegade clique sends its troops marching into Czechoslovakia and imposes "international dictatorship" over the people of that country. Tomorrow, under the pretext of "safeguarding" something else, it can send aggressor troops marching into another of its "fraternal countries" in the "socialist community" or into countries outside this so-called "community" to violate their territorial integrity and sovereignty. In fabricating the theory of "international dictatorship," a theory for fascist aggression, the Soviet revisionist renegade clique has a completely vile purpose in mind.

Our great leader Chairman Mao has pointed out: "The

governments of the imperialist countries, though they engaged in counter-revolutionary activities every day, had never told the truth in their statements or official documents but had filled or at least flavoured them with professions of humanity, justice and virtue." The Soviet revisionist social-imperialists are no exception. To deceive people, the Soviet revisionist renegade clique decked out the completely fascist theory of "international dictatorship" in the cloak of "internationalism." But their counter-revolutionary activities nail them down as having completely betrayed proletarian internationalism. Behind the slogan of the theory of "international dictatorship" is concealed the ugly, vicious counter-revolutionary aggressor's face.

The theory of "international dictatorship" preached by Soviet revisionism is aimed at realizing its ambitions to redivide the world in collusion with U.S. imperialism, and to meet its needs in collaborating and contending with U.S. imperialism. This "theory," on the one hand, serves U.S. imperialist aggression and legalizes its military occupation; on the other hand, it can be used to contend with U.S. imperialism for spheres of influence and designate at will any country as being within Soviet revisionism's own sphere of "international dictatorship." U.S. imperialism supports Soviet revisionism in instituting "international dictatorship" within its own sphere of influence; and in like manner, Soviet revisionism supports U.S. imperialist aggression against other countries under the shameless lie of "defending the free world." This is the filthy bargain these two have struck.

There isn't the slightest difference between this theory of "international dictatorship" and the fascist excuses for aggression. The German fascist gangsters once ran up the rag of the "New Order of Europe" and carried out wanton aggression against other countries. In invading China and Southeast Asian countries, the Japanese pirates clamoured about setting up a "Greater East Asia Co-Prosperity Sphere." After World War II, U.S. imperialism advocated an "international government." Aren't all these precisely the same as the Soviet revisionist theory of "international dictatorship"? The Soviet revisionist social-imperialists and all the imperialists and fascists are jackals from the same lair, and their "theories" are cut from the same cloth.

The renegade, hidden traitor and scab Liu Shao-chi is a running dog of U.S. imperialism, Soviet revisionism and all reaction. He frantically pushed a counter-revolutionary revisionist line, vainly trying to restore capitalism in China and realize the rabid ambitions of U.S. imperialism and Soviet revisionism to subvert socialist China. The Great Proletarian Cultural Revolution has overthrown Liu Shao-chi and company and smashed their conspiracies. Like a cornered beast, the Soviet revisionist renegade clique recently resorted to armed provocations against China and carried out armed invasion of Chinese territory Chenpao Island, and it was duly punished for this. The Soviet revisionist renegade clique has committed crimes against the Chinese people as well as against the Soviet people. The people of China and the Soviet Union share a profound revolutionary friendship. We are convinced that the proletariat and other working people of the Soviet Union will surely rise to overthrow the bourgeois fascist rule of the clique of a handful of Soviet revisionist renegades and cut off its vicious aggressive claws. As our great leader Chairman Mao has pointed out, "The Soviet Union was the first socialist state and the Communist Party of the Soviet Union was created by Lenin. Although the leadership of the Soviet Party and state has now been usurped by revisionists, I would advise comrades to remain firm in the conviction that the masses of the Soviet people and of Party members and cadres are good, that they desire revolution and that revisionist rule will not last long."

Chairman Mao teaches us: "We must be clear-headed, that is, we must not believe the 'nice words' of the imperialists nor be intimidated by their bluster." Armed with Mao Tsetung Thought, the workers at the Taching Oilfield profoundly understand this great teaching of Chairman Mao's. The Soviet revisionists, in co-ordination with the U.S. imperialists, imposed an economic and technical blockade on China in an attempt to strangle us on the question of petroleum. But we were not overwhelmed by this. Led by Chairman Mao and guided by invincible Mao Tsetung Thought, the workers at the Taching Oilfield have persisted in self-reliance and, by relying on their own efforts, built up a big oilfield that ranks with the best in the world. This has dealt the Soviet revisionist renegade clique a telling blow. From now on, no matter what tricks the U.S. imperialists, the Soviet revisionists and their lackeys play or what their pretexts are, if they dare to continue to invade our country we will resolutely, thoroughly, wholly and completely wipe out them. Holding high the banner of opposing imperialism and revisionism, we pledge to unite with the revolutionary people the world over to bury, once and for all, imperialism, revisionism and all reaction.

Away with all pests!

Our force is irresistible.

61. RADIO BROADCAST: ON THE UNITED NATIONS (November, 1970)*

> *For the twentieth time in twenty-one years, the People's Republic was denied admission to the United Nations primarily because of U.S. opposition, as well as U.S. support for the Nationalist government on Taiwan. However, at the twenty-fifth session of the General Assembly in 1970, Peking gained for the first time a simple majority, with 51 in favor, 49 against, and 25 abstentions. Although it was still not admitted at that time because of the requirements of a two-thirds majority, Peking's interpretation was that of "major victory."*

Peking, November 22 (Hsinhua)—The General Assembly of the United Nations concluded on November 20 the debate on the restoration to the People's Republic of China of its legitimate seat in the organization. Amid thunderous applause, the General Assembly approved with 51 votes for, 49 against and 25 abstentions the draft resolution of 18 countries including Albania and Algeria which demands the restoration to the People's Republic of China of its legitimate seat in the U.N. and the immediate ousting of the Chiang Kai-shek clique from the organization. This is a serious defeat for the policy of U.S. imperialism which, in its obstinate stand of hostility towards the Chinese people, has for the past 20 years manipulated the voting machine of the U.N. and installed in the U.N. the Chiang Kai-shek clique which has long been spurned by the Chinese people. It is an important victory for the Chinese people and the people of various countries upholding international justice. It proves that "a just cause enjoys abundant support while an unjust cause finds little support," and that the dyke of hostility towards China built by U.S. imperialism in the U.N. has begun to collapse.

*From *Background on China*, B. 71-37 (July 20, 1971).

According to reports by Western news agencies, the approval of the resolution of 18 countries including Albania "raised a storm of applause in the assembly" and "a great burst of applause broke out and continued for several minutes." After the voting, representatives of the countries standing for the restoration to China of its legitimate seat in the U.N. congratulated one another and made "a torrent of triumphant statements."

The countries voting for the 18-nation draft are: Afghanistan, Albania, Algeria, Austria, Britain, Bulgaria, Burma, Burundi, Byelorussia, Canada, Ceylon, Chile, Cuba, Czechoslovakia, Denmark, Equatorial Guinea, Ethiopia, Finland, France, Ghana, Guinea, Hungary, India, Iraq, Italy, Kenya, Libya, Mali, Mauritania, Mongolia, Morocco, Nepal, Nigeria, Norway, Pakistan, the People's Republic of the Congo, Poland, Romania, Somalia, Southern Yemen, the Sudan, Sweden, Syria, Tanzania, Uganda, Ukraine, the United Arab Republic, the U.S.S.R., Yemen, Yugoslavia and Zambia.

Mustering a handful of accomplices and lackeys such as the reactionary Sato government of Japan, U.S. imperialism had once again put forward the so-called "important question" draft resolution in an attempt to keep the Chiang clique from being ousted from the United Nations and the legitimate seat of the People's Republic of China in the organization from being restored even though the People's Republic of China might have the support of a majority of votes. This illegal draft was adopted at the General Assembly with 66 votes for, 52 against and 7 abstentions. Compared with last year, the votes for the draft dropped by 5, those against it increased by 4 and the abstentions increased by 3. Silence prevailed at the Assembly when the draft was passed. Even those who voted for the draft did not applaud. The different scenes and atmosphere that followed the voting of the two resolutions reflected the popular feelings at the General Assembly as well as the guilty conscience and the unprecedented isolation of U.S. imperialism and the handful of its accomplices and lackeys. During the debate in the past few days, the representatives of many countries of Asia, Africa, Latin America and other regions continued to denounce the U.S. imperialist policy of hostility towards and aggression against China. Cuban representative Ricardo Alarcon Quesada pointed out that the Chiang Kai-shek clique which is now prolonging its feeble existence in China's Taiwan Province is a "pure invention of imperialism" and the result of U.S. imperialist aggression. Referring to the U.S. policy of hostility towards China, Yugoslav representative Lazar Mojsov said that in international life, it is impermissible for one country "unilaterally to prevent another country, especially when it is a question of such a big country as the People's Republic of China, from taking its legitimate place in the United Nations. Such a practice is contrary to the spirit of the Charter and it jeopardizes the foundations of the United Nations."

Representatives of many countries also exposed and condemned the so-called "important question" resolution unscrupulously concocted by U.S. imperialism and its plot to create "two Chinas." Ceylonese representative H. Shirley Amerasinghe said that the so-called "important question" resolution submitted by the United States is an "abuse of the (U.N.) Charter" and "one of the greatest miracles of intellectual confusion in our time". He added that obviously the question of representation required only a simple majority. Representative Vernon J. Mwaanga of Zambia pointed out that such a U.S. practice "is not only undemocratic and unrealistic, but also extremely harmful to the sacred interests of the (U.N.) organization." French representative Jacques Kosciusko-Morizet said that the United States adopted "with regard to the People's Republic of China an attitude both legally ill-founded and politically unrealistic". He pointed out that the question of restoration to China of its seat "is not one of admission to a new state, and is therefore not provided for by the Charter." He added that China, "as a founding member of the United Nations and permanent member of the Security Council", "is the People's Republic of China". Representative Padma Bahadur Khatri of Nepal said, "there has been a growing realization now that no international problem could be meaningfully discussed ... without the participation of the People's Republic of China." He declared that Nepal categorically rejects any "two Chinas concept", adding that "such misleading techniques have often been adopted to deny ... the lawful rights of the People's Republic of China in the United Nations." Many representatives pointed out in their speeches that "there exists only one China, since Taiwan is a part of China" and that the "two Chinas" scheme is entirely "untenable".

Representatives of U.S. imperialism and a handful of its followers including the reactionary Sato government of Japan at the session put up a feeble defence for their draft resolution on "important question". U.S. representative Christopher Phillips, seeing that the U.S. imperialist plot to obstruct the restoration to China of its legitimate seat in the United Nations could hardly be continued, hypocritically stated that "the United States is as interested as any in this room to see the People's Republic of China play a constructive role among the family of nations." But Phillips emphasized that the United States firmly opposed the ousting of the Chiang Kai-shek clique from the United Nations. This shows that U.S. imperialism changed its tone for the sole purpose of misleading others so as to facilitate its intensified pursuance of the "two Chinas" or "one China, one Taiwan" plot. This is what the Chinese people can never permit.

Parroting the tune of his U.S. master, the delegate of the reactionary Sato government of Japan made an eight-minute speech at the session, stressing Japan's opposition to the ousting of the Chiang Kai-shek clique from the United Nations. Sato admitted in a television programme on November 18 that the question of China is "the most annoying problem" for him. According to a report of *Tokyo Shimbun*, Japan's foreign minister Aichi "could not sleep the whole night" during the last few days when the question of China's representation was debated in the U.N. General Assembly. The Japanese reactionaries who obstinately follow U.S. imperialism and take a hostile stand toward the Chinese people will definitely come to no good end.

Among the over 50 delegates who spoke at the U.N. General Assembly session during the debate on the restoration to China of its legitimate seat, the overwhelming majority stood for this, and only a handful of U.S. accomplices and lackeys parroted the tune of U.S. imperialism. To obstruct the passage of the draft resolution of the 18 countries, U.S. imperialism had worked intensely both inside and outside the Assembly before the draft was put to the vote. Reuter reported that "the United States, fighting a fiercest rear guard action, today tried desperately to keep Peking from gaining a majority of votes for admission to the United Nations". It added that "the lobbying of American diplomats in the U.N. was reinforced by the activities of American ambassadors in national capitals", and that to prevent such an outcome, the United States "had lobbied with unprecedented intensity". But all this had failed to save the U.S. imperialist scheme from defeat. A Western news agency reported from the United Nations: "The big loser today (November 20), in the view of many observers was the United States, which for 21 years engaged in an intensive diplomatic campaign, first of all to prevent the Assembly even from discussing Chinese representation and then, through the two-thirds majority tactic, from allowing a decision by a simple vote." A UPI report lamented that the outcome of the vote for the 18 countries draft was "despondent".

Our great leader Chairman Mao pointed out 14 years ago: "The present situation in which the United States controls a majority in the United Nations and dominates many parts of the world is a temporary one, which will eventually be changed." The outcome of the vote for the draft of the 18 countries including Albania and Algeria in the U.N. General Assembly has testified to the wise prediction of Chairman Mao. The baton of U.S. imperialism in the United Nations has become more and more ineffective, and it has become increasingly difficult for U.S. imperialism to continue to manipulate the U.N. voting machine. An increasing number of countries have risen against the crime of U.S. imperialism and its accomplice in playing power politics and practising hegemony in the United Nations. If U.S. imperialism and its accomplice continue their course of wilful action and conspiracy in the United Nations, they will either face an even more shameful defeat for themselves or bring failure to the United Nations, which will be made to embark on a beaten path similar to that of the League of Nations after the First World War.

62. CHINESE EDITORIAL: WELCOME THE ESTABLISHMENT OF DIPLOMATIC RELATIONS BETWEEN CHINA AND CANADA (October, 1970)*

The 1970's provide convincing evidence that China desires and is willing to establish or to improve diplomatic relations with all countries, regardless of their social systems, on the basis of the Five Principles of Peaceful Coexistence (except with the Nationalists on Taiwan), as illustrated in the following editorial.

*From *Jen-min Jih-pao* (October 15, 1970).

The Chinese Government and the Canadian Government have decided to recognize each other and establish diplomatic relations in accordance with the principles of mutual respect for sovereignty and territorial integrity, non-interference in each other's internal affairs and equality and mutual benefit. We welcome this major development in the relations between China and Canada.

There is a traditional friendship between the Chinese and Canadian people. During our War of Resistance Against Japan, the friend of the Chinese people Dr. Norman Bethune dedicated his life to the cause of the Chinese revolution. In recent years, intercourse between the two countries has developed. The decision of China and Canada now to formally establish diplomatic relations reflects the common aspirations of the two peoples and conforms to their interests.

Our great leader Chairman Mao has pointed out: "We firmly maintain that all nations should practise the well-known Five Principles of mutual respect for sovereignty and territorial integrity, non-aggression, non-interference in each other's internal affairs, equality and mutual benefit, and peaceful coexistence." Abiding precisely by these Five Principles, China has in the past 21 years established diplomatic relations with countries having different social systems. On the basis of these Five Principles, China has developed relations of friendship and co-operation with many countries. We do not encroach on the sovereignty and territory of other countries, and we never allow other countries to encroach on our sovereignty and territory. We do not interfere in the internal affairs of other countries, and we never allow other countries to interfere in our internal affairs. Practice has proved that among nations with different social systems, the Five Principles of Peaceful Coexistence are correct principles in handling relations between one country and another.

The Government of the People's Republic of China is the sole legal government representing the entire Chinese people. It is really the height of absurdity for the Chiang Kai-shek clique, long ago overthrown by the Chinese people and now coiling itself up in China's Taiwan Province under the protection of U.S. imperialism, to call itself a "government." Ever since the founding of New China, U.S. imperialism has never given up its policy of hostility towards the Chinese people. It has been obstinately clinging to Chiang Kai-shek, a political mummy, and has done its utmost to concoct the plot of "two Chinas." However, the international prestige of the People's Republic of China has become higher and higher, and its influence in international affairs greater and greater. The "two Chinas" fallacy has been spurned by public opinion in more and more countries. In these circumstances, U.S. imperialism was forced to make some superficial changes and dish up the new gimmick of "one China, one Taiwan." It tries vainly by this stratagem to slice off China's territory and attain its criminal purpose of forcibly occupying Taiwan permanently. The Chinese people absolutely will not permit this. The Chinese people are determined to liberate their sacred territory of Taiwan!

Canada is a big country on the continent of America. The White Book on foreign policy issued by the Canadian Government last June reflects its desire and will to pursue an independent policy. This shows that the attempt of one or two "superpowers" to control the internal and external policies of other countries has become more and more unfeasible.

The Chinese people welcome the establishment of diplomatic relations between China and Canada. We wish the continuous growth of friendship between the people of China and Canada and the daily development of relations between the two countries.

63. CHINESE EDITORIAL: DOWN WITH THE DOCTRINE OF BIG-NATION HEGEMONY (January, 1971)*

The following is one of the major changes with respect to Chinese foreign policy themes on Latin American countries in the 1970's.

The struggle of the Latin American countries and people against U.S. imperialist control and aggression and for the defence of their national interests and state sovereignty is surging ahead vigorously. Of late, the member states of the Andean Pact Organization took joint steps to restrict the operations of U.S. capital and defend their national economies; Panama valiantly stood up and confronted U.S. imperialism on the canal question; nine countries, including Chile and Peru, held a conference on defending their ocean rights, firmly opposing the superpowers' domination and division of the seas;

*From *Jen-min Jih-pao* (January 23, 1971).

and, since the beginning of this year, Ecuador has defied brute force and seized 11 U.S. piratical fishing boats which had intruded into her territorial waters. All this shows that the struggle of Latin American countries against the doctrine of big-nation hegemony has become an irresistible trend of history.

For many years U.S. imperialism has regarded Latin America as its "backyard," committing all sorts of evil and doing what it likes in that region. Without exception, almost every Latin American country has been or is being subjected to oppression, enslavement and devastation by this "good neighbour." Not only has U.S. imperialism avariciously plundered the wealth of these countries, it has also crudely interfered in their internal and external affairs. The contradictions between U.S. imperialism on the one hand and the workers, peasants and petty bourgeoisie in the Latin American countries on the other are irreconcilable. U.S. imperialism and the national bourgeoisie in these countries also have a clash of interest. The sharpening of these contradictions and conflicts is impelling more and more countries to rise to oppose in varying degrees the power politics of U.S. imperialism.

A common fate and common aspirations will certainly give rise to a new situation of unity in struggle. The Latin American countries are becoming more united; they are gradually establishing a united front against U.S. imperialism on different issues and in various forms. A striking case in point is their joint struggle in defence of their sovereign right over their territorial waters. The formation and development of the anti-U.S. united front has greatly stimulated their struggle against the doctrine of hegemony.

The powerful struggle of the Latin American countries and people has effected a breakthrough in the "inter-American system" used by U.S. imperialism for years to bind them hand and foot. U.S. imperialism has always employed the "Organization of American States" to dictate to Latin American countries and do as it pleases. Now, this organization is divided by a confrontation between U.S. imperialism on one side and the Latin American countries on the other. Ignoring U.S. imperialism, more than 20 of the latter held meetings on their own of the "Special Committee for Co-ordination of Latin America" at which they unanimously opposed U.S. plunder and control. This is unprecedented in Latin American history. What is more, Latin American countries have further strengthened their militant unity with Afro-Asian countries. From the Third Conference of Heads of State and Government of Non-Aligned Countries to the 25th Session of the United Nations General Assembly, the countries of the three continents, Asia, Africa and Latin America, have been uniting more closely in their struggle against the doctrine of big-nation hegemony. The fence U.S. imperialism built round its "backyard" is falling apart in whole sections.

The present situation shows that the Latin American countries and people are no longer victims which U.S. imperialism can oppress and enslave at will. These countries have gradually thrown aside the myths about U.S. imperialism in the course of their struggle. When they first touched this huge monster to test it, they found that there was nothing terrifying about it. Later, they dared to defy the orders of U.S. imperialism, dared to stand up to its pressure and dared to take the wind out of its sails. U.S. imperialism can no longer continue its power politics in Latin America! Its position as an overlord on that continent is caving in!

In the world today, more and more small and medium-sized countries are rising against the doctrine of big-nation hegemony. Nations, big or small, should be equals without distinction. But one or two superpowers consider themselves entitled to order other nations about, bully them and damage their interests. Who gave them this "right"? Why should big nations be superior to others? By their overbearing and tyrannical actions, they have made themselves the enemy of the people the world over. These are the harsh facts: Whoever wants to trample others underfoot, ride roughshod and lord it over them will meet with the concerted attack of the people of the whole world till his complete destruction.

Our great leader Chairman Mao has pointed out: "We firmly maintain that all nations should practise the well-known Five Principles of mutual respect for sovereignty and territorial integrity, non-aggression, non-interference in each other's internal affairs, equality and mutual benefit, and peaceful coexistence." Following Chairman Mao's teaching, the Chinese Government and people have faithfully abided by these principles in handling relations among nations. We never permit other nations to encroach upon our sovereignty and interfere in our internal affairs. We on our part will never encroach upon other nations' sovereignty or interfere in their internal affairs. This is our stand today; it will be the same in the future.

U.S. imperialism is now calling China a "potential super-power," implying that China may also squeeze into the ranks of the superpowers some day. Thank you, American lords, but China will never accept this kind of compliment! China will never seek the so-called big-power position. We will for ever stand side by side with all nations subjected to aggression, control, intervention or subversion by superpowers; we will for ever stand side by side with all oppressed people and oppressed nations. The Chinese people will fight together with the people of the whole world to resolutely smash the doctrine of big-nation hegemony!

64. NEWS COMMENTARY: MULTIPURPOSE USE ON INDUSTRIAL FRONT (February, 1971)*

For the first time since the founding of the People's Republic, China began to initiate a policy to combat pollution of the environment, as demonstrated in the following news commentary, published in February, 1971.

Studying and applying Chairman Mao's brilliant philosophical thinking in a living way and breaking with metaphysics, staff members and workers on China's industrial front are going all out for multi-purpose use, thus opening up broad prospects for developing industry with greater, faster, better and more economical results.

Turning "Waste" Into Something Valuable

Chairman Mao has taught us: "In given conditions, each of the two opposing aspects of a contradiction invariably transforms itself into its opposite as a result of the struggle between them. Here, the conditions are essential. Without the given conditions, neither of the two contradictory aspects can transform itself into its opposite." According to this teaching, what is "waste" and what is valuable are the unity of opposites in a thing. In given conditions, "waste" can be transformed into

*From *Peking Review* (February 5, 1971), pp. 8-10.

what is valuable and the useless into the useful. Revolutionary staff members and workers on the industrial front have studied and mastered this dialectical relationship. Their subjective dynamic role unreined, they have gone all out for comprehensive use and devoted themselves to turning "waste matter" into useful wealth.

Tail gases belching from the chimney of a Shanghai oil refinery used to foul the air. These gases have been transferred to a nearby chemical plant via a 2-kilometre-long channel set up by the workers who analysed, separated and purified them, obtaining ethylene, propylene and butane from this noxious exhaust. After being synthesized, the gases were transformed into many kinds of chemical materials. They were then delivered to Shanghai's textile mills, plastic and pharmaceutical factories and machine-building plants, which processed them into light, abrasion-resistant and anti-moisture artificial wool, dacron, capron and other synthetic fibre goods, as well as various plastic goods needed for industry and the people's livelihood, insecticides, medicines and medical equipment.

A sugar-cane chemical plant in Kwangtung Province had to spend a hundred thousand yuan annually to ship pulverized cinders, filtered mud and pyrite slag and dump them into the sea. Now it can change them into raw materials for making cinder bricks, cement, carbon steel and pig iron. Since last year, just by making use of these wastes alone, it has created wealth worth hundreds of thousands of yuan for the state. In the spirit of the Foolish Old Man who removed the mountains, workers in a Shanghai steel plant produced well over 1,500 tons of iron and steel by comprehensive use of the steel slag that had piled up as high as three storeys.

The revolutionary committee of a Peking chemical plant fully mobilized the masses to completely explode the myth about the electronics industry. Through their own labour and indigenous methods, they used a large amount of the plant's tail gases to make polycrystal silicon, an important material for the electronics industry, in a matter of 37 days. This has opened up broad vistas for developing China's electronics industry. Comprehensive utilization of agricultural and side-line products by many small chemical plants set up in the rural areas of Kiangsu and other provinces has enabled them to use cotton seed hulls, corncobs, rice husks, sugar-cane residue and castor oil to

produce alcohol, furfural, acetic acid, acetone, glucose, anti-
biotics and other chemical products.

Making What Is Harmful Beneficial

Pollution of the environment is not only unhealthy to
people, it is destructive to nature. It destroys crops, creates
countless hazards for animal and fish life and is unbalancing
nature. What to do about the garbage of industrial production is
a big question all over the world, particularly in the capitalist
world where profits get priority. In China this problem is now
being tackled. Industry is at work to control pollution and
re-cycle waste materials.

Large amount of waste acids, liquid and gases emitted from
Shanghai's metallurgical, chemical, electroplating, dyeing and
printing and paper-making enterprises. The revolutionary staff
members and workers went about dealing with the waste acids
and gases with a will. Their all-out efforts for comprehensive
utilization turned what had been harmful into something
beneficial.

By making an all-round and dialectical analysis of the copper,
nickel and acids found in various waste liquids, workers at a
small plant realized that the harmful could be made beneficial.
Through decomposition, they created wealth amounting to
more than 1.7 million yuan for the state last year. The copper
oxide obtained from such "industrial rubbish" as waste liquids
meets the demand for pigment in the country's enamel
industry.

The big amount of daily waste gases and liquids emitted from
a factory had damaged 700 *mu* of farmland every year and
caused a loss of 50,000 yuan in income from farming there.
Collecting and utilizing the waste gases and liquids, the workers
obtained a lot of valuable resources, enabling the factory to
acquire an additional income of 3 million yuan each year.
Moreover, they have done away with the big destructive factor
causing great harm to farmland and the people's health.

Making One Thing Serve Many Purposes

Through practice in production, the workers' understanding
of the need to fully tap the potential of material resources has

deepened step by step and in many respects they have made one thing serve many purposes.

In addition to producing sugar in which sugar-cane was the chief raw material, the Kiangmen Sugar-cane Chemical Plant in Kwangtung Province has made comprehensive use of waste sugar-cane residue and liquids to make more than ten kinds of light industrial and chemical products. These include pulp board, glazed and wrapping paper, furfural, cementing material, alcohol, yeast and "702" farm chemical made from waste sugar-cane residue and other wastes. Formerly, this plant was in operation half a year and lay idle for the other half. This situation now has been completely reversed. Cutting across the limits set, it has changed into a multiple-producing factory making light industrial products such as sugar, paper and artificial fibre pulp as well as steel, iron, chemicals, medicines, building materials and polycrystal silicon.

On the basis of constantly summing up practical experience, workers have made new advances in recent years in comprehensively using pigs. From bristles, they extracted protein fibre which is used as textile material and obtained glue and lard from pig bones which, when ground to powder, become potassium fertilizer used in helping crops grow. When made into a powder, pig blood can be used as an industrial material. From the visceral organs of pigs and their glands and throat-bones, medicines such as bile acid and chondroitin are manufactured. Brain lipoid can also be obtained from pig brains, each kilogramme worth several thousand yuan.

Turning the Old Into the New

An important aspect in multi-purpose use, turning the old into the new reflects the proletariat's and other working people's fine quality of working hard and living simply and their practice of being industrious and frugal. As a result, it becomes possible to make the maximum use of material resources.

Alongside the rapid growth of industry and agriculture, large quantities of new machines, equipment, tools and packing boxes or containers are needed. All things gradually become old or damaged in the course of use. This is the natural law of the development of things. After an all-round analysis of damaged equipment, workers have become aware of the fact that something that is damaged is bad in one respect but this does not mean everything about it is bad. After being repaired or restored, old or damaged equipment becomes greatly changed and very serviceable.

In 1969, a Shanghai shop repairing old electric machinery and a bearing repair plant fixed more than 400 electric machines, 200 water pumps, 500-odd blowers and over 100,000 sets of bearings. Provided they are ground smooth and the saw-teeth are sharpened, processed or reproduced, damaged saws, files and other similar tools are serviceable again. This has saved the state a large amount of material. Old or cast-off iron buckets, cardboard and wooden boxes and other packing boxes can also be restored. A cardboard-box shop in recent years has repaired boxes weighing over 16,000 tons, thus saving more than five million yuan.

China has a vast expanse of land and is rich in resources. It abounds in mineral, agricultural and forest resources and in aquatic and animal products. Their tremendous potential remains to be tapped further. Multi-purpose use on China's industrial front means that still greater success will take place.

65. RADIO BROADCAST: TIENTSIN MAKES ADVANCE IN RECYCLING INDUSTRIAL WASTE (April, 1971)*

Tientsin is one of the most important military and industrial seaports of China. It is located in eastern Hopeh Province where the Pai River and Grand Canal join to form the Hai River. The Grand Canal links it with the two greatest Chinese rivers, the Yellow and the Yangtze. The following announcement serves as an illustration of China's efforts to combat pollution problems in her industrial cities in the 1970's.

Tientsin, April 30 (HSINHUA)—Workers, cadres and technical personnel in North China's important industrial city of Tientsin have achieved big successes in the multi-purpose use of industrial waste. This movement is guided by the party organizations and revolutionary committees at all levels.

Statistics to hand show that 70 chemical, light industrial, textile, metallurgical, building material and commercial units and local industries devised 190 kinds of multi-purpose uses up

*From *NCNA International Service in English* (April 30, 1971).

to last March. Over 46 per cent are in serial-production. They have provided the state with 35,000 tons of chemicals and chemical products, 170 million medicinal tablets and 500 tons of non-ferrous metals. They have smelted 2,500 tons of iron and steel from scraps and saved 1,000 tons of grain for industrial use. The city has recovered 35,000 tons of waste acid, equal to the annual production of a medium-sized sulphuric acid plant. It has produced 60 million bricks by utilizing waste heat and gas, 4,000 tons of cement from water quenched slag and other waste materials and irrigated 13,330 hectares of farmland with sewage water. Polycrystalline silicon, cadmium, titanium, manganese, coagulants and other important products have been extracted.

Tientsin factories made some achievements in multi-purpose use before the Great Proletarian Cultural Revolution. But, the renegade, hidden traitor and scab Liu Shao-chi and his agents spread idealist metaphysics, pushed the counterrevolutionary revisionist line, insisted on a minute division of labour and advocated "putting profit in command". This held back the multi-purpose use of industrial waste.

The city's cadres and workers made a living study and application of Mao Tsetung Thought, roundly criticized Liu Shao-chi's counter-revolutionary revisionist line and repudiated various kinds of erroneous ideas last year to encourage the multi-purpose use of industrial waste.

People used to think metaphysically that waste consisted of unusable things. The workers and cadres studied Chairman Mao's philosophic thinking and came to understand that "every thing divides into two" and that waste materials can be transformed into useful things.

The Tientsin insecticide plant used to find it very difficult to deal with its sewage water, waste gas and slag. It stored the smelly and poisonous waste of ethyl sulfide from hydroxyethyl sulfide in boxes in the open air. The boxes rotted and the ethyl sulfide was lost. This wasted ten to twenty thousand yuan annually. After the workers studied Chairman Mao's philosophic works, they used materialist dialectics to analyze the properties of ethyl sulfide. They finally produced a highly effective anodyne. Now the plant has seven projects for multi-purpose use of 80 per cent of the plant's waste. They produce 2.5 million yuan of value every year. The Tientsin pharmaceutical works used its waste liquid to trail-produce fodder containing tetracyclin, sodium acetate, potassium iodide, ammonia water, plasma substitute and other products.

The cadres and workers in the Tientsin factories and workshops recognize that the multi-purpose use of industrial waste is of great importance in production and involves a deep-going ideological revolutionization. Only when the thinking of the people is revolutionized, is it possible to make good use of industrial waste.

A chemical works in Tientsin used to discharge 1,000 tons of waste liquid daily. Some of the cadres wanted to ask for a large government investment to build a modern recovery system. The workers criticized this idea of blind faith in big and foreign projects, which can be traced back to Liu Shao-chi's influence. The workers set to work themselves. They dug ditches and laid pipes to lead the waste liquid into a reservoir where it is filtered before being used. The problem of recovering useful material from waste liquid was thus quickly solved. This was a profound education to leading cadres in the factory. They mobilized the workers to start a mass drive for other multi-purpose utilization. In less than one month, they recovered 109 tons of chemical products with a total value of 240,000 yuan.

Workers and staff members at the Tientsin winery have fostered the concept that a socialist enterprise should make full use of things to serve the people. This followed criticism of the revisionist fallacy spread by Liu Shao-chi and his agents that "the purpose of a winery is to turn out wine to make big profit". The leading cadres went to the workshops and teams to carry out experiments with the masses. They made poly-crystalline silicon from recovered waste gas and insecticide and artificial ice from waste liquid and residue.

Tientsin's industrial enterprises cooperated to investigate possible multi-purpose use of material, breaking through the rigid division of labour between different trades. They are using the waste gas, liquid and residue from chemical works to make iron and steel or grow polycrystalline silicon and extract chromium, cadmium and lithium. They also use residue from food-processing and other light industry factories to produce yeast, perrlycin, tetracyclin and other medical [supplies]. Bringing their wisdom into full play, the workers and revolu-tionary technicians strive to develop new techniques and processes to make the fullest use of material and create more wealth for the country. The Chinku winery extracts a medical material and makes three insecticides and a wine from residue. Workers of the Tientsin sulphuric acid works have tried out a new process for making acid and steel.

66. GOVERNMENT STATEMENTS: CHINA AT THE UNITED NATIONS (October 29, November 15, 1971)*

As almost predicted by Peking a year ago (see Document 61), the General Assembly of the United Nations voted on October 25, 1971—with 76 in favor, 35 opposed, and 17 abstentions—to admit the People's Republic in place of the Chinese Nationalists on Taiwan to the United Nations.

A week later, on October 29, the Acting Foreign Minister of China, Chi Peng-fei, sent a cablegram to United Nations Secretary General U Thant: "I have received your telegram of 26 October informing me that at its 26th session the General Assembly of the United Nations adopted on the 25th of October the resolution restoring to the People's Republic of China all its rights in the United Nations and expelling forthwith the representatives of Chiang Kai-shek from the place which they unlawfully occupy at the United Nations and in all the organizations related to it. I have also noted that you have notified all the bodies and related agencies of the United Nations of this resolution adopted by the United Nations General Assembly and believe that the above-mentioned resolution will be speedily implemented in its entirety. I now inform you that the Government of the People's Republic of China will send a delegation in the near future to attend the 26th session of the General Assembly of the United Nations. The name list of the delegation will be sent to you later. Please accept the assurances of my highest consideration."

*From Hsinhua News Release, October 29, 1971, reprinted in *Peking Review*, November 5, 1971, p. 6, and New York *Times*, November 16, 1971. (The title is the editor's.)

On November 2, 1971, Chi Peng-fei sent two more cablegrams to the secretary general informing him of the composition of the Chinese delegations: Chiao Kuan-hua, chief delegate; Huang Hua, deputy head; Fu Hao, Hsiung Hsiang-hui, Chen Chu—representatives; Tang Ming-chao, An Chih-yuan, Wang Hai-jung, Hsing Sung-yi, and Chang Yung-kuan—deputy representatives, all in the General Assembly; Huang Hua, permanent representative to the Security Council; and Chen Chu, deputy representative. These delegates together with a staff of forty-seven members arrived in New York City from Peking on November 11. A historical moment began in the United Nations.

The first group of delegates from China represents experienced professionals and indicates that China attaches great importance to its entry into the United Nations. For instance, China's chief delegate, Chiao Kuan-hua, is Vice Minister of Foreign Affairs and has been responsible for the ministry's two most important departments: the Department of West Europe, American, and Australian Affairs and the Department of Soviet and East European Affairs. He served as the principal adviser to Premier Chou En-lai at the 1954 Geneva Conference on Indochina and the 1962 Geneva Conference on Laos, as well as being the chief negotiator at Sino-Soviet border talks. Huang Hua, the permanent representative, is one of China's most trusted diplomats and was the first Chinese ambassador to Canada. Other delegates include four career foreign affairs specialists: Fu Hao (Asian affairs), Hsiung Hsiang-hui (American affairs and a graduate of Western Reserve University in Cleveland), Chen Chu (Middle East and African affairs), and An Chih-yuan (Soviet-bloc affairs). Other specialists include Tang Ming-chao (specializing in intelligence and an editor of a Chinese daily in New York City from 1945 to 1949), Hsing Sung-yi, and Chang Yung-kuan (military affairs). Last but by no means least, a woman delegate, Wang Hai-jung, has been serving as deputy protocol officer in the Foreign Ministry and is a niece of Chairman Mao Tse-tung's.

*In the last analysis, China's entry into the United
Nations will undoubtedly accelerate a whole series of
realignments on the international scene, as illustrated
below in two major policy statements: (I) First
official reactions of the Chinese government upon
notification of its admission to the world organization; and (II) First policy statement issued by Chiao
Kuan-hua at the United Nations on November 15,
1971.*

I

At its 26th session, the General Assembly of the United
Nations adopted on October 25, 1971, by an overwhelming
majority the resolution put forward by Albania, Algeria and 21
other countries demanding the restoration of all the lawful
rights of China in the United Nations and the immediate
expulsion of the representatives of the Chiang Kai-shek clique
from the United Nations and all the organizations related to it.

This represents the bankruptcy of the policy of depriving
China of her legitimate rights in the United Nations obdurately
pursued by U.S. imperialism over the past 20 years and more
and of the U.S. imperialist scheme to create "two Chinas" in
the United Nations.

This is a victory of Chairman Mao Tse-tung's proletarian
revolutionary line in foreign affairs and a victory for the people
of the whole world and all the countries upholding justice.

The Governments of Albania, Algeria and the other sponsor
countries have made outstanding contributions in this struggle.
Many friendly countries, especially the royal Government of
Cambodia under the leadership of Samdech Norodom
Sihanouk, have over a long period of time made unremitting
efforts for and played an important role in the restoration of
the legitimate rights of our country in the United Nations. The
Chinese Government and people express their hearty thanks to
the Governments and people of all the friendly countries which
uphold principle and justice.

The outcome of the voting at the present session of the U.N.
General Assembly reflects the general trend of the peoples of
the world desiring friendship with the Chinese people. At the
same time, it indicates that the one or two superpowers are

losing ground daily in engaging in truculent acts of imposing their own will on other countries and manipulating the United Nations and international affairs.

All countries, big or small, should be equal; the affairs of a country must be handled by its own people; the affairs of the world must be handled by all the countries of the world; the affairs of the United Nations must be handled jointly by all its member states—this is the irresistible trend of history in the world today. The restoration of the legitimate rights of the People's Republic of China in the United Nations is a manifestation of this trend.

However, not reconciled to their defeat, the U.S. and Japanese reactionaries are continuing to spread the fallacy that "the status of Taiwan remains to be determined" and are frenziedly pushing their scheme of creating "an independent Taiwan" in a wild attempt to continue to create "one China, one Taiwan" which is in effect tantamount to "two Chinas."

While instigating the representatives of the Chiang Kai-shek clique to hang on in some specialized agencies of the United Nations, they are even vainly attempting to let the Chiang Kai-shek clique worm its way back into the United Nations under the name of a so-called "independent Taiwan." This is a desperate struggle put up by them, and their scheme must never be allowed to succeed. The just resolution adopted by the U.N. General Assembly must be speedily implemented in its entirety. All the representatives of the Chiang Kai-shek clique must be expelled from the United Nations organization and all its bodies and related agencies.

Aggression and interference in others' internal affairs are incompatible with the U.N. Charter. The Government of the People's Republic of China and the Chinese people have consistently opposed the imperialist policies of aggression and war and supported the oppressed nations and peoples in their just struggles to win national liberation, oppose foreign interference and become masters of their own destinies. The Chinese people have suffered enough from imperialist oppression. China will never be a superpower bullying other countries.

The Government of the People's Republic of China will soon send its representatives to take part in the work of the United Nations. The People's Republic of China will stand together with all the countries and peoples that love peace and justice and, together with them, struggle for the defense of the national independence and state sovereignty of various countries and the cause of safeguarding international peace and promoting human progress.

II

Mr. President, fellow representatives:

First of all, allow me in the name of the delegation of the People's Republic of China to thank you, Mr. President, and the representatives of many countries for the welcome they have given us.

Many friends have made very enthusiastic speeches expressing their trust in as well as encouragement and fraternal sentiments for the Chinese people.

We are deeply moved by this and we shall convey all this to the entire Chinese people.

It is a pleasure for the delegation of the People's Republic of China to be here today to attend the 26th session of the General Assembly at the United Nations and to take part together with you in the work at the United Nations.

As is known to all, China is one of the founding members of the United Nations. In 1949 the Chinese people overthrew the reactionary rule of the Chiang Kai-shek clique and founded the People's Republic of China.

Since then the legitimate rights of China in the United Nations should have gone to the People's Republic of China as a matter of course.

It was only because of the obstruction by the United States Government that the People's Republic of China was deprived of its legitimate rights for a long time and that the Chiang Kai-shek clique, long repudiated by the Chinese people, was able to usurp China's lawful seat in the United Nations.

This was a gross interference in China's internal affairs as well as a willful trampling on the Charter of the United Nations. Now such an unjustifiable state of affairs has finally been put right.

On Oct. 25, 1971, the current session of the General Assembly of the United Nations adopted by an overwhelming majority the resolution restoring to the People's Republic of China all its lawful rights in the United Nations and expelling forthwith the representatives of the Chiang Kai-shek clique from the United Nations and all the organizations related to it.

This proves the bankruptcy of the policies of hostility towards the Chinese people and of isolating and imposing a blockade upon them. This is the defeat of the plan of the United States Government in collusion with the Sato Government of Japan to create two Chinas in the United Nations.

This is a victory for Chairman Mao Tse-tung's revolutionary line in foreign affairs; this is a common victory for the people all over the world.

Upholding principle and justice the sponsor countries for the resolution—Albania, Algeria, Burma, Ceylon, Cuba, Equatorial Guinea, Guinea, Iraq, Mali, Mauritania, Nepal, Pakistan, the People's Democratic Republic of Yemen, the People's Republic of the Congo, Rumania, Sierra Leone, Somalia, the Sudan, Syria, the United Republic of Tanzania, the Arab Republic of Yemen, Yugoslavia and Zambia—have made unremitting and fruitful efforts to restore China's legitimate rights in the United Nations.

Many friendly countries which supported this resolution have also made contributions to this end.

Some other countries have expressed their sympathy for China in various ways.

On behalf of the Chinese Government and the people I express heartfelt thanks to the government and the people of all these countries.

Twenty-six years have elapsed since the founding of the United Nations. Twenty-six years are but a brief span in human history. Yet, during this period profound changes have taken place in the world situation.

When the United Nations was first founded there were only 51 member states and now the membership has grown to 131.

Of the 80 members that joined later, the overwhelming majority are countries which achieved independence after World War II.

In the past 20 years and more, the peoples of Asia, Africa and Latin America have waged unflinching struggles to win and safeguard national independence and oppose foreign aggression and oppression. In Europe, North America and Oceania, too, mass movements and social tides for the change of the present state of affairs are rising. An increasing number of medium and small countries are uniting to oppose the hegemony and power politics practiced by the one or two superpowers and to fight for the right to settle their own affairs as independent and sovereign states and for equal status in international relations.

Countries want independence, nations want liberation and the people want revolution. This has become an irresistible trend of history.

Human society invariably makes constant progress, and such progress is always achieved through innumerable revolutions and transformations. Take the United States, where the United Nations headquarters is situated. It was owing to the victory of the Revolutionary War of 1776 led by Washington that the American people won independence. And it was owing to the great Revolution of 1789 that the French people rid themselves of the yoke of feudalism. After mankind entered the 20th century, the victory of the 1917 Russian October Socialist Revolution led by the great Lenin opened up a broad path to freedom and liberation for the oppressed nations and peoples of the world.

The advance of history and social progress gladdens the hearts and inspires the peoples of the world and throws into panic a handful of decadent reactionary forces who do their utmost to put up desperate struggles. They commit armed aggression against other countries, subvert the legal governments of other countries, interfere in other countries' internal affairs, subject other countries to their political, military and economic control and bully other countries at will.

Since World War II, no new world war has occurred, yet local wars have never ceased. At present, the danger of a new world war still exists, but revolution is the main trend in the world today. Although there are twists and turns and reverses in the people's struggles, adverse currents against the people and against progress, in the final analysis, cannot hold back the main current of the continuous development of human society.

The world will surely move toward progress and light, and definitely not toward reaction and darkness.

Mr. President and fellow representatives, the Chinese people have experienced untold sufferings under imperialist oppression. For one century and more, imperialism repeatedly launched wars of aggression against China and forced her to sign many unequal treaties. They divided China into their spheres of influence, plundered China's resources and exploited the Chinese people. The degree of poverty and lack of freedom suffered by the Chinese people in the past are known to all.

In order to win national independence, freedom and liberation, the Chinese people, advancing wave upon wave in a dauntless spirit, waged protracted heroic struggles against imperialism and its lackeys and finally won the revolution under the leadership of their great leader, Chairman Mao Tse-tung, and the Chinese Communist party. Since the founding of the People's Republic of China, we, the Chinese people, defying the tight imperialist blockades and withstanding the terrific pressures from without, have built our country into a socialist state with initial prosperity by maintaining independence and keeping the initiative in our own hands and through self-reliance. It has been proved by facts that we, the Chinese nation, are fully capable of standing on our own feet in the family of nations.

Taiwan is a province of China and the 14 million people who live in Taiwan are our fellow-countrymen by flesh and blood. Taiwan was already returned to the motherland after World War II in accordance with the Cairo Declaration and the Potsdam Proclamation, and our compatriots in Taiwan already returned to the embrace of their motherland.

The U.S. Government officially confirmed this fact on more than one occasion in 1949 and 1950, and publicly stated that the Taiwan question was China's internal affair and that the U.S. Government had no intention to interfere in it.

It was only because of the outbreak of the Korean war that the U.S. Government went back on its own words and sent armed forces to invade and occupy China's Taiwan and the Taiwan Straits, and to date they are still there. The spreading in certain places of the fallacy that "the status of Taiwan remains to be determined" is a conspiracy to plot "an independent Taiwan" and continue to create "two Chinas." On behalf of the Government of the People's Republic of China, I hereby reiterate that Taiwan is an inalienable part of China's territory and the U.S. armed invasion and occupation of China's Taiwan and the Taiwan Straits cannot in the least alter the sovereignty of the People's Republic of China over Taiwan, that all the armed forces of the United States definitely should be withdrawn from Taiwan and the Taiwan Straits and that we are firmly opposed to any design to separate Taiwan from the motherland. The Chinese people are determined to liberate Taiwan and no force on earth can stop us from doing so.

Mr. President and fellow representatives, the Chinese people who suffered for a long time from imperialist aggression and oppression have consistently opposed the imperialist policies of aggression and war and supported all the oppressed peoples and nations in their just struggles to win freedom and liberation, oppose foreign interference and become masters of their own destiny. This position of the Chinese Government and people is in the fundamental interests of the peoples of the world and is also in accord with the spirit of the United Nations Charter.

The United States Government's armed aggression against Vietnam, Cambodia and Laos and its enchroachment upon the territorial integrity and sovereignty of these three countries have aggravated tension in the Far East, and met with strong opposition of the people of the world, including the American people.

The Chinese Government and people firmly support the peoples of the three countries of Indochina in their war against U.S. aggression and for national salvation and firmly support the Joint Declaration of the Summit Conference of the Indochinese Peoples and the seven-point peace proposal put forward by the provisional revolutionary government of the Republic of South Vietnam. The U.S. Government should withdraw immediately and unconditionally all its armed forces and the armed forces of its followers from the three countries of Indochina so that the peoples of the three countries may solve their own problems independently and free from foreign interference; this is the key to the relaxation of tension in the Far East.

To date, Korea still remains divided. The Chinese people's volunteers have long since withdrawn from Korea but up to now the U.S. troops still remain in South Korea. The peaceful unification of their fatherland is the common aspiration of the entire Korean people. The Chinese Government and people firmly support the eight-point program for the peaceful unification of the fatherland put forward by the Democratic People's Republic of Korea in April this year and firmly support its just demand that all the illegal resolutions adopted by the United Nations on the Korean question be annulled and the "United Nations Commission for the Unification and Reha-bilitation of Korea" be dissolved.

The essence of the Middle East question is aggression against the Palestinian and other Arab peoples by Israeli Zionism with the support and connivance of the superpowers. The Chinese Government and people resolutely support the Palestinian and other Arab peoples in their just struggle against aggression and believe that, persevering in struggle and upholding unity, the heroic Palestinian and other Arab peoples will surely be able to recover the lost territories of the Arab countries and restore to the Palestinian people their national rights.

The Chinese Government maintains that all countries and peoples that love peace and uphold justice have the obligation to support the struggle of the Palestinian and other Arab peoples, and no one has the right to engage in political deals behind their backs, bartering away their right to existence and their national interest.

The continued existence of colonialism in all its manifestations is a provocation against the peoples of the world. The Chinese Government and people resolutely support the people of Mozambique, Angola, and Guinea (Bissau) in their struggle for national liberation, and resolutely support the people of Azania, Zimbabwe and Namibia in their struggle against the white colonialist rule and racial discrimination. Their struggle is a just one, and a just cause will surely triumph.

The independence of a country is incomplete without economic independence. The economic backwardness of the Asian, African and Latin-American countries is the result of imperialist plunder. Opposition to economic plunder and protection of national resources are the inalienable sovereign rights of an independent state.

China is still an economically backward country as well as a developing country. Like the overwhelming majority of the Asian, African and Latin-American countries, China belongs to the Third World. The Chinese Government and people resolutely support the struggles initiated by Latin-American countries and peoples to defend their rights over 200-nautical-mile territorial sea and to protect the resources of their respective countries.

The Chinese Government and people resolutely support the struggles unfolded by the petroleum-exporting countries in Asia, Africa and Latin America as well as various regional and specialized organizations to protect their national rights and interests and oppose economic plunder.

We have consistently maintained that all countries, big or small, should be equal and that the five principles of peaceful coexistence should be taken as the principles guiding the relations between countries. The people of each country have the right to choose the social system of their own country according to their own will and to protect the independence, sovereignty and territorial integrity of their own country. No country has the right to subject another country to its aggression, subversion, control, interference or bullying. We are opposed to the imperialist and colonialist theory that big nations are superior to the small nations and small nations are subordinate to the big nations. We are opposed to the power-politics hegemony of big nations bullying small ones or strong nations bullying weak ones. We hold that the affairs of a given country must be handled by its own people, that the affairs of the world must be handled by all the countries of the world, and that the affairs of the United Nations must be handled jointly by all its member states, and the superpowers should not be allowed to manipulate and monopolize them.

The superpowers want to be superior to others and lord it over others. At no time, neither today nor ever in the future, will China be a superpower subjecting others to its aggression, subversion, control, interference or bullying.

The one or two superpowers are stepping up their arms expansion and war preparations and vigorously developing nuclear weapons, thus seriously threatening international peace. It is understandable that the people of the world long for disarmament and particularly for nuclear disarmament. Their demand for the dissolution of military blocs, withdrawal of foreign troops and dismantling of foreign military bases is a just one. However, the superpowers, while talking about disarmament every day, are actually engaged in arms expansion daily.

The so-called nuclear disarmament which they are supposed to seek is entirely for the purpose of monopolizing nuclear weapons in order to carry out nuclear threats and blackmail. China will never participate in the so-called nuclear disarmament talks between the nuclear powers behind the backs of the non-nuclear countries. China's nuclear weapons are still in the experimental stage. China develops nuclear weapons solely for the purpose of defense and for breaking the nuclear monopoly and ultimately eliminating nuclear weapons and nuclear war. The Chinese Government has consistently stood for the complete prohibition and thorough destruction of nuclear weapons and proposed to convene a summit conference of all countries of the world to discuss this question and, as the first step, to reach an agreement on the non-use of nuclear weapons.

The Chinese Government has on many occasions declared, and now on behalf of the Chinese Government, I once again solemnly declare that at no time and under no circumstances will China be the first to use nuclear weapons. If the United

States and the Soviet Union really and truly want disarmament, they should commit themselves not to be the first to use nuclear weapons. This is not something difficult to do. Whether this is done or not will be a severe test as to whether they have the genuine desire for disarmament.

We have always held that the just struggles of the people of all countries support each other. China has always had the sympathy and support of the people of various countries in her socialist revolution and socialist construction. It is our bounden duty to support the just struggles of the people of various countries. For this purpose, we have provided aid to some friendly countries to help them to develop their national economies independently.

In providing aid, we always strictly respect the sovereignty of the recipient countries, and never attach any conditions or ask for any privileges. We provide free military aid to countries and peoples who are fighting against aggression. We will never become munition merchants. We firmly oppose certain countries trying to control and plunder the recipient countries by means of "aid."

However, as China's economy is still comparatively backward, the material aid we have provided is very limited, and what we provide is mainly political and moral support. With a population of 700 million, China ought to make a greater contribution to human progress and we hope that this situation of our ability falling short of this wish of ours will be gradually changed.

Mr. President and fellow representatives, in accordance with the purposes of the United Nations Charter, the United Nations should play its due role in maintaining international peace, opposing aggression and interference and developing friendly relations and cooperation among nations. However, for a long period the one or two superpowers have utilized the United Nations and have done many things in contravention of the United Nations Charter against the will of the people of various countries. This situation should not continue.

We hope that the spirit of the United Nations Charter will be really and truly followed out. We will stand together with all the countries and peoples that love peace and uphold justice and work together with them for the defense of the national independence and state sovereignty of various countries and for the cause of safeguarding international peace and promoting human progress.

APPENDIX A

Draft of the Revised Constitution of the People's Republic of China, 1971*

Chapter One: General Principles

Article 1: The People's Republic of China is a socialist state of proletarian dictatorship led by the working class (through the Chinese Communist Party) and based on the alliance of workers and peasants.

Article 2: Chairman Mao Tse-tung is the great leader of the people of all nationalities in the entire country, the Chief of State of the proletarian dictatorship, and the supreme commander of the whole nation and the whole armed forces. Vice Chairman Lin Piao is Chairman Mao's close comrade-in-arms and successor and the deputy supreme commander of the whole nation and the whole armed forces. Mao Tse-tung Thought is the guiding compass of all the work of the people of the whole nation.

Article 3: All power in the People's Republic of China belongs to the people. The organs through which the people exercise power are the people's congresses at every level, with the deputies of workers, peasants, and soldiers as the main body. The people's congresses at every level and other state organs all practice democratic centralism. Deputies to the people's congresses are elected through democratic consensus. The original electoral units and the electorate have the power to supervise and, in accordance with the provisions of law, to recall and replace the elected deputies.

* From the secret text of the Ninth Central Committee of the Chinese Communist Party held August 23-September 6, 1970 (not published). The editor wishes to acknowledge with thanks the permission to reprint the text from *Comparative Communism* (January, 1971); the text (preamble omitted) has been translated by the editor and his father, Dr. Ch'u Chai. The replacement of Lin Piao by Chou En-lai or a team of high officials is expected.

Article 4: The People's Republic of China is a unitary multinational nation-state, with national autonomous regions as inseparable parts of the People's Republic of China. All the nationalities are equal and are opposed to great nationalism and parochial nationalism. All the nationalities have the freedom to use their own spoken and written languages.

Article 5: At present, the main categories of ownership of means of production in the People's Republic of China are twofold: socialist ownership by the whole people, and socialist collective ownership by the masses of working people. The State permits nonagricultural individual laborers, under the central management of urban and township street organizations and production teams of rural people's communes, to engage in individual labor within permissive legal provisions and not exploit others. They are in the meantime to be guided step by step onto the road of socialist collectivization.

Article 6: The state sector of the economy is the leading force in the national economy. All mineral resources and waters, as well as state forests, undeveloped lands, and other resources, are the property of the whole people. The State may purchase, appropriate, or nationalize both urban and rural land, as well as other productive resources, in accordance with legal provisions.

Article 7: The rural people's commune is an organization in which government and commune are combined into one. At present, the economy of collective ownership in the rural people's communes generally operates under three levels of ownership—namely, ownership by the commune, by the production brigade, and by the production team as the basic accounting unit. Provided that the development of the collective economy of people's communes is guaranteed and occupies absolute priority, members of a people's commune may operate small pieces of land for private operation.

Article 8: Socialist public property is inviolable. The State guarantees the consolidation and development of socialist economy and prohibits anyone from using any means to sabotage the interests of socialist economy and public property.

Article 9: The State practices the socialist principles of "no work, no food," "to each according to his ability," and "distribution according to one's labor." The State protects the citizens' right to own income from labor, savings, houses, and other means of subsistence.

Article 10: Political work is the lifeline of all activity. The State acts to retain revolution, promote production and work, and to prepare for defense, as well as to promote the systematic and proportional development of socialist economy, so that on the basis of continually elevating social productivity, the material and cultural life of the people will be gradually improved, and the independence and security of the State will be consolidated.

Article 11: All working personnel of state and other organs must study and apply creatively the Thought of Mao Tse-tung, place special emphasis on proletarian politics, oppose bureaucratism, align closely with the workers and peasants, as well as all laboring masses, and serve the people with whole heart and devotion. Working personnel of all organs must participate in collective labor. All state organs must practice the principle of simplified administration; their leadership organs must practice the revolutionary three-in-one combination of military men, cadres, and masses, and of the old, the middle-aged, and the young.

Article 12: The proletariat, which must be established in the superstructure including the various cultural fields, exercise total dictatorship over the bourgeoisie. Culture, education, literature, arts, and scientific research must all serve proletarian politics, serve the workers, peasants, and soldiers, and unite with productive labor.

Article 13: Blooming and contending on a big scale, big-character posters, and great debates are new forms of socialist revolution created by the masses of people. The State protects the use of such forms by the people in mass movement, to create a political situation where there is democracy and yet centralism, discipline and yet freedom, collective will and yet individual pursuit of mental gratification, so as to consolidate proletarian dictatorship.

Article 14: The State safeguards the socialist system, suppresses all treasonable and counterrevolutionary activities, and punishes all traitors and counterrevolutionaries. The State according to law deprives landlords, rich peasants, reactionary capitalists, counterrevolutionaries, and other undesirable elements of their political rights for a specific period of time; meanwhile it provides them means to earn a living, in order to enable them to reform through labor and become citizens who can earn their livelihood by their own labor.

Article 15: The Chinese People's Liberation Army and militia are the children and brothers of workers and peasants under the leadership of the Communist Party of China, and the armored power source of the whole nation. The Chinese People's Liberation Army is perpetually and simultaneously a combat unit, a work unit, and a production unit. The duty of the armed forces of the People's Republic of China is to safeguard the socialist revolution and the achievements of socialist construction, to defend the sovereignty, territorial integrity, and security of the State, and to guard against the subversion and aggression of imperialism, social-imperialism, and their lackeys.

Chapter Two: The State Structure

Section I: The National People's Congress

Article 16: The National People's Congress is the highest organ of state power under the leadership of the Communist Party of China. The National People's Congress is composed of deputies elected by provinces, autonomous regions, municipalities directly under the central authority, armed forces, and Chinese residents abroad. A number of patriotic personalities may be invited to participate when necessary. The National People's Congress is elected for a term of five years, which may be extended under special circumstances. The National People's Congress meets once a year, but under special circumstances it may be convened sooner or postponed.

Article 17: The functions and powers of the National People's Congress are: To make and to amend the Constitution, to make laws, to appoint and remove the premier of the State Council upon the recommendation of the Central Committee of the Communist Party of China, to examine and approve the state budget and the state accounts, and to exercise such other functions and powers as the National People's Congress considers necessary.

Article 18: The Standing Committee of the National People's Congress is the permanent working organ of the National People's Congress. Its functions and powers are: To interpret the laws to the sessions of the National People's Congress, to adopt decrees, to appoint and recall plenipotentiary representatives, and to ratify and nullify treaties concluded with foreign states. The Standing Committee of the National People's Congress is composed of the chairman, the vice chairmen, and other members, to be elected or removed by the National People's Congress.

Section II: The State Council

Article 19: The State Council is the Central People's Government. The State Council is accountable to the National People's Congress and its Standing Committee and submits reports to them. The State Council is composed of the premier, the vice premiers, the ministers, the chairmen of commissions, and others.

Article 20: The functions and powers of the State Council are: To formulate administrative measures and issue decisions and orders in accordance with the Constitution, laws, and decrees; to coordinate and lead the work of ministries and commissions and the work of local administrative organs of state throughout the country; to formulate and put into effect the national economic plan and the provisions of state budget; to direct the administrative affairs of the State; and to exercise such other functions and powers as are vested in it by the National People's Congress or its Standing Committee.

Section III: Local People's Congresses and Local Revolutionary Committees

Article 21: Local people's congresses at every level are local organs of state power. The term of office of people's congresses in the provincial and municipal level is five years; that of people's congresses of special districts, cities, and counties, three years; that of people's congresses of rural people's communes and townships, two years.

Article 22: Local revolutionary committees at every level are the standing organs of local people's congresses and, at the same time, local people's governments. A local revolutionary committee is composed of the chairman, the vice chairmen, and other members, to be elected or recalled by the people's congress of the corresponding level. A local revolutionary committee is accountable to the local people's congress and to the next higher state organ.

Article 23: Local people's congresses at every level and members of local revolutionary committees ensure the implementation of laws and decrees in their respective areas, stimulate the enthusiasm of local organs at every level to the utmost, provide leadership for local socialist revolution and socialist construction; examine and approve local budgets; protect revolutionary order; and safeguard the rights of citizens.

Section IV: Organs of Self-government of National Autonomous Areas

Article 24: The organs of self-government in autonomous regions, autonomous *chou*, and autonomous counties are the people's congresses and revolutionary committees. The organs of self-government of national autonomous areas may exercise, in addition to the functions and powers of local state organs as prescribed in Chapter Two, Section III of the Constitution, autonomy as provided by law. Higher state organs at every level should fully safeguard the exercise of autonomy by organs of self-government in national autonomous areas and actively support the various minority nationalities in carrying out socialist revolution and socialist construction.

Section V: The Judicial and Procuratorate Organs

Article 25: The Supreme People's Court, local people's courts at every level, and special people's courts exercise judicial authority. The people's courts at every level are accountable to the people's congresses and their standing committees and submit reports to them. The permanent organs of the people's congresses at every level appoint or remove presidents of the people's courts. The exercise of procuratorial and trial authority shall follow the mass line. Mass discussion and criticism are to be conducted in serious counterrevolutionary and criminal cases.

Chapter Three: Fundamental Rights and Duties of Citizens

Article 26: The most fundamental rights and duties of citizens are: To support Chairman Mao Tse-tung and his close comrade-in-arms, Vice Chairman Lin Piao; to support the leadership of the Communist Party of China; to support the proletarian dictatorship; to support the socialist system; and to abide by the Constitution and laws of the People's Republic of China. It is the highest responsibility of every citizen to defend the motherland and to resist against aggression. And it is the glorious duty of citizens to perform military service according to law.

Article 27: All citizens who have reached the age of eighteen have the right to vote and stand for election, except those deprived by law of such rights. Citizens have the right to work and the right to education. The working people have the right to rest and leisure and the right to material assistance in old age and in case of illness or disability. Women enjoy equal rights with men. The state protects marriage, the family, and the mother and child. The state protects the just rights and interests of Chinese residents abroad.

Article 28: Citizens enjoy freedom of speech, freedom of correspondence, freedom of press, freedom of assembly, freedom of association, freedom of procession, freedom of demonstration, and freedom to strike. Citizens enjoy the freedom of religious belief and the freedom of iconoclasm and of propagating atheism. The freedom of person and the homes of citizens are inviolable. No citizen may be arrested except by decision of a people's court or with the sanction of public security organs.

Chapter Four: National Flag, National Emblem, Capital

Article 30: The national flag of the People's Republic of China is a red flag with five stars. The national emblem is: in the center, Tien An Men under the light of five stars, framed with ears of grain and with a cog wheel. The capital of the People's Republic of China is Peking.

APPENDIX B Decision-making Chart of China's Foreign Policy*

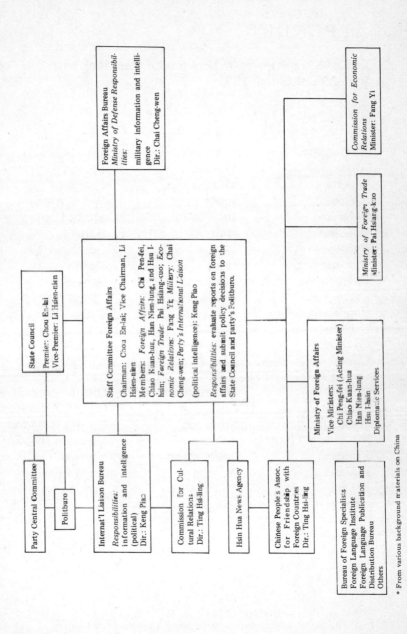

Party Central Committee

Politburo

State Council
Premier: Chou En-lai
Vice-Premier: Li Hsien-nien

Foreign Affairs Bureau
Ministry of Defense Responsibilities:
military information and intelligence
Dir.: Chai Cheng-wen

Staff Committee Foreign Affairs
Chairman: Chou En-lai; Vice Chairman, Li Hsien-nien
Members: *Foreign Affairs:* Chi Pen-fei, Chiao Kuan-hua, Han Nien-lung, and Hsu I-hsien; *Foreign Trade:* Pai Hsiang-kuo; *Economic Relations:* Fang Yi; *Military:* Chai Cheng-wen; *Party's International Liaison* (political intelligence): Keng Piao

Responsibilities: evaluate reports on foreign affairs and submit policy decisions to the State Council and Party's Politburo.

Internat'l Liaison Bureau
Responsibilities: information and intelligence (political)
Dir.: Keng Piao

Commission for Cultural Relations
Dir.: Ting Hsi-ling

Hsin Hua News Agency

Chinese People's Assoc. for Friendship with Foreign Countries
Dir.: Ting Hsi-ling

Ministry of Foreign Affairs
Vice Ministers:
Chi Peng-fei (Acting Minister)
Chiao Kuan-hua
Han Mien-lung
Hsu I-hsin
Diplomatic Services

Ministry of Foreign Trade
Minister: Pai Hsiang-kuo

Commission for Economic Relations
Minister: Fang Yi

Bureau of Foreign Specialists
Foreign Language Institute
Foreign Language Publication and Distribution Bureau
Others

* From various background materials on China

APPENDIX C

List of Countries with Diplomatic Relations with the People's Republic of China, 1971*

Afghanistan	Germany (East)	Peru
Albania	Guinea	Poland
Algeria	Hungary	Rumania
Austria	India	San Marino
Belgium	Indonesia[1]	Sierra Leone
Bulgaria	Iran	Somalia
Burma	Iraq	Southern Yemen
Burundi	Italy	Sudan
Byelorussian SSR	Kenya	Sweden
Cameroon	Korea (North)	Switzerland
Cambodia (exile)	Kuwait	Tanzania
Canada	Laos	Tunisia
Ceylon	Lebanon	Turkey
Chile	Libya	Uganda
Congo (Brazzaville)	Mali	Ukrainian SSR
Cuba	Mauritania	USSR
Czechoslovakia	Mongolia	United Arab Republic
Denmark	Morocco	United Kingdom
Equatorial Guinea	Nepal	Vietnam (North)
Ethiopia	Netherlands	Yemen
Finland	Nigeria	Yugoslavia
France	Norway	Zambia
Ghana[1]	Pakistan	

* As of November 15, 1971.
1 Temporarily severed or suspended diplomatic relations.

APPENDIX D

Chinese History, 1000 B.C. to A.D. 1949*

CENTURY	EXTERNAL RELATIONS	DYNASTIES (Non-Chinese Underlined)	POLITICAL STRUCTURE	INTERNAL DEVELOPMENTS
B.C. 1000	Chinese Expansion	WEST CHOU	FEUDALISM	
900				
800	Barbarian Invasions			
700		EAST CHOU		Rise of philosophic schools: Confucianism, Taoism, Mohism, Legalism
600				
500				
400		WARRING STATES		
300				Coinage
200	Chinese Expansion	CH'IN		Great Walls built / Peasant revolts / Establishment of bureaucracy
100	Caravan Trade / Introduction of Buddhism	WEST HAN		Confucianism as a state cult
A.D. 1	Chinese Expansion	EAST HAN		Reforms of Wang Mang A.D. 8-23
100				Peasant revolts (Yellow Turbans, etc.)
200		THREE KINGDOMS		Beginning of the decline of the Northwest and growth of the Southeast
		WEST CHIN	MONARCHY AND BUREAUCRACY OF THE GENTRY	
300	Barbarian Invasions	BARBARIAN STATES / EAST CHIN		
400	Beginning of Maritime Commerce	WEI / FOUR CHINESE DYNASTIES		Buddhism flourished
500		BARBARIAN STATES /		
600	Chinese Expansion	SUI		Canal to Ch'ang-an / Government and Civil Service examination system perfected
700	Foreign Religions	T'ANG		Golden Age of art and literature / Rebellion of An Lu-shan
800	Foreign Invasions			Invention of Printing
900	Foreign Invasions	FIVE DYNASTIES / TEN STATES		Peasant revolts (Huang Ch'ao, etc.) / Widespread use of paper money
1000		LIAO / NORTH SUNG		Reforms of Wang An-shih 1069-85
1100				Capital transferred to coast
1200	Foreign Ideas and Maritime Commerce	CHIN / SOUTH SUNG		Neo-Confucianism, Chu Hsi
1300		YUAN		Canal to Peking
1400	Chinese Expansion / Naval Expeditions			Peasant revolts
1500	Foreign Invasions / Europeans Came by Sea	MING		
1600				Peasant revolts
1700	Chinese Expansion	CH'ING		
1800	War with the West			T'ai-p'ing Rebellion, 1851-64 / Modernization and Reform
1900	Cultural Impact of the West / Two World Wars / Soviet Influence	REPUBLIC		Revolution of 1911 / Nationalist government
		PEOPLE'S REPUBLIC		Communist government

STRONG UNITY—CENTRALIZATION .... ☐   WEAK UNITY—DECENTRALIZATION .... ▥   DIVISION .... ▨

* Area Handbook for Communist China (Washington, D.C., U.S. Government Printing Office, 1967).

Current Scene, Vol. VII, No. 17 (September 1, 1969)

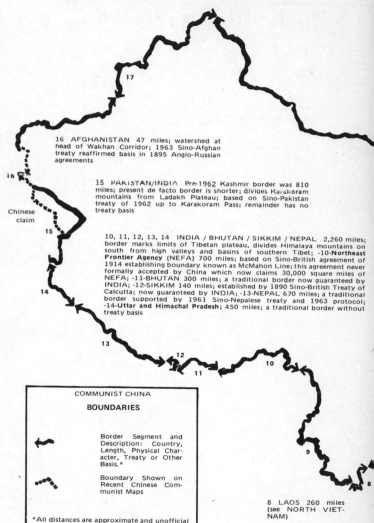

17 USSR 1,850 miles in Sinkiang province; series of angled border segments alternately following mountain ridges and crossing valleys; Tadjik SSR border based on Anglo-Russian agreement of 1895, but never formally accepted by China; Kirgiz and Kazakh SSR borders based chiefly on multilateral treaties of 1860, 1864, amplified by later agreements

17

16 AFGHANISTAN 47 miles; watershed at head of Wakhan Corridor; 1963 Sino-Afghan treaty reaffirmed basis in 1895 Anglo-Russian agreements

16

Chinese
claim

15 PAKISTAN/INDIA Pre-1962 Kashmir border was 810 miles; present de facto border is shorter; divides Karakoram mountains from Ladakh Plateau; based on Sino-Pakistan treaty of 1962 up to Karakoram Pass; remainder has no treaty basis

15

10, 11, 12, 13, 14 INDIA / BHUTAN / SIKKIM / NEPAL 2,260 miles; border marks limits of Tibetan plateau, divides Himalaya mountains on south from high valleys and basins of southern Tibet; -10-**Northeast Frontier Agency** (NEFA) 700 miles; based on Sino-British agreement of 1914 establishing boundary known as McMahon Line; this agreement never formally accepted by China which now claims 30,000 square miles of NEFA; -11-BHUTAN 300 miles; a traditional border now guaranteed by INDIA; -12-SIKKIM 140 miles; established by 1890 Sino-British Treaty of Calcutta; now guaranteed by INDIA; -13-NEPAL 670 miles; a traditional border supported by 1961 Sino-Nepalese treaty and 1963 protocol; -14-**Uttar and Himachal Pradesh**; 450 miles; a traditional border without treaty basis

14

13

12

11

10

COMMUNIST CHINA

BOUNDARIES

Border Segment and Description: Country, Length, Physical Character, Treaty or Other Basis.*

Boundary Shown on Recent Chinese Communist Maps

*All distances are approximate and unofficial

9

8

8 LAOS 260 miles (see NORTH VIET-NAM)

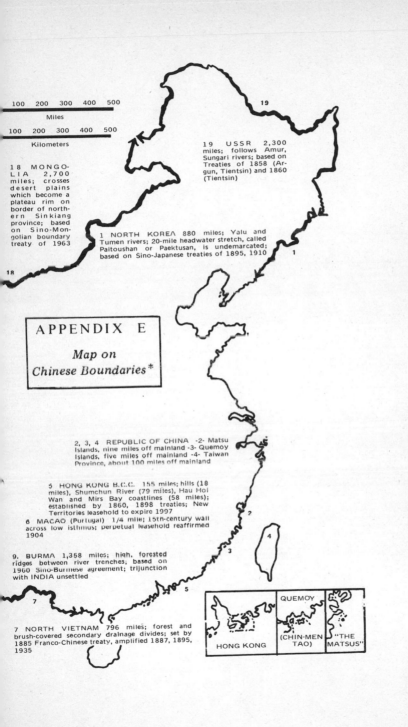

18 MONGO-
LIA 2,700
miles; crosses
desert plains
which become a
plateau rim on
border of north-
ern Sinkiang
province; based
on Sino-Mon-
golian boundary
treaty of 1963

19 USSR 2,300
miles; follows Amur,
Sungari rivers; based on
Treaties of 1858 (Ar-
gun, Tientsin) and 1860
(Tientsin)

1 NORTH KOREA 880 miles; Yalu and
Tumen rivers; 20-mile headwater stretch, called
Paitoushan or Paektusan, is undemarcated;
based on Sino-Japanese treaties of 1895, 1910

APPENDIX E

Map on Chinese Boundaries *

2, 3, 4 REPUBLIC OF CHINA -2- Matsu
Islands, nine miles off mainland -3- Quemoy
Islands, five miles off mainland -4- Taiwan
Province, about 100 miles off mainland

5 HONG KONG B.C.C. 155 miles; hills (18
miles), Shumchun River (79 miles), Hau Hoi
Wan and Mirs Bay coastlines (58 miles);
established by 1860, 1898 treaties; New
Territories leasehold to expire 1997

6 MACAO (Portugal) 1/4 mile; 15th-century wall
across low isthmus; perpetual leasehold reaffirmed
1904

9. BURMA 1,358 miles; high, forested
ridges between river trenches; based on
1960 Sino-Burmese agreement; trijunction
with INDIA unsettled

7 NORTH VIETNAM 796 miles; forest and
brush-covered secondary drainage divides; set by
1885 Franco-Chinese treaty, amplified 1887, 1895,
1935

HONG KONG

QUEMOY
(CHIN-MEN
TAO)

"THE
MATSUS"

APPENDIX F

Information Guide on China's Foreign Trade Corporations: Their Principal Exports and Imports*

China Travel Service, Ltd.
Yu To Sang Building
Queen's Road
Central, Hong Kong

Official agency for travel and visa arrangements.

China National Chemicals Import and Export Corporation
Erh Li Kou, Hsi Chiao, Peking
Cable: SINOCHEM PEKING

Rubber, rubber tires, and other rubber products, petroleum and petroleum products, chemical fertilizers, insecticides and fungicides, pharmaceuticals, medical apparatus, chemical raw materials, dyestuffs, pigments, etc.

China National Native Produce and Animal By-Products Import and Export Corporation
82 Tung An Men Street, Peking
Cable: CHINATUHSU PEKING

Tea, coffee, cocoa, tobacco, bast fiber, rosin, feeding stuffs, timber, forest products, spices, essential oils, patent medicines and medicinal herbs, as well as other native produce, bristles, horse tails, feathers, down, feathers for decorative use, rabbit hair, wool, cashmere, camel hair, casings, hides, leathers, fur mattress, fur products, carpets, down products, living animals, etc.

* U.S. Consulate General, Hong Kong.

China National Light Industrial Products Import and Export Corporation
82 Tung An Men Street, Peking
Cable: INDUSTRY PEKING

Paper, general merchandise, stationery, musical instruments, sporting goods, toys, building materials and electrical appliances, fish nets, net yarns, leather shoes, leather products, pottery and porcelain, human hair, pearls, precious stones and jewelry, ivory and jade carvings, lacquer ware, plaited articles, furniture, artistic handicrafts and other handicrafts for daily use, etc.

China National Textiles Import and Export Corporation
82 Tung An Men Street, Peking
Cable: CHINATEX PEKING

Cotton, cotton yarns, raw silk, steam filature, wool tops, rayon fibers, synthetic and man-made fibers, cotton piecegoods, woolen piecegoods, linen, garments and wearing apparel, knitted goods, cotton and woolen manufactured goods, ready-made silk articles, drawn works, etc.

China National Cereals, Oils and Foodstuffs Import and Export Corporation
82 Tung An Men Street, Peking
Cable: CEROILFOOD PEKING

Cereals, edible vegetable and animal oils and fats, vegetable and animal oils and fats for industrial use, oil seeds, seeds, oil cakes, feeding stuffs, salt, edible livestock and poultry, meat and meat products, eggs and egg products, fresh fruits and fruit products, aquatic and marine products, canned goods of various kinds, sugar and sweets, wines, liquors, spirits of various kinds, dairy products, vegetables and condiments, bean flour noodles, grain products, canned goods, nuts and dried vegetables, etc.

China-National Machinery Import and Export Corporation
Erh Li Kou, Hsi Chiao, Peking
Cable: MACHIMPEX PEKING

Machine tools, presses, hammers, shears, forging machines, diesel engines, gasoline engines, steam turbines, boilers, mining machinery, metallurgical machinery, compressors and pumps, hoists, winches and cranes, transport machinery (motor vehicles) and parts thereof, vessels, etc., agricultural machinery and implements, printing machines, knitting machines, building machinery, machinery for other light industries, ball and roller bearings, tungsten carbide, electric machinery and equipment, telecommunication equipment, electric and electronic measuring instruments, scientific instruments, complete industrial plants, technical knowhow, etc.

China National Metals and Minerals Import and Export Corporation
Erh Li Kou, Hsi Chiao, Peking
Cable: MINMETALS PEKING

Steel plates, sheets and pipes, steel sections, steel tubes, special steel, railway materials, metallic products, pig iron, ferro-alloys, nonferrous metals, precious rare metals, ferrous mineral ores, nonferrous mineral ores, nonmetallic minerals and products thereof, coal, cement, hardware, etc.

Sinofracht Chartering and Shipbooking Corporation
Erh Li Kou, Hsi Chiao
Peking

The chartering of vessels and booking of shipping space required for Chinese import and export cargoes. Also, similar business on behalf of principals abroad. Canvassing cargoes for ship owners.

Complete Plant Export Corporation
Fu-Wai Street
Peking

Exporters only: of complete factories, works, and production units, usually, but not exclusively, as part of an economic-aid agreement.

Publications Centre Guozi Shudian
P. O. Box 399
Peking

Import and export of books and periodicals in Chinese and foreign languages. Arranges subscriptions to Chinese newspapers and periodicals on behalf of foreign readers.

Foreign Trade Transportation Corporation
Erh Li Kou, Hsi Chiao
Peking

Arranges customs clearance and delivery of import/export cargoes by land, sea, and air, or by post. May act as authorized agents clearing and delivering goods in transit through Chinese ports. Arranges marine and other insurance and institutes claims on behalf of cargo owners on request.

SUGGESTED FURTHER READINGS

Barnett, A. Doak, *A New U.S. Policy Towards China.* Washington, D.C., Brookings Institution, 1971.

Blum, Robert, *The U.S. and China in World Affairs,* A. Doak Barnett, ed. New York, Council on Foreign Relations, 1966.

Chai, Winberg, *New Politics from Communist China.* Pacific Palisades, Calif., Goodyear Publishing Co., 1972.

Chen, Lung-chu, and Lasswell, Harold, *Formosa, China and the United Nations.* New York, St. Martin's Press, 1967.

Clubb, O. Edmund, *China and Russia. The Great Game.* New York, Columbia University Press, 1970.

Cohen, Jerome Alan, ed., *The Dynamics of China's Foreign Relations.* Cambridge, Mass., Harvard University Press, 1970.

——*et al., Taiwan and American Policy.* New York, Praeger, 1971.

Deutscher, Isaac, *Russia, China and the West.* New York, Oxford University Press, 1970.

Doolin, Dennis J., *Territorial Claims in the Sino-Soviet Conflicts.* Stanford, Calif., Hoover Institution Press, 1965.

Eckstein, Alexander, ed., *China Trade Prospects and U.S. Policy.* New York, Praeger, 1971.

Friedman, Edward, and Selden, Mark, eds., *America's Asia.* New York, Pantheon Books, 1970.

Gittings, John, *Survey of Sino-Soviet Disputes.* New York, Oxford University Press, 1968.

Hinton, Harold C., *China's Turbulent Quest.* New York, Macmillan, 1970.

413

Johnson, Cecil, *Communist China and Latin America, 1959-1967.* New York, Columbia University Press, 1970.

Lall, Arthur, *How Communist China Negotiates.* New York, Columbia University Press, 1968.

Larkin, Bruce D., *China and Africa, 1949-1970.* Berkeley, Calif., University of California Press, 1971.

North, Robert, *The Foreign Relations of China.* Belmont, Calif., Dickenson Press, 1970.

Ojha, Ishwer C., *Chinese Foreign Policy in an Age of Transition.* Boston, Beacon Press, 1969.

Robinson, Thomas, *et al., The Cultural Revolution in China.* Berkeley, Calif., University of California Press, 1971.

Simmonds, J. D., *China's World: The Foreign Policy of a Developing State.* New York, Columbia University Press, 1971.

Stoessinger, John G., *Nations in Darkness: China, Russia and America.* New York, Random House, 1971.

Tang Tsou, ed., *China's Policies in Asia and America's Alternatives.* Chicago, University of Chicago Press, 1968.

Van Ness, Peter, *Revolution and Chinese Foreign Policy.* Berkeley, Calif., University of California Press, 1970.

Whiting, Allen, "What Nixon Must Do to Make it in Peking." *The New York Review of Books,* Vol. XVII, No. 5 (October 7, 1971).

INDEX